THE JUMBIES' PLAYING GROUND

Map by Bill Pitts

Lesser Antilles

INTRODUCTION

Similarities between disguised performance traditions in the West Indies and those in West Africa and Western Europe warrant investigation. *The Jumbies' Playing Ground* explores cross-cultural knowledge transfer relating to transatlantic art influences. This interdisciplinary study examines how Afro-Creole masquerades evolved and looks for possible precursors in the regions from which Caribbean populations were drawn. More specifically, it examines the elements of Old World masquerades adopted in the Lesser Antilles in terms of appearance, roles, and behavior. In so doing, this research provides a detailed exploration of the origins of New World cultural practices as well as cultural transfers between European and African descendants starting with Caribbean colonialism. Other studies in this area usually have been only side issues in debates focusing on another topic, have focused on a single group, or have otherwise been limited in scope. By taking a broader perspective, *The Jumbies' Playing Ground* brings new depth to the study of the international dimensions of cultural interchange. It transcends established academic boundaries and interacts with other areas while adding to village-based studies on the arts of island-cluster communities and how they have intersected with broader currents of global interchange.

This book examines the making of Afro-Creole masquerades, which are an important part of mas' (masquerade) within the vernacular mode of Caribbean music and dance. This book focuses on masquerades of the Eastern Caribbean—Barbados and the Leeward Islands of the Northern Lesser Antilles—and only on early prototypes containing residues of Old World beginnings. It is not intended as a compendium of Leeward Islands' masquerades but rather highlights certain practices that date back to the beginning of the plantation economy. The Old World section concentrates on the masquerades of Upper Guinea, especially the Mande diaspora, though the Igbo and other West African groups are also discussed. In Western Europe, the focus is on Britain (especially the West Country), Ireland, the Nordic regions, and Scandinavia. The Leeward Islands include Antigua, Barbuda, St. Kitts–Nevis, Anguilla, Montserrat, and the U.S. Virgin Islands (USVI),[1] but the study also examines Dominica, St. Vincent, Grenada, and Carriacou in the Windward

Islands as well as Barbados. Jamaica appears because as a significant part of the former British West Indies (BWI), it has more in common with the Lesser Antilles than it does with its neighbors in the Greater Antilles, Cuba and Hispaniola. As part of the cultural network of the Atlantic Rim region, North Carolina and Newfoundland also appear in this account.[2]

The traditions explored in this book overlap with but are essentially different from those of the Latin Carnaval that spread to the New World during the late sixteenth and seventeenth centuries when Spain, Portugal, and France began colonizing parts of the Americas. For example, the dance in the Leeward Islands known as Plait Pole (Maypole) bears a marked similarity to the Danza de las Cinta (Ribbon Dance) performed by the masked dancers of San Juan Totolac in Mexico (Mauldin 2004, 162), but such parallels are not pursued here. New World carnivals are explored in other worthy books (see, e.g., Kinser 1990; Mauldin 2004), as are expositions of Bakhtinian notions of "liminality" and "inversion" (Bakhtin 1984; Turner 1969, 1974). In Montserrat, the enslaved's adoption of St. Patrick's miter as a headdress for their principal masquerade is seen as a rite of reversal. The Leeward Islands' inversion of social norms during Christmas mas' is shared with Mardi Gras and carnivals held in Trinidad, Mexico, Bolivia, and Brazil but differs in that the carnivals, connected as they are to Catholicism, represent pre-Lenten revelry for which participants typically atone in the fasting and sobriety of Lent. With the exception of hangovers and empty pockets, there was no period of atonement following Leeward Islands festivities.

This book is based on certain assumptions. Masquerading is multivoiced, providing whole theater that combines other arts—music, dance, performance, and visual decoration. Art has the ability to provide glimpses of an underlying reality in the here and now as well as of the universal in a particular instance—universal human values, the collective unconscious, or folk perceptions of ancestors. Arguments for an Old World provenance of masquerade genres assume that these traditions have been resilient over time. Although European genres are quite well documented in the literature, there are fewer historical records about the sorts of West African masquerades of the seventeenth through nineteenth centuries to which enslaved Africans en route to the Caribbean might have been exposed. However, masquerades documented in the first half of the twentieth century are fair representations of long-established traditions, and some surviving African masking traditions are known to have remained little changed for hundreds of years: the horned Ejumba masquerades of the Jola (Diola) of Senegambia (Mark 1992); the Kankuran bush masquerades of the Mandinka (De Jong 2007); and the Zooba masquerade of the women's Sande society in Liberia (Monts 1984).

Charry (2000, 197–98) confirms such continuity in Upper Guinea: "Accounts written by Europeans over the past several centuries describe dance events similar to those seen in villages nowadays." Furthermore, while many of the West African masquerades proposed here as exemplars remain operant in the twenty-first century, the same does not hold true to the same degree for Western European practices. Although a few stalwart performers preserve the tradition, this dearth is particularly poignant in England's West Country, which was historically strong in wassailing. Accordingly, this research draws broadly from Western European regions to generate a field of likely prototypes, some still active, recognizing that similarities existed among peasant communities; indeed, a common masquerading ethos seems to have once encompassed most of Europe. What Margaret Fay Shaw witnessed in the Scottish Hebrides at Halloween in the early 1930s can be considered a cultural fossil, though at that time it was also common in Scandinavia and the Nordic Regions. According to Shaw (1955, 14), "One little boy spent the day carefully removing the entire skin off the head of a sheep so he could slip it over his own head like a bag, with ears intact." Compare this practice to the paintings of Romans in Alexandria in 1344 wearing heads of a donkeys, monkeys, goats, and bulls (E. K. Chambers 1903/1967, 1:frontispiece) or to John Hadman's 1433 King of Christmas parade in Norwich, England, where revelers, "dressed as devils, chased the people," while others were "wearing skin dresses, and counterfeiting bears, wolves, lions, and other animals" (Coffin 1973, 134).

A comparison of Old World and Leeward Islands masquerading is necessarily a broad study containing lots of diverse information, but the weft has been systematically separated from the weave and information presented in a systematic and unambiguous manner. The rigorous use of tangible proof in historical research is critical, but it is important to remember that the absence of evidence is not evidence of absence. At a certain level of antiquity, the sociopolitical roles of masquerades in Western Europe seem comparable to West African traditions—similar enough in many aspects to provide a conterminous bedrock to this study.

The research examines the interaction between intercontinental and interisland diffusion. Customs from diverse societies migrated into the Caribbean, and more localized transmission occurred as well. Most of the Leeward Islands were once part of the former BWI, and this commonality provided shared British influences and allowed for cultural interchange among the islands. Such sharing extended to the Danish West Indies (DWI, now the USVI) because the Danes did not import their folk culture into the Caribbean in any substantial way. Although Danes administered the islands, most plantation managers and planters were English, Irish, or Scottish. Nevertheless, peasants in Denmark had a vibrant mumming culture, and although the Julebukk was outlawed in 1668, straw effigies continued. This familiarity might have encouraged straw dolls such as John Hog and endorsed the Straw Bear in the DWI. Raffia masquerades such as the Straw Bear are somewhat generic to the West Indies, West Africa, and Western Europe, but in the Eastern Caribbean, only two named the bear were uncovered—one in the Virgin Islands and one in Barbados. Are the two connected? Following emancipation in 1848, the Danish islands experienced an influx of laborers from the former BWI, including Barbados, Antigua, and St. Kitts–Nevis. Some became actively involved in social issues: For example, the activist Queen Mary of the 1878 Fireburn fame hailed from Antigua. Although masquerading occurred in the preemancipation Virgin Islands, the new arrivals doubtless boosted it. Marshall, the premier Mocko Jumbie in St. Croix during the early twentieth century, came from Barbados. This research examines whether the Virgin Islands' bear originated in Barbados or was derived independently from a confluence of Danish and Irish customs.

Chapter 1 spells out the book's ideas and themes and includes a discussion of masquerade derivation, costumes, and behavior. What is a Jumbie, what constitutes play, and what is the significance of the playing ground? Chapter 2 looks at masquerade group membership, performance calendar, and class composition as well as the logistics and economics of masquerading. Chapter 3 investigates aesthetics, including dressing up and dressing down; costume and mask types; and stilts, horns, and whips, followed by an examination of musical and percussion instruments and rhythm and song texts. Chapter 4 describes eighteen masquerade types in the Eastern Caribbean, while chapters 5 and 6 look at the Old World provenance of masquerade exemplars in West Africa and Western Europe, respectively. Chapter 7 compares Old and New World masquerades in both secular and spiritual realms and describes a Leeward Islands Saturnalia. Finally, the conclusion examines religious censure in a historical context in each of the three regions and considers the past, present, and future of masquerading in the Eastern Caribbean.

Chapter 1

MASQUERADE DERIVATION, COSTUMES, AND BEHAVIOR

I became interested in masquerade performances while getting my degree in art in London. A Yoruba artist, Taiwo Emmanuel Jegede of the Keskidee Arts Center in England, taught us that the artist's duty is to feed society's soul. I was intrigued by a masquerade's quality of "whole theater," combining the other arts.[1] I eventually researched the masquerade culture of the Igede people of Benue State, Nigeria. Although once used to ready warriors for war or to commemorate battle victories, Igede masquerades such as Onyantu, Aitah, Ogrinye, and Abakpa now appear primarily during funerals or during the New Yam Festival, which demarcates each agricultural year. I found that a masquerade's performance is one of many voices within an event where an enhanced aesthetic is initiated by the conjunction of different art forms (Nicholls 1997, 64).[2]

During my research among the Igede, I found that ancestors were viewed as being of the dawn or the beginning and as conservative and concerned with the continuity of tradition. Yet because the dawn recurs each day, they are also connected with rebirth and renewal, creation and creativity. This viewpoint suggests not only that old things can be regenerated as new things but that old ancestral things such as masquerades can possess an immediacy that makes them appear as vital and new. In modern day soca and calypso parlance, the word *wind* (pronounced "wine") refers to the pelvic rotations characteristic of many African-derived dances. Similarly, *work* (pronounced "wuk") is currently used to refer to dance. It might be assumed that these are relatively modern terms, probably not more than thirty or forty years old. Yet more than two centuries ago, Moreton (1790, 14–15) documented a dance song in Jamaica that includes these terms:

Hipsaw! my deaa! You no shake like a-me!
You no wind like-me! Go, yondaa!
Hipsaw! my deaa! You no jig like a-me!
You no work like a-me! You no sweet him like a-me!

This lyric exposes the vintage of the customs that are researched here as well as the context that implies that they can appear fashionable and new despite their age. Authentic masquerades possess something of this quality, seeming fresh and novel on each encounter. Although Ronald Hutton (1997, 94) launched his academic career by calling the antiquity of the British animal disguises of the early nineteenth century into question, he concedes that the "nature of the entertainment," if not the physical artifact, has "remained consistent" over the years and that the impression of antiquity cannot be denied. Furthermore, he points out,

> E. C. Cawte shrewdly commented that the experience of being inside a hooden horse has an odd character of its own, involving a sense of slackening responsibility for what occurs as the role of playing the creature takes over. The present author, who has had that experience, must agree, and testify to the nervousness in the laughter of most spectators at the approach of something that is, and yet is not, a human being.... These customs do have a way of communicating something genuinely archaic, whatever their actual age. (94)

On arriving in the Virgin Islands (VI), I was pleased to discover that Caribbean masquerading did not simply consist of John Canoe in Jamaica but was part of the heritage of the Eastern Caribbean. Professor Ruth Beagles (pers. comm., July 10, 1995) told me that when she was growing up in Christiansted, St. Croix, she would hear the "jing-jing-jing" of the steel triangle in the Christmas celebration and run to the window of her two-story house to throw coins down to a small group of musicians and a masquerade, maybe Lucifer with horns, or Donkey Mas' dancing to the tune "Donkey want water, hold him down." I decided to explore Eastern Caribbean masquerading in more depth and thereby to discover its historical influence on today's carnivals.[3]

Each Caribbean Island has a carnival, but they are held at different times of the year. Dominica, Guadeloupe, Martinique, and Trinidad keep their carnivals true to Catholic tradition as pre-Lenten bacchanals ending on Ash Wednesday, like the New Orleans Mardi Gras. Anguilla, Antigua, Grenada, and Tortola hold their carnivals at the beginning of August to commemorate emancipation in the former British West Indies (BWI); St. Kitts–Nevis, Montserrat, St. Croix, and the Bahamas hold their festivals at Christmas, perpetuating ancient turn-of-the-year traditions. (Nevis also features Culturama in August.) Still others hold their carnivals at distinctive times. In Barbados, the carnival is held in June or July and is a continuation of the old Crop Over

Festival, which celebrates the sugarcane harvest. St. Martin holds its carnival on April 30, the birthday of Queen Beatrix of the Netherlands. St. Thomas also has its carnival at the end of April, simply to extend the tourist season.

The masquerades of the different islands are similar, though their festivals' Creole names may vary. Dominica has a Mocko Jumbie stilt masquerade known as Bwa Bwa; a donkey or burrokeet; a cow-horned shaggy masquerade known as Sensay Bull; and a raffia bear, which is the Sensay proper. (Plate 46) These masquerades are particularly prominent during the pre-Lenten carnival, Mas Domnik. Modern carnivals evolved from the earlier street masquerading that occurred primarily during the Christmas period and the New Year. S. B. Haynes (1872, 202) reports that on Three Kings' Day 1872, "we had the unusual amusement of seeing the whole population of St. Thomas en masque. . . . The people were so delighted at exhibiting themselves in party-colored garments and false faces. . . . And we can never forget the striking effects produced by groups of these brilliantly tinted costumes beneath the glowing tropic sky, with the white West Indian houses for backgrounds." A similar scene occurred in the first decade of the twentieth century: "What with the bright sunlight and the brighter colors displayed by the crowd of masqueraders, the Main Street from one end to the other seemed a kind of rainbow" (*St. Thomas Bulletin*, January 8, 1907). Literati described Caribbean slaves' Christmas revels as a "Saturnalia" or "Bacchanalia." Held in December, Saturnalia was an ancient Roman agricultural festival that was characterized by a symbolic reversal of power relations, whereby the meek appeared mighty and the mighty appeared meek. Tuckerman (1837, 24), for example, describes the 1836–37 Christmas and New Year's activities in St. Croix as a "complete Saturnalia": "The houses of the proprietors of slaves are thrown open; and long processions of slaves . . . with banners and music, enter at will the habitations to which they determine to go . . . are served with cakes and wine by their owners . . . and dance till they may be disposed to depart."[4] Throughout most of the nineteenth century, playing mas' turned the world topsy-turvy at Christmas, and disguised performers roamed the streets. Mock aristocracy and their retinues performed Plait Pole (Maypole) in yards and pastures; ritualized battles broke out between Zulus and "Wile Injuns"; men dressed as women, and vice versa; tall Jumbies danced on stilts; Bluebell Girls tantalized bystanders with glimpses of frilly petticoats and pantalets; David and Goliath reenacted their epic battle on street corners; and the Shaggy Bear and Wild Bull chased children and danced to the music of the fife and drum.

For the Jola and others in Upper Guinea, transitioning to manhood involved becoming "a bull," dancing in a horned mask and generally embodying masculine values: "strength, sexual potency, and . . . aggressive retaliation" (Mark 1992, 53). Such statements hold true for the Caribbean as well, although jocularity should be added because the Caribbean Bull was often comical. Although the literature might suggest that the involvement of women is less common elsewhere, in the Danish West Indies and in other parts of the Leeward Islands, women wore masks within women's troupes such as Mother Hubbard and dressed down within Cane Cutters troupes, as the literature, oral reports, and photographs attest. (For women's costumes as vehicles of enhancement rather than the disguise, see Franco 1998; Bettelheim 1998.)

Contemporary carnivals often give old masquerades a new lease on life and perpetuate the ancient custom as a living tradition. St. Thomas is a case in point. Carnivals were held in 1912 and 1914 but then lapsed until 1952, when Carnival was reestablished as an annual event. The roster of the 1952 and 1953 Carnivals shows that the parade drew on established Christmas masquerades. For example, Magnus the stilt-dancing Mocko Jumbie appeared in 1952 and 1953, as did the bear, Plait Pole, Indians, Zulus, clowns, and big heads. In the 1952 carnival, David and Goliath and a Down South troupe (blackface minstrels) appeared; the following year saw women's Blue Belles, Old Fashioned Pantalets, and Mother Hubbard troupes as well as an entry dubbed Old Fashioned Masquerade. In most cases, island carnivals liberally showcased traditional masquerades or modified or borrowed from them. Following the Trinidadian model, Caribbean carnivals expanded to include majorettes, steel bands, large troupes, and elaborate floats (Liverpool 2001). Nevertheless, carnivals in the twenty-first-century Virgin Islands include Mocko Jumbies, Indians, Zulus, clowns, queens, and kings, while the Blue Belles and women's contingents of yesteryear have been replaced by large troupes such as Hugga Bunch, Gypsies, or the Infernos that include women in skimpy costumes or spandex body stockings.

SCOPE OF THE STUDY

A masquerader is a street performer who entertains by dancing and other antics while disguised in a costume and usually a mask. In the Caribbean, masquerades historically were performed in the open air—on village greens, in urban compounds, in market squares, in yards, and on street corners. In colder climates, troupes might be invited into the parlor. In Britain, the terms *guiser*, *mummer*, *hoodener*, and *wassailer* are commonly used, along with more localized names such as Johnny Funny. More urbane characterizations included Merry Andrew and Jack Pudding and in earlier times a *device*, a *droll*, or an *antick*. According to the ethnic tongue, Africans have various names for disguised dancers, but in the English language, African guisers are generally referred to as masquerades or simply maskers. In the Upper Guinea, the Mandingo (Mandinka) masquerade, the Mumbo Jumbo, has been superseded by Kankuran, while I describe the horned Ejumba of the Jola (Diola), other West African masquerades, and Afro-Caribbean masquerades by their local names.

Barbados, the first British colony, had a Shaggy Bear (bush masquerade), Tilt-Man (Stilt-Man), Mother Sally (shemale), Donkey (tourney horse variety), and Donkey Man. Other early masquerades in the BWI included animal disguises such as the horse and the bull, including Cowhead Jonkonnu, and various clowns and Caribbean-style Merry Andrews, such as the Antiguan Highlanders. These characters unquestionably contain the residue of formative Old World seeds, but what Old World elements were adopted by Afro-Creole masquerades in the Eastern Caribbean, and how did transmission occur? The study looks for correspondence in appearance, roles, and behavior; where similarities arise, it fleshes out influences and potential attributive links. Social and spiritual roles of masquerading are discussed. Descriptions of the general appearance of a score of Caribbean masquerades are provided, including characteristic masks and costumes and musical components such as drum rhythms and song performances. Customary behavior and purposes are examined in areas of dancing, whipping, perambulations, demeanor, quêtes (traditional begging for food or alms to the accompaniment of folk song, specifically as part of a folk play), milieu, and social impact.

Paradigms of "dressing up" versus "dressing down" are explored. Dressing up uses a form of exaggerated realism and enhances rather than conceals the wearer (e.g., the Carnival Queen; see Cynthia Oliver 2009). In contrast, dressing down costumes lean to abstraction, are more amorphous, disguise the wearer, and may involve wearing sackcloth, raffia, and/or rags. For example, a bush masquerade such as the Shaggy Bear resembles nothing less than a mobile haystack. Pitchy Patchy and many of the Dominican Sensay masquerades are colorful cloth versions of the bush masquerades. (Plate 42) Moreover, some masquerades, such as the devil or bull, espouse an antisocial character. Because the Virgin Islands clown, Pitchy Patchy, and Montserrat masquerade are stylish and the Mocko Jumbie stilt masquerade is elegant, they might be considered dressed up. However, like the bush masquerades and animal representations, authentic renditions are totally disguised. In the past, gloves and stockings ensured that all human flesh was concealed. This fact, along with the name, *Jumbie*, connotes ancestral beliefs and interaction with the spirit world. Interviewed on television during the 2009 VI Carnival Parade, Carl Callwood, director of the Tropical Masqueraders Clown Troupe, explained that the masquerades "are based on our ancestors" and that their traditional function was "to scare away Jumbies." Women's genres include the dressed-down Cane Cutters in burlap costumes and the masked Mother Hubbard troupes with their tamarind whips.

A *Jumbie* (synonymous with *Duppy*) is a ghost or spirit. Referring to Guyana, Scoles (1885, 60) states, "Now Jumbie be it known is a great power out here, and . . . a sort of public pet, for so many things have been given or dedicated to him . . . such as trees, flowers, seeds, berries and birds." This is generally true of the Lesser Antilles, where one finds not only Jumbie beads (*Abrus precatorius*) and Jumbie trees (e.g., *Ceiba pentandra*) but also Jumbie peppers (*Rivina humilis*), a shrub that has toxic berries used locally to treat diarrhea; Jumbie fingers, the seedpod of the pomshock tree (*Inga laurina*); Jumbie parasols, small white umbrella-shaped fungi; Jumbie crab, a small reddish land crab; Jumbie bird, the nightjar, with its eerie whirring warble; and Jumbie horse, the vernacular name for praying mantis.

The word *Jumbie*, like *zombie*, may derive from the Kimbundu word *zumbi* or *nzambi*, which generally means a spirit or deity, or from the Kikongo word *njambi*, which refers to a major deity (Gerhard Seibert, pers. comm., March 13, 2001; see also Kubik 1999, 24). However, it may have a duel provenance, because an alternative possibility from the Upper Guinea region exists in the Senegambian word *bajumbi*. Bajumbi is a pea-sized red and black seed of a vine (*Abrus precatorius*) that is believed to provide protection from bad spirits. Bajumbi seeds give their name to the Ejumba mask of the Jola in the Casamance region, a mask associated with male initiation ceremonies: "The ejumba mask covered with red seeds protects the new initiate" (Mark 1992, 103). (Plate 13) In the Eastern Caribbean, *Abrus* seeds (Jumbie beads, John Crow beads in Jamaica) are made into necklaces and bracelets to serve as protection against Jumbies and malevolent forces. Masquerades may also be decorated with *Abrus* for the same reason.

The term *Jumbie* reflects animistic ideas of spirits that inhabit natural phenomena such as trees and rocks and equates to African notions of the ancestors, particularly deceased kinfolk. Barbadians around 1817 "believed in the existence of spirits, which they call Jumbees, and sometimes spread victuals on graves . . . that their spirits might return and eat" (Watson 1817, 17). In St. Vincent, for some time after Nine Night (a funeral wake), "one is likely to see the first drops of any liquid being drunk thrown on the ground whether for the daddies (as the ancestors are called) or for a specific dead person. This is especially important to do at the crossroads or where people congregate in public" (Abrahams 1983, 180). Using edible offerings to remember the deceased was fairly common both throughout the Caribbean and in

West Africa.[5] Jumbies can be good or bad, but mostly they are mischievous. Tobagoans believe that "jumbies are restless spirits, the undead who pass their time playing tricks on the living" (Iaconetti 1997, 42). Theresa Lewis (1990, 43) explains the importance of "knowing whether it was a good jumbie or a bad jumbie. Bad jumbies could bring you the worst possible luck. . . . On the other hand, a good jumbie could also influence your surroundings and help to protect you." Asta Williams (pers. comm., August 3, 2001) points out, "Spirits provide omens; they can alert you to a lot." Regarding the Virgin Islands, Lito Valls (1981, 7) writes of a "Bapoo," which he describes as a "Jumbee in a bottle": "Bapoos are sometimes placed on fruit trees to keep children away." In Jamaica, the term "dressing a garden" means "setting Obeah for the thieves" (Bell 1889/1970).

In relation to Jumbie protection, a confluence of Old World ideas occurred in the Caribbean. There is an old belief in Europe that wearing clothes inside out, wearing underwear outside of one's regular clothes , or cross-dressing renders one invisible to evil spirits. In the VI, Frank Charles (pers. comm., July 1, 1996) recollects that "when going home late at night, someone might wear their clothes inside out to ward off ghosts." The same is true for Antigua, where Samuel Smith states, "women use to turn their dresses over their head when walking at night and men use to turn their shirts on the wrong side" (Smith and Smith 1988, 67). This practice also occurs in Tobago and elsewhere (Iaconetti 1997, 42). If a ghost was felt to be in the vicinity, an Antiguan woman would throw her skirt over her head, stoop, and show the ghost her bloomered backside while uttering curse words (Lornetta Prince, pers. comm., August 2, 1995). The fact that the protective power is in the textile is evidenced by the fact that in the Virgin Islands, "You could prevent a jumbie from entering your home by turning your clothes inside out and hanging them on a line across the room. The jumbie will walk up and down outside, but it could never enter" (Schrader 1993, 89). Although she is now in her thirties, Crucian Tracy Warner (pers. comm., August 30, 1996) confirms that she will still "put on her pajamas inside out" to ward off ghosts.

Mocko Jumbie now refers exclusively to Caribbean stilt-dancing masquerades; in the Eastern Caribbean, however, the term previously referred to all masquerades. Furthermore, as a consequence of both the dialect of the informant and the partiality of the chronicler, there are many spelling variations of *Mocko Jumbie* (and *Jonkonnu*, for that matter). Moreover, the name both describes what it is and what it does. As an adjective, *mock* means "sham" or "artificial"; as a verb, the word means "to mimic" or "to ridicule." A Mocko Jumbie, therefore, is an effigy—a supernatural scarecrow—that ridicules and scares away ghosts (Leona Watson, pers. comm., August 9, 1996). *Mocou* in

Fig. 1.1. Mocko Jumbie dancing in St. Croix, ca. 1900. Note raised skirt revealing the petticoat and musicians, including flute and triangle players, to the right. Photo by Alfred Paludan-Müller. Courtesy Royal Library, Copenhagen, Department of Maps, Prints, and Photographs.

colloquial Spanish means "spirit" or "ghost." Some Virgin Island folktales tell of Jumbies dancing and being dispersed with a whip. In Antigua, the noise of stamping feet can dislodge spirits from a yard or from inside a house. A Mocko Jumbie's presence is believed to have a negative effect on malevolent spirits and sorcerers. The Mande of Upper Guinea perceive the bush as a place of *dibi* and the world of sorcery as submerged in it. Masks are described as *dibi-finw* (things of *dibi*) that enter the world of obscurity to fight treachery and sorcery (McNaughton 1982, 58). Mama Konta, a Senegalese folklorist, discussed similar ideas at the Smithsonian Folklife Festival in Washington, D.C., in 1990. She said that when villagers dance in Senegal, they stamp their feet to keep away the evil spirits, which then take refuge in the trees, where only the stilt dancer can reach them to mock them and get rid of them. Jumbies in trees, stamping feet, and cracking whips are all familiar concepts in the Eastern Caribbean. Through Creolization processes, bloomers, petticoats, clothes turned inside out, and clothes of the opposite gender were seen as weapons to be used against Jumbies. Historically in the Virgin Islands, stilt masquerades often dressed in women's clothes and would raise their outer skirts, show their underwear, and flutter or feather their petticoats to drive off evil spirits. According to Rudy Farrell (pers. comm., August 2, 1995), when his father, Magnus, would perform as a Mocko Jumbie, he would make a fast series of shuffling backward jumps, waving his petticoats in the air to ward off spirits.

The use of small decorative mirrors also demonstrates a confluence of Old World traditions. The little mirrors that Mocko Jumbies wore symbolized their invisibility: Viewers would see only themselves reflected back. In both European and West African cultures, mirrors are thought to dispel evil. British mummers and morris dancers often decorate their hats and jackets with small mirrors "as a means of reflecting away evil" (Helm 1981, 40). Ejumba masquerades of the Jola of Senegambia are adorned with small mirrors, which are believed to unmask and reveal witches (Mark 1992, 104). In Sierra Leone, Temne diviners use mirrors to identify evildoers (Nunley 1985, 97), while the antiwitchcraft masquerades of the Banyang of southeastern Nigeria wear mirrors as clairvoyant "eyes" that discern witchcraft activity (Robert Farris Thompson 1974, 209), as do the Anogiri masquerades of the Okpella in Nigeria's Bendel State (Borgatti 1988, 71). The notion of clairvoyance leads into an interpretation of Mocko Jumbie stilt masquerade as a seer and sorcerer. The name *Mocko Jumbie* is phonetically similar to *Mumbo Jumbo*, and according to Daniel Crowley (1956, 198), the standard definition of *Mumbo Jumbo* is a magician who protects his people.

When I interviewed older people, I found that *Mocko Jumbie* previously was used in a wider sense to describe disguised performers in general. Alfred M. Williams (1896, 117) writes about festivities in St. Kitts that involved stilt dancers, horned masks, Indians, men dressed as women, and sailor masqueraders, all of which he called "moka jumbic dances." In the same vein, Richard Schrader (1989, 2) refers to a "Mrs. Langley, an old lady in the village who played a moko jumbie" in St. Croix. Langley actually belonged to a Mother Hubbard troupe of maskers. All masquerades possessed the ability to interact with Jumbies to a degree. Historically, Mocko Jumbies were believed to be able to bestow good luck and beneficence. They still appear on stilts at housewarmings and business openings. In Charlotte Amalie, they invariably visit the hospital grounds at Carnival time to dance for patients, who look out the windows.

COSTUME CHOICE

Various theories can be propounded regarding communal choices of a masquerade and its costume. Perceptible parallels exist among masquerades in

Africa, Europe, and Caribbean, and these parallels are often explained via a diffusion model, which explores attributive links of a cause-and-effect nature. The word *Creole* implies that eclecticism and Caribbean masquerading emerged from a fusion of styles. I hypothesize that indentured servants and other Europeans introduced peasant culture into the Caribbean, where it blended with Africans' culture to produce a distinctive form of expression. However, other explanations also exist, foremost among them a consideration of parallel evolution, which suggests that similar cultural artifacts can emerge independently in diverse regions.

Parallel Evolution

Some psychologists assert that humans share a macrolevel collective unconscious and that the imagery of one group is potentially intelligible to members of an unrelated group. This theory suggests that all humans possess a fount of imagery that is little affected by time and place and that by means of individual inspiration, comparable notions can emerge independently in diverse localities.[6] The artistic output of Native American shamans is sometimes attributed to introspection and vision quests, which uncover subconscious aesthetic forms. According to this theory, such archetypal forms as a horned figure, a therianthrope, a shaggy bush monster, or a shemale are universal and might influence masquerade representation in different places. However, research in Africa has shown that when new masquerade costumes are attributed to dream inspiration, they are seldom completely novel but instead generally stay within the parameters of established aesthetic conventions (see Strother 1998). This book does not pursue parallel inspiration theories. Nevertheless, festivals are times to construct costumes, and individual performers draw on their inherent creativity and strive to make original choices and inspired commentary.

Another form of parallel evolution suggests that like circumstances produce like results. Before acetate and celluloid became common media in the twentieth century, cultural diffusion involved live performances and direct contact between people, and John Storm Roberts (1972, 248) states that it is "logical to assume that the encounter of similar factors from two musical cultures—West African and British—in the West Indies and in West Africa produced somewhat similar results independently." Roberts's argument for parallel evolution is fallacious, however, because he omits a consideration of social class. The West African and the West Indian experiences are different. In West Africa before the twentieth century, the colonial presence was less pervasive than in the West Indies. West Africa saw few European settlers other than slavers in the early era and later sailors in the seaports; the European working class had only a minor presence. Accordingly, West African cultures did not become significantly Creolized, and Europeans had little impact on masquerading. In contrast, in the West Indies, indentured servants, deported prisoners, and general immigration introduced European peasant culture, where it blended with Africans cultures to produce a distinctive form of masquerading. Those Creolisms that eventually appeared in West Africa resulted from an out-migration of cultural ideas from the Caribbean starting around 1800. (See appendix 2.)

Practical Expediency

Pursuant to the idea that like circumstances produce like results, another form of parallel evolution might result from the selection of dance costumes as a result of expediency. The poverty of peasants is a historical commonality in the three regions, and raffia masquerades historically appear in West Africa, Western Europe, and the West Indies. A convenience principle suggests that parallel development can occur because raffia, whether dried leaves or straw, is cheap and locally available in all of the three regions being considered. In Africa, raffia masquerades are found in many farming communities. For example, the Igede have a masquerade known as Onyunwunyu that dressed in shaggy raffia and danced at the New Yam Festival (Nicholls 2006a). (Plate 7) The Panther Men of the Wé ethnic group of Ivory Coast are another of the many African masquerades who wear dried foliage costumes. Raffia costumes have also been popular in rural Europe. In Germany, Czechoslovakia, and England, straw masquerades are known as Straw Bears, while in Ireland they are Strawboys. Raffia bush masquerades also existed in Barbados, Dominica, and the Virgin Islands. The Caribbean Shaggy Bear was usually dressed from head to toe in a bulrush or plantain flag costume, often made of dried banana leaves. Elick the Bear appeared in the 1914 Carnival in St. Thomas, while Koka the Bear was one of the best known twentieth-century performers.

An examination of cultural manifestations in West Africa, Western Europe, and the West Indies should, therefore, consider the influence of parallel evolution as a result of pragmatic choices. But the principle becomes moot with regard to animal-hide costumes, which are virtually nonexistent in West Africa, although pelts and fur might embellish costumes. For example, the masquerades of Ode–Lay hunting societies may wear a vest with "a variety of animal skins, including civet, baboon, and bush antelope, hang[ing] from the front and the back" (Nunley 1987, 126). In this area, similarities are more noticeable between Western Europe and the West Indies. Moreover, despite an

Fig. 1.2. Kumpo at a cultural festival, Ziguinchor, Casamance, Senegal, 1994. Note how assistant's foot serves as a pole prop for Kumpo's gyrations. Courtesy Ferdinand de Jong.

early prevalence in Jamaica, reports of bull-hide costumes did not surface in the Leeward Islands. The animal decoy disguises that were used to facilitate prehistoric European hunting might also have been worn during celebrations as a matter of expedience—Why create a new costume when an existing one is already close at hand? The later pastoral Celts had a plentiful supply of domestic cattle hides from the annual prewinter culling. As large tracts of arable land came under the plow in the Middle Ages, horses became common for burden and for transport, and their carcasses were generally available, as were those of other farm animals. The choice of animal hides as costumes seems to include pragmatic considerations. Church literature of the fourth century A.D. contains accounts of both stag masquerades in Spain and stags and horses in Algeria (Nicholls 1988). Clergymen complained about local citizens donning the skins of stags, bulls, and horses during new year or midwinter festivals in Barcelona in A.D. 370 and Seville in A.D. 636. The use of a bull-hide costume was recorded in 1656 in Evershot, Dorset, England (Besse 1753). In Jamaica in 1797, it was reported that the "John Canoe . . . exhibited by the Butchers, is clad in the hide of an ox with horns, which is held up with a rope" (Anonymous 1797/1976, 22). The fact that this masquerade was performed by butchers suggests an element of expediency. The horned headdresses of the Ejumba of the

Jola in Senegambia come from cattle slaughtered to commemorate the male initiation ceremonies.

However, in other cases, costume choices seem to involve more than mere practicality. Although wearing antlers may have been a practical choice for early hunters, in other times and places it comprises a more arcane or fanciful option. The Abbots Bromley horn dancers of Staffordshire, England, performed dances during the seventeenth century that involved six men carrying reindeer horns at shoulder level (Heaney 1987). Reindeer have been extinct in Britain for millennia, and a radio-carbon-dating test on the horns shows they came from reindeer that lived during the eleventh century. Hutton (1997, 90) thus suggests that "the antlers must have been imported from Scandinavia, or even further afield." In this instance, the choice of reindeer horns clearly was not pragmatic and based on local availability.

An examination of shemale masquerades further includes the possibility of parallel evolution resulting from practical choices made in situ. Here again, most of the parallels occur between Europe and the Caribbean. For three-quarters of a century starting around the 1870s, the standard uniform of the Mocko Jumbie stilt dancer in the Virgin Islands was a European-style woman's dress. The appropriation of a female dress to save money was doubtless a factor: Such a costume is cheap and easily obtained—the performer simply co-opts a fanciful dress from his wife's or sister's closet. That this choice was purely one of convenience is supported by the fact that for the Mocko Jumbie, it did not involve additional padding or artificial breasts, and the masker did not mince around parodying female behavior. In contrast, at virtually every J'ouvert in the Eastern Caribbean, young men don women's dresses, sometimes displaying bloomers and underwear, and here the intent is to lampoon the opposite sex.

Cultural Diffusion

Although pragmatism might bear some consideration with bush masquerades and the bull-horned Jonkonnu, the situation changes when we consider the House Jonkonnu, named after the effigy of a house or a ship worn as a headpiece. The Jamaican report that describes the dress of the House Jonkonnu in 1797 appears to present it as an innovation: "Many of their present figures claim attention for the fantastic modern cut of their cloaths, often of silk and sometimes enriched with lace, a quantity of hair on the head as preposterously dressed as some European beaux: and over that a representation of an edifice . . . in the stile of a baby house, shewing different fronts with open doors, glazed windows, stair cases, plazas and balconies, in which diminutive figures are placed" (Anonymous 1797/1976, 21). In one of many such descriptions from Jamaica, Belisario (1837) drew such a "House John Canoe" in 1836: The masquerader is wearing a humanesque mask, possibly of wire mesh. Clement Bethel (1977, 10) declares, "Junkanoo only appears to have occurred in those countries which have some English influence." Although not recorded in the Carolinas, such a "house ghost" appeared in the New Year's Junkanoo parades in Bahamas (Bethel 1977, 10). It is also remembered by an anonymous source in Tortola in the British Virgin Islands (BVI) in 1843 as the "harmless pageant of Jonkanoo [that] with its little emblem of Noah's Ark [had] fallen into disuse" (Abrahams and Szwed 1983, 294). Moreover, similar headpieces were worn by white villagers in Newfoundland during Christmas Janneying: In the mid-1800s, costumes included cocked hats surmounted with paper models of houses or ships (Story 1969, 171). Such paper models are intricate and finely made. In this case, expediency is not a factor, and diffusion rather than parallel evolution is at play.

A mixture of the practical tempered with the arcane is apparent throughout the range of costumes. For example, is the practice of wearing clothes turned inside out simply a folk superstition, or does the principle of expediency deserve consideration here also? Warner (1977, 6) explains that among Russian peasantry, "the customary exchange of clothing between men and women and the habits of wearing clothes inside out [was prompted by] the desire to hide or protect one's person by disguise from the attention of the evil spirits." A similar idea once existed in Devonshire and Pembrokeshire in England, where the notion of being "Pixy-led" (led astray by Pixies) was combated by turning one's garment inside out (J. B. Smith 2010, 8).[7] Lucy Broadwood describes the pace eggers' costume of Heysham, Lancashire, in 1893 as "simply a nightshirt worn over the clothes, ornamented with tags of coloured ribbon and paper sewn in all direction" (Cass 2001, 50). These beliefs crossed over to the Caribbean and contributed to the Creolization process. Furthermore, the use of mirrors as costume elements demonstrates a confluence of Old World traditions. Parallel evolution is hardly a possibility; instead, it seems that when the mirror was adopted in a territory, certain ideas came along with it. In Europe, shiny things contained the essence of the sun, a major deity. Ultimately, abundant evidence shows that in the Caribbean, costume choices involve more than mere expediency. Stilts, for example, are an arcane rather than a practical choice.

THE PLAYING GROUND: PLAY, RITUAL, AND REDRESS

The words to one well-known myal song that accompanies a Jonkonnu performance at Nassau, St. Elizabeth, Jamaica, show how the earth, containing the souls of the ancestors, is honored. Particular honors go to the ground of the family yard where the dancing is taking place, the ring—the Jumbies' playing ground. Kenneth Bilby (1999, 56; 2010, 191) explains,

> If the play is not generating enough heat, and the spirits are slow to make their presence felt, the following myal song, specially designed for the purpose, may be sung to hasten the process:
>
> *Oy-oh, eh-de-oy, eh-de*
> *Roll de band a yard*
> *Det a grong a me fren [literally, the ancestral dead in the earth/cemetery are my friends]*
> *Seh duppy a me fren [the spirits are my friends]*
> *Seh duppy a me fren*
> *Roll de band a yard*
> *Det a grong a me fren*
>
> The song is meant to honour the family "yard" of which the ancestors are part . . . in the hope of cajoling the disgruntled spirits to come forward and manifest themselves.

Play is a singularly important term in a discussion of West African enactments and is regularly used by native practitioners to indicate a broad range of activities that are simultaneously serious and lighthearted. This book uses a concept of play derived from Africa but also found in the Caribbean. In the parlance of the Hausa of Sahelian Africa, *wasa* (play) describes a wide range of recreational activities, particularly music and dance. Among the Mande, "the term *nyènajè* (entertainment) or the more general term *tulon* (play) is used in several contexts to refer to drumming and dancing"—for example, the dancing that celebrates the return of circumcised children to the village is considered *tulon* (Charry 2000, 209–10). Among the Igede of Nigeria, the patron of a music association is known as Ada'ilo (Ada Ayilo), which translates as "father of play." The literature variously describes the Igede *ojiya*, a clearing in the village forest edged by giant trees, as the "town square" (Ikoni 1988, 30), "the central meeting ground" (Ranung 1973), and "Igede stadium" (Eru 1988, 7); the local people, however, invariably refer to it as the "playground," even though it has traditionally been the site of serious activities such as trials, public debates, and ritual sacrifices as well as funerals, music and dance activities, and children's games, including soccer in the modern era. The Idoma, neighbors to the Igede, refer to their "playground" as *ojila*. There is some suggestion that *play* may be a euphemism for other more earnest activities involving dance and ritual and that the term has been used to ease colonial administrators' fears. Bilby (2010, 209) supports this rationale, arguing that "preservation of the bond with ancestral spirits . . . most likely required a particular kind of disguise of its own. . . . The Jankunu tradition had to mask (that is, pose) in public . . . as Christianity's harmless opposite—a 'secular' form of 'play.'" However, the concept is more far-reaching than simply a defense maneuver.

Roger D. Abrahams and John Szwed (1983, 35) show that *play* was historically prevalent in the Caribbean and referred broadly to music and dance activities: "Any holiday may be called a *play-day*, as was a wake." Accounts from as early as 1729 relate that the slaves in Barbados held "plays"—Sunday gatherings with spiritual overtones "in which with various instruments of horrid music howling and dancing about the graves of the dead, they [give] victuals and strong liquor to the deceased (Handler and Frisbie 1972, 14). In Jamaica around 1788, the term was used to describe the "violent exercise" of singing and dancing, and slaves traveled many miles to dances or events "which they style plays" (Marsden 1788, 33). Furthermore, in 1823, it was observed that *play* is the slaves' term for any of a range of "licensed nonsense occasions" (Stewart 1823/1969, 270). Abrahams and Szwed (1983, 33) discuss the contrast between "serious" and "play" and argue that the latter focuses "on situations of style- and code-switching . . . which have to do with the assertion of value—and culture—differences in performance terms."

Sidney Kasfir (1982, 47) has studied the concept of play and identifies Idoma associational masks as "bush spirits." Moreover, she contends, "Masks control danger by bringing aspects of the wild into the controlled environment of the village playground (*ojila*)" (1988, 86). In many West African mask performances, Kasfir points out, "elements of both 'play' and 'ritual' may be present in a single enactment," and "in the Nigerian village where I lived masquerades were both a primary form of enactment or religious ritual and the most popular form of entertainment" (3).[8] In an article on an Idioma artist, Ojiji, Kasfir (1989, 44) writes, "In contrasting his life with that of Westerners like me, Ojiji used to say, 'We only do three things here: farm, hunt, and play.' 'Play,' in the deep meaning of the word, is what Ojiji's life was principally about. He was not only a successful woodcarver but also a diviner, dancer, and Anjenu [river spirit] priest."

In contrast to the West, where sacred and secular are represented as a dichotomy, in traditional Africa, the sacred is omnipresent and indivisible from the mundane. According to Kasfir (1988, 3), "In this context, the sacred/secular distinction made little sense, since masking was clearly perceived as *both* play and ritual. . . . Even the most frivolous, outrageous or absurd masked figure is nonetheless *ekwu*, 'a spirit.' He is not simply an actor playing a role, but a being from the netherworld." Thus, Kasfir suggests, it "becomes possible to view masking as a transformational process which, when enacted as ritual, reflects the cosmic order, and when enacted as play, belongs to the social order. . . . It is more accurate to say that mask performances *mediate* between play and ritual" (5). Or play and nonplay. Discussing Ode-Lay masquerades of Sierra Leone, John Nunley (1987, 177) writes, "What might appear to be play at times may be interpreted as the real thing, or what appears to be a nip may at times be read as a bite." Furthermore, "in the region where art, magic, and religion overlap, humans have evolved *the metaphor that is meant* (190).

Ideas of spirits and the netherworld are not limited to Africa; Europeans believed that visits from the ancestral world were possible during the seam between the old year and the new year. Referred to as Daft Days by the Galoshin mummers in Scotland, this was a liminal period when normal conventions were in abeyance and abnormal conduct was permitted. Research conducted by Ülo Tedre (2007, 387) suggests that the mumming of the Estonian Jõulupoisid (Christmas Boys), who visited farms to dance, joke, and wish people a merry Christmas and good luck, was "a mixture of a magical-ritual function and entertainment." Vento (2007, 357) explains, "The Indo-European calendar, based on the moon, had to allow for the difference of twelve days between the solar and lunar year. This 'twelve-day phenomenon' would thus explain the rites and frolicking that accompanied the Saturnalia festival of the Romans . . . and likewise the Nordik midwinter feasting and the 'time of the spirits' of the Finns." Such seasonal rites of renewal aimed at the regeneration of power through celebration, thanksgiving, and good-luck sharing. Nonetheless, in Europe, the enigmatic relationship between play and ritual is no longer as apparent as it once was. Play seems to be at the forefront, although camouflaged ritual elements such as coats turned inside-out often provide subtexts in play activities.

Music, dance, and costumed performance might be seen as entertainment in each of the three regions, but such performances historically encoded complex cultural messages related to continuity and change and made the local ideology salient to the populace. Performance directed at creating behavioral change can be considered normative because the intent is that listeners heed the commentary and correct objectionable behavior. By providing the opportunity to experiment with novelty within the safety of an artistic "pretend" situation, the revels were instrumentally transformative. Discussing a Kittitian troupe known as Niega Business (Neagar Business) whose charter was to bring local scandal to the street at Christmas, Mills, Jones-Hendrickson, and Bertram (1984, 11) state, "These members of the lowest stratum in our society often used this medium not only to caricature bukra man [white man] and the middle class, but to laugh at them, to imitate and to mock them, and even to expose their social and moral depravity and corruption. . . . This license and ridicule that bordered on slander was only temporary, that is, it would only last during the Christmas Season." This group made a point of dressing down: "Wire masks may or may not be worn, and occasionally one may have his entire face covered with soot and locomotive grease. The clothes were extraordinary: a derby on the head, long black scissor-type frockcoats, rumpled tie or big bow tie, and trousers sometimes decorated with coloured rags sewn thereon" (9).

Various masquerades encoded cultural messages and by means of parody and inversion mediated between the different segments of society. Shaming either individuals or modes of behavior in song and mocking them in masquerade are forms of coercion that can lead to behavior modification or at least an increased awareness of the situation. The same holds true for larger institutions and social processes, demonstrating that music, dance, and masquerading can go beyond merely criticizing the social order to lead to change in the status quo, as is exemplified by the disbanding of the militia following the St. Croix Gombay confrontation of Christmas 1852. (See appendix 3.) In extreme situations, "play" and "reality" merge, and masquerades can initiate sociopolitical transformation, as in the case of Arthur Sixteen's confrontation with Antiguan sugar boss Sir Alexander Moody-Stuart. However, those who acclaim the revolutionary potential of Black Saturnalia tend to overlook how the African ethos of pragmatism was perpetuated in the Caribbean. Despite intermittent clashes, island populations showed themselves to be resilient, essentially seeking improvements in their daily lives. While the toppling of the system might not be immediately achievable, tackling the many small problems could lead to real practical changes in the here and now.

OLD WORLD ANTECEDENTS

The similarities between disguised performance traditions in the West Indies and those in West Africa and Western Europe warrant investigation.

The Amerindian heritage affected some aspects of Caribbean culture but not masquerades, and there were no cattle or horses in the Caribbean prior to Columbus's arrival.[9] The fact that the bull, horse, and donkey were subsequently represented in costume betokens cultural diffusion. Therefore, formative influences can be credited to antecedent masquerades in Western Europe and in West Africa, and attributive links can be speculated. Masquerade prototypes in the Leeward Islands were formed primarily from a fusion of styles from the Upper Guinea region of West Africa—loosely defined as stretching from Senegal to the northwestern Ivory Coast—and Western Europe, especially Britain's West Country and Scotland, Ireland, and Wales.

Although early arriving groups made critical contributions to the establishment of a masquerading template, late-arriving groups often generated more observable "Africanisms" than those groups whose cultures were established early and subsequently absorbed. McDaniel (1998, 104) notes that between 1843 and 1865, Grenada had more than six thousand "late-to-arrive" Yoruba, while McNeal (2010, 194) points out that postemancipation Trinidad "received a relatively large infusion of Yoruba-speaking West Africans who came not as slaves but indentured immigrants between 1838 and 1870 and who brought elements of traditional Orisha praxis with them." The Yoruba similarly affected Bahia in Brazil (Falola and Childs 2004). Fon traditions of voodoo from the Benin Republic were consolidated in Haiti (Herskovits and Herskovits 1938). By the same token, the Abakua masquerade of Cuba is akin to the Ekpe leopard society masquerade of the Efik and Ejagham of Nigeria (Miller 2009; see also Miller 2005; Bettelheim 1991, 75; Palmié 2010).

What does masquerading or mumming represent in West Africa, Western Europe, and the West Indies? What social and spiritual roles were fulfilled? Because most of West Africa was not affected culturally by colonial forces until the early twentieth century, many of the roles of masquerading in that region are still expressed. In contrast, European peasant culture was subjugated by the church and feudalism, and masquerading has long since been stripped of most of its communal functions and relegated to society's margins. What remains are mere phantasms of formerly viable spiritual and sociopolitical entities. Despite this devaluation, vestiges of comparable spiritual agencies and egalitarian regulatory models can be traced.

West African masquerading unashamedly dealt with spiritual manipulation and was ably expressed as a device for sociopolitical control. Thus, the "rule-application" function of West African masquerades provides the most thoroughly articulated model. European agrarian communities once used masquerades for communal regulation, though this function had become limited by the time those communities enter human history. At that point, a marked difference already existed between the West African and European models. In West African deep history, masquerades tended to be conservative in that they affirmed the existing social order. By medieval times in Europe, in contrast, the use of masquerades was more radical and activist. Vestiges of grassroots sociopolitical control models can be seen within skimmingtons, while inversion rites such as the Lord of Misrule games and yearly pageants of transition such as carnivals also served as critiques. Elements of both skimmingtons and Saturnalia existed in the West Indies. At the local level, the communal regulation and behavior modification (especially of children) was apparent until recent times, while annual street festivals and carnivals still represent a form of Saturnalia, albeit muted. West African and Western European populations and their masquerades can be identified as part of the genesis of Caribbean masquerading.

Western Europe

British (English, Scottish, and Welsh) and Irish migrants, especially those from southwestern England, were prevalent among the early colonists in Barbados, St. Kitts–Nevis, Antigua, and Montserrat. Eltis (2000, 41) proclaims that the islands "were settled and carried firmly into the plantation export sector of the Atlantic economy with the aid of a mainly European, rather than African or Amerindian, labor force." Various other European nations also have had interests in the Caribbean. The Spanish and Portuguese made the initial inroads, but Dutch, French, British, Swedish, and Danish nationals were involved in the slave trade as well. At the outset of colonization, the Caribbean was frontier territory, and adventurers and speculators of many nationalities strived to make their mark. According to Eltis (2000, 235), "There was greater diversity in the English West Indies than in the Chesapeake." Visiting Barbados in 1655, Henry Whistler (1900, 146) wrote, "This Island is inhabited with all sortes: with English, french, duch, Scotes, Irish, Spaniards thay being Jues." The French were conspicuous in Martinique and Guadeloupe in the Windward Islands, while the Danes were notable in the Danish West Indies (DWI). However, few Danish farmhands or rural workers migrated to the DWI, and the Danish inhabitants were mostly of the administrator class. As a result, although Danish was the language of officialdom, it was never the common tongue. The Dutch had previously been major players in the region, making considerable contributions to the culture, especially the language, before the vernacular changed from Dutch Creole to English Creole.

Until sugar production necessitated African labor, the majority of settlers were white, and indentured servants were the principal workforce. Ronald

Tree (1972, 14) writes that the colonization of Barbados "proceeded rapidly, and within three years of the arrival of the first settlers, between 1,500 and 1,600 persons were living on the island. . . . The holdings for the most part were small, and were worked by the settlers themselves." Immigrants fell into three categories: "Firstly, those who possessed of some means . . . with which they bought leaseholds or small properties" (15). The second group comprised indentured servants, who "were for the most part on a three- to five-year indenture and who, during that period, voluntarily sold themselves into slavery in return for passage and clothing—at the end of which they were given 300 lbs of tobacco with which to start a new life" (15). The final group, enslaved people from West Africa, "on the whole were treated better than the indentured whites; being slaves in perpetuity, they were of greater value to their owners" (15). According to Robert Haynes (1934, 67), a descendant of Richard Haynes, a Royalist who was forced to emigrate to Barbados in the time of Oliver Cromwell, "In 1640 the labour problem was so acute that even foreign servants were welcomed, some kidnapped Frenchmen fetching 900 lbs of cotton per head." This need for labor meant that the indentured servants' found their time of indenture as much as doubled as a consequence of supposed infractions.

Barbados's population began to shift from predominantly white to predominantly black with the adoption of the sugar economy in the 1630s. Prior to the introduction of sugar, the island had consisted of small estates held mostly by formerly indentured servants on which vegetables, cotton, and tobacco were grown. In 1645, the island had six thousand black slaves and thirty-seven thousand whites, most of them indentured servants. Fifteen years later, the Barbadian white and black populations were approximately in balance, though whites remained more numerous elsewhere in the British Caribbean. By 1685, Barbados's European population fell to seventeen thousand, while the number of black island inhabitants rose to forty-six thousand (Conniff and Davis 1994, 77; Eltis 2000, 41).

By 1655, Barbados had 745 sugar plantations, and the island's council voted for a consignment of one thousand Irish boys and an equal number of Irish girls for their "other" West Indian colonies (Robert Haynes 1934, 65). In the same year, Barbadian planters claimed to have twelve thousand prisoners of war as servants, including representatives of Ireland, Scotland, and England (Niles 1980, 16), including "jailbirds from Newgate prison" (Rediker 1989, 28). Furthermore, Cromwell had dispatched many Irish prisoners of war to Montserrat following his victory at Drogheda in 1649. As a result, Montserrat eventually had a majority-Catholic population, St. Patrick's Day is a national holiday, and the headdresses of the Montserrat masqueraders resemble St.

Patrick's miter. "The bulk of white migration to Barbados occurred before the more restrictive Navigation Acts of the early 1660s cut off the influx of Scottish indentured servants and after the flow of prisoners from Scotland and Ireland had ended" (Eltis 2000, 235). Nevertheless, "the sugar islands received over three-quarters of the prisoners leaving England after 1660" (52).

West Countrymen in the Leeward Islands

As a consequence of the English Civil War, the commonwealth seized Royalist estates and forced their owners to go abroad, further affecting migration to Barbados. "Most of the immigrants came from the West Country [Cornwall, Somerset, Devonshire, Gloucestershire, Dorset, and Wiltshire], Bristol being the port from which most of the West Indian trade was conducted" (Tree 1972, 16). As such a prominent port city, Bristol also was a major supplier of sailors. Tree (1972, 35) writes, "After the Battle of Worcester [Gloucestershire] in 1652 the first mention is made of Royalists having been brought out to Barbados and sold as slaves for fifteen hundred pounds of sugar each, according to their ability to work. . . . On arrival in Barbados they were sold as chattels and employed on grinding the mills, attending the furnaces and digging in the hot sun—whipped at the whipping post as rogues" (35).

Records show that the early colonists also included country folk from Wales, Scotland, and Ireland (Burton 1997, 15). The southwestern region of England supplied 78.6 percent of the total number of servants shipped from Bristol to Barbados in the seventeenth century (Niles 1980, 24). Members of Barbados's poor white population were known as Red Legs and comprised farmers and townsfolk from Devon and Somerset who supported the Duke of Monmouth's abortive 1685 attempt to capture Bristol and who were sent with ten-year indentures to the West Indian colonies: "Over eight hundred were packed into ships and sent off to the colonies, to be sold in batches on arrival to the planters. . . . Some ran away and hid in caves of the Scotland district, where they formed themselves into bands which ultimately became villages" (Tree 1972, 39).

According to Vincent Cooper (1999, 380), the first Englishmen in St. Kitts "came from the southwestern area of England—Cornwall, Somerset, Devonshire—as well as from Suffolk, Essex, Bedfordshire and Oxfordshire." The fenland area of Cambridgeshire had similar folk traditions to the West Country, which is documented as historically strong in Christmas wassailing, including animal disguises (bull and horse) and beribboned mumming traditions (also found in neighboring Hampshire). In describing slave recreation in Surinam (an extension of the Caribbean), J. G. Stedman (1796/1971, 376), a military officer, writes, "The [African] men also cudgel and wrestle; yet I think them

Fig. 1.3. Halloween disguise with mask in Uist, Outer Hebrides, Scotland, ca. 1930s. Photo from Margaret Fay Shaw, *Folksongs and Folklore of South Uist* (1955). Courtesy Routledge Taylor and Francis, London.

inferior to either those of Cornwall or Devon." In his correspondence, Richard Chidlaw of Gloucestershire (pers. comm., July 15, 2010) points out that "Dursley Methodist Church [Gloucestershire] was founded in 1799 and William Jenkin, its first minister, a Cornishman from St. Keverne in the Lizard, was sent to St. Kitts before he came to us. . . . The Irishman, Walter Griffiths, the founding Wesleyan evangelist of this area had been to St (Christopher's) Kitts some time before this." Chidlaw does "not see Wesleyans helping with the transporting of folk culture" but nonetheless adds that, "the early Methodists weren't teetotal at all." Their errant parishioners were more likely the culture-bearers. With the growth of sugar estates and increased importation of West Africans, the system of indentured white labor waned. "By the end of the 17th century, the importation of white labour had practically ceased. Some former servants established themselves as smallholders and a few even rose to own estates. But the majority went to swell the ranks of the 'poor whites'" (Robert Haynes 1934, 68).

The Gaelic groups that arrived in the Caribbean during the early period furnished strong animal disguise and/or bush masquerade traditions. The Scottish Highlands' traditions include Hogmanay dancers in bull-horned and hide costumes and straw-covered guisers such as the Skeklars from the Shetland Islands. In South Wales, the Mari Lwyd horse was a prominent animal disguise. The Irish have the Lair Bhan horse disguise and Strawboys' bush

Fig. 1.4. Straw Bear and handler, Whittlesey, Cambridgeshire, England, 1909. Note collection box. Photo by Bowker Weldon from lantern plates belonging to Henry Slater. Courtesy Folklore Society, University College London Library Services, Special Collections.

costumes that were the equivalent of the Scandinavian Straw Staffan, while the Straw Bear of the fenland area of England's Cambridgeshire, notably Whittlesey, has a counterpart in Walduern, Germany.

British Folk Traits in the Caribbean

Abrahams (1967, 461) suggests that European folk activities became diffused throughout the West Indies and developed by people of predominantly African descent after being "introduced by the European peasant groups with whom the Negroes have lived and worked, such as the French fisher folk, the British 'White Bajan' or the Madeira Portuguese." Alternatively, these practices "may have been taught by the overseer who was often of rural British origin, and was a member of the white . . . community with whom the slaves had the greatest contact." That British migrants like to reconstitute their folk culture when far from home is evinced by the performances of Jack in the Green in Tasmania from 1843 to 1873 (Leech 1989). An account of Sir Humphrey Gilbert's 1583 voyage to Newfoundland to claim the island for Elizabeth I shows that on some occasions, masquerade costumes—in this case, a hobbyhorse "to delight the savage people"—could be deliberately stowed aboard vessels on transatlantic voyages (Hayes 1589/1958, 250).

In Barbados and the Leeward Islands, indentured servants from Britain and Ireland lived in a state of deprivation. Barbadian administrators particularly despised the Irish servants. Eltis (2000, 237) reports that infractions of a

1652 Barbados statute empowering the Governor's Council to inflict corporal punishment on those who used mutinous language "involved far more Irish than other groups, including African." Because of their disenfranchisement, the Irish servants evidently showed sympathy toward enslaved Africans and were known to have joined with them in dissent. In 1655, the Barbados Council noted various reports of "severall Irish Servants and negroes out in rebellion in ye Thickets and thereabouts" (Eltis 2000, 237). During the seventeenth century, contact of various kinds between servants and slaves provided an opportunity for lateral interchange.

But overseers and masters might also become agents of vertical transmission, especially when British, Scottish, and Irish servants completed their indenture and rose in the ranks of authority. John Luffman (1789, 99) commented in 1789 that in Antigua, "white overseers [are] generally poor Scotch lads who, by their assiduity and industry, frequently become masters of the plantations, to which they came out as indentured servants." A hundred years later, Samuel Smith, a black Antiguan, recalled his experience of masquerading in St. John's, the island's capital: "New Year's Day 1899 was the first New Year's Day I spent in town. . . . [A]ll the music, the dancing, the masquerading clowns and the whole New Year's jump up [festival] was white people. . . . Sometime later the Goodwin's tell me that the merry makers was Scotchmen and they were the ones that brought Christmas celebration to Antigua" (Keithlyn B. Smith and Smith 1988, 93). Officials at the Antiguan Ministry of Education, Culture, Sports, and Youth Affairs (n.d., 1), however, believed that "it may be more correct that Christmas celebrations were a fusion of the cultures, and that the Scottish with their long tradition of New Years Day (Hogmanay) celebrations successfully transplanted them to Antigua." Johan Lorentz Carstens's (1997, 132) description of New Year's perambulations on St. Thomas involving European and African descendants between 1725 and 1740 supports the idea of cultural interchange occurring during seasonal holidays: "When the masters and the slaves have one and all gotten well drunk together, one master visits the other in the company of his slaves. The slaves are obliged to walk in groups, in front of and behind the masters, playing on instruments, including the . . . *Asen-kiefte* [jawbone of an ass with horsehair strings] and other stringed instruments. They also blow on tutu horns [conch shells] and various reed flutes. All the while shots from both small and large arms are fired off into the air. Also air and water squibs are thrown on people, livestock, houses and in the water, giving the island the appearance of being on fire through the night." Carstens condemns "these barbaric festivities," pointing out that various governors "have not been able to achieve their goal of having them abolished." This condemnation is in tune with Sylvester Hovey's (1838, 30) later report:

"Most of the managers and overseers in Santa Cruz [St. Croix] are foreigners and many of them are Irishmen. . . . [N]ot a few of them lead the most dissolute lives. The influence of their example is often among the greatest obstacles which the missionary has to encounter in the moral improvement of the slaves." Although neither Carstens nor Hovey mentions masquerading, festive visiting was typical of New Year's celebrations in rural Europe, and mumming commonly occurred at these times. J. B. Moreton (1790, 156) compares dances of the enslaved at Jamaican funerals and weddings to similar occasions in Ireland: "I never saw anything that so nearly resembled the amusements . . . held . . . by the vulgar peasantry in Ireland, where to the music of a rotten bagpipe, or crazy fiddle, they dance to 'tire each other down.'"

West Africa

Upper Guinea Groups

The Afro-Creole prototype of masquerading, like the Creole dialect, seems to have emerged at the outset of the plantation economy in the Eastern Caribbean; therefore, West Africans who were enslaved early are likely to have contributed a major influence. Once established, the template tended to remain constant and, despite being modified or embellished by subsequent waves of West Africans and Western Europeans, was not radically altered. A study by Crahan and Knight (1979) supports this idea. They found that as a result of the supply and demand cycle for slaves, the West Indies experienced an influx of "ethnic and culturally cohesive cohorts and allowed for the establishment of certain societal norms to which later arrivals, regardless of their customs, would have to conform" (11). In light of the fact that particular Old World regions provided many early migrants, inspecting their masquerade traditions is instructive.

Upper Guinea groups were critical in establishing the early masquerade prototypes, although other ethnic groups, especially the Igbo, also played their parts. The examination of ships' logs and historical records shows that during the initial phases of colonization, people from the Upper Guinea region were well represented in the New World, especially in Barbados and the Leeward Islands. Even ecological aspects such as the introduction of savannah trees and tree lore support a geographical connection. The baobab and the tamarind, which flourish in arid regions of the Western Sudan, were imported into the Eastern Caribbean beginning in the seventeenth century. The tamarind is considered a spirit tree in that region and gives its name to Dakar (Wolof), the capital of Senegal. In the Virgin Islands, it is known as a Jumbie tree. The baobab is the major "palaver tree" in Upper Guinea—that is, a large ancestral tree where political or communal assemblies are held, sometimes including dance festivals. In the Eastern Caribbean, baobabs are honored as ancestral trees. St. Croix has more baobabs than any other island in the Eastern Caribbean (Nicholls 2006b).

The Upper Guinea region encompasses Senegambia, south to Guinea Bissau and the Bissago Islands, through to Guinea, Sierra Leone, Liberia, and the northwestern Ivory Coast. Senegambia's terrain encompasses the Senegal and Gambia Rivers, but it is more than merely a geographical area: It is "a region of homogeneous culture and a common style of history. . . . The people of Senegambia have lived as neighbors for many centuries, and there has been a steady interchange of people among them" (Curtin 1975, 1). In addition, the culture of Upper Guinea bore a heavy Mande overlay as a consequence of the influence of waves of conquerors, immigrants, and refugees (Gwendolyn Midlo Hall 1992, 29). Linguistically, the widespread Mandinka of Senegambia and Guinea-Bissau (as well as based in Mali, Ivory Coast, and Burkina Faso) are members of the Mande subfamily, which includes the largest number of Manding speakers in the Western Savannah and the Malinke and Bamana (Bambara) of Mali, the Susu and Mende of Sierra Leone, and the Maninka, Duranko, and Wangara. The Dyula (Jula) of the Bondoukou region of Ivory Coast are another core group of Mande (McNaughton 1982, 54). All of these people speak mutually intelligible dialects and share major aspects of culture and social organization, including kinship, politics, and economy (Gwendolyn Midlo Hall 1992, 45; Weil 1988, 184). Linguistic relationships revealed by the Manding tongue show that the Mande cultural overlay also includes the Vai-Kono and the Toma (Looma), who are Southwestern Mande (Vydrin 2009, 108). The Upper Guinea slave trade was well established before 1700, and Upper Guinea ethnicities that were transported to the Caribbean include the groups listed previously as well as the Jola of the Casamance; the Baga and the Kono of Guinea; and the Dan (Yacuba), who are Southern Mande and straddle the border region of Guinea, Liberia, and Ivory Coast. Petridis (2012, 30) states that "the Mende language spoken by the Dan is similar to that of their Kono, Diomande, Mau, and Tura neighbors in the north and east, and their Mano, Kpelle, and Toma neighbors in the west." Furthermore, he points out that "culturally, though not linguistically, they also have much in common with their eastern and southern Kru-speaking neighbors." Around 1850, S. W. Koelle took an inventory of slave cargoes recaptured at sea by the British following the abolition of slavery and then released in Sierra Leone. The hundreds of groups represented demonstrate the wide reach of the slave trade, with the list including such Upper Guinea groups as the Wolof, Fulbe, Diola (Jola), Bolanta (Balanta), Bijago, Bambara, Baga, Temne, Susu, Malinke, Kono, Toma, Mende, and Vai (Curtin 1969, fig. 20).

The Jola and many Upper Guinea groups were both victims and perpetrators of the slave trade. According to Baum (2010, 143), the Jola of Esulala conducted most of their "raids against the two Diola groups that raided them the most: the Djougoutes and the Huluf." He continues, "Unransomed captives were sold to Afro-Portuguese, Bainounk, and Mandinka traders or to Diola intermediaries who carried them to larger slave trading centers" (144). Furthermore, "through the ransom or sale of captives, a successful raider could acquire livestock, guns, iron, and cloth" (148). While both the Mandinka and Bambara are Mande peoples, the Mandinka were major slave traders and concentrated on selling the Bambara, in part because of religious differences: "While the Mandinga were the proselytizers of Islam, the struggle against Islam was an important component of Bambara identity until the late nineteenth century" (Gwendolyn Midlo Hall 1992, 41). Significant numbers of Bambara were shipped to Louisiana in the eighteenth century as part of the French slave trade. Paul Oliver (1970) sees the Bambara as core "savannah syncopators" who made major contributions to jazz and blues in the United States. When ships stopped at the French islands of Grenada, St. Domingue, and Martinique to replenish supplies, local administrators seized many Bambara, who became part of the islands' enslaved population (Gwendolyn Midlo Hall 1992, 58). The Jola predominate in the Lower Casamance but are not linguistically related to the Mandinka; however, centuries of contact have led to mutual influence. Jola dancing, for example, "with torsos bent parallel to the ground and outstretched arms flapping like birds' wings, resembles Mandinka dancing" (Charry 2000, 22). Similarly, the Baga, who are neighbors to the Maninka and occupy a small strip of land on the coast of Guinea, "have an extensive drumming and mask dancing tradition that is part of a larger West Atlantic tradition that reaches north to the *kankurang* fiber masked figure of Gambian Mandinka" (22).

After the Portuguese established slaving posts in West Africa, slaves from the Upper Guinea region became dominant in the early era. From 1526 to 1640, enslaved people came primarily from Senegambia, Guinea-Bissau, and Sierra Leone as well as from Cameroon and Angola. Although records of early slave shipments are scarce, Buhnen (1993) has determined the ethnic origins of Peruvian slaves. The records reveal the magnitude of Upper Guinean shipments and show the importation of the Jola, Mandinka, Bainunk, Balanta, Fula, Jolofo (Wolof), and Sape (the forebears of the Baga and Temne). For example, ten thousand Folupo (Jola) from Senegambia were shipped to Peru

Fig. 1.5. Kankurang and one of his guardians dressed up like a woman, Ziguinchor, Casamance, Senegal, 2004. Courtesy Ferdinand de Jong.

during the first four decades of the seventeenth century, and many of them likely witnessed bull-horn headdresses—indeed, some men probably wore them during their circumcision ceremonies before leaving Africa. Slaves imported to Spanish territories in the Greater Antilles also would have encountered this practice. (Plate 10)

The Upper Guinea people, particularly the Mande, provided a primary masquerade stimulus (Young 1807, 258; Bettelheim 1979, 52–53; Nicholls 1999, 57–58, 2009, 146–47). Bush masquerades are strongly represented, including the Kankouran and Sengko of the Mandinka and Kumpo of the Jola. Animal disguises include the Simba (Zimba, lion dancer) of the Wolof, the Ejumba and Kebul bulls of the Jola, and the Red Spear of the Mandinka. Mamapara is a stilt masquerade dancer in Gambia, while the Kono, Toma, Guerzé, and Kissien people of Guinea and the Dan (Yacuba) of Liberia are all noted stilt masqueraders, as are the Temne of northern Sierra Leone and the Mende of Sierra Leone and Liberia. Moreover, the Man, Mahou, Karadjan, Danane, Biankouma, Touba, and Seguela of Ivory Coast all have stilt masquerades. Ortiz (1921, 32) reports that in the nineteenth century, the structure and motifs of Cuban festivities resembled those of the Yolofes (Wolof) of Senegambia and that many of the masquerade groups were named *Mandinga* or variations thereof (e.g., Mandinga Mocu Azul, which might translate as "Mandinka Blue Spirits," since *mocou* in colloquial Spanish means "spirit" or "ghost"). French artist Frederic Mialhe's painting of Three Kings' Day in Havana, Cuba, ca. 1850, *Dia de Reyes: The Holy King's Day*, shows both a stilt masquerade and a bull-horned dancer among masked and costumed revelers in the streets of Havana.

West Africans in the Leeward Islands

In the early literature, tribal designations are often ambiguous. Some remain current, while others are archaic. Writing about Virgin Islanders in the eighteenth century, missionary C. G. A. Oldendorp (1770/1987) lists recognizable names such as Fula, Mandinga (Upper Guinea), Akkran, Fante (Ghana), Ibo, Karabari, and Mokko (Nigeria) along with more obscure names. Ethnic identification of African nation dances existed in Jamaica as late as the emancipation period, 1820s–30s, as evidenced by Kelly's (1838, 21) observation that at Christmas, "the Mangolas [perhaps enslaved people from Angola], the Mandingoes, the Eboes, the Congoes, etc., formed into exclusive groups [to perform] the music and songs . . . peculiar to their country." Of the nine African nation dances of Carriacou (which do not necessarily include masquerading; see appendix 4), the Manding of Senegambia and the Temne of Sierra Leone represent the Upper Guinea region, while the Moko, Chamba, and Igbo from Nigeria's Bight of Biafra are included, as are the Kongo from central Africa, the Arada from Benin Republic, and the Cromanti (Akan) from Ghana. The Akan of Ghana contributed significantly to Caribbean culture, and because many were warriors who were taken prisoner, they engineered a number of rebellions. Despite their eventual numerical prevalence, however, "masquerades are not now, and probably were never, products of Akan societies" (Bravmann 1979, 44). Thus, the Akan of Ghana (including Cromanti, Asante, Twi, Fante, Akuapem, and Agona ethnicities) can be ruled out as a masquerade-importing group.

"The Bight of Biafra was the most important source of slaves for the southern Caribbean, but in the Leeward Islands, Central Africa and Senegambia dominated" (Heuman and Walvin 2003, 390). Barbados was the first island colonized by the British, and slave shipments from the Upper Guinea region were considerable in the early era. Gwendolyn Midlo Hall (1992, 31) explains that generally, "Senegambia had been the main source of the Atlantic slave trade during the mid–sixteenth century, but after 1640, it probably never furnished more than 10 percent of the trade." Before 1700, none of the British Leeward Islands were capable of handling a complete transatlantic shipment of slaves, depending on Bridgetown, the capital of Barbados, as a major distribution center for both slaves and merchandise. Ligon (1673/1970, 46) provides a glimpse of African arrivals in Barbados around 1657: They emanated from "Guinny and Binny [the Gold Coast to the Bight of Biafra], some from Cutchew [Cacheo, in Upper Guinea], some from Angola, and some from the River of Gambia" (see also Eltis 2000, 247). In addition to Upper Guinea region, those areas represent Akan and Igbo/Ibibio/Ejagham regions as well as the western coast of southern Africa. The demographics of the slave supply changed over time, with the number of Gold Coast (Akan) slaves steadily increasing throughout the Caribbean. Discussing Barbados and Jamaica, Eltis states, "After 1713, first the Bight of Biafra took over from the Akan/Aja region and then was itself replaced, though less completely, by Angola" (257). Bridgetown was eventually superseded by Port Royal in Jamaica, and both Barbados and Jamaica became important slave distribution centers for the Spanish Americas. Africans from Upper Guinea, the Bight of Biafra, and Angola were overrepresented in this intra-American trade. In the 1680s, for example, the Company of Royal Adventurers in Jamaica "sold a complete shipment from the Gambia to the Spanish" (Eltis 2000, 246).

Sir William Young (1807, 283), governor of Tobago, observed the arrival of enslaved Africans in the central Windward Islands in April 1792: "Went on board a Guinea ship, the Active, from Sierra Leone." Sierra Leone is in the Upper Guinea region and is home to the Mende ethnic group. The previous December, Young recorded, "The ships came from distinct districts and with people of different nations on board: The Pilgrim of Bristol, with 370 Eboes [Igbos] from Bonny. The Colus of Liverpool with 300 Windward Negroes from Bassa. The Anne of Liverpool, with 210 Gold Coast Negroes from Whydah" (251). "Windward Negroes" refers to the Windward Coast, an area that broadly overlaps modern-day Liberia and Ivory Coast on Upper Guinea's southern boundary. According to Kingsley (1877, 248), "In 1867 there were in Montserrat 400 squatters, holding lands. . . . These people lived without paying taxes, and almost without law or religion. . . . The south-west corner of Montserrat is almost entirely settled by Africans of various tribes—Mandingos, Foulahs, Homas, Yarribas, Ashantees, and Congos." Again, Upper Guinea is represented by Mandinka and Fulani, Nigeria by Yoruba, Ghana by Ashanti, and Central Africa by Congo. The Igbo are conspicuous by their absence.

The Igbo

Some authors point to the Kongo, the Yoruba and Igbo of Nigeria, and Ghanaian groups as having influenced Caribbean masquerading (Barringer, Forrester, and Martinez Ruiz 2007; Cooper 1992; Douglas B. Chambers 2001; *Musical Traditions* 1993). However, the influence of these other groups was limited to modifying the Mande templates, the main features of which remained constant. Although Belisario's (1837; reproduced in Barringer, Forrester, and Martinez Ruiz 2007) lithographs of "Christmas Amusements" are later than the early masquerades featured in this study, they depict customary street performance genres in Kingston, Jamaica, around 1817—the Women's Sets, the Actor Boys (which Belisario describes as a "class of John Canoe"), and the House John Canoe. Robert Farris Thompson (in Barringer, Forrester, and Martinez Ruiz 2007, 89) proposes a possible prototype for the house headdress in a Kongo tradition, *zungukunu*, that refers to "moving about with a small model of a house carried on the head of a dancer, as a symbol of the exaltation of a lineage." Barbaro Martinez Ruiz (in Barringer, Forrester, and Martinez Ruiz 2007, 112, 114) concedes that the "houseboat's significance and intended use may be Central African in origin" but points to "conceptual connections with houseboats among the Ijo, Ibo, Ibibio, Yoruba, and Agoni people in the Cross River Delta in Nigeria." Kenneth Bilby (in Barringer, Forrester, and Martinez Ruiz 2007, 132, 130) concurs with Thompson that "there are grounds for believing that the strongest parallels [with regard to Jankunu] are to be found specifically in West Central Africa" but notes that Long (1774) witnessed "Jankunu processions in Kingston in the mid-eighteenth century," when Africans' "geographic and ethnic backgrounds were still indexed with some degree of specificity." Long himself (1774, 2:424–25) reports, "In 1769, several new masks appeared; the Ebos, the Pawpaws, etc, having their respective Connus, male and female, who were dressed in a very laughable style." Bilby translates "Pawpaws" as "Papa"—Ewe, Aja/Fon, and people from neighboring areas in the Ghana/Togo/Benin region. Thompson clarifies that he is not contending "that Jánkúnu is pure Kongo art in Jamaica. Far from it" (89). Rather, Jonkonnu is an example of "intra-African fusions," a genuinely Creolized form of culture: "Local creativity long ago complicated Kongo traits in the festival with, for example, visual elements from Mande and Mande-influenced tradition namely the bush cow mask" (89).

Because later-arriving groups reinvigorated existing Caribbean masquerade genres, it is enlightening to look at the interaction of incoming groups with what might loosely be termed the Mande masquerade prototype. Long's (1774) report from Jamaica ties the Igbo to Jonkonnu. Although large numbers of Igbo were not part of the earliest shipments to the Caribbean, they eventually reinvigorated the masquerades they found in their new home. Calabar and Bonny were two important slaving outlets in the Bight of Biafra. About 1.7 million people were exported from the Bight of Biafra, 1.5 million of them after 1700. Although shipments included Ibibio, Moko (Efik), and various Ejagham groups, the majority were Igbo. The Igbo had a flourishing masquerade tradition in West Africa and are known as an entrepreneurial people. With their arrival in the Caribbean, they adapted indigenous prototypes to better reflect Igbo aesthetics.

The Mocko Jumbie stilt masquerade is a case in point. The earliest account in the literature is that of Young, who was in St. Vincent in the Windward Islands on December 24, 1791. There, he saw a stilt masquerade: "It was the Moco Jumbo and his suite. The Jumbo was on stilts, with a head, mounted on the actor's head, which was concealed, the music was from two baskets, like strawberry baskets, with little bells within, shook in time. The swordsman danced with an air of menace, the musician was comical, and the Jumbo assumed the 'antic terrible,' and was very active on his stilts" (Young 1807, 258). A note probably added by editor Bryan Edwards identifies the "Moco-Jumbo" with the "Mumbo Jumbo of the Mendengoes [Mandinkas]." This assumption is almost certainly correct, because the same evening Young was entertained by visiting slaves who executed a "lascivious dance" to the music of a "Balafo" with "handkerchiefs folded tastefully about their heads and gold ear-rings and necklaces" (259). A balafon is a wooden xylophone used by the Mandinka, the Wolof, and neighboring peoples, and according to Charry (2000, 135), "the Maninka xylophone, called bala or balafon, is used wherever Maninka peoples have migrated," while De Jong (2007, 125) states that xylophones are "claimed by the Balanta to be part of the cultural heritage," Dirks (1987, 5) also describes the Mocko Jumbie as "a Mandingo import."

A report from St. Vincent published by Charles William Day (1852, 85) identifies the performer as an Igbo stilt dancer assisted by some of Igbo soldiers of a "negro regiment"—no doubt a British West Indies Regiment stationed in St. Vincent. The stilt dancer's costume combines African and European elements (cowrie shells and grenadier's cap), and he is referred to not as a Mocko Jumbie but simply as "De Jumbee" or "De Jumpsa-man." However, Day explains, "'De jumbee' was of course an imitation of the genuine"—that is, mock: "On stilts six feet high. . . . He was dressed in a guernsey-frock and long striped trousers made very wide which concealed his feet. His face was covered with a mask of scarlet cloth, ornamented with cowrie shells; and having a huge wig and beard, with a grenadier's hairy cap on his head, he looked unearthly" (85). This seems to be a clear example of the appropriation of a Mande archetype by Igbo people.

Other examples are not quite as blatant. Bettelheim (1979) points to horned masquerades of the Mande and related groups in the Upper Guinea region as possible exemplars for the Jamaican "Cowhead Jonkonnu." Cattle-horned headdresses (masks and caps) with a pair of real horns are evident among the Jola and Mandinka and include the Ejumba, Kebul, and Red Spear. The description of the "John Connu" mask (ca. 1760s) by planter-historian Edward Long (1774, 2:424) is often quoted: "In the towns, during the Christmas holidays, they have several tall or robust fellows, dressed up in grotesque habits, and a pair of ox-horns on their head, sprouting from the top of a horrid sort of visor, or mask, which about the mouth is rendered very terrific with large boar tusks. The masquerader, carrying a wooden sword in his hand, is followed with a numerous crowd of drunken women, who refresh him frequently with a cup of aniseed-water, whilst he dances at every door, bellowing out John Connu." Another description of the Jamaican Jonkonnu states, "The Negroes have their droll, which, however it may be dressed is always called a John Canoe; a whimsical character. . . . Sometimes they wear two faces . . . usually they have but one, which is often rendered hideous by beards and boar's tusks" (Anonymous 1797/1976, 21). This character was escorted through the town by a throng beating metal objects and executing a call-and-response refrain. In addition, "They carry a stick in their hands, which they flourish somewhat in the form of a cudgel-player, and when two of those accidentally meet in their walks, they exchange several grimaces before they pursue their respective ways" (22). Although bull-horned Igbo masks are discussed below, Igbo in the West Indies may have modified the prototype by adding tusks, which are not usual among the Mandinka and their neighbors and do adorn some non-horned Igbo masquerades. Apart from the false-face masks of the Dan and Mano of Liberia, which feature tumors, other disfigurements, and occasionally snaggle teeth (see Adams 2010, figs. 4, 5), masks rendered hideous by tusks are unusual in West Africa and are a rarity in Upper Guinea (with the exception of a Bamana horned and tusked helmet mask that became defunct [Gray and Dochard 1825]). However, tusked masks appear with regularity among the Igbo. For example, the mouth of an Igbo mask in the Nigerian Museum in Lagos is distorted by the addition of five crooked teeth and real tusks. The item comes from a village northeast of Onitsha and is composed of a basketry helmet plastered with gum, is topped with a dozen or so horns of wild animals, and is decorated with red seeds, probably *Abrus* seeds (Eyo [1980], 29). According to Boston (1960, 56), the masks of the Nri-Akwa of the northwest corner of Igboland include composite headdresses that consist of a helmet surmounted by a cluster of horns. These hunting trophies are normally "narrow pointed horns of various kinds of antelope." In this region, broad buffalo horns became obsolete, apparently because of declining animal populations, but elsewhere wooden masks with carved crescent-shaped buffalo horns are still created—for example, the Igbo Atu Ejeogu bush cow mask that appears in the Enugu Mmanwu Festival.

Although the dark Okoroshi (Okorosia) beast masks that are used in the Owerri region do not sprout horns from the head, they often are tusked. They appear during the annual six-week masking season that heralds the New Yam Festival. Okoroshi masks fall into two classes. The benign ones are Okoroshi Oma, identified as "beautiful spirits." The Igbo word *oma* means "good," "pretty," and "light." Carved with delicate features, they manifest female spirits, and fewer of these white-faced, white-dressed characters come out than their aggressive beast counterparts. The larger grotesque dark masks manifest male spirits; many of the latter group have distorted, enlarged features and include snaggle teeth. They are accompanied by a male entourage carrying clubs and singing dirges about war and conquest (Cole and Aniakor 1984). *Chimpanzee*, a dark wooden apelike mask collected at Nwaozo around 1960 and now in the collection of the Fowler Museum of Cultural History at the University of California–Los Angeles, has a distorted mouth with large snaggle teeth made of bleached scallop shells and a protruding tusk that extends up the right cheek almost as far as the eye. Cole and Aniakor (1984, fig. 305) include a photograph of *Death Has No Friend* (a name taken from a proverb), an Okoroshi Ojo mask from Mgbala Agwa, west of Owerri, in the Nigerian National Museum at Lagos. It has a skeletal face, crooked teeth, and a pair of tusks. (Plate 14) Can the tusked John Canoe mask with his cudgel-wielding entourage be equated to the dark beast masks of the Igbo and their neighbors?[10]

Despite specifically mentioning the Igbo and the Papa, Long's (1774, 2:424) statement that "in 1769, several new masks appeared; the Ebos, the Pawpaws, etc." is ambiguous. His silence regarding the ethnic groups implied by his "etc." is deafening, and what he meant by "new" is open to conjecture—new styles, new performers, new arrivals? Does it imply that horned masks were by that time considered old, so that *new* therefore refers to nonhorned masks such as the House Jonkonnu? Whatever the specifics, a general blending of cultures occurred over time, combining elements from diverse nations.

EUROPEAN VERSUS AFRICAN INFLUENCES

John Canoe

Scholars have not reached a consensus regarding the meaning of the name *John Canoe*. Long (1774, 2:424) suggests that "This dance is probably an honorable memorial of John Conny, a celebrated *cabocero* [*cabecera*] at Tres Puntas, in Axim, on the Guiney coast; who flourished about the year 1720." A *cabecera* is a headman, and Conny was a notorious African slave trader on the coast of Ghana, apparently a mulatto. However, Cassidy (1967, 200) cites Long's (1774, 2:425) specific reference to Ewe speakers in suggesting that *John Canoe* is a combination of the Ewe words *dzono* (sorcerer) and *kunu* (something deadly, a cause of death). Fayer and McMurray (1999, 61) bring up the possibility that there are multiple etymologies for the term. Antigua has a horned John Bull masquerade, but in England John Bull is an icon, the equivalent of Uncle Sam to Americans. John Bull's surname is reminiscent of the alleged English fondness for beef, as reflected in a French nickname for English people, *les rosbifs* (the roast beefs). The name *Bull* was used to indicate the English, as when Thurlow Weed (1866, 346) describes festivities in which a black man beats his drum "as proudly as Ole Bull draws his cat gut"—that is, as an Englishman plays his violin. The name *John* is more enigmatic and in the BWI often describes playful dance activities, including dances such as the John John, Joan-Johnny, and Jo and Johnnie (Alexander 1833, 157; Spencer 1974, 5). John's namesake Jack Pudding is a British term for a clown "dressed in the rough clobber of the yokel" (Speaight 1955, 27). Johnny Jack was a character in British mummers' plays, for example in Burghclere and Overton in Hampshire and in Bury Town near Manchester (Tiddy 1923/1969, 189, 195; Cass 2001, 123–24). Furthermore, "Little Johnny Jack, also known as Little Happy Jack and Saucy Jack, is very common across the south of England" (Cass and Roud 2002, 37). Jack or John Finney (Vinney), the "doctor's" assistant, is rare in Wiltshire but common in Gloucestershire (37). Jolly Jack Tar, replete with nautical associations, accompanies Lord Nelson of the Furness Morris Men (Cass 2001, 104). He also appears around 1880 with the Cumbrian Jolly Boys (Cass and Roud 2002, 25). Jack in the Green was a green-leaf masquerade. Furthermore, the West Country pronunciation "Jan," as in "Janneying," describes Christmas mumming in Newfoundland, and Jolly Jacks are found among Newfoundland mummers (Halpert 1969, 56).

Rashford (1984) explores the uses of the name *John* in Jamaica, where it denotes the vulture John Crow as well as the John Crow bead, the red and black *Abrus precatorius* seed known as the Jumbie bead in the Eastern Caribbean and the Bajumbi in Upper Guinea, which also gives its name to the Jola's bull-horned Ejumba. The Afro-Creole adoption of *John* may relate to obeah charms known in the American South as John de Conquer Root, about which Muddy Waters and other bluesmen have sung. In the words of Henry Louis Gates Jr., High John de Conquer "embodies joy over misery. . . . Those who are still deprived of material wealth discover that their principal asset is spiritual wealth, rhythm, and laughter" (Hurston 1995, xx). Zora Neale Hurston (1995, 139–40) explains that the spirit of High John de Conquer followed the slave ships from Africa and can be seen in the resilience of enslaved Africans: "John de Conquer was walking in the very winds that filled the sails of the ships. . . . The sign of this man was a laugh, and his singing symbol was a drum beat. . . . It helped the slaves endure. They knew something better was coming. So they laughed in the face of things and sang. . . . And the white people who heard them were struck dumb that they could laugh. In an outside way, this was Old Massa's fun, so what was Old Cuffy laughing for?" Mocko Jumbie practitioners similarly use the masquerade to rise above adversity. According to John Cupid, a Trinidadian masquerader, "The Moko Jumbie, if you asked him, he would say from under his masked face that he has been walking all the way across the Atlantic Ocean from the West Coast of Africa. Laden with many, many centuries of experience and, in spite of all the inhuman attacks and encounters, yet still walking 'tall, tall, tall'" (Stegassy 1998, 99). In both cases, a spirit that emanates from Africa is seen as a source of power that buoys social well-being, an echo of Taiwo Jegede's definition of art as feeding society's soul. (Plate 41)

Determining Masquerade Ancestry

The issue of determining ancestry is fraught and loaded and in most cases is tentative at best. While some people of African descent may have an ideological and even subjective attachment to theories reflecting the African ancestry of Afro-Creole masquerades, Europeans generally have not contemplated the issue and are not prepared to concede the high ground to African ancestry as a form of political correctness. Dedicated scholars, however, should be prepared to consider the evidence and reach their own conclusions. Although Leeward Islanders of African descent predominate among performers, many masquerades have a mixed cultural ancestry. The European heritage is evident in Maypole, in quadrille balls, and in hero-combat mummers' plays. The festival calendar often follows that of Europe, and the historical performance circuit—touring the streets and visiting houses to solicit gifts—reflects Europe's Christmastime mumming patterns. The term *Afro-Creole* recognizes that within the Caribbean, people of African descent have been in the majority, with a relative wealth of African influences; where European influences have been incorporated, African aesthetic sensibilities have been applied.

To the extent that their culture was not wrung from them, Africans brought their aesthetic sensibilities to the Americas. A Mandinka or a Jola arriving in the Eastern Caribbean would have found the physical environment familiar in many ways—similar fruit trees, palm tree fiber for matting, sacred silk cotton trees, and even the vines with *Abrus bajumbi* seeds that provided spiritual protection were available. However, the process of enslavement in the New World meant jettisoning West African social institutions. The age-grade initiation ceremonies of the Mande and their neighbors could not occur in the Caribbean. For example, the Jola lost the context in which fathers sacrificed bulls to make horned headdresses for their sons, and that absence would adversely affect the continued existence of bull masquerades such as Ejumba in the new locality. In West Africa, masquerades are crucial constituents of life-cycle rituals—most notably, initiations and funerals—which were jeopardized in the new environment. In this new context, joining a Caribbean masquerade group might serve in part to inculcate traditional values.

The existence of African nation dances shows that newly arrived Africans identified with members of their ethnic group and that expressions of group socialization and solidarity were channeled into the Sunday dances and especially Christmas festivities. However, as Crahan and Knight (1979, 10) emphasize, "reconstitution of any specific ethnic group overseas did not necessarily re-create the original conditions for the propagation of the basic African culture in all its authentic dimensions. For we are not dealing with free individuals in families, but with slaves in slavery." Caribbean masquerades drew from different elements among the available exemplars, and "blending occurred not only between European and African traditions, but also within the varied traditions of a multitude of African ethnic groups" (Bilby 1985, 183). The boundaries between discrete masquerades with established protocols crumbled as more generic Afro-Creole varieties emerged.

On Montserrat, Messenger (1973, 55–56) explains, "It is apparent to anyone well acquainted with both African tribal and Irish peasant cultural milieu that most of Montserratian culture today is a composite of African and Irish retentions, regional borrowings and internal innovations." Regarding the Carriacou mas', which Fayer and McMurray (1999, 59) describe as a Caribbean Creole artifact, "Opinions vary as to relative strength of West African and Western European components, but the influences of both are dramatically illustrated in the performances." In any particular case, one might ask which influences predominate. Creolisms can be seen as falling somewhere on a sliding scale between African and European poles. The exploration of the provenance of the stilt-dancing masquerade shows it to be derived from Upper Guinea counterparts and modified by the Igbo and other Africans, with few apparent European stimuli; it therefore lies closer to the African end of the continuum. In contrast, the Maypole, quadrille, and hero-combat mummers' plays such as *St. George and the Dragon* and *David and Goliath* are closer to the European end.

In their own time, the colonialists in the West Indies dismissed the masks worn by African-descended peoples as exotic, overlooking comparable practices in Europe's Carnival or rural areas. However, a number of early-nineteenth-century writers in Jamaica did connect Caribbean masquerades with those of Britain. For example, Matthew G. Lewis recognized that "the John-Canoe is a Merry Andrew" (1834/1999, 36). During Christmas 1839, Joseph John Gurney (1840, 26) saw "a merry-andrew" during a "negro Saturnalia" in the Virgin Islands. Michael Scott (1836/1999, 249, 253) compared John Canoe to a "Jack Pudding" and asserted that "the Gardeners came nearest of anything I have seen before to the Mayday boys in London, with the advantage that their Jack-in-the-Green was incomparably more beautiful." In *The Red Set Girls and Jack-in-Green*, Belisario (1837) sketched a Jamaican Jack in the Green in which palm fronds were substituted for conventional British greenery.[11]

Discussing the mixing of cultures in St. Kitts, Abrahams (1967, 461) assumes British influences when he ponders the question, "How was the St. George Mummers Play or the Christmas Bull introduced into the slaves' manner of celebrating Christmas on some islands?"[12] Others think that Caribbean masking, especially the bull, has an African provenance. For example, Richard D. E. Burton (1997, 65) argues that the early Jonkonnu with bull horns "is clearly a neo-African or indigenized, rather than creolized, cultural form," while Antigua Museum literature (in possession of the author) states, "John Bulls were replicas of the grotesquely masked African Witch Doctor with a bull's horns on the head." The Caribbean Bull, for example, was influenced by West African masquerades but nourished in an environment conducive to Christmas bull perambulations on a European model. This lends support to Abrahams's (1967, 462) conclusion that "what emerged was a folklore tradition which had traits of both peasant Europe and aboriginal Africa and a feeling which is more identifiably West Indian as time passes."

Chapter 2

AESTHETICS OF MASQUERADING

Masquerade performances provide enjoyment—masquerading is fun—but the pleasure provided is not trivial; rather, it contains psychosocial benefits. It brings aesthetic experiences into the community and disseminates values. Moreover, masquerading provides informal education, especially in the affective domain. For example, the Caribbean Bull has been shown to embody masculine values of strength, jocularity, sexual potency, and aggressive retaliation. Eike (2007b, 103) talks about mumming participation in Norway as a type of *rite de passage*. Similarly, Kaivola-Bregenhøj (2007, 538) argues that youthful mumming in Finland served as a socialization agent, offering "the boys and girls of the same age who were in mixed groups a chance to meet [so] that shy boy from Satakunta could really come to life."

INVERSION

Inversion is common in masquerading. In the British West Indies (BWI), Abrahams (1967, 477) writes, "the most colorful and widespread expression of the desire to turn the world upside-down is found in the masking and the masquerades. In these costume groups, there is a high incidence of social and sexual role-reversals." Abrahams and Szwed (1983, 35) distinguish between "dressing up" and "dressing down" during seasonal "play days": Both indicate the taking on of unaccustomed roles in which "antinormative motives" are channeled. Disguise can be contrasted to dressing up in grand clothes that enhance but do not conceal the wearer. Dressing up uses a form of exaggerated realism and often involves the adoption of prestigious positions within elaborate hierarchies such as mock military or mock aristocracy (for example, Carnival Queen). In contrast, in dressing down, the disguise is normally more thorough, the intent is often to affront people's sensibilities or challenge social norms. The costumes may be more informal or abstract and may involve wearing rags, patches, raffia, sackcloth, or the like—"to 'scruff up' wearing old clothes and sooted faces" (Cass 2001, 1; Nicholls 2001). Within the dressing

Fig. 2.1. Bull, Frederiksted, St. Croix, ca. 1900–1910. Courtesy St. Croix Landmarks Society and Archives, Ovesen Collection.

down mode, "One direction which these changes take is to espouse an anti-social character role, such as those of . . . the devil . . . and brutal animal (such as the bull)" (Abrahams 1967, 477).

The dressing up/dressing down dichotomy is less applicable to West African regions, where other dichotomies may exist. The Frafra and Bulsa warriors of northeast Ghana were dressed up in their antelope-horned helmets and pelt and coral regalia, as were the Jola *usikoi* initiates in their bull horns. The same is true of Ejumba, for although fearsome, with its enhanced appearance, the masquerade is dressed up. In former times, cowrie shells were currency, so wearing cowrie and coral garlands sent a message similar to that conveyed by the town queens in Charlotte Amalie in 1871 when they "sewed on the bosom of the dress bank-notes and gold doubloons" (S. B. Haynes 1872, 201). Moreover, dressing down by scruffing up has particular significance in Western Europe and the West Indies but is less important in West Africa, where portraying the figure of an insubordinate outsider in rags and soot lacks a sense of political importance because society lacks the classic class-based or class- and race-based features that were present in Britain and the Caribbean, respectively. Some African groups do dress down, but the context is different. The Igede of Nigeria, for example, have a few masquerade groups that portray pollution. Ranung (1973) describes the *ayilo uchih* (dirty or foolish music) of the Akatangka association, whose members engaged in abnormal behavior (eating from a pit in the ground) and whose musicians and masquerades dress in tattered costumes. Discussing the Ode-Lay masquerades of Freetown, Sierra Leone, Nunley (1987, 177) points out, "Purity is defined by what is considered impure or what is considered polluted. Without pollution, purity is meaningless and . . . the key frames [phases] in a successful masquerade present the opportunity to cope with pollution." Rather than a dressing up/dressing down dichotomy, Freetown has opposing dualisms of fanciness and fierceness that are represented by masquerades (128) and are not dissimilar to the two classes of Igbo Okoroshi masquerades: light delicate masks that manifest female spirits, and dark grotesque masks that manifest male spirits.

Dressing Up

In the Caribbean, enhancement rather than disguise was typical of the balls held by the free colored of the preemancipation era and of the slaves' visits to the Great Houses. Abrahams (1967, 477) notes the era's fascination with prestige hierarchies: "A number of the earliest groups employing elaborate hierarchies were patterned on military organizations (perhaps inspired by the tradition of the militia each year at Christmas, whose maneuvers were one of the major attractions of that season). One such costume marching group was the 'Landship,' found on Barbados, St. Vincent, and other islands." For much of its history, soldiers and militiamen regularly paraded through the streets of the Virgin Islands' towns. The islands also served as a port of call for naval and commercial shipping, meaning that foreign sailors were frequent visitors. In the nineteenth century, military apparel was sometimes represented in masquerade costumes. During the 1866 New Year's festivities in St. Thomas, "innumerable costumes [included] soldiers (main and halt) [and] Generals" (*St. Thomas Tidende*, January 3, 1866). St. Croix's New Year celebrations in 1893 featured a large model ship drawn through the streets accompanied by revelers dressed as "sailors in uniform," among them "a plentiful supply of officers of various grades . . . from admirals down" (*St. Croix Avis*, January 4, 1893). One of the most notable expressions of the adoption of prestigious roles was the existence of mock royalty. Prior to emancipation, queens and their consorts served as the centerpiece of dance troupes that visited estate houses at Christmastime (Cynthia Oliver 2009).

Dressing Down

Most animal disguises fall into the dressing down category. Masquerades in the stylized likeness of animals include the bull, bear, and donkey. The bull was the fiercest, the donkey was mostly comical, and the bear fell somewhere in between. Such animal disguises did not aim at naturalistic portrayals, and although the raffia bear costume was shaggy, it did not directly simulate fur. In the Leeward Islands, the intent to astound audiences influenced the costumes, and abstraction was derived from aesthetic sensibilities inherited from West Africa. Unlike European classical art, African-derived art does not strive to provide naturalistic realism but instead depicts the more surreal world of the spirits. A masquerade's appearance is meant to be strange and bizarre; as a manifestation of the otherworld, it is expected to be, paraphrasing abstract expressionist Wassily Kandinsky (2006), a mysterious expression of the mysterious. Accordingly, many masqueraders aimed simply at anonymity rather than at identifiable renderings. This trait baffled elite classes in the Virgin Islands and led to accusations that maskers did not dress in character. For example, the January 7, 1865, *St. Thomas Tidende* describes New Year's festivities and "groups of people dressed in masquerade" but bemoans the absence of typical British pantomime and mumming characters, wishing that there had been "a semblance of Pantomime . . . and the characters personifying something either tragic or comic. . . . If it only undertook to represent Colombine, the Domino, Doctor Sangredo, Punch and Judy, Malbrooks, the Gamin, and others of the innumerable characters that have made the masquerade universal and notorious. [But] the costumes simply represented or meant nothing." The tone of these criticisms means that glimpsing the bull in nineteenth-century accounts often requires reading between the lines. For example, the January 8, 1870, *St. Thomas Tidende* notes that during the Three Kings' Day festivities of two days earlier, there were "masks . . . in every variety of costume . . . where silk and gold lace predominated. . . . Coarser materials were also seen, producing laughable effects." Some costumes in the dressing down mode were made from burlap, while others were made of vegetable fiber. Although African cultures believe that raffia contains spiritual qualities derived from the wild forces of nature, the literati of the Virgin Islands considered sackcloth or raffia costumes to be poor and paltry. Thus, the "coarser materials" mentioned by the *Tidende* probably included burlap or raffia costumes such as were worn by the bull and the bear. Similarly, the April 9, 1890, *Tidende* complains of the "degenerated" costumes that appeared on Easter Monday of that year: "What we do reprehend is the disporting on the streets of ragged and unsuitably-swathed individuals, unacceptable to both sight and taste." Another disparaging report from the *Tidende* describes Whitmonday 1893, when "a contingent of masqueraders kept the streets lively [but] the number of riff-raff were larger" (May 24, 1893). Again, the "ragged" and the "riff-raff" were probably marginal and deviant characters such as the bull, the bear, and the devil. These figures represented by the dressing down mode shocked the sensibilities of Europeans and elites, signifying an alien world beyond their understanding.

Realism in Disguise

Thus far, disguise has been linked to abstract portrayals and dressing down (e.g., the bull), while personal enhancement has been equated to realistic representation and dressing up (e.g., queens). Other categories exist, however. For example, a genre of pretty masquerades, Pitchy Patchy, combines disguise and dressing up with abstract representation. Whether the masqueraders were adorned in sparkling and colorful cloth or in rags, skins, and straw, the disguise element renders them equal in terms of spiritual status. Another genre of realistic portrayals combines disguise with dressing up, a form of make-believe that was probably a familiar European tradition and consequently provided a comfort level to European and elite audiences. Normally, such realistic portrayals represent human heroic figures. In the modern era, an Elvis Presley or Batman impersonator would fall into this category, as would a host of mythical figures and matinee idols. The nineteenth-century equivalent of movie stars was the famous and influential personages of the era, who were depicted realistically by masqueraders whose identity was disguised. The March 28, 1883, *St. Thomas Tidende* reports the Easter Monday presence of "young gentlemen who, assuming the characters of celebrated men, wore masks the very similitude of the personages they represented. These were William I, Napoleon I, Napoleon III, Victor Emanual, Arabi Pasha, Cetewayo, Zulu Chief, Bismarck, Washington, Sultan, Gambetta Moltke, Victor Hugo, Rochefort, Duc d'Aumale, John Bull, Plon Plon, Grévy, Hypocrate." This group included kings and emperors, military and civil officers from Turkey and North Africa, U.S. and German political leaders, a noted French author, and an ancient Greek physician as well as the generic British icon. The appearance of the Zulu chief, Cetewayo, would have struck a responsive chord with the Afro-Caribbean spectators and probably was the forerunner of the Zulu troupes that cavorted with Indians in the late nineteenth century—for example, on Whitmonday 1893. These Zulu manifestations predate those of Mardi Gras in New Orleans, where the Zulu Social Aid and Pleasure Club was formed in 1909 and first entered the Carnival parade seven years later (Berry 2004, 313). A Zulu troupe based in the town of Savan appeared in the 1914 St. Thomas Carnival (Rufus Vanderpool, pers. comm., August 3, 1995). In the Virgin Islands, the Zulus were often associated with the Indians because of the mock battles staged at New Year's and other holidays. When the St. Thomas

Carnival was revived in 1952, the Zulus were among the entries, but following the 1950s they fell into a slump, in part because of their caricatured appearance—onlookers said their white loincloths looked like diapers. However, since 2002, Zulus dressed as authentic South African warriors have appeared, led by bodybuilder Charles Matthew and his peers billed as King Shaka of the Zulu Nation.

COSTUMES AND MASKS

Many factors influence the choice of a masquerade costume, including cultural authenticity, the context of the performance, aesthetics, and utilitarian considerations. It was important for Leeward Islanders to see local circumstances depicted in the costumes. Clacia Hendrickson (pers. comm., July 2, 1996) points out, "A little bit of everything that went on in the island appeared in the festivities and the costumes reflected the local economy." In earlier years, frugality was at play, and performers utilized available bull hides, banana leaf raffia, burlap sugar bags, and Gold Medal flour bags. An outfit could be made from the sturdy white fabric of flour or chicken-feed sacks, which was the same material used to make men's shorts and women's baggy knee-length bloomers and skirts. The fabric was washed but retained the original brightly colored decals and floral designs. Old clothes were shredded and used for patches and ribbons.

West African aesthetic preferences, including a predilection for pluralism, were applied to masquerade costume construction and performance in the Eastern Caribbean. Adams (1989, 72) uses the term *heteroglossia* to describe the pluralism of masquerade and other African performances and argues that the enactment is composed of "multiple voices." This pluralistic orientation was fostered in costume design, as is evidenced by the multipatterned, multitextured, layered assemblage that constitutes a masquerade's apparel. Made of multiple strands of dried vegetal material, the traditional raffia costume has a shaggy look. Pitchy Patchy, raffia's cloth counterpart, is similarly rough textured. Other masquerade costumes are constructed in layers or have attachments. According to Maurice Thomas (pers. comm., July 7, 1995), individuals would artistically expand on a theme—for example, by taking ordinary clothes and enhancing them by adding patches of cloth, ribbons, small mirrors, spangles, little bells, medallions, and other paraphernalia. Patched clothes were common mas' wear. Large unbroken areas of a smooth material were rare, and even women's costumes were textured, with cuffs and collars, berthas, hems, pockets, ample lace trim, multiple petticoats, and sometimes aprons. Petticoats are usually highly textured. The can-can petticoat that William Richardson wore to flare the skirt of his Mocko Jumbie costume looked like many petticoats, but it was really one garment, with seven layered flounces of different colors. The same pluralistic principle figured in the choice of textiles, and bright, richly patterned materials were generally favored over solid colors. Patterns, large or small, geometric or floral, were popular for women's skirts, whether Mother Hubbard, Bamboula, or quadrille, as exemplified by madras cloth. Masquerades' hats usually are also multitextured and sport appendages such as plumes and streamers. Hats are often conical or triangular, like an admiral's hat. Helen Joseph (pers. comm., July 4, 1996) describes hats made from cardboard and paper with strips of brightly colored paper pasted on and hanging down about three inches from the brim.

Leeward Islanders appreciated creativity in costume design, and an important consideration was a costume's ability to arouse spectator interest, often using shock and surprise. Again parallels are found in Africa, as Biebuyck (1979, 78) observes in his discussion of initiation art of the Lega of the Congo: "The Lega initiates have no difficulty in replacing one visual symbol by another. . . . They take delight in the unusual combinations and manipulations of objects to heighten the element of surprise." Attention is generated by inventive juxtapositions, bizarre combinations of colors, and the clustering of symbols and artifacts. Some Virgin Island masqueraders mix styles: In Stanley Jacobs's (pers. comm., June 30, 1996) words, "Performers might dress up by wrapping dry banana leaves around them and wearing a tall top hat." This anomalous juxtaposition is depicted in a photograph of Paddy Moore taken around 1925 on St. Croix that is part of the Landmarks Society's Ovesen Collection (Nicholls 1998, fig. 6). Many masquerades are a onetime creation and do not fit into the standard categories. An aesthetic sensibility that favored originality meant that some performers took pride in making new costumes for each outing. According to Alexander Petersen (pers. comm., July 10, 1995), Paddy Moore devised original costumes out of goat or cow leather, out of canvas sailcloth used to filter sugar, and out of leaves, vines, and grass sewn onto cloth.

A Caribbean masquerade wears a mask or is otherwise disguised to ensure anonymity and add to the fun. Some masquerades impersonated Jumbies, while others represented the power of particular guilds within the community. For many individuals, masquerading was simply the adoption of a temporary persona to manifest a more frivolous side of the personality. A mask might have features or be featureless—simply a piece of cloth over the face. Sometimes burlap balaclavas were used. The bull or bear, for example, might wear a brown crocus bag blackened with soot and with holes for the eyes, nose, and mouth. Not all disguised characters wore face masks. Other forms of disguise include soot, flour, or paint to color the face; false beards or mustaches; men dressed as women; and women dressed as men. (Plate 64) European females in eighteenth-century Antigua considered cloth masks and veils à la mode. Luffman (1789, 35–36) reports that "the [white] ladies . . . seldom walk the streets, or ride in their wiskys, without masks or veils[; they are] frequently seen at a distance unmasked, but as soon as they are approached near, on goes the vizor, thro' which, by a couple of peep-holes, about the size of an English shilling, they have the opportunity of staring in the faces of all they meet. . . . Custom has established it . . . as fashionable."

African masks were not regenerated in the Caribbean because they were too provocative for the colonial classes. The archetypal African mask is carved from wood or constructed of fibers, is worn on multiple occasions, and is relatively long-lasting. Indeed, some ethnic groups believe that masks accrue spiritual power as they age and are used (Picton 1974). However, even in West Africa, wooden masks are not universal; many cloth and vegetal masks exist, while some groups simply do not have masked dancing. Caribbean masks and costumes are often but not always short-lived. Some disguises, such as face paint, are removed at the close of the day. Some costumes are worn once and discarded, while costumes of dried leaves or colored paper are fragile and have to be reconstituted for each outing. As a result of their temporary nature, many Caribbean disguises possess a mutable quality, and their appearance changes during the course of an outing. Soot or face paint, for example, can become smeared and mottled, rendering the wearer's appearance more grotesque. Fragile masks made of papier-mâché, starched cloth, or cardboard are similarly vulnerable to heat, sweat, and exertion. Antiguan masks were made from the thick black wax covering from imported Sheffield hams: A wax imprint could be made of an individual's face and a neat, fitted mask with clearly defined features created. However, in the heat of the sun, such masks often distorted into shapeless masses with amorphous designs (Edgar Lake, pers. comm., August 13, 1996). The changeable nature of some costumes has aesthetic ramifications. For example, a costume might start out as dressing up but during the course of the revelry become disheveled and gravitate more toward dressing down. Whether this mutable quality of Caribbean costumes is simply incidental or suggests an aesthetic preference is debatable.

Some Leeward Island masqueraders had costumes that could be reused, as with donkey costumes that appeared in several performances (Helen Joseph, pers. comm., July 4, 1996). Imported papier-mâché masks cast from a mold using pulp paper and then painted had shaped facial contours and were available from merchants, as were some wire-screen masks, which Bettelheim (1988, 59) reports "were originally exported to the Caribbean and South America in the late 1800s from the Tyrol region of Austria." Before holidays, local newspapers carried advertisements for different types of masks, providing not only price information but also their country of origin (Rufus Vanderpool, pers. comm., July 9, 1995). Commercial masks appear to have been relatively durable, and wire-mesh masks were often but not always periodically repainted and reused. In the late 1930s and early 1940s, members of a Christiansted, St. Croix, family wore wire masks that were so old that the paint had smeared or disappeared, and many were not recognizable as faces (Arnold Golden, pers. comm., January 20, 1996). Were such masks also considered to accrue spiritual power as they aged?

In the Leeward Islands, mesh masks are known as safe-wire masks because they were often made from the wire gauze used to cover food safes prior to the advent of refrigerators. Most such masks were homemade, although enterprising individuals might make them for sale: Purchasers could paint on eyes, eyebrows, and a mouth. A good mesh mask followed the contours of the face. During the 1950s and 1960s, Mocko Jumbie William Richardson had his masks made by a man from St. Kitts residing in Charlotte Amalie, St. Thomas. He poured plaster into a well-formed mask to obtain a form on which subsequent masks were shaped. Thin metal strips cut from a biscuit tin were folded and attached to the sharp outside edges (William Richardson, pers. comm., July 15, 1996). Some masks were edged with tape or cloth—maybe the same textile as the costume. The mask might also be decorated with shells or mirrors. More recently, masks made of plastic gauze have begun to replace wire mesh and are often trimmed with artificial fur in bright colors. (Plate 58)

Screen or net masks can claim antecedents in both Europe and West Africa. Huet (1978, 27) reports that the masks worn by African Kono and Dan stilt dancers are made of "a net of palm-tree fiber." Sidro (1987, 459) explains that flower petals, candy-sugar confetti, plaster, and baker's flour were liberally thrown around at nineteenth-century carnivals in Nice, France, meaning that "one had to be . . . protected . . . from flour and plaster dust. To spare one's face; one had to wear a wire-meshed mask similar to a fencer's." Ash Wednesday, the first day of Lent, got its name from the practice of putting ashes on the forehead as a sign of penitence. Similar to the carnivals of Nice, during Christmas and New Year's festivities in the Leeward Islands in the first half of the twentieth century, people who ventured out without costumes were dashed with flour or confetti, so that they, too, became costumed (Philip Rhymer, pers. comm., July 18, 1996). Mrs. A. C. Carmichael (1834, 293–94) remembers that in St. Vincent, "The giving out the Christmas allowances is a very merry scene: they flour each other's black faces and curly hair, and call out, 'look at he white face! and he white wig.'" Furthermore, because West Africans believed that fire was the ultimate means of decontamination, participants in purification rituals often whitened their skin with ashes. At wakes, for example, ashes were used to reflect the marginal status of the bereaved. Moreover, during Poro society initiations in Liberia and Sierra Leone, novices are painted with white clay to symbolize that they are temporarily dead. This sensibility may have crossed over into the Caribbean.

Leroy Arnold (pers. comm., July 8, 1995) argues that it would have been too racially provocative for performers to overtly whiten their faces. The early clowns, who emulated the European circus clowns, were an exception. An example can be seen in a photograph of Washie Roebuck and his companions in the Donkey Parade in Christiansted in the Danish era (Rezende and Walbom 2009, 100). Arnold suggests, however, that Mother Hubbard's mask, representing a character in a European nursery rhyme, was used as a means of subtly satirizing the white population. Such masks were painted light pink with rosy cheeks, blue eyes, and red lips, while the males had thin painted mustaches. Ethel McIntosh (pers. comm., July 9, 1995) concurs, noting, "The eyes were light blue because it was a white people's mask." Some of the masks undoubtedly satirized Europeans, but at Christmas, everything and everyone else was also being lampooned. Conversely, spirits in Africa are often believed to be white or colorless, and white masks in Africa generally indicate spirit masquerades. A genre of white face masks representing female spirits was once popular among groups in southeastern Nigeria, including the Igala, Idoma, and Igede, and is exemplified by the Agbogho Mmuo "maiden spirit" masquerade of the Nri-Akwa area of northern Igboland. Bilby (2010, 195 n. 22) remembers, "During my fieldwork among the Aluku Maroons of French Guiana and Suriname during the 1980s, I very frequently saw spirit mediums in a variety of religious contexts with faces coated in *pemba doti* (powdered white clay)." He also points out that "among Garifuna performers in Belize and Honduras, wire-mesh masks . . . are painted white or pink and are . . . sometimes being given additional features, such as mustaches and goatees, meant to show that they represent Europeans." Bilby addresses these dual interpretations and refers to "multiple layers of meaning" projected by masquerades: "Both of the meanings suggested here could have come into play at different points and in different contexts" (195 n. 21).

Some masks were constructed of heavily starched and painted cloth or the gauze used to strain molasses with holes cut for eyes. Richardson (1984, 91) describes a process for stiffening cloth that involved starch, borax, and a small amount of candle grease. Older residents of St. Thomas recall that the skin of the triggerfish (*Balistes vetula*), known locally as the old wife fish, was sometimes dried, shaped, lacquered, painted, and made into a plastic-like mask (Alfred Lockhart, pers. comm., August 19, 1995). The twentieth century saw the increasing popularity of the stocking mask, which has now become part of the characteristic clown costume. (Plate 48) Originally intended to be worn beneath the mask to cover the ears and neck, the stocking is now itself used as a masquerader's disguise, especially among clowns and some Mocko Jumbie stilt dancers. These genres also favor dark featureless cloth masks that render the wearer faceless. (Plate 59)

The design and construction of the Mocko Jumbie's mask is further guided by utilitarian and practical concerns, and on that level, choices seek to maintain a level of safety and comfort. Many are characterized by wide open mouths and eye sockets. Stilt dancing is a strenuous activity that requires an ample oxygen supply. Whereas an uncut cloth mask may limit effective breathing, an open space around the mouth facilitates it. Mocko Jumbie performers also need good peripheral vision, especially in parades, when people come up close to the stilts. Today, wire-screen masks and their nylon counterparts meet these requirements, as does a fine net fabric that acts as a veil. (Plate 61) Some current Mocko Jumbie masks are made of fabric—sometimes the same fabric as the costume. Willard John decorates his fabric masks by attaching mirrors, cowrie shells, and various seeds. At the 1990 Smithsonian Folklife Festival in Washington, D.C., John's mask was a hood of a thick, metallic fabric with holes for his eyes and mouth, while John McCleverty wore a red hood that extended down to his chest and had its facial area patterned with beads and cowrie shells. (Plate 62)

Hats worn by Mocko Jumbies come in various shapes and sizes, and most are topped by plumes, pennants, or streamers. Alternatively, triangular hats can be worn sideways (that is, with the points toward the front and back). Some of Kombo Omolara's masks incorporate the facial covering and conical hat into one unit. Some performers wear straw hats, either made in the Caribbean or sturdy Fulani hats imported from West Africa. Some headdresses, such as the one worn by John McCleverty at the 1990 Folklife Festival, resemble delicate horns. McCleverty's headdress consisted of a horizontal fringed bar with a pair of red plumes on each end. For her 1995 St. Thomas Carnival entry, Naomi Baylarian used conical thread spools as hornlike appendages from which feathers sprouted. Various accessories complete the costume. In addition to wands or whips, necklaces and bracelets made of different seeds and beads may be worn.

A Mocko Jumbie performer requires strong, firmly tied stilts. Stilts are traditionally made of wood, although lightweight aluminum stilts are available. Gerard Luz James makes his stilts from Douglas fir, which is commonly used in the building trade. He buys a twelve-foot-long two-by-four, splits it down the middle, and adds a rubber pad to the bottom to protect the wood. Tall stilts can place the top of the performer's head as high as seventeen feet from the ground. However, increased height results in less control. A performer cannot dance at above fifteen feet, and to walk or run at that height requires the extra support of stilts tied around the thigh. Beginners start with shorter stilts, with accomplished performers frequently at about twelve feet off the ground. Such stilts end just below the knee, allowing the performer to bend his legs for dancing. Although straps can extend along the shins, they must be most firmly secured around the feet. Protective padding prevents the wood from chafing the skin. Many old-time Mocko Jumbies wore long stockings and danced without shoes. Rudy Farrell, like his father, Magnus, uses thick reinforced stockings but now prefers light flexible slippers.

The colors and design of a Mocko Jumbie's costume and the movements of his dance interact aesthetically. Some performers include special design features to dramatize the flow of its movement. Rudy Farrell's costumes have little pockets that act as handles, enabling him to manipulate the garment to emphasize shifts in body posture. Clothes with vertical stripes are popular because they add height to the image, and tall hats topped by long peacock feathers are worn for the same reason. The choice of fabric is guided by pragmatic as well as aesthetic concerns. According to Alli Paul (pers. comm., July 10, 1995), "You get too hot in taffeta cloth and it sticks to the skin. When it gets wet it catches and rips easily. I use a stronger fabric—cotton breathes, rayon does not." For this reason, cotton bloomers are preferable to silk, which retains the heat. The costume design is dictated by the demands of an individual's performance style. For example, if a Mocko Jumbie performer is very agile—spreading the legs, bending over backward, throwing a leg up and holding onto it—a skirt is generally more practical than pants, but not if it is a stiff or heavy fabric or has too many petticoats. An agile performer must wear loose pants with extra fabric built into the crotch. Sometimes, as in William Richardson's costume, what appear to be trousers are really separate leggings that come only halfway up each thigh, with the tops concealed by the skirt or the shirt.

In towns, cow horns and cow meat were obtained from local abattoirs or simply from local markets. Like the popular bull's foot soup, bull's heads were sought after because they were good to eat. When cattle died on Virgin Island farms, the skull could be prepared as a headpiece: "Men used to take the head and clean it out. And they fix it, dig it out, sand it, clean it out and fit it to their face" (Jamsie Brewster, interview by Vincent Cooper, 2002). Arthur Sixteen customarily wore a wire-screen face mask or, later in his career, after he had achieved notoriety, no mask at all, but sometimes he wore the whole skull as a helmet mask. Moreover, nineteenth-century chronicler Michael Scott (1836/1999, 251) describes a Jonkonnu "clothed in an entire bullock hide, horns and tail . . . the whole of the skull being retained." Preparing a bull's cranium as a helmet mask was laborious, as George Farrell (pers. comm., November 13, 2002) explains:

> They clean it out, they get it, they sun it, they do everything to it, burned it out, sit down on it every day, sandpaper, every single day. . . . When they finish it come out white, white, white, white, because the chemical is there, the system you call lime. They soak it in lime, throw a lot of lime on it and leave it there a couple of days. And there's meat whatever meat, because they get it fresh from the market. They throw lime all over, inside every crevice and that lime [gets] everything out. So when they reach a point they just carry it to water, the cattle drink-water [cattle trough] and wash it out right there, and get sandpaper and well scrub. Get down all them sharp edges of the bone and then fit it.[13]

More common than a skull that fit over the performer's entire head was a headpiece of a quarter of the skull or pate with horns attached or a hemispherical calabash skullcaps with horns attached. According to the Antigua Museum (in possession of author), John Bull "had a cow's horn clamped onto a rigid piece of cloth. His head was padded with a big 'catacoo,' which was a soft support." After arriving in St. Thomas, Farrell discarded the horned pate for the half calabash secured to his head with a small buckled belt. Eighty-five-year-old Reginald Ryan told Donoghue (2001, 44) that in Montserrat, "the bulls used to wear horns fixed to a tin that was wide enough for the head. You then bore the tin with a sharp instrument for the mouth and eyes." Furthermore, "To heighten their already ferocious appearance the horns of the bulls were tipped with red paint."

For the bull, mask-wearing was the norm. (Plate 34) George Farrell's mask was of the wire-screen variety. Burlap hoods were sometimes used, or the face was covered with black substances. Payne (2005) cites an informant who remembers a participant in Antiguan Christmases who would "mak[e] up his face with charcoal and ash . . . and [scare] the village's children half to death." According to the Antigua Museum literature (in possession of author), "The John Bull generally wore a mask, but sometimes they reverted to blackening their face with grease and paint and sprinkling with a little fine chalk dust. They looked very grotesque." (Plate 33) Lornetta Prince (pers. comm., December 26, 1994) remembers Sam "Miate" Williams, who performed as John Bull in Urlins Village, Antigua, in the 1960s. Williams, a light-skinned man in his fifties, daubed "pot smut" (soot) on his face to emphasize the whites of his eyes, which he rolled menacingly and which became increasingly bloodshot as a result of drink and exertion. Even scarier was John Jude, who played the bull not only with blackened face but also with eyes circled with red paint, frightening adults as well as children.

Whether raffia or burlap, the bull and the bear often shared costume styles. Crocus or crooter bags (the rough burlap sacks used for brown sugar) were made into costumes. According to Crucian Ethel McIntosh (pers. comm., July 9, 1995), the bear was completely covered by his costume, a plain robe made out of crooter bags with no colors or cloth attachments. A bag would be tied so that the head appeared to have two bear's ears. Some earlier incarnations had a tail made of stuffed burlap. On St. Thomas, Rufus Vanderpool reports (pers. comm., July 9, 1995), a bear covered his head with a crooter bag with holes cut out for the eyes. Tied around his waist was a rope, the other end of which was held by the bear master.

The bull's costume on St. Thomas around 1916 resembled that of the bear with the addition of real bull horns with some of the animal's hide and fur retained to make the performer look as fierce as possible. In addition to eye holes, the burlap helmet had burlap ears attached, and the tail consisted of a stuffed burlap tube. According to the Antigua Museum (in possession of author), the bull's "costume was sometimes just a sugar crocus bag with the head cut out and two armholes, with a big piece of rope around the waist." In the Virgin Islands, just before the bull fell into disuse around 1950, Maurice Thomas (pers. comm., July 7, 1995) saw one in Christiansted. The performer had horns and a burlap costume, but his face was neither masked nor blackened.

To the costume's base of burlap bags, dried leaves of one kind or another usually were attached. Charles Turnbull (pers. comm., June 19, 1996) says that Koka the Bear's costume was made of rough brown crooter bags with straw. Such raffia costumes are known in the Leeward Islands as bulrush, after the reeds that grow in swampy areas, but they might be constructed of cane shag shafts, guinea grass, banana leaves, or a combination of these materials. Dried banana or plantain leaf costumes ("banana shaggy") are standard. Antiguans often use the term *plantain flag*, while Jamsie Brewster (interview by Vincent Cooper, 2002) refers to it as "banana shak." In the Eastern Caribbean, *shak shak* refers to various maracas and rattling seedpods such as those found on the tibet tree (*Albizia lebbeck*, also known as rattlebush or woman's tongue). In addition to giving a gigantic appearance, the rustling sound of the raffia provides an acoustic quality that supplements the beat of the drum. Mary Seales (pers. comm., July 5, 1996) remembers Crucian Paddy Moore as a gifted entertainer: "He would come down the street swinging his arms while his costume made a noise like a shek shek. He would try and scare the children and they would run and laugh." According to Hortencia McIntosh (pers. comm., July 3, 1995), Moore's costume consisted of a skirt and a blouse made of crocus sugar sacks with dried leaves sewn onto them. He would wear a wire-mesh mask or blacken his face and wear an old hat, maybe over a madras head tie. Raffia bear or bull costumes sometimes involved long, shaggy one-piece robes that stretched from neck to ankle. The St. Croix Landmarks Society in Frederiksted has a photo of a bull masquerade around 1910 that shows a performer in a shaggy ankle-length gown with bull horns on his head and accompanied by a clown in a baggy one-piece costume. Aggie Bough (pers. comm., July 1, 1996) relates that a one-piece raffia robe was constructed by cutting a circular neck hole out of a piece of burlap so that the remainder of the bag hung down, covering the arms. Banana shaggings were then arranged in tiers of fringes in horizontal layers, "like a flapper's dress from the 1920s." The same arrangement is used for the construction of Pitchy Patchy's costume.

The costume of the Antiguan John Bull was designed to absorb whip blows. Staff at the Antigua Museum (in possession of author) write, "To absorb the blows from the whip they would stuff the back with grass or straw, like a hunchback." George Farrell's (pers. comm., November 13, 2002) two-piece costume consists of a plantain flag skirt and a heavily padded burlap blouse. The bottom layer is a T-shirt, topped by "the bag. . . then banana leaf you peel all the leaf off the stalk . . . and we stuff between the bag and my shirt, the plantain flag leaf them, you shove it all around." Farrell calls the long neck-to-ankle raffia costume a "shroud," or one-piece. By stretching further down the legs, this costume offers more protection from the whip. The bull's costume was decisively organic, reflecting the local environment. The whip man and drummers wore ordinary clothes or might be dressed down in shabby clothes or clad in festive colors.

Most troupes included at least one character with a whip, usually homemade. A three-foot tamarind cane decorated in bright colors was the trademark of the Mother Hubbard troupes, with each member carrying one. In Montserrat, the bull's minder uses a hunter, a cart whip made out of leather strips of plaited cow skin. Such whips, which can be eight or nine feet long, were formerly used by slave drivers (Donoghue 2001, 10–11). They are also used by members of the St. Kitts–Nevis Red Bull troupe (Mills, Jones-Hendrickson, and Bertram 1984, 29). Cart whips are harsher than the Antiguan whips and the Virgin Islands clap whips, which are made of pounded plant fibers, such as the century plant (*Agave*) whip, or dagger, used by the bull masquerade minder in Antigua. Mocko Jumbies, clowns, and other traditional masqueraders had clap whips made from "gwana tail" or iguana tail (*Sansevieria*, best known as a decorative houseplant), which was beaten and plaited and noisily cracked for effect by the clowns in St. Thomas (Myron Jackson, pers. comm., July 20, 1995). The whips of the Shakespeare Mas' troupes of Carriacou are made out of telephone or electrical cable wrapped in plastic tape (Fayer and McMurray 1999, 66).

In the "John Koonering" that Warren (1885, 201) observed in North Carolina in 1829, the leading character's footwear consisted of "sandals of the skin of some wild 'varmint.'" Although George Farrell (pers. comm., November 13, 2002) now wears socks and sneakers, he used to go barefoot: "Them days we don't have money to buy shoes, you understand, so your foot on the hot road, but it become nothing to us because we are accustomed to it." Bare feet were not protected against the lash of the whip, however, and on one occasion, Farrell remembers, "the end of the whip catch my big toe, and raise that nail up, and it punish me." He felt pain and fatigue only when he stopped performing: "When I started dancing I don't feel it, but the minute I stand up for five minutes, it starts to get me in a trouble." Nevertheless, Farrell "play out the day. Feel much more better going and going all day."

MUSICAL INSTRUMENTS

The Eastern Caribbean has an impressive array of musical instruments. In addition to fifes, flutes, horns, and stringed instruments, there are many kinds of drums and other percussion instruments. Most were handmade from local materials. Stanley Jacobs (pers. comm., November 26, 2005) described how fifes were made from papaya or bamboo stalks, ukuleles from sardine cans, triangles from the steel rods in old-fashioned automobile brake systems, and ass pipes (bahas) from car exhaust systems. Some instruments were derived from European models, but more were adaptations of African instruments. While Upper Guinea masquerades dance to open-ended drums, in Europe and in the Leeward Islands, open-ended drums and masquerading are an anomaly. The Jola Ejumba masquerades of Upper Guinea dance to a slit drum (*emumbi*) and a large open-ended drum (*fujundum*) or to a set of three or four large open-ended drums (*bugarab*) played by a single person. The Mandinka Kankuran masquerades customarily dance to the open-ended drums of the Mandinka three-drum ensemble, *kutirindingo*, *kutiriba*, and *sabaro*. Eastern Caribbean masquerades are more likely to dance to double-ended drums of the tabor or dundun variety, while open-ended drums are more commonly used to accompany African-style drum dances like Gombay and Bamboula. The portable dundun of the Mande comes in different sizes and bears comparison to the British tabor and the bass and kettle drums of the Eastern Caribbean.

The fife-and-drum bands that historically played with the Mocko Jumbie and other masquerades are often assumed to have a military genesis based on European models, and it is true that military and militia marching bands entertained the general public in the Eastern Caribbean on official occasions. But parallels also exist in the Upper Guinea region, where flutes made from grain canes such as millet stalks are popular instruments. Flutes may be open-ended or stopped and have mouth holes for blowing at the top (vertical flute) or at the side (transverse flute). Flutes are played solo by herdsmen or played with drums or other instruments. The Fulani (Fulbe) play a side-blown flute known as *serdu*, and their skills are widely appreciated (Charry 2000, 21). The double-ended dundun accompanies the flute, and this combination bears comparison with the bass drum and fife of Caribbean masquerade bands. The flowing and bubbling melodies of masquerade flute tunes in the Leeward Islands bear more resemblance to those of Fulani flute players than to those of the four-square melodies of European military bands.

The musical instruments played by the enslaved in eighteenth century Virgin Islands were locally made and consisted of stringed instruments (lutes, harps, and violins); wind instruments (the conch shell horn [tutu] and flutes made from reeds); drums made from barrels, tree trunks, calabashes, and pots; plus other percussion instruments such as calabash shakers and iron beaters. According to Carstens (1997, 78), among the instruments used at a wedding celebration in the 1730s were "the asen-kiefter, that is, the jawbones of donkeys, strung with horse hairs. These are draped with several silk ribbons, yellow, red, and blue in color. There are also various small pipes or flutes and tutu horns." The missionary Oldendorp (1770/1987, 249) observes that the slaves "find great pleasure in instrumental music; quite early the children make a kind of fiddle for themselves, constructed by stretching several horse hairs over a shingle and then stroking them with a bow or plucking them with their fingers." Instruments in the 1760s also included drums: "A skin stretched over a small barrel or a calabash, or if need be, even a pot serves as a drum and animates their dances" (249). These drums also caught the attention of literati during the following century: Tuckerman (1837, 25), for example, says that Christmas and New Year's holidays on St. Croix "are welcomed in by the beating of drums." During a dance at the plantation house, "the noise of the music, which was of drums and kettle drums, made it impossible that the voice should be heard." S. B. Haynes (1872, 200) reports of a Christmas perambulation in 1871 in which drums are mobile: People "parade the streets in gangs . . . preceded by a drum, which is sometimes accompanied by an accordion and triangle, to the sounds of which they [sing] in chorus."

The pipe and tabor apparently were sometimes used as a unit in the British West Indies. An anonymous article in the *Colombian Magazine* (1797/1976, 23) reports that music heard in Kingston, Jamaica, at Christmas included "winding of the postmen's horns, beating militia and negroe drums, the sound of pipe and tabor, negro flutes, gombas, and jaw-bones, scraping on the violin, and singing of men, women, and children." Music at Crop Over festivities in "one or two of the Leeward Islands," Bayley (1830, 437), reports, involved "an empty barrel . . . with a large piece of parchment on the top, a kettledrum, a tambourine, a pipe, a gumbay [and] bonja [banjo]." In Montserrat, Messenger (1973, 56) saw a counterpart to the Irish bodhran in the form of large and small tambourines known respectively as "Jumbie drum" and "babala": "Both instruments closely resemble the Irish *bodhran* and are struck in the Irish manner with the back of the hand rather than with the palm and the front of the fingers as in Africa, where the flat drum is not a traditional instrument."

Only a few of Upper Guinea's diverse musical instruments crossed the Atlantic to the New World. Along with Mande xylophones, harps, and lutes, there are many different types of drums in Upper Guinea, including slit drums, hourglass drums, and open-ended, closed-ended, and double-ended drums of different shapes and sizes, including the ubiquitous *jembe*. Charry's (2000, 197) assessment that "the combined wealth of these drumming traditions reflects a culture in which dancing is essential to everyone, although some are recognized as excelling in it" holds true not only for Mande culture in Africa but also for the Mande diaspora in the Eastern Caribbean as well as for most of West Africa. Whereas in Europe and the Caribbean, double-ended drums take precedence for masquerades (with the exception of some frame drums such as the tambourine and bodhran), in Upper Guinea, both single-ended open drums and double-ended drums are used. Even the all-wooden slit drum is used for masquerading in Jola initiation ceremonies within the sacred forest and for some Igede and Igbo masquerades as well. Reports of transplanted Africans using this instrument in the Eastern Caribbean have not surfaced. However, it did appear in Congo Square, New Orleans, during dance festivals that were held by African descendants in the latter half of the eighteenth and the first half of the nineteenth century. New Orleans is often considered an extension of the Caribbean, and Congo Square, which was formerly a ceremonial ground of the Oumas Indians, was situated where Beauregard Square is today. The instruments that appeared with the transplanted Africans in Congo Square included a wooden instrument that is recognizably a slit drum. Latrobe (1819/1969, 181) described it as "a block cut into something in the form of a cricket bat with a long deep mortice down the center. This thing made a considerable noise being beaten on the side by a short stick." Some pre-Columbian Caribbean inhabitants used a hollow-log slit drum (Manuel 1995, 5; Rouse 1992, 11). The Tainos who occupied the northern Leeward Islands used both slit drums and rattles, in the form of maracas, to accompany recreational dancers and ceremonies such as those celebrating the deeds of ancestors. But although the use of maracas, which are also found in West Africa, continued, the slit drum did not.[1]

Charry (2000, 195) notes the "the broad sahel and northern savanna distribution of tama-like and dundun-like instruments," traditions that "are rooted in the practice of having at least one drummer take the role of accompanist and one drummer act as leader. In Mali dunduns can be played in pairs in this way." The Mande dundun drum does not resemble the dundun of the Yoruba of Nigeria, which is a tama-like, hourglass drum called *kalangu* by the Hausa and known as a talking drum. A tama is held under one arm, and the tone of the note is tensioned by squeezing the longitudinal thongs with the elbow while beating the skin with a curved stick held in the other hand. Tama drums are used, for example, by the Laniboy stilt masquerade of Ninibou village, near Macenta, Guinea (Appia 1943). Laniboy is acoustically outfitted. Two small bells are attached to the tip of his hat, while two larger bells hang from his skirt, and leg rattles are attached to the base of his stilts. Laniboy dances to the music of two instrumentalists playing hourglass drums. Similar masquerades are performed among the Toma, Guerzé, and Kissien people of Guinea. While the Mande dundun-like drum crossed the Atlantic, the hourglass drum did not, possibly because it is complicated technically, more fragile than regular drums, and more conspicuous. In West Africa, where tamas are paired with dunduns, the latter plays the accompaniment, while the former plays the lead.

In northern Nigeria, Niger, and Sahelian terrain through northern Ghana, Mali, Guinea, and Senegal, the double-ended dundun is a routine drum that can be a solo instrument or take part in a variety of ensembles. It is slung low over the left shoulder and in the Sahel is played with a curved stick held in the right hand. Further south, in the savannah area, straight sticks may be used. In Mali, large and small dunduns are generally paired, while in Guinea they are played in sets of three ranging in size. The larger dundun is about twenty-seven inches long and thirteen inches in diameter. The left hand commonly holds a cone-shaped bell, the *nganga* or *nege* (meaning "metal"), hung around two fingers by a short string and struck with a ring worn on the thumb on the same hand (Charry 2000, 230). In southern Mali, the small dundun is usually played without a bell. According to Charry (2000, 229, 231),

"Among the Xasonka in the region of Kayes in western Mali the dundun is a solo instrument that is played by jelis [griots] usually accompanied by a second dundun": "Dundun patterns consist of a combination of bounces and presses where the stick is pressed into the skin, momentarily deadening it. An accompanying dundun part generally consists of short patterns with little allowance for variation. A lead dundun part for a piece may consist of one or more patterns identified with that piece, leaving room for improvising within the patterns." As an all-round drum, the dundun can accompany jembe drums as well as tamas, and much Malian and Guinean Maninka dancing is rooted in ensembles consisting of jembes and dunduns. The high-toned jembe is now common and typically is about twenty-four inches tall. Jembes are often played with three large flexible oval metal plaques attached to the drum. The plaques have small metal rings inserted so that when the drum is struck, the rings jingle (Charry 2000, 217).[2] However, the jembe did not migrate to the Eastern Caribbean, although Luffman (1789, 135) points out that Antigua's toombah drum "is similar to the tabor, and has gingles of tin and shells." This description is reminiscent of the jembe's plaques; however, Luffman also describes the toombah as having a "hollow sound," which seems more like a dundun than the high tone of the jembe's taut skin. A preference for adding a vibrating or textured quality to a drumbeat gives rise to the use of a snare—that is, a wire, gut, or hide string stretched across a drumhead to produce a rattling sound. Hausa and Gwari (Gbagyi) dundun-like drums are often fitted with a thin leather cord across the beaten head. Charry provides a musical transcription that includes a jembe, a snare drum, and a dundun and "shows how the dundun part has been used as a bass line" (227).

A musical style known as jinkgouing in Barbados and jenkoving in Jamaica is described as clapping of hands on the mouth of two jars (Leslie 1739, 326; Spencer 1974, 4). In 1688, Sloane saw dancers in Jamaica who wore leg and wrist rattles that were shaken in time with an instrument that seems like a kind of idiophonic pot drum. Sloane writes that the musician "makes a sound on the mouth of an empty gourd or jar with his hand" (1707, 46). This musical technique is similar to playing the Udu musical pot, an Igbo rhythm instrument. The Udu is unusual: Made of fired clay and pear-shaped, with a cylindrical hollow neck, it has an approximately two-inch-diameter hole in its side. Like a slit drum, it is classed as a concussion idiophone, but unlike the slit drum, which is beaten with sticks, it is played by alternately beating each hole with the flattened palm of the hand. This technique produces a rhythmic gulping sound not unlike the talking drum of the Yoruba. Jinkgouing seems likely to have produced similar gulping rhythms. The Udu is known as *otahubah* (literally "pot drum") among the Igede, who are northern neighbors to the Ezza and Izzi Igbo, and is heard to good effect on *The Igede of Nigeria* (1991, track 13). This drum is also known as the *kimkim* among Ibibio people and has now spread throughout north-central Nigeria, especially within Christian church ensembles (Ames and Gourlay 1978; Ahuwan 1992).

Leg rattles, ubiquitous in West Africa, appeared in the Caribbean and are mentioned by James Edward Alexander (1833, 96) in what was then British Guyana: "Outside the house in the moonlight, a musician seated himself, with his drum on the grass, and commenced singing an African air, when the circle of men and women, linked hand in hand, danced round him with rattling seeds on their legs, and joined in the chorus." In the twenty-first century, some Montserrat masqueraders wear tinkle bells attached to straps around their ankles, while St. Kitts–Nevis and Virgin Island clowns have bells attached to their shoes. When in Barbados, Alexander witnessed another African air, this time accompanied by a calabash rattle: "One evening whilst sitting in the marble veranda at Enmore . . . I heard the lively sound of a drum at some distance, and immediately repaired to where the negroes were amusing themselves. . . . On a level spot surrounded by small houses of coloured and black people, was a bench, on which stood a man shaking violently a calabash fitted with small stones and reeds and singing with contortions an African air. The crowd formed a ring, and those who wished to dance the Joan-Johnny stepped forward, presented the leader of the band with a bit" (157). Oldendorp (1770/1987, 264) describes a shaker consisting of a calabash containing "seeds and small stones" and "attached to a stick or handle." Day (1852, 47) describes "de shot" as "a small gourd as large as an orange, filled I understand with shot, and having a handle." John Stewart (1823/1969, 270) describes Jamaican rattles as "being small calabashes filled with seed of a plant called by the negroes *Indian shot*." The two shakers, "like strawberry baskets with little bells within" that Young (1807, 258) saw with the Moco Jumbo, sound similar to those common in West Africa but rarely reported in the West Indies.

While Young's Moco Jumbo danced to the rhythm of two basket shakers, Day (1852, 85) reports the "De Jumpsa-man" in St. Vincent danced to the music of drums: He saw "two tum-tums, beating the drum they call alloo, and five or six wenches from the Granadines singing an African chorus, and clapping their hands as accompaniment. . . . The dance consisted of various contortions of the body, sufficiently droll. [The dancer] alternately amused and frightened the women for twenty minutes." In Barbados, Day saw the drums at an open-air Joe and Johnny dance event held during the Christmas season "at a place called Cullumore Rock, a short distance from Bridgetown" (46): "Our music consisted of fiddles, with a rude African looking tambourine . . . a 'tum-tum' or 'tump,' a piece of parchment stretched over what seemed to be a small iron-looped pail . . . and 'de shot'" (47). He continues, "The tum-tum was played by an alternate thump of the open-handed knuckles on the parchment, and then a slap of the palm on the wood" (47). At another Joe and Johnny held on New Year's Day, "a triangle was added to the instruments" (48).

Metal objects were often spontaneously converted into instruments. On some islands, scrap iron has been used, and the automobile wheel hubs of Trinidad steel bands are well known. The iron bands of Antigua have also garnered some repute, and similar youth bands appear on other islands. Lena Schulterbrand (pers. comm., June 30, 1996) remembers biscuit pans being used in the Virgin Islands. According to Amy Gill (pers. comm., July 1, 1996), the blade of a pitchfork would be struck, while Charles Turnbull (pers. comm., June 19, 1996) recalls two empty milk cans being knocked together. Parallels are found in Upper Guinea: For example, young Jola women line up in the central square for performances of Kumpo and sing and dance, "using old spades for rhythmical accompaniment" (De Jong 2007, 156). The squash or guiro of the Eastern Caribbean is a serrated tubular gourd scraped with a toothed metal stroker to create a rasping sound. Sometimes, metal cheese graters are used to provide a strident percussive rasp, and an equivalent instrument is used by the Mande in the form of a foot-long iron rasp known as *nege* or *karinyan* (*karignan*), described as "a notched narrow metal tube held in one hand while the other hand rhythmically scrapes it with a thin metal rod" (Charry 2000, 87). In the hands of a master such as Alexander Michael, better known as Ciple, a kerosene container could be a formidable instrument. Ciple composed his own songs and accompanied his singing on a five-gallon kerosene can that he played like a tambourine. When Harry S. Truman visited St. Croix on February 23, 1948, Ciple played at a reception in the U.S. president's honor at the Annaly home of Mr. and Mrs. Ward Canaday. Ohaldo Williams recalls that Ciple's "fingers were light and they moved like a bee on the pan with a lick here: PAM . . . and another there BAM, and RAM. . . . When Ciple played the island stopped and listened" (Schrader 1993, 11–12). Ciple's songs featured local news and scandal. Leroy Arnold (1979) remembers "All I Want I Get It," a song about a real incident where a married lady arranges to meet a flute player after a dance.

Signal horns were historically used in West Africa to alert villagers in case of fire or attack and, like the European bugle, to issue directives to warriors in battle. Among the Igede of Nigeria, the *ekureh* was two-toned and made from the horn of the bush cow, while the smaller *opikeh* had a piercing call and was made from an antelope horn. More recently, such horns punctuate ensemble music (Nicholls 1993, 251). Among the Igede and the Igbo, horns have martial connotations and are also associated with hunting. Although some ensembles in the region use horn bugles, they are more often military associations rather than masquerade associations. Horns are blown, for example, to orchestrate the renowned Ohafia War Dances (McCall 2000). During Igbo Okonko festivals in Isu Njaba near Nkwerre, musicians who accompany masquerades comprise a large number of men rapping horns with sticks as percussion instruments. Both cow horns (*abeng* in Jamaica) and conch shells have been used as signal instruments throughout the Caribbean. One of the earliest to appear in the literature is the tutu horn—the shell of the conch mollusk (*Strombus gigas*) blown as a trumpet. The conch shell was a signal instrument for the pre-Columbian Taino and Carib Amerindians and is still occasionally used by local fishermen in the Eastern Caribbean to advertise fish for sale. A conch shell trumpet fulfils legal status as a boat's horn since it can be heard for two miles (Robert Cole, pers. comm., November 21, 1994). On Bonaire, the conch shell bugle is known as *carco* and was traditionally used to report missing persons, to announce the harvest festival, and to call people to midnight mass at Christmas (Brenneker 1977, 62). Although Carstens (1997, 132) also describes the tutu horn in a musical context within a New Year's procession, it was used primarily as a signal instrument that orchestrated the slaves' working day. It was blown by the *bomba* (field supervisor) and is described by Carstens on St. Thomas around 1725–40 and by Haagensen (1758, 49–50) on St. Croix around 1740–50: "At three to four o'clock in the morning, a shell . . . is blown on all the plantations. This extremely large shell produces a sound much like a horn." At 6:30 in the evening, "the bomba blows the shell once again to bring them in." In the modern Virgin Islands, the conch shell is considered a "liberation instrument" because it rallied slaves for emancipation (1848) and laborers for the Fireburn (1878 labor revolt). It is blown annually on Emancipation Day, July 3, and on other commemorative occasions.

The prototype of the banjo in the form of a skin-covered lute is found in Upper Guinea. Although the tradition of singing to lute accompaniment is widespread in the Western Sudan, Cecelia Conway (1995, 28) sees Senegambia as providing a link, "especially between a Wolof musical instrument, the *halam*, and the American banjo." Michael Theodore Coolen (1984, 117) points out that *halam* is sometimes spelled *khalem*, *xalam*, or *kalem*. As with the American banjo, both four-string and five-string lutes are found in the Western Sudan. The *kôla-lemmé* of the Diawara of Mali, which "looks much like an early folk banjo," has four strings, as does the *gambaré* of the Soninké (123). In contrast, the Wolof *xalam* and *tidinit* of Mauritania have five strings (121), as does the Mandinka *kontingo* (124). In the Eastern Caribbean, the banjo provided music for Mother Hubbard and other masquerades that utilized string bands. It continues to be featured today in scratch bands or fungi (foonji) bands. In the Virgin Islands, experts include King Derby and Edgy, who plays with Stanley and the Ten Sleepless Knights. The banjo is strummed rather than picked and often sounds more like a percussion instrument, played quickly and with cross rhythms, making it different from U.S. techniques, such as used with the five-string banjo of bluegrass.

Early descriptions of the banjo derived from the African calabash lute are found in Barbados, Surinam, the Virgin Islands, Antigua, and Jamaica. In Jamaica in 1688, Sir Hans Sloane (1707) described "instruments in imitation of lutes [which are] made of small gourds fitted with necks, strung with horse hair, or the peeled stalks of climbing plants." Leslie (1739, 326–27) describes a "bangil" in Jamaica that is "not unlike our lute." Before 1770 on a Jamaican plantation, Thomas Thistlewood "broke Job's banjar to pieces in the mill house" (D. Hall 1989, 12). European observers documented names such as Creole bania (Surinam), bangil (Barbados, Jamaica), banshaw (St. Kitts) and merry-wang (Jamaica). For Stedman (1796/1971, 375–80), in Surinam around 1775, "The Creole-bania . . . is like a mandoline or guitar, being made of a half gourd covered with sheepskin to which is fixed a very long neck. . . . This instrument has but four strings. . . . [I]t is played by the fingers." Luffman (1789, 135–36) states in a March 14, 1788, letter from Antigua, "The banjar is somewhat similar to the guittar, the bottom, or underpart, is formed of one half of a large calabash, to which is fixed a wooden neck, and is strung with cat-gut and wire. This instrument is the invention of, and was brought here by the African negroes, who are most expert in the performance thereon which are principally their own country tunes. I do not remember ever to have heard anything like European numbers from its touch." Bryan Edwards (1794, 86) lists the "Banja or Merriwang" among Jamaican instruments, while Pinckard (1806, 264–65) describes Virgin Islands instruments including the "Banjar . . a coarse and rough kind of guitar." Later banjos and ukuleles were made from circular cheese boxes and, in the Virgin Islands, large sardine cans.

Because of a masquerade's perambulatory aspect, acoustic instruments that could be played while walking were used. Thus a differentiation can be made between the mobile drums used for masquerading and the stationary drums used for drum dances such as the Bamboula. The stationary method of playing is described by Pinckard (1806) and Leaf (1948).[3] Belisario's (1837) sketch from Jamaica, *Band of the Jaw-Bone John Canoe*, shows a perambulating group with a musician striking a horse's skull with a stick and two musicians with drums suspended from their necks. One beats a square frame drum (bench drum) with his hands, while the other has a large double-ended European-style bass drum, which he beats with padded sticks. Harriet Jacobs

(1861/1987, 118) describes the "Johnkannaus" band in North Carolina that "dancers keep time to": "A box, covered with sheepskin, is called the gumbo box. A dozen beat on this, while others strike triangles and jawbones." A jawbone, normally from a horse, has clattering teeth. It serves as a rasp, rattle, and a percussion instrument. Jacobs's gumbo box is probably the square single-skinned, open-ended frame drum depicted in Belisario's sketch. Oldendorp (1770/1987, 264) describes a frame drum during an Antiguan funeral: "The drums consist of small square boxes over which skins had been stretched." The square frame drum is most often referred to as a "gombay drum," which is how it was known among the Maroons of Jamaica. It is no longer used in the Leeward Islands, but it crossed back over the Atlantic to Sierra Leone in 1800 with repatriated Maroons, and the drum and the name subsequently spread to Ghana and throughout West Africa (Bilby 2011; Collins 2001). The kettle drum and its companion bass drum have skins at both ends and are beaten with sticks—two drumsticks in the case of the kettle drum, and a single beater with a padded end in the case of the bass drum. The drums are suspended from the players to allow mobility. Although the Caribbean kettle (kittle) drum has no resemblance to the huge kettle drum used in European orchestras, the title has long been used in the region. Ligon (1673/1970, 48), for example, notes that "kettle drums" were played for Sunday dances in Barbados in the seventeenth century. In today's usage, the term *kettle drum* is often used interchangeably with and resembles the *snare drum*: Both are relatively small and light and have a skin at each end, although the kettle drum lacks the snare.

The basic masquerade band consists of bass drum and kettle drum as well as a steel (triangle), a tailpipe (ass pipe or baha, often literally a four- to five-foot piece of a car's exhaust pipe), or perhaps a fife (especially for a stilt masquerade). A cow-horn bugle was played for the John Bull ensemble in Urlins, Antigua. Sometimes a squash (guiro, scraped calabash) might be added. A David and Goliath ensemble had drums, squash, and fife, which provided the fife-and-drum quality of military music that the "soldiers" could march to.

Paddy Moore (1979) used to make masquerade drums. For the kettle drum, he used the skin of ram goat; for the bass drum, he used a ram goatskin at one end and a ewe goatskin as the striking head. After he removed the hair from a skin, he soaked it in rum, not water as is customary. Frank Charles played for masquerades on a bass drum he made from a keg with a goatskin at each end. The drumstick is a sturdy dowel with a tennis ball attached to one end. He would hang the drum around his waist and beat the striking skin with the drumstick held in his right hand, using his left hand to dampen (or muffle) the skin. His drum was much heavier than comparable Gwari drums of northern Nigeria. The smaller kettle drums can be slung from the shoulders with a harness but are more often hung from the waist. The Jam Bull ensemble that currently performs in the St. Thomas Adult Parade consists of a kettle drum, bass drum, and steel. (Plate 35) During his days in Antigua, George Farrell (pers. comm., November 13, 2002) used only the drums, which he refers to as "kittle" and "boom." Matheson (1983, 13) describes the instrumentation of the St. Kitts bull ensemble: "The music of the Bull troupe had a rather jerky rhythm. The instruments were the goat skin drum or tambourine played by hand, maracas . . . a [metal] grater, . . . a gourdie [guiro] and the baha, a piece of one-and-a-half inch pipe or section of bamboo which was blown into and which provided bass effects." The band that accompanied the Virgin Islands' Cane Cutter troupe included drums, guiro, a cowbell (metal gong), fife, tailpipe (baha), and a banjo.

A differentiation can be made between drum music and the music made by a string band. Drummer Irvin "Brownie" Brown (pers. comm., August 16, 1996) explains that a string band, or fungi band, includes guitar, ukulele, banjo, and fife. A tailpipe was often substituted for the bass drum. Mills et al. (1984, 9) describe instrumentalists with Niega Business masqueraders in St. Kitts: "The players were often cane labourers or fishermen, generally three or four, and were accompanied by a small band of musicians with guitar, quatro [small lute,] triangle and baha." Perambulating Mother Hubbard troupes in the Virgin Islands danced to string music, which musician Sylvester "Blinky" McIntosh (pers. comm., July 8, 1995) reports was comprised of two or three guitars, a banjo, steel, squash, and tailpipe. The tailpipe was essential for Mother Hubbard, and Paddy Moore (1979) was acclaimed as a tailpipe player and was proud of his ability to produce two distinct tones. The various Party Girl sets utilized a similar band, and the early clowns also danced to string band music.

Not all masquerade music was formalized, and as Charles Turnbull (pers. comm., June 19, 1996) relates, people improvised by knocking together pieces of metal or other items. Scratch, fungi, or quelbe bands still include some instruments that appeared in the old-time street festivities—fife, maracas, tambourine, tailpipe, guiro (squash), steel (triangle), and stringed instruments such as a banjo, guitar, or ukulele. Although essential to old-time masquerading, bass and kettle drums are seen less often today, replaced by conga drums and in carnival parades by drum machines.

RHYTHM

Crucian Stanley Jacobs (pers. comm., June 30, 1996) remembers that there was less "noise pollution" in the old days, when masquerade drums, especially the

Fig. 2.2. Mocko Jumbie in woman's dress with cap in hand, St. Croix, ca. 1910. Note big drum on left. Courtesy St. Croix Landmarks Society and Archives, Ovesen Collection.

heavy sound of the bass drum, could be heard all over Christiansted. Richard Schrader (pers. comm., July 7, 1995) remembers how drums of troupes in different parts of Frederiksted could be heard simultaneously from strategic locations such as Custom House Square on Strand Street. The varied masquerade rhythms are rapped out on the kettle drum, while the bass drum provides a regular metronome pulse. According to George Farrell (pers. comm., November 13, 2002), a great deal of skill is required to play the kittle drum because it provides the rhythm for the dance movements, whereas the bass "is just boom, boom, boom, boom, he just keeps that steady beat." However, if the boom "don't make a steady beat he could hamper everybody. . . . You have to mix the skill with the two, keep a regular beat. You have to just keep that beat straight and riding on, rattling that drum, doing what he have to do. But if [the boom] stops he will hamper you the [masquerader]. Yes, he will even hamper the whip man if it is time for the whip, the man is using the whip, started using the whip and he making the boom boom without care, I could get hurt, somebody behind could get hurt by going back with the whip." In other words, the whole performance is based on the music. Leona Bryant (pers. comm., July 23, 1996) confirms Frank Charles's statement that each masquerade genre had its own unique signature rhythm, enabling people to determine which masquerade was approaching even before it was visible. In most cases, the distinctive rhythm was rapped out on the snare drum while the bass drum provided a regular pulse. The bass pulse might be faster for the Indians, or slower in the case of David and Goliath. In contrast, the bass drumbeat for the Mocko Jumbie was not a regular metronome pulse but was distinguished by a double beat or stutter. As a child on Denmark Hill, Gertrude Melchior (pers. comm., August 9, 1995) would know a Mocko Jumbie was approaching at Christmastime when she heard the double beat.

Irvin "Brownie" Brown (pers. comm., August 16, 1996) confirms that the Mocko Jumbie bass rhythm was characterized by a double beat:

On one occasion, Paddy Moore played the bass drum for Magnus while Hostaman played the snare drum. According to Moore (1979), "I remember Ciple told me anytime that I hear a man start to roll a kettle drum for the Mocko Jumbie, don't follow that, only you [sing]":

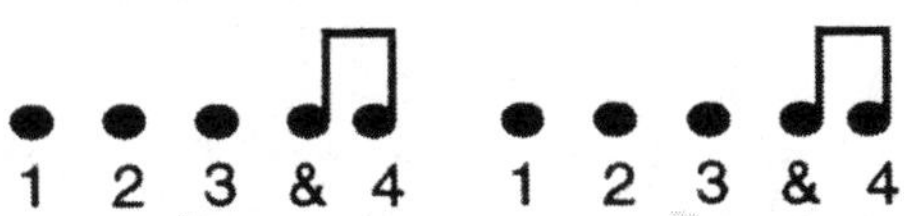

Moore continues, "And I go on the same way. But then Hostaman give a roll and chop, and when he starts to chop, I give the double rock, then I step back":

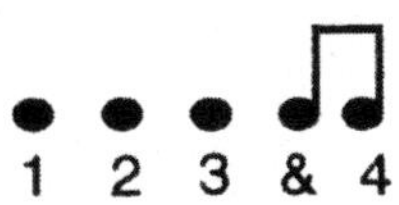

"You see all the time so. Good music man!" The rhythmic examples provided by Melchior, Brown, and Moore are essentially the same. Only the position of the first beat of the bar varies in Paddy Moore's example, where the double beat falls at end.

In West Africa, there are techniques for committing drum notation to memory that involve spoken sounds. If the sounds consist of intelligible words, they are referred to by ethnomusicologists as burden texts; if they consist of nonsense syllables, they are known as vocables. Lacking written scores, these forms or oral notation preserved drum rhythms from generation to generation (Nicholls 1992, 164–70). Any given piece might be represented by both a burden text and/or vocables. The same technique was used in the Virgin Islands. Aggie Bough (pers. comm., July 1, 1996) recalls that Thomas Church, who was her grandfather and Frank Charles's father, told her that the drums were saying, "Up the shallow down the deep, Up the shallow down the deep. Aah we [all of us], move up, move up. Aah we, move up, move up. Aah we, move up, move up." This constitutes the burden text. The burden text can also be expressed in vocables, the first line of which Bough renders as, "Tum pa tu ku, Tum pa tuk, Tum pa tu ku, Tum pa tuk." Similarly, Irvin "Brownie" Brown (pers. comm., August 16, 1996) remembers "straw hat" masquerade music, which resembled what the Indians play today: "Straw hat is a rhythm word, because the drums would play 'I'm straw hat, I'm straw hat, I'm straw hat.'"

SONGS AND DANCES

The songs that support masked dancing are generally perfunctory and motivational. An 1797 report from Jamaica shows that, as is common in West Africa, the songs performed for the John Canoe masquerade consisted of short refrains delivered in call-and-response formula: "This character . . . was attended thro' the town by a great number of negroes, beating old canisters, or pieces of metal, singing 'ay, ay John Canoe' in the time expressed by three quavers and two semiquavers, but with little inflexion of the voice: the word 'ay, ay,' being frequently repeated like a chorus" (Anonymous 1797/1976, 22). This call-and-response song formula is found throughout the Caribbean and is typical of West African songs accompanying masquerade performances—for example, those of the Igede people:

Example 1. *G'ehwong j'abwo*

(Nicholls 1988)

Most Caribbean animal disguises had an ostinato refrain that audiences sang while the masquerade danced. In the Virgin Islands, the donkey danced to a string band and had a distinguishing tune: "Donkey want water, hold him down" or "hold him Joe." The musicians played the tune, while a lead singer would outline a refrain and the onlookers would join in the chorus. The donkey(s) would prance back and forth, and the performer acted as if he/she were trying to hold down the thirsty donkey, much to the delight of the audience (Asta O'Bryan James, pers. comm., July 3, 1996). In St. Kitts–Nevis, performers had a special song for the bull, "Bull Passing." In Antigua's Urlins Village, Lornetta Prince (pers. comm., December 26, 1994) reports that John Bull was also called Potato Bull or Tatie Bull, and a chorus, "C'mon C'mon Potato Bull," was sung to him. Her uncle, Romic Williams (pers. comm., September 22, 1996), remembers, "Come ya [here], Come ya, Tatie Bull," and according to his sister, "Everyone was pleased to see John Bull and would dance and shake their rumps, 'Shake a bull, shake a bull,'" winding their waists and rotating their buttocks. George Farrell (pers. comm., November 13, 2002) recalls that the bulls "have a song, 'The Bull wouldn't wuk [work] but he wants more money.' . . . It has a lot more to it but that is the chorus. . . . People would sing that, especially when the money's here." According to Philip Rhymer (pers. comm., July 18, 1996), the bear's song was, "Rum tum tee. The bear got away." Charles Turnbull (pers. comm., June 19, 1996) points out that the masquerades would dance in character: Koka danced like a clumsy bear, and the devil had a wild, wicked, and menacing dance. Magnus's masquerade dances included a shuffling movement in which he made a fast series of backward jumps, fluttering his petticoats to ward off spirits. When the Moco Jumbo that Young (1807, 258) documented "assumed the 'antic terrible,'" he "was very active on his stilts," while the dance that "De Jumpsa-man" performed "consisted of various contortions of the body, sufficiently droll" (Day 1852, 85).

The characteristic call-and-response technique and topical nature of songs performed for dancing are noted by plantation owner Matthew G. "Monk" Lewis (1834/1999, 80):

> The principal part of the music to which they dance is vocal, one girl generally singing two lines by herself, and being answered by a chorus. . . . To make out . . . the . . . meaning of the words, was out of the question. But one very long song was about the Duke of Wellington, every stanza being chorused with,
>
> *"Ay! hey-dey! Waterloo!*
> *Waterloo! ho! ho! ho!"*

> I had a great deal to do in the business, for every third word was 'massa'; though how I came there, I have no more idea than the Duke.

A call-and-response song about a "massa" and his sexual appetite synchronized the strokes of oarsmen in Barbados in the first half of the nineteenth century, with "the whole crew joining in the chorus in the intervals between every stroke of the oars," as Trelawny Wentworth (1834, 1:242) documents:

> *Massa cum from London town,*
> *Fine time o' day.*
> *Massa is a hansome man,*
> *Fine time o' day.*
> *Massa is a dandy man,*
> *Fine time o' day.*
> *Him hab de dollar, plenty too,*
> *Fine time o' day.*
> *Massa lub' a pretty girl,*
> *Fine time o' day.*
> *Him lub 'em much, him lub 'em true,*
> *Fine time o' day.*
> *Him hunt 'em round de guaba bush,*
> *Fine time o' day.*
> *Him catch 'em in de cane piece,*
> *Fine time o' day.*

Moreton (1790, 157) admits being "amaz[ed] to think with what agility [Jamaican dancers] twist and move their joints:—I sometimes imagine they were on springs or hinges from the hips downwards; whoever is most active and expert at wriggling is reputed to be the best dancer." A report by Day (1852, 53) uses the present-day term *soul* to describe the feeling enslaved Barbadians invested in dance: "Not one within the witchery of the music could keep still. Black nymphs sleek as moles, showed by their contortions how impossible it was. Arms involuntarily went up and down, and dark feet writhed like eels. . . . This was dancing with the soul in it."

Chapter 3

MASQUERADING IN THE EASTERN CARIBBEAN

MASQUERADE GROUP MEMBERSHIP

In discussing the composition of masquerade groups, a distinction must be made between large troupes (eight to twenty or more members), smaller groups, and solo performers, some of whom were accompanied by musicians. A further distinction can be made between masqueraders who performed regularly as the same character and those who adopted different disguises each time. In the Virgin Islands, the former included Koka the Bear, Smokey Joe the Bull, and Magnus the Mocko Jumbie, while the latter is exemplified by Paddy Moore, who played a range of characters including the bear and the Indian. Viggo Roberts of Christiansted, St. Croix, was similarly versatile, playing the devil, the donkey, and sometimes a bat, with outstretched wings. Joe Barilla led large mixed-gender troupes in Christiansted that appeared in different disguises for each outing, including Mother Hubbard, Bluebells, or Down South (blackface minstrels). Nellie Scott of Frederiksted organized Mother Hubbard, Bluebell Girls, Cane Cutters, and other predominantly female troupes.

What is the relationship between members of masquerade groups in the Eastern Caribbean? Anthropological studies often distinguish between common descent and common residence—that is, between family lineage ties and neighborhood-based ties. Family ties are vertical, involving people of different ages and generations, while cohort ties based on common residence are more horizontal and often involve people of similar ages. Horton (1971, 93) discusses cross-cutting institutions in West Africa that "ignore, cut across and even work against the lineages and the lines of division they create." In the early Caribbean, when relocated Africans were still identified along tribal lines, relationships based on ethnicity were routine, as exemplified by the African nation dances. Later, music and dance societies existed primarily on plantations, and relationships were based on common residence, although some family ties might be involved. In the postemancipation era, plantation villages or neighborhood bases were paramount, while certain families came to be associated with specific troupes. Although lineage-based masquerade societies exist in West Africa, masquerades are more often associated with cross-cutting institutions such as secret societies or age-grade institutions. Similarly, in the Eastern Caribbean in the twentieth century, cohort groups of unrelated people of similar ages usually formed the basis of masquerade ensembles.

Prior to emancipation, rivalries often existed between plantations. In one of the songs collected by Weed (1866, 349) on St. Croix at New Year's 1845, members of the Wheel of Fortune Estate's dance troupe disparage rivals on Betty's Hope Estate. In this era, stratification was labor-based, and differentiation existed, for example, between house slaves, craft slaves, and field slaves. Around 1845, according to Weed (1866, 347), "In the town the Free Colored People and House Slaves form their parties, elect their Kings, Queens, etc., in like manner" to the plantation slaves. Such ties based on social strata were evident among the Virgin Islands women's societies, whose members "adopt common principles [and] give support to one another" (Tyson 1995, 8). This suggests that one of preemancipation dance troupes' foremost functions was as a mutual aid society with a supplementary musical component; within the limitations of a slave-based economy, such groups served to some extent as lobbying and political entities. In 1845, the words of a woman's song, "sung by a fine looking gang of slaves . . . as they came into town from the Wheel of Fortune Estate on New Year's morning," especially the line, "King Christian has sent to say he will crown us all," anticipates the 1848 emancipation.

> *All we girls must keep heads together; King Christian has sent to free us all;*
> *Governor Scholten had a vote for us; King Christian has sent to grant us all;*
> *We all have signed for independence; we all have signed for liberty;*
> *Our Crown Prince had a vote in it; our Gracious Queen had the highest vote;*
> *King Christian has sent to say he will crown us all.*
> *Oh, yes! oh, yes! hurrah! hurrah! (Weed 1866, 348)*

Lineage relationships were prevalent in some masquerade troupes in the twentieth century. For example, Arnold Golden (pers. comm., January 20, 1996) remembers that in Christiansted between 1937 and 1942, one family in particular masqueraded every Christmas. Different generations and genders would turn out, most of them young to middle-aged adults, with some elders and children. Myron Jackson (pers. comm., July 20, 1995) emphasizes the neighborhood base for masquerading in Charlotte Amalie but also says that certain families in such neighborhoods as Savan, Pollyberg, and Upstreet were affiliated with specific troupes, among them clowns and Indians.

The dance society's role as a vehicle of solidarity united under a common head is best exemplified by the preeminence of queens and kings. The traditions of mock royalty continued into the twentieth century—for example, masked queens and kings within Plait Pole groups. By this time, however, the queen's authority, the length of her reign, and the number of her adjuncts was diminished. Both Eulalie Rivera on St. Croix (pers. comm., July 3, 1995) and Philip Rhymer on St. Thomas (pers. comm., July 18, 1996) remember kings and queens marching around the streets leading their retinues. Before Christmas, each Mother Hubbard troupe would call a meeting and elect an outspoken woman as queen. The queen was distinct from the owner or sponsor of the troupe, and there were no princesses or ladies-in-waiting. The queen dressed more richly than the others and wore a crown. She would decide when the troupe would stop to perform and when it would move on.

A one-man act had the simplest organization, and the primary responsibility was paying the musicians, who were often hired for an agreed fee rather than a share of the proceeds. Good musicians were generally feted and would be enticed with food and beverages. One New Year's Day, Drattie Drake, a tail-pipe player with a Mother Hubbard troupe, was too intoxicated to continue; the troupe sent a dish of fungi (foonji) and callaloo and three bottles of rum to Paddy Moore (1979), who then agreed to play for the balance of the afternoon for ten dollars.

Every masquerade group had principal figures who oversaw the smooth running of the association and the quality of the entertainment. Foremost was the owner or leader of the troupe, who had the support of interested constituencies and had a reputation as an efficient organizer. This individual brought together the various elements and controlled administrative functions. Although troupes had some inherent democracy and members had input into decision making, organizers would usually oversee costume construction, manage timetables of rehearsals and events, and hire musicians. Another member coordinated troupe activities for the duration of the event. This forthright person would be the queen or maybe the captain, but any vigorous and proficient performer could execute this role. Because a masquerade's vision is usually impaired by the mask, in a bull group, the whip man invariably assumed the position of coordinator. George "Pope" Farrell (pers. comm., November 13, 2002) states, "Any whip man in a masquerade, in a Jam Bull, is the man responsible for that bull," relating how the whip man got the day started: "By the time it's time to get dressed, my whip man will come and say, 'Good morning Mr. Farrell,' that's my father, 'Ah, where is Pope?' He say,

Fig. 3.1. Masked king, Christiansted, St. Croix, ca. 1914. Courtesy St. Croix Landmarks Society and Archives.

'Pope he does drink his tea.' 'Well, okay fine.' Then I get dressed and when I finish he hold up my shoulder, asking me how is my feeling, and all such. So me tell him, 'Well.' He'd cheer you, like that right, 'It'll be good for you to make it today? You know, while maybe I say something like, 'What question you ask me, where's the rum?' He says, 'Well the rum there.'"

A group's treasurer bore responsibility for guarding the proceeds and dividing them up at the end of the day. Performers had various means of collecting donated coins. An upturned hat might be placed on the ground or passed around. Regina Williams (pers. comm., July 11, 1995) remembers a big yard in Christiansted where a laundered white flour bag was laid on the ground and onlookers would throw in money. Before the members of the troupe moved on they would pick up the bag by the four corners and empty it into a smaller bag. Evelyn Richardson (1984, 147–48) recalls that when David and Goliath troupes in Frederiksted around 1910 "played before the home of judge or some other official they received money thrown from the balcony into their small baskets." On other occasions, money would be tossed haphazardly and coins would scatter on the street. Whoever picked up the money was duty bound to give it to the group's treasurer. According to Eulalie Rivera (1987, 17), "The money they collected helped to pay for their costumes, some of which were quite elaborate. One member of the masquerade troupe was responsible for collecting the money, and no matter which masquerader picked up the money, it was always given to this designated person. Later the money would be divided up among the musicians and members of the troupe." Individuals occasionally might not pass all the coins to the treasurer, and rewards were not always monetary, for it was customary to provide performers with food and drink. Aggie Bough (pers. comm., July 1, 1996) remembers an occasion when a musician hid a bottle of sorrel donated by her mother in the guiro (squash gourd). The band members continued playing, waiting for their gift, until the infraction was finally discovered.

Some costumes were homemade, while others were sewn by professional seamstresses, an important individual in larger troupes, though most were not members. A seamstress's expertise was crucial to the troupe's success. Performers might provide their own cloth, though many seamstresses had access to a variety of fabrics. Philip Rhymer (pers. comm., July 18, 1996) remembers that St. Thomas seamstress Bertha Gomez was quite busy before Christmas: "You would take cloth to her and tell her what you wanted and she would make it up."

THE MASQUERADING YEAR

On French-influenced islands in the Lesser Antilles, the major festive performances take place as a pre-Lenten bacchanal, Mardi Gras, ending at Ash Wednesday. After visiting the West Indies in 1807, John Augustine Waller (1820, 70–71) noted the ease with which the British seized the island of Marie Gallante, a dependency of Guadeloupe, because their attack coincided with carnival masquerading: "Whether by accident or design, the attack was made early in the morning at the day which succeeded the last evening of the carnival. . . . The whole town of Grandbourg, is then one masquerade, where harmony and conviviality predominate. . . . At sun-rise the next morning few are to be found out of their beds, except some of the most determined dancers with their masquerade dresses, who could not present any great obstacle to an invading enemy. About 200 men were landed. . . . They marched along the shore without opposition, and arrived at the town between six and seven o'clock unperceived."

Most Leeward Islands, however, have a festival season that follows that of the British West Indies (BWI). The Christmas cycle generally begins with Guy Fawkes Day (November 5) and continues through Christmas Day, Boxing Day, and New Year's Eve before ending on Twelfth Night, the beginning of Epiphany. In Britain, Guy Fawkes Day and its bonfires echo the Celtic New

Year, Halloween, and All Souls' Day (November 2). Other Caribbean holidays are Easter, Crop Over, May Day, and Whitsun. May Day and Crop Over reflect the natural seasons; May Day is inherited from Europe, while Crop Over is determined by the Eastern Caribbean's agricultural year. The timing of many holidays is determined by Easter and consists of celebrations coinciding with religious days. These occasions include not only Ash Wednesday and the beginning of Lent but also Whitsun, which falls on Pentecost and is followed by Whitmonday, which was often the last masquerading holiday until the start of the Christmas cycle. Evelyn Richardson (1984, 147) remembers that around 1910, when she was a child, masquerades would perform in Frederiksted on Easter Monday, Whitmonday, and Christmas Second Day: "On those special days the custom was that some of the adult troupes masked with guitars, mandolins, and dry gourds would rap at the front door of influential families and would be invited into the living rooms to dance for the occupants. In turn they would be given money and a few drinks. Besides these masqueraders, there were Mocko Jumbies (high stilt walkers), the Wild Indians, and the Devil.... Then there was the David and Goliath troupe.... They drew quite an audience around them."

After the United States acquired what are now the U.S. Virgin Islands in 1917, other holidays emerged there. July 4 was sometimes celebrated with masquerading and is now the date of the St. John Carnival. More recently, Crucians have begun to celebrate Emancipation Day on July 3 with speeches, traditional reenactments, and masquerading.

Christmas

In his eighteenth-century report of the slaves' year, Oldendorp (1770/1987, 227) states, "During the three major holidays—Christmas, Easter, and Whitsuntide—they are given the first two days of each holiday entirely free." Half a century later, according to Weed (1866, 346), the holiday was extended by popular practice. On St. Croix in 1844–45, "the holidays of the slaves commence with Christmas, and although the law gives them that and the following day, they contrive, in imitation of our Congress, to do very little work between Christmas and New Year." The holidays took place despite the fact that Christmas coincided with the ripening of the cane, as Thomas Rasmussen points out: "Christmas day [1861] was in the middle of a crop and the greatest holiday for the negroes. Often it was the only holiday allowed them throughout this busy time" (Tyson 1995, 22).

Rehearsals preceded Christmas. According to Weed (1866, 346), "For several weeks preceding Christmas they are busied with preparations for their festivities," while the *St. Thomas Tidende* reported on November 22, 1890, that "the various drum dances . . . are being organized by their respective 'kings' and 'queens.' . . . By some 'troupes' the shrieking of the singers and thumping of drums . . . have fairly begun." Amos Frett (1979) remembers that in the early twentieth century, "They set up the drum on the Fifth of November. We used to light a bonfire and start to practice from that night . . . that was Guy Fox [Fawkes] day; they knock bamboula from that night, practicing for Christmas." Rehearsals normally occurred at night, when participants had free time.

Christmas celebrations have long begun with serenading, normally starting as early as 3:00 on Christmas morning, when groups traveled with their instruments from estate to estate in the country or house to house in town, singing Christmas songs; householders would give the visitors guavaberry drink and cake. In Antigua in the early nineteenth century, Flannigan (1844, 2:130) writes,

> "Christmas Day" is ushered in with the sound of fiddles and drums; parties of negroes going around the town about four o'clock in the morning, playing on these instruments for the purpose of breaking people's rest . . . and then they have the assurance to call at the different houses during the day for payment. At the conclusion of the serenade, or waits . . . the musicians generally raise their voices to the highest pitch, and call out, "Good morning to you massa; good morning to you missis; good morning to you, ladies and gentlemen all!" A flourish is then given with the fiddle and drum, and they march off to disturb another quiet household.

Joseph John Gurney (1840, 26) describes celebrations in St. Thomas during Christmas and New Year 1839–40, when he saw "a merry-andrew" during a "negro Saturnalia": "The slaves being allowed a perfect liberty from Christmas to New Year's day, to drum, fiddle, dance and sing." This mention of a Merry Andrew confirms that maskers were included prior to emancipation in the Danish West Indies. Little masquerading took place on Christmas Day—people went to church or simply spent the day with family or visiting friends. But during the evening and on Boxing Day (also known as St. Stephen's Day and Christmas Second Day), individuals donned disguises and took to the streets. Visby-Petersen (1917, 26) describes Christmas in St. Thomas around 1892: "The festivals . . . were characterized by parades, in carnival style. The merriments were only allowed to begin after 4 P.M.; but already in the morning one would meet figures in disguise. . . . An unnerving sight to behold was the traditional 'Mumbo-Jumbo' or Mukka Jumbe, as the Blacks call him . . . do an insane dance on tall stilts. . . . The public eagerly awaits his appearance . . . and that of the two devils who form part of the tradition on these occasions."

In the Virgin Islands, Christmas and other holidays were also celebrated with a Plait Pole (Maypole). The January 3, 1866, *St. Thomas Tidende* reports that at the island's recent Christmas and New Year's celebrations, "One troupe . . . executed the 'peasant dance' around a . . . Maypole so famed in England. Each dancer held a ribbon fastened to the top of the pole, [and the dance] was continued until the ribbons became so tightened as to deny the dancers any further progress, the ribbons were then undone in like manner." Other accounts describe Plait Pole performances at New Year's 1893 in Christiansted and on Three Kings' Day 1900 in Charlotte Amalie. In the early days, mixed-gender groups participated, dressed in masks and fancy clothes and led by a king and queen; later, however, Plait Pole came to be primarily a women's dance, and masks were abandoned. The pole was mobile and could be moved to different locations. In the meadows, the pole might be placed in a hole, whereas a wooden frame base was used in the streets.

New Year's

New Year's was also celebrated by masquerading. During the second quarter of the eighteenth century, Carstens (1997, 132) noted that the people of St. Thomas "observe only one general celebration during the year. It commences on the evening of the last day of the year and lasts until the following evening on New Year's Day." In 1831–32, Nissen (1838, 164) describes New Year's perambulations in St. Thomas. Celebrants are no longer masters and slaves perambulating together but African descendants, free and unfree: "It is the custom here, especially among the colored persons, to celebrate old year's night with music, dancing and singing. . . . As early as four o'clock in the afternoon, [they are] passing in crowds through all the streets crying in their Creole tongue, 'Old Year's Night.' At 9 o'clock they pass through the streets with music and continue . . . the whole night."

Hovey (1838, 36) states, "The Christmas holidays are . . . spent in feasting, visiting, and dancing." He continues, "It is customary at this time, for slaves on the different plantations, attired in their choicest dress, to go in a body to the house of their master, and to receive admission to his best apartments; where they set up the music of the banjo and commence dancing. The family make it a point to be present, and not unfrequently join in the dance" (36). The literati highlighted the visiting aspect of the celebrations. In the nineteenth century, slaves' visiting included seasonal calls on "massa" and his family at the Great House. Of St. Croix around 1818–21, Captain J. Johnson writes, "On New Year's eve and on the morning of the New Year [the Negroes] enter the house of the Master dancing and singing" (Tyson 1995, 3). On large estates, greeting the enslaved could be a lengthy process. James Smith (1840, 79) spent Christmas 1839 at the house of a prominent St. Croix physician: "This gentleman is the proprietor of one or two hundred slaves, and it was no inconsiderable task to greet so many, it occupied much of the morning." Slaves did not limit their visits to their own master's Great House or confine their calls to rural estates. During Christmas 1839, large numbers of revelers paraded through the streets and visited Smith's residence in Christiansted: "Christmas day and the day thereafter . . . our boarding-house was visited by several hundreds, who danced for our amusement" (79). Following emancipation, the cycle of visiting continued, only now the proprietors of the great houses were no longer slave owners. In Rasmussen's 1866 description, the manager received visits from the black population of the Lower and Upper Love plantations: "The women dressed in most gaudy colors and came in a long parade marching up past the manager's house to beg the permission to start the dance. . . . Cakes which are baked of cornmeal and rum are passed around. . . . All of a sudden a whole mob would line up and march out going to the next plantation where the whole show would be started over again and a new mob would arrive in their place" (Tyson 1995, 22). Masquerade groups also customarily visited the governor and other dignitaries. H. F. Garde describes Christmas and New Year's 1851–52 in St. Thomas: "Early in the morning of New Year's day [bands of negroes] gather at Government House to sing, dance and give a cheer. The Governor made a short speech and scattered coins. . . . One gang of negroes succeeded another. . . . [T]he dispensing of coins . . . ceased due to lack of coins. The Governor's speeches also ended" (Tyson 1995, 13). At New Year's 1866, "Each group or party assumed their own fancy. . . . [M]any . . . presented themselves to different family mansions and asked to be allowed to dance. . . . One troupe . . . executed the 'peasant dance' around a . . . Maypole. . . . This troupe danced in all the principal squares and streets and gathered very large crowds. . . . One group of Equestrians . . . proceeded to the residence of the Vice-Governor, where . . . three chosen for the purpose, presented an address" (*St. Thomas Tidende*, January 3, 1866).

Three Kings' Day

After emancipation, some islands celebrated Twelfth Night, which occurs on January 6, Three Kings' Day, and co-opted it as a day for masquerading, extending the festive season by nearly a week. The January 8, 1870, *St. Thomas Tidende* reports that on Three Kings' Day, "His Excellency kept open house, and many of the Masks paid their respects. In several private houses they danced during the evening." The occasion "closed the holidays." In 1871–72 on both St. Croix and St. Thomas, according to S. B. Haynes (1872, 200) "the Christmas holidays were celebrated . . . by the colored people. . . . [F]or more than a week they are completely exempt from labor, and devote the days . . . to the pleasure of dancing. They commenced at two o'clock on Christmas morning . . . to parade the streets in gangs numbering from twenty to a hundred, males and females. . . . On New Year's Day, of which they think even more than of Christmas, some of the town queens are gorgeous in silk or satin. . . . They also commemorate Twelfth-night, or 'Three Kings' Day,' as they call it here." For Three Kings' Day 1881, "the general public amusement [was] the masquerade . . . having their music to accompany them" (*St. Thomas Tidende*, January 8, 1881). In 1899, the *Tidende* stated, "Three Kings' is usually a half holiday, but there was no half about yesterday—it was from morn to eve. . . . There were crowds of masqueraders running around the town" (*St. Thomas Tidende*, January 7, 1899). The turn of the twentieth century was marked in the usual style in St. Thomas: "From the early afternoon crowds of masqueraders were on the streets and these attracted the customary crowds of spectators. The presence ashore of hundreds of Russian and German soldiers added greatly to the bustle. The principal features of the masking were the pole plaiting, an old time favorite, and the revival of the 'moko-jumbi'—walking on stilts" (*St. Thomas Tidende*, January 8, 1900).

Leroy Arnold (pers. comm., July 8, 1995) maintains that most masqueraders in the Virgin Islands were people on the rural estates and that few townspeople dressed in costumes. Troupe members assembled where the leader lived and performed at different estates. The masqueraders started in the country in the morning and spent some hours traveling among different estates before coming into town, whether Christiansted or Frederiksted in St. Croix or Charlotte Amalie in St. Thomas. Under Danish law, performances could not take place in town prior to 3:00 P.M. and must cease by dusk, 6:00 P.M.. Alma Doward (pers. comm., July 6, 1995) remembers that on the Annaly Estate around 1920, when she was a child, the masquerade troupes would assemble in their costumes on Christmas Second Day. If their leader had a mule cart, they would ride, but more often they walked. Acoustic instruments—drums, fife, tailpipe, squash, and steel—could be played while walking, although the bass drum and the tailpipe were a little burdensome. In town, masquerades stopped to dance on street corners and in compound yards, where little crowds gathered. The route they took was not systematized, and the different troupes perambulated according to their own inclinations, stopping where participants knew residents. Arnold Golden (pers. comm.,

January 20, 1996) remembers that masqueraders would move down Christiansted's King Street and up Company Street and visit the big yard near the cemetery. He recalls the devil, David and Goliath, and the Indians. As much as half an hour might pass between the departure of one group and the arrival of the next. Mary Seales (pers. comm., July 5, 1996), who lived near St. Paul's Church in Frederiksted, confirms the randomness of the perambulations: "We children would wait expectantly for the masquerades. . . . One group would perform then another group would arrive." Some onlookers watched from second-story windows and threw money down. Masquerader Paddy Moore (1979) remembers, "At 6 P.M. we had to stop playing. So we went into a yard and played there until 7 P.M." Troupes at times assembled at Faster Field, on the edge of Frederiksted.

Many of St. Thomas's festivities centered on Charlotte Amalie, the capital of the Danish West Indies, which had a more freewheeling atmosphere than existed elsewhere. Dancing was permitted there after dusk on the major holidays, although masks had to be removed so that performers' identities could not be concealed (Philip Rhymer, pers. comm., July 18, 1996). Masquerade groups came into town from different parts of the island, gathering in the field that is now Lionel Roberts Stadium and performing together like a mini-carnival. In centrally located Market Square, people would put out benches so that they could sit and watch. Groups would then move all around Emancipation Gardens or by the old district courthouse. Masquerades also performed on side streets such as Garden Street (Commandant Gade), where well-to-do residents lived. Gertrude Melchior (pers. comm., August 9, 1995) lived on Denmark Hill as a child in the late 1920s, and from this vantage point she could hear the different performers. From Market Square, the Mocko Jumbies and other masquerades climbed the hill to visit her house. According to Charles Turnbull (pers. comm., June 19, 1996), masqueraders who performed particularly well were feted and invited into homes for refreshments.

In Antigua, the twelve days of Christmas were touring season for masquerades. George "Pope" Farrell (pers. comm., November 13, 2002) reports that the Highlanders and clowns he saw as a child in All Saints Village visited various settlements scattered throughout the southern countryside, among them Freeman's Village, Liberta, Swete, Ebenezer, Jennings, John Hughes, Old Road, Parham, English Harbor, Nelson's Dockyard, and Falmouth. Later, when performing as the bull, Farrell traveled to many of the same places. Masquerade groups had to report their planned itineraries to the police, so a police station was the first stop. Officials would then alert other stations along the route. Sometimes one or two policemen would escort the ensemble to the village to help keep the revelry under control. Young men in particular could spoil the fun. According to Payne (2005), "One 'John Bull' . . . had to end the Christmas act he brought to my village early because he had taken a rum-break and left his costume unattended. A bunch of little boys carefully wove some stinging nettles into the thatch and the consensus was there was never a better or more energetic dance ever done by a 'John Bull.' . . . I wonder if that's one of the reasons my village has never been famous for the 'John Bull.'" On his trips to town, Farrell would put on his costume at the St. John's Police Station and then entertain the police. Starting from St. John's Market, the masquerades would gravitate up the hill toward more upscale residential areas. In the words of some Antigua Museum literature (in possession of author), Christmas performers "would visit the homes which were mainly at that time concentrated in the city when the big houses were on the streets in the business section—High Street, Long Street, Newgate, St. Mary's, Redcliffe and Market Streets, on the 'Paroch' or Thames Street. Each was occupied by families of the business and professional sections of the community." According to Farrell (pers. comm., November 13, 2002), six, seven, or more bulls would gather to compete. An informal hierarchy existed among bull performers: A local bull might generate a crowd of onlookers in his home village, but when a bull with elevated status appeared, the local would make himself scarce. When Clovelle Philip (pers. comm., December 4, 1996) dressed up as a bull, he "tied two cow horns to my head and wore my grandmother's dress. I sewed banana shaggy around me like a skirt. The children ran from me. Then I saw a real John Bull coming and I stripped off my mask and ran like hell."

Easter

Easter is a movable feast, not fixed in relation to the civil calendar and marking the end of Lent.[1] Dominica, Guadeloupe, Martinique, and Trinidad hold their carnivals as a pre-Lenten bacchanal ending on Shrove Tuesday, the day before Lent begins. Although Carnival is not held at this time in St. Thomas, Easter Monday was an occasion for celebrations: The April 9, 1890, *St. Thomas Tidende* reports, "The Easter holidays were observed in the usual manner. . . . Monday kept up its reputation as a time for picnicking and in the afternoon there was some bustle on the streets with the appearance of maskers." By the early twentieth century, women participated: "Easter Monday was made unusually lively by the appearance in town of a fine cavalcade of maskers dressed as clowns, 46 horsemen comprised the parade, and a number of female maskers followed the procession on foot" (*St. Thomas Tidende*, April 15, 1903).

Whitsun

In the West, the earliest possible date for Whitsun is May 10 and the latest June 13. Whitmonday follows Whitsunday and was a bank holiday in the United Kingdom until 1967. In the Leeward Islands, Whitmonday was known for horse racing and masquerading. On May 24, 1893, the *St. Thomas Tidende* reported, "Whitmonday was observed yesterday in the customary manner—by picnics at day-time and dances in the evening. From 4 o'clock in the afternoon a contingent of masqueraders kept the streets lively. . . . Fortunately the pugilistic tendencies of these 'wile injuns' and 'Zulus' affected none but the men themselves." The "wile" Indians danced aggressively, whooping and shaking their braids. In the early twenty-first century, the Indians still perform in the Virgin Islands Carnival, one of the only troupes that continues to use traditional drums to beat out their fast rhythms, advancing a legacy that is well over a century old. Amos Frett (1979) remembers masquerading in Tutu in the Danish era: "We had Mas' out here in the country. . . . Men used to wear woman frock and thing; we went to Tutu; I think it was Whit Monday, it broke up, we would Mas' all about. I was one—I hade a frock on too; we had string music: guitar . . . lute and guiro and ass pipe [tailpipe]."

Crop Done

Crop Done, alternatively known as Crop Over, was celebrated on St. Croix and other islands, including St. Vincent, Trinidad, and Barbados. F. W. N. Bayley (1830, 437) states, "I believe in one or two of the Leeward Islands it is more usual for the august assembly of sable revellers to carry on their [Crop Over] gaieties on the green lawn before the dwelling of the proprietor. . . . An empty barrel 'par exemble,' with a large piece of parchment on the top, a kettle drum, a tambourine, a pipe, a gumbay or bonja [banjo], with sundry other instruments, and these aided by the vocal efforts of men and women, boys and girls, do verily emit sounds of most terrific merriment." Elaborate Barbadian Crop Over celebrations are now commemorated annually as part of the island's Carnival. This harvest festival was previously a high point of the agricultural year, occurring when the last sugarcane was cut. Harvest usually commenced in February or March (Johan Christian Schmidt in Tyson and Highfield 1994; West 1793). The festival was commemorated with music and dance and in Barbados with masquerading featuring the Straw Bear. John Chester Greville (1869, 81–82) relates, "A cart laden with the last canes is drawn by mules decorated with ribbons, and attended by a crowd of labourers; the principal women being attired in white muslin" (62). According to Schrader (1989, 40), Crop Done in the Virgin Islands was marked by "pomp and circumstance—Crucian style": "The last cart, truck and tractor loads of sugarcane brought to the factory from the fields were decorated with lovely red flambouyant. Even the horses, mules, and donkeys were trimmed with this beautiful flower. People sat on top of the sugar cane in their vehicles, waving red flags, a symbol of joy that a period of tough labor has ended."

May Day

May Day was celebrated on May 1 in much of the BWI. May Day celebrations invariably involved dancing around the Maypole, more commonly known as the Plait Pole, and dancers in the late nineteenth and early twentieth centuries wore masks. A photograph taken on May Day 1912 in St. Croix shows masked male and female dancers around a Plait Pole (Axel Ovesen Collection, St. Croix Landmarks Society, Frederiksted). Leona Bryant (pers. comm., July 23, 1996) recalls May Day celebrations in the Field in St. Thomas involving a May Queen dressed in white on a throne. Similarly, Aggie Bough (pers. comm., July 1, 1996) took part in May Day festivals in St. Croix that featured a May Queen and Maypole dancing.

LOGISTICS OF MASQUERADING

Two dominant truisms emerge in discussions of masquerading in the Eastern Caribbean. The first is that it was engaged in solely by the lower classes; the second is that events were spontaneous and not planned. While these assumptions are so patently true they have become clichés, an examination of the exceptions can help determine the soundness of the stereotype. The view of masquerading as a lower-class activity originated in Europe and generally does not hold for West Africa. Cass and Roud (2002, 40) point out that in England, "almost without exception, mumming was a *working* or *labouring class* custom. The local middleclass and gentry sometimes viewed such customs with scorn." Similarly, one of Tedre's (2007, 408) informants states, "Goats [animal disguises] were poorer people, cottagers. Others did not go in for it." Comparable attitudes are expressed in the Eastern Caribbean, and street masquerading in the Virgin Islands was an activity for those whom Rufus Vanderpool (pers. comm., August 3, 1995) calls "working class" and Ruth Moolenaar (pers. comm., August 10, 1995) labels "lower socioeconomic status." Helen Joseph (pers. comm., July 4, 1996) says that "in the past, masquerading

Fig. 3.2. Plait Pole troupe, St. Croix, ca. 1900–1910. Courtesy St. Croix Landmarks Society and Archives, Ovesen Collection.

was looked on by the upper crust as something vulgar. It was okay to be entertained by them and give them a few pennies, but it was not something you would want your child to do." While some elites came to watch, others did not, and the more straitlaced viewed masqueraders with disdain. According to Eulalie Rivera (1987, 18), Sister Nanca Schoern, matron of Frederiksted's Ebenezer Home Orphanage before 1917, disapproved of Ana Mills, a masquerade troupe leader, mostly because she was garrulous and had "a boisterous and infectious laugh." Schoern "would often use Miss Mills as an example of how not to act when she was teaching us ladylike manners." According to Charles Turnbull (pers. comm., June 19, 1996), in the mid-twentieth century, members of the middle and upper classes observed masquerades from a distance to avoid appearing to participate. They would look from their windows or gather with friends on their porches or balconies. Children from these families were not allowed on the street but would toss money down because "it was the right thing to do." According to Mills, Jones-Hendrickson, and Bertram (1984, 3, 14) "practitioners of the art" of masquerading in St. Kitts–Nevis were "working class people all, and overwhelmingly rural"; moreover, "The production and execution of [these] activities have always been seen by the upper and middle classes as the unenviable and exclusive preserve of the poor and black lower classes."

Nevertheless, the assumption that masquerading invariably involved only one class is incorrect. In Denmark, rural elites as well as laborers engaged in mumming, as is evident in Bregenhøj and Larsen's (2007, 212) account of Shrovetide mumming, which involved the rural elite and was very grand. In a highly stratified society such as the preemancipation Danish West Indies, music and dance societies distinguished social strata. Victor Schoelcher identified different women's societies with "the two classes of color—the Negroes and the mulattos" (Tyson 1995, 8). Weed (1866, 347) likewise distinguished between the mid-1840s town masquerade troupes formed by the free colored people and those of the house slaves. Moreover, the masqueraders who appeared on Easter Monday 1883 were described as "young gentlemen" who impersonated such erudite men as Victor Hugo and Hippocrates, showing that quite a high degree of scholarship was involved (*St. Thomas Tidende*, March 28, 1883). Spectators, too, came from many classes. According to the January 8, 1856, *St. Croix Avis*, the entertainment provided by processions of members of the "laboring populations" drew "crowds of people, not of the ordinary class." Spectators became involved to varying degrees, participating by clapping, mingling with maskers, dancing, and generally blurring the distinction between performer and spectator. Some elites even helped sponsor activities.

Stereotypes depict old-time masquerading as spontaneous, with small groups of masqueraders informally touring the streets and stopping to perform according to their own inclinations. Although this assessment is generally accurate, exceptions occurred, including large-scale parades involving significant numbers of people. S. B. Haynes (1872, 201) describes Christmas festivities involving revelers and queens' processions "parad[ing] the streets in gangs numbering from twenty to a hundred." Moreover, an equestrian procession involving three to four dozen mounts requires planning and prior communication with the affected neighborhoods. Such cavalcades occurred on Easter Monday 1903; Three Kings' Day 1907, when a parade of thirty-four donkeys "ridden by gaily dressed fellers" took place in Charlotte Amalie (*St. Thomas Bulletin*, January 8, 1907); and Valentine's Day 1914, which featured a cavalcade of "54 handsome costumed riders, including ladies" (*St. Thomas Tidende*, February 21, 1914).

A spectacle of the magnitude of a large parade stands out (see Rezende and Walbom 2009, 101). On January 4, 1893, the *St. Croix Avis* reports, "New Year's day falling on a Sunday did not prevent the people of" Christiansted from enjoying the holiday "to the full on Monday. We had the streets thronged all the afternoon, the attractions being masqueraders, pole plaiters, and a guitar band, but above all, a model ship of considerable size drawn through the streets. There was a numerous crew, who . . . walked behind. [It was pulled] by four small ponies. . . . The sailors were all in uniform." Such a display involved sophisticated levels of organization and planning. Historian George Tyson (pers. comm., July 5, 1995) agrees that by the end of the nineteenth century, New Year's festivals were more coordinated, with high levels of organization; however, he doubts that overall annual themes existed, as is the case with current carnivals. Despite some exceptions, therefore, the paradigm of masquerading as a small-scale, informal, working-class activity remains intact. Random perambulations were the norm and were decidedly less regimented than parades. Although the revels tended to have a leveling effect, reducing the distance both literally and metaphorically between different social strata, the majority of the performers were working-class people of African descent, and masquerading reflected the vox populi.

ECONOMICS OF MASQUERADING

The splendor of the Christmas festival was thrown into high relief by the grinding poverty of the rest of the year. The contrast between feast and famine could not have been greater, as Stewart (1823/1969, 274) tersely noted in Jamaica: "The Negresses must, however, have their annual display of fine clothes and suitable ornaments, [even] if they should go in filth and raggedness all the rest of the year." How might this ostentation and flaunting of attire on the part of the poorest sections of society be explained? Illiffe (1983, 21) observes that conspicuous hedonism and displays of wealth feature within manifestations of the African notion of the "good life." Saturnalia possessed an omnipresent larger-than-life quality. One aspect of masquerading involves financial considerations. Constructing costumes inevitably entails time, labor, and money, and Christmastime saw an exchange of resources—entertainment in return for gifts. Such exchanges may not seem to represent major transactions in the grand scheme of things, but within the slaves' and later the laborers' purview, the practice implied considerable outlays that could bring significant rewards. Troupe members' savings, elite patronage, and the remunerations earned through performance financed the activities.

Nineteenth-century celebrations demonstrate an increasing level of extravagance. During Christmas 1831 in St. Croix, William E. Canning notes, "They make quite a display of dress especially the females, some of whom wear, not only fashionable, but costly articles" (Tyson 1995, 4). Such flamboyance is more characteristic of the dressing up genre of masquerading than the dressing down, which is the focus of this book. Regardless, the costumes of Mocko Jumbies, Montserrat masqueraders, Pitchy Patchy, Highlanders, and clowns often use distinctive textiles, finely sewn and elaborate. An account of a dance contest in the Danish West Indies that involved dressing up describes a competition between the Oxford and La Grange plantations to see who could "dress best, dance best, and spend most money" (Tyson 1995, 14). According to this account, "The tourney was commenced by the Oxford King throwing with dignified nonchalance, $10 in 5 stiver pieces, full in the face of the La Grange royalty. This unexpected maneuver, completely routed the unfortunate King's plans, he was defunct for the rest of the festivities." The penchant for using money as adornment was observed in the queen, "upon [whose] bosom reposed a $10 gold piece and below a doubloon," and in the captain, who had "a five dollar bill pinned on his bosom."

Allowances and Earnings

How were the music and dance associations financed? How did slaves and later laborers, the most impoverished section of society, mount extravagant costumed dance exhibitions? Prior to emancipation, the slaves largely supported their revelry by their own earnings, dearly wrenched from the environment. Tyson and Highfield (1994) obtain useful information about slave finances from the writings of individuals, most of them Danes, who witnessed the slave system firsthand. Every week, each plantation slave received an allowance of food—usually six to eight pieces of Baltic herring and six quarts of flour in the form of kiln-dried corn meal, supplemented occasionally with some pork or beef. According to Hovey (1838, 26), "An equivalent is sometimes given in yams or other vegetables." Furthermore, "They not unfrequently sell part of their meal and fish . . . or exchange them for meat or clothing, and other things which they prefer." West (1793; in Tyson and Highfield 1994, 132) reports, "Every night, those Negroes stationed within a mile or more from the towns carry grass to the towns for the horses of the inhabitants. . . . Likewise, they sell the firewood used in all the hearths in the town as well as in the country." Other produce, including fruit, was also found growing wild and then sold in the towns. Charles Boudens, Vicomte de Vanderbourg (1798; in Tyson and Highfield 1994, 156) reports that slaves also spend time "cultivating some nutritional plants and fruits in the mountainous parts of the island." Other slaves increased their income by shooting blue doves or other wild game birds or by fishing (134). Brady (1829; in Tyson and Highfield 1994, 162) reports, "They are not permitted to possess boats, but they go out to fish upon rafts," returning with "fish, land crabs, and occasionally a turtle."

All slaves above the age of ten were provided with gardens, which were tended on Sundays and provided an additional source of food and income. According to Vanderbourg, the gardens consisted of "small plots of land that are loaned to them every year so that they might grow yams, corn, millet, potatoes and such" (Tyson and Highfield 1994, 156). Moreover, "the Negroes . . . supplement the deficit in their rations . . . in raising poultry, pigs, and goats" (156). Some slaves made and sold craft items such as straw hats and woven baskets. These items and foodstuffs were sold at Sunday markets, where both white and African-descended people obtained much of their vegetable and meat supplies. However, as West (1793; in Tyson and Highfield 1994, 133) points out, "The finer fruits—avocados, pineapples, mesples [mespels], grapes and the like . . . are sold from the gardens of whites or free Negroes." According to Weed (1866, 352), in the mid-1840s, the "Negro Market . . . is eligibly situated upon a square, where the female slaves exhibit poultry, eggs, vegetables, fruit, herring, etc., spread out upon the ground under small Tamarind trees. . . . The slaves save the meal and herring from their rations. The vegetables and fruits are the product of their grounds. Most of the meal used by the townspeople is purchased from the slaves. . . . The market is a scene of much animation from twelve till three o'clock. The colored women, to the number of two or three hundred, bring their products to market in trays upon their heads, from the different plantations, the most distant of which are from six to seven miles."

Some young men hired themselves out as laborers on Sundays. According to Brady, "About two shillings and a pint of rum each person, is the ordinary rate of payment" (Tyson and Highfield 1994, 171). Payments in rum, of course, were easily squandered. Otherwise, as Dookhan (1974, 152) states, "The money so earned was used to buy necessities and luxuries not otherwise provided, or else saved to purchase freedom. . . . Slaves were permitted and sometimes encouraged to buy the clothes they needed or desired out of the money they earned through the sale of their provisions, livestock or services."

Money earned from these endeavors was set aside for the costumes worn during the Christmas revelry, and dance troupes pooled their resources to ensure that queens were grandly adorned. James Smith describes one queen's decorations as "furnished by contributions of the slaves" (Tyson and Highfield 1994, 202). Following emancipation in 1848, S. B. Haynes (1872, 201) states, "Each party has a chosen queen, attired according to her own or collected means." The *Pennsylvania Freeman* mentions the part that savings played in revelers' Christmas celebrations: "The negroes . . . save their earnings for the holidays, when whiz! it flies as freely as though lavished by a prince of the blood, and they enter upon the new year with sick heads, debts and tattered finery, but with the pleasing reminiscence that while the fun lasted it was royal" (Tyson 1995, 14). The January 4, 1856, *St. Croix Avis* describes the king and queen and their Gombay Troupe retinue as an "absurd exhibition of mock royalty," lamenting the "needless extravagance" of the troupe, whose members were "richly attired in silks and satins—the cost of which no doubt, was defrayed from the hard earned savings of a whole year." Nevertheless, some twenty years later, S. B. Haynes (1872, 202) reports that on St. Thomas, "On New Year's Day . . . some of the town queens are gorgeous in silk or satin, and occasionally . . . will have sewed on the bosom of the dress bank-notes and gold doubloons."

Gift Giving and Seasonal Rewards

At Christmas, the slaves received an annual allotment of food and clothing. Various reports specify what food, fabrics, or items of apparel were given. Tuckerman (1837, 24) states, "At Christmas, every slave receives six pounds of white flour, six pounds of pork, and about four pounds of sugar, and a bottle of rum." Schoelcher lists "four pounds of lard . . . twelve yards of bamboo [woolen cloth], 24 yards of brown [heavy cloth], and two bonnets every year" (Tyson and Highfield 1994, 207). On St. Croix, Brady writes, "the legal annual allowance of clothing for each man" during the late 1820s consisted of "seven yards of osnaburg, which will make a shirt and a pair of trousers. Three and a half yards of a coarse kind of woolen cloth, called bamboo, which is usually made into a coat or cloak. The allowance for the women is the same, except that they have an additional yard of osnaburg. . . . Each man and woman receives a blanket every two years. At — —, each male is annually allowed a hat; each woman, two cotton handkerchiefs" (Tyson and Highfield 1994, 163). The annual allowance might include cash, as Hovey (1838, 89) states: "This is the occasion, when presents are distributed among them of provisions, clothing, or even of money. The feelings of the slaves towards their master, through the year, depend very much on the treatment they receive at these times." According to a song by Wheel of Fortune slaves collected in 1845 by Weed (1866, 350),

> *Massa Walker give them the best Madrass*
> *Good brown and bamboo—and care dem well*
> *Come along! come along!*

The visitations and gift giving continued into the twentieth century. Recollects Maud Andreas (1989),

> When Christmas [came], they all would like to go to the manager's house, and sing Christmas songs, and dance for the manager, and he would give them presents, give them money and thing[s]. . . . This was a song they were singing:

Good morning to you, Massa Gyllich
Yeah, how we like all we Enfield girl.
To you in prosperity.
Hope you may live to enjoy many more.

Oh, le' we go, le' we go,
Le' we go La Reine, le' we go,
Le' we take an enticing walk La Reine
If the master insult us, right back home!

Slave visitors did not limit themselves to their own plantation houses but ventured further afield. During these visits, they might receive refreshments and cash gifts. Tuckerman (1837, 25) describes one St. Croix man who was "obtaining small Danish coin, in exchange for two doubloons, for distribution among the slaves who would be at his house . . . on a visit." As in mumming in Ireland, Britain, and Newfoundland, annual calls were not reserved exclusively for local benefactors, and visits to friends and neighbors were commonplace.

As the various masquerade groups moved to different locations, performing on street corners, in big yards, or inside houses, spectators customarily provided the performers with cash or food and drink. In the twentieth century, the token gift giving is symbolized by johnnycake (journey cake) and guavaberry drink. When she was young, Evelyn Richardson (1984, 146) belonged to a Mother Hubbard troupe whose leader, Petronella, "took us to the homes of many of the rich and the not-so-rich. There we would dance and sing for them. They in turn gave us candy and lemonade and buns." The reciprocal nature of Christmas gifting demonstrates that the raison d'être was not simply to obtain succor but instead an exchange. The dancers provided festive entertainment. Creativity was appreciated, and the financial rewards could be considerable, especially for solo performers, who only had to pay musicians. Paddy Moore (1979), a renowned Crucian masquerader, reports that he made as much as three hundred dollars on one particular day in the early 1930s. Coercion may have been a factor; Flax (2004) has childhood memories of John Bull masquerades visiting St. John's, the capital of Antigua: "Boxing Day was the day that fife bands and John Bulls or John Canoe came out. I remember as a child hearing the drums from the John Bull in the distance and was terrified knowing that he was coming. The tradition was that the John Bulls came through the streets of St. John's, each on a different route, with a drummer, a whipper and a fife (wind pipes) band behind him. The whipper would whip the John Bull which will entice him to run kids off the street with his bull horns on his head. The only way to prevent that was to throw him some money then he would leave you alone."

George "Pope" Farrell (pers. comm., November 13, 2002) remembers that he and his Jam Bull ensemble would sometimes earn twenty dollars in a village, "and it's a plenty." The money was divided equally among the masquerade, the whip man, and the musicians.

Sponsorship

The Virgin Islands literature offers little information regarding sponsorship or gifts or loans of clothes provided to masqueraders by whites or elites. Leroy Arnold (pers. comm., July 8, 1995) reports, however, that Danish-era plantation owners, managers, and other Europeans sometimes helped sponsor performances, providing dresses or materials or loaning phaetons in which kings and queens could ride. Literature from Jamaica provides examples of the kind of support and sponsorship that probably occurred elsewhere in the BWI. Matthew G. "Monk" Lewis (1834, 54) describes the New Year's Day celebrations of 1816 and the support that his "landlady," Miss Edwards, provided to the Blue Girls: She "had, indeed, contributed one of her female slaves to sustain a very important character in the show." W. J. Gardner (1873, 183) states, "At the Christmas carnival the younger women adorned themselves with all the finery they could procure: this was often of a superior kind, for their savings for months were devoted to the purpose. Nor would their mistresses, whether white or colored, refuse to assist them, either with gifts or the loan of jewellery and other ornaments." However, in his time, Stewart (1823/1969, 74) believed that the New Year's queen parades were in decline because "the mistresses of the slaves, who were the patronesses of them, and at whose expense much of the requisite finery was provided, find they cost more money and trouble than they can well spare." Some wealthy individuals invested in performers' costumes as a moneymaking ventures: Lewis (1834/1999, 53) records that "this year, several gentlemen in the neighborhood of Black River had subscribed very largely towards the expenses of the show." He continues, "The John-Canoes are fitted out at the expense of the rich negroes, who afterwards share the money collected from the spectators during their performance, allotting one share to the representator himself." In his description of Actor Boys, Belisario (1837) shows how costumes could be recycled: Following the festivities, costumes might be passed on for use by other masqueraders. An Actor Boy's costume apparently cost about "five Doubloons, equal to about 15 Pounds Sterling." Should the costumes "escape uninjured, they are disposed of after the holidays to the negroes in the country, at a considerable loss, who apply them to the like purpose in the ensuing year."

SPIRITUALITY OF CARIBBEAN MASQUERADES

Data demonstrating overtly spiritual aspects of masquerading in the Eastern Caribbean are marginal. In her study, Bettelheim (1979, 277) concludes that Jonkonnu "is fundamentally secular in nature." Nevertheless, the possible religious or ritual significance of masquerades continues to interest observers. Kenneth Bilby (1999, 48) states, "Although present-day participants in Jamaican Jonkonnu street festivities almost universally characterize their traditional as a kind of 'jollification' without any deeper significance, this has not prevented a number of writers from surmising that at an earlier period these festivities might have been closely tied to African-derived religious observances." Bilby's research reinforces this connection.

Some striking parallels exist between the Sensay masquerade of Dominica and the Kankuran of the Mandinka: Both combat malevolent forces. In Upper Guinea, the Kankuran costume is made from the shredded bark of the *fara* tree, which is believed to combat wickedness, and raffia Kankuran and Kumpo masquerades with the supposed ability to dispel malevolent forces were brought out intermittently to cleanse the community. These masquerades were valued as witchcraft-fighting devices and were used to undo hexes and identify sorcerers. The Sensay masquerade takes its name from a frizzled feathered chicken that has short irregular plumage and a shaggy look. According to J. D. Elder (1988, 35), "The Ashanti are held to have introduced . . . divining with sensay (*asense*) fowl." In her survival studies among Georgia's coastal African Americans, Mary Granger (1940, 171) states, "A frizzled chicken is known as a wise chicken and is used to find lost articles. If something has been buried and its place forgotten, a frizzled chicken can, according to the islanders, find the place and scratch up the lost article." From correspondence with Granger dated October 10, 1938, Melville Herskovits says, "Frizzled chickens are prized both in Africa and in the New World for their ability to find and scratch up evil magic buried against the owner (1958, 233 n. 13a). He reports that "in Atlanta, Mrs. Cameron was informed, 'if a frizzled hen is kept in the yard she will scratch up and destroy all conjuration which will cause discomfort for the family.' The ascription of this function to these peculiar fowl has been recorded several times from the [U.S.] South; hens of this kind are to be found performing the same task in West Indian Negro yards no less than in West African compounds" (237) In Dominica, the bird and by association the masquerade historically are linked with obeah finding and "duppy [Jumbie] catching" (Richards 2006, 40). In addition to spiritual protection, Sensay, like Kankuran, ostensibly served as instruments of social control.

Bilby's research in remote parishes in the hills of Jamaica has unearthed Jonkonnu masquerades with a spiritual aspect associated with myalism practices and Gombay dances. Myalism has generally been regarded as an art by which the obeah man could be counteracted. The Reverend A. J. Emerick states that the use of myalism to combat obeah developed "until eventually to 'dig up Obeah' became its principal differentiation from witchcraft" (Joseph J. Williams 1932, 148). He continues, "The mysterious operations of Mialism consists in communicating with spirits or deaths ('dets' as the Jamaican terms it). The persons who are so favoured with communications with spirits are called mial people. They are said to be 'fo-eyed,' that is four-eyed, by which it is meant that they can see spirits and converse with them. Both sexes make pretensions to this power" (148). Joseph J. Williams (1932, 155–56) envisages myalism as a thing of pride, arguing that whereas "Obeah is secretive and malicious; Myalism is open and benevolent. When the 'shadow' is 'pulled' at the cotton tree, or 'caught' at the funeral, just as when Obeah is 'dug up,' the larger the body of witnesses the greater is the satisfaction of the Myal man in this good deed which he performs."

Lewisohn (1964, 58) discusses the similarity between Virgin Island Jumbie practices and that of obeah: Jumbies are "supernatural beings [that] were to St. Croix what voodoo was to Haiti and Obeah to Jamaica." In the past, when people were trying to contact dead relatives, they would visit a silk cotton tree on a moonlit night. These trees were also the focus of "shadow catching" rites involving music and dance that were aimed at restoring the stolen souls of obeah victims. In Tortola, according to Eadie (1931, 289), "in Negro folklore, as in that of many other races, a person's spirit was identified with his shadow." Writing from the Danish West Indies, Oldendorp (1770/1987, 198) confirms that this identification occurred among two Ghanaian groups, the Amina and the Watje. Moreover, "the Calabar [Nigerian] word for soul is that used for shadow" (Waddell 1863/1970, 139). According to Joseph J. Williams (1932, 153), "One of the supposed avocations of the Obeah man was to catch the shadows of the living and nail them to a cotton tree." These stolen souls were hidden and kept spellbound at the base of the silk cotton tree, with dire effects on the victim. Emerick (1916) describes myal men pulling shadows from imprisonment in trees via a process that involves singing and dancing, special costumes, the sacrifice of chickens, and pelting the tree with eggs. Gardner (1873,

461) discusses these rituals in Jamaica in 1842 and reports that the myal men danced in tree branches.

Bilby's research on Jonkonnu in the country district of Coker, nestled in the Nassau Mountains of western Jamaica, was guided by Martha Beckwith's and Helen Roberts's accounts from the early 1920s. His research shows that the Jonkonnu complex forms an integral part of a living folk religion centering on spirit possession and a local cult of ancestors (Bilby 1998, 5). Both Beckwith and Roberts report on a "House John Canoe" that focuses on the display of a relatively large house or "temple" rather than on a mask. Furthermore, Beckwith (in Bilby 1999) reports that Ewan, a Jonkonnu dancer, "was a notorious *myal* man in Lacovia, that is a man who held communication with the spirits of the dead," and that that the same is very likely true of Swabe, another Jonkonnu dancer. As described by Roberts (in Bilby 1999), the temple of the Lacovia John Canoe company had two stories and was about three feet tall: "Strips of brightly colored paper . . . were twisted and fastened from stick to stick forming walls. Bits of mirror, silver paper and wallpaper furnished the decoration." The musicians consisted of "three drummers and a triangle player." Roberts states, "We met them on the road beyond the store. The old man was dancing, notwithstanding the heavy little temple on his head, the singers were swaying, and bending the knees in time to the music, and the drummers . . . were absorbed in creating the most complicated and fascinating rhythms. A small crowd of young people were following them, dancing out of the way of the long lash which tradition permits the man to carry." Prior to the temple's appearance on the first night of Christmas, the preparations are kept private: "The building of the temple and the rehearsing of the songs is done in the greatest secrecy, at night, in the weeks just preceding Christmas." The John Canoe's spiritual nature is consolidated: "The temple is carried to a graveyard and left over night for the duppies, as the ghosts of the dead and disembodied spirits are called, to initiate into its coming duties. . . . After the holidays, the temple loses its power and is destroyed."

Roberts (n.d., 76–77) saw another John Canoe company at Prospect, Manchester, Jamaica, in January 1921: "The temple was . . . oblong, with two floors and a small porch in front. It looked not unlike a doll's house. Every temple shelters a small doll. . . . This is called the baby, although its clothes are not baby's clothes." Beckwith (in Bilby 1999) provides a similar account and in the 1920s stated that "John Canoe companies led by a John Canoe dancer carrying a model of a house still survive in St. Elizabeth and St. Mary, and I am told also in the western parishes. In St. Elizabeth . . . the dance is definitely connected with obeah practices." Beckwith states that in the interior of the house is set "a little bell suspended from the top to tinkle with the motion of the dance." Furthermore, before the house is built, "a feast must be given consisting of goat's meat boiled without salt, together with plenty of rum. As the building progresses, other feasts are given. On the night it is brought out in public, it is taken to the cemetery, and there the songs and the dances are rehearsed in order to 'catch the spirits of the dead,' which henceforth accompanies the dancer until, after a few weeks of merriment during which performances are given for money at the great houses and at a village crossroads, it is broken up entirely. For 'as long as it stays in the house the spirit will follow it.'"

On January 11, 1991, in Nassau, St. Elizabeth, Bilby was led to a makeshift shed. On a tall stool "was a beautifully decorated model of a house fashioned from wood, cardboard, multicolored paper streamers, and aluminum foil" (Bilby 1999, 54). "Inside, on the second story," Bilby "could see a plastic doll and a carved wooden figurine. My escort turned to me and said, 'this is what we call the Jangkunu.' I looked around and noticed a gumbay drum in the corner of the shed, of the same rectangular design seen by Beckwith and Roberts in the 1920s. 'You almost came too late,' continued my guide. 'Tonight is the night the Jangkunu will be destroyed and we dance myal'" (54). Bilby (1998, 5) itemizes the components of the Coker Jonkonnu complex: "House headdress, itself called 'Jonkonnu.' . . . leading drum called gumbay—the same distinctive square shape . . . other percussion, such as instruments called kata. . . . [F]inally there is a female lead singer called the maam, whose solo vocals were answered by the chorus." The gombay drum is a principal component and key to the Jonkonnu performance. This square single-skinned, open-ended frame drum is depicted in Belisario's (1837) *Band of the Jaw-Bone John Canoe*, as is the gumbo box of North Carolina's Johnkannaus band, and Oldendorp (1770/1987, 264) describes a square frame drum at an Antiguan funeral. Bilby (1999) suggests that the presence of a gombay drum indicates a strong probability that spiritual factors are also present but are kept secret from outsiders. The gombay is not just a drum in Nassau, St. Elizabeth, but a year-round dance that includes spirit visitation. The Gombay Play includes a special category of songs known as *myal sing* (myal songs) that "are used to invoke ancestral spirits, who, if things are done properly, will eventually come and take possession of the myal-man" (56). The Gumbay Play conjoins with Jonkonnu within seasonal observances that occur only during the Christmas holidays: "As early as November a small hut called the *Jangkunu house* must be built to shelter the headdress while the latter is still under construction. During the process of construction, this hut receives frequent visits from vigilant ancestral spirits (sometimes referred to as 'watchman'), some of whom may manifest themselves from time to time in the form of an animal, such as a lizard or a toad" (57). Entry to the Jangkunu house is restricted and the headdress kept covered with a sheet. "The Jangkunu builder . . . is always a myal man with special training in his art. This myal-man is referred to as *massa*, or 'master,' of the Jangkunu" (58). Among the costumes designed for dolls in recent years are miniature versions of policemen's and nurses' uniforms:

> Considerable pride goes into the building of the Jangkunu. During the period of construction, Gumbay Play is held frequently; singers and dancers organize special practice sessions in preparation for Christmas holidays, at which time the Jangkunu will finally be brought outside and paraded in public. As Christmas approaches, periodic feasts may be offered to the spirits of ancestors at the graveyards; if ignored these ancestors are prone to show their displeasure by causing sections of the house headdress to become torn or tattered. Each individual Jangkunu is given a personalizing name by its builder; among some of the better known names given to headdresses in years past are Grand Queen, Big Wonder, Blue Mam, Grand Mam, Little Wonder, and Little Mam. (58)

Bilby (2010, 190) reports that early on Christmas Eve, the entire community is summoned to a major Gombay Play by the blowing of a conch shell. Reports one longtime participant, Percel Titus, "The living hear, and the dead hear" (Bilby 2010, 190). Bilby (1999, 58) states, "On Christmas Eve a major Gumbay Play is held. As the night wears on, the time comes for the Jangkunu to turn out. . . . Down at the two major family graveyards, the ancestral spirits are fed with white rice, the blood of a chicken, and a specially prepared concoction known as 'egg punch.'" Bilby (2010, 191) elaborates, "Back up at the neighboring dancing ground, the myal man and his assistants remove the sheet that has up to this point covered the Jangkunu (as the house headdress itself is known), and carry the beautifully decorated object out into the open for all to see, placing it on a bench in the central performing space in Big Yard, known as the 'ring.'"

Bilby (1999, 58–59, 60) states,

> Shortly before dawn, the myal-man, with the help of his assistants, hoists the Jangkunu onto his head and proceeds down to the cemeteries of Rhoden Town and Brown Town, where he dances and displays his creation so that its beauty can be enjoyed by the entire community of ancestors. . . . The Jangkunu dancer and his

> entourage return . . . to the main dance ground at Big Yard. . . After daybreak, the crowd moves out onto the road, marching along with the musicians through the different sections of the community. . . .
>
> Only after December 25 does the Jangkunu ensemble from Nassau go outside to perform in other communities. [Later] when the Christmas spirit has begun to fade away, the ancestors provide indications that the time has come to 'mash up' the house headdress. [At this time] the Jangkunu is turned over to those younger males who wish to have a final dance of their own with it. [The crescendo is reached when] the surrounding crowd pounces upon it, rapidly tearing it to pieces.

The idea of displaying a masquerade in the graveyard finds a parallel in an Ode-Lay Egungun, Agbaru Agbadu (Black Snake) of Sierra Leone. Nunley (1987, 126) states, "This masquerader appears at cemeteries on Easter Monday, when all the ancestors of the societies are presented sacrifices. . . . The agbaru agbadu informs the people of the underworld that a play is about to be held in their honor."

Bilby (2010, 189) explains that the Coker variant of "Jankunu performance" differs conspicuously from the standard forms found elsewhere in Jamaica today. The full complex is rarely found in the more recent companies, which practitioners call simply *masquerade* rather than *Jonkonnu*. Edward Long (1774, 2:424) does not describe the drum, but female singers are implied by the mention of the "numerous drunken women" who follow the John Connu and refresh him with "aniseed-water." Bilby (1999, 65) consequently suggests that many of the fundamentals indicative of spirituality were always present, but the only documented activity began and ended in the public spaces where the literati encountered performances: "The European observers who set down their impressions of Jonkonnu performances in past centuries considered these cultural practices as little more than curiosities—colourful diversions that struck them by turns as pleasing to the eye, and grating to the ear. These European writers did not bother to search behind the performers' masks for deeper meaning."

In the past, House Jonkonnus also performed in the Bahamas, the British Virgin Islands, and elsewhere in the British West Indies, and a deeper meaning may also apply to these other masquerades. However, in the Coker version of the Gombay Play, with its Jonkonnu headdress, the spiritual meaning lives on and "even today forms part of a subterranean cultural and spiritual world, of which outsiders remain almost totally ignorant" (Bilby 1999, 65). In this community, the Jonkonnu complex forms an integral part of a living folk religion.

Bilby (2010, 180) elaborates on the perceived spirituality of Jonkonnu and the apparent contradictions involved. He opens with Caribbean poet and historian Kamau Brathwaite's assertion that the Jonkonnus "that we know throughout Plantation America are the visible publicly permitted survival icons of African religious culture." In contrast, as Bilby points out, "Jankunu today is characterized by most local commentators, including the majority of practitioners themselves, as a fundamentally 'secular' tradition." He then asks, "How could a tradition almost universally perceived as 'secular,' and said by participants themselves to be devoid of spiritual significance, be interpreted by a leading scholar and cultural 'insider' as an iconic embodiment of religiosity? What might explain this apparent contradiction?" (180).

Bilby (2010, 182–83) minimizes the views of modern practitioners: "For a scholar interested in long-term historical processes unfolding over time, statements made by present-day Jankunu practitioners, although not to be dismissed, need not carry much weight in attempts to determine what the tradition might have meant to participants during its heyday in the eighteenth and nineteenth centuries." He continues, "Meanings that held sway centuries ago could easily have been replaced by others in more recent times; original religious or spiritual meanings could have been lost or become submerged over time" (183). Moreover, "theorizing about the historical origins and possible spiritual foundations of Jankunu brings us squarely into [a] largely uncharted epistemological terrain" (184). Bilby examines Jonkonnu in Jamaica, Belize, and Cat Island in the Bahamas. His significant findings in Jamaica have a vague echo among the Garifuna in Belize, but regarding the Bahamian Junkanoo, he states, "What I found is a complex duality suggestive of a history of resistance and accommodation—a separation of performance contexts into two symbolic domains, one thought of as 'inside' and explicitly 'religious' or 'spiritual,' and the other as 'outside' and 'worldly.' This division clearly reflects the impact, on an island with a long history of intensive Christian missionization, of Western theological principles" (195).

Bilby concludes (2010, 215) that Brathwaite's "summation neatly, and I believe accurately, encapsulates both the historical reality of Jankunu, and what it has become. Jankunu emerged in the Americas as an aspect of African religious culture that survived, remained visible, and was publicly permitted only because it succeeded in 'masking' the African spiritual presence it embodied with an appearance of secularity [play]." Such contextual camouflage undoubtedly is a feature of much Leeward Islands' masquerading.

Ultimately, therefore, within the current manifestations, other considerations—ideological and psychological—come into play, and *play* is the operative word.

Chapter 4

SPECIFIC MASQUERADE TYPES

MOCKO JUMBIE

Unlike the bear and the bull, the Mocko Jumbie masquerade seems not to have a shared European and African ancestry—there are only marginal European influences. However, stilts were worn by shepherds and hunters in France and by hop twiners in Britain. Alli Paul (pers. comm., July 10, 1995), a Mocko Jumbie performer, uses the term stilt *dancers* to differentiate Mocko Jumbies from stilt walkers, who appear in European circus rings and elsewhere. The Mocko Jumbie stilt-dancing masquerade historically appeared in many places in the Eastern Caribbean, including Anguilla, Antigua, Barbados, St. Vincent, St. Kitts–Nevis, St. Lucia, and Trinidad. In the past, one or maybe two individuals would appear, accompanied by a band consisting of a fife, bass drum, and snare drum, beating out the Mocko Jumbies' "stutter" rhythm. Now, however, during Carnival, Harbor Night, or other festive occasions, troupes of seven or more Mocko Jumbies appear, dancing to larger bands on a truck or to recorded music. A 1791 description from St. Vincent provides a Mandinka designation (Young 1807, 258), whereas Day's (1852, 85) report, also from St. Vincent, calls the stilt masquerade "De Jumpsa-man" and describes it as "an exhibition by an African Ebo [Igbo] negro."

Documentation regarding the Virgin Islands Mocko Jumbie's costume shows it to have changed little from about 1870 to 1940. An 1871 line drawing in the Danish National Museum captioned, "Mocha Jumpy—Christmastime," reveals a stilt dancer in a women's dress. A raised whip is in the performer's right hand, while the left is lifting the skirt's hem. The performer wears a pale mask and a tall conical hat topped by a pennant, and his feet, which are not visible, are about three feet from the ground. A photograph taken in Frederiksted, ca. 1910, shows a Mocko Jumbie wearing a woman's frock that ends just below the knees and with mid-toned stockings. His feet are about three and a half feet above the ground. His pale, finely painted mask was probably purchased commercially, with clearly defined eyes, eyebrows, lips, and cheeks. He wears a tall conical hat and is holding a cap in his right hand (see figure 2.2). A photograph of a U.S. Virgin Islands Jumbie that appeared in *National*

Geographic in 1940 is very similar: His mask is pushed back, and he wears a decorated conical hat. His feet are some five feet from ground, and he holds a wand in his hand. Considering the seventy-year span between the Danish line drawing and the 1940 photo, the similarity of the costumes is remarkable.

The late Magnus (John Farrell) and Marshall (Fritz Isaiah Sealey) were well-known Mocko Jumbies who performed in the Virgin Islands until the 1950s. In a 1966 newspaper column reproduced in a St. Thomas Carnival program (in possession of author), Rufus Martin catches the flavor of a Mocko Jumbie performance: "Ah remembah de periods of de late thirties and early forties wen Magnus performed alone and was indeed ah one man karnivul. Yes sir, dose were de days wen masquerading had hit ah low ebb an Magnus an ah fungi ban [scratch band] use to keep things lively on holidays. He performed in all sections of de tung, all day, dancing on dose two high stilts, doing arl kine ah antics, showing de folks ah numbah of diffrunt colored petticoats and fancy underwear." The fact that Magnus was showing "diffrunt colored petticoats and fancy underwear," like the "Mocha jumpy" in the 1871 drawing, speaks to the Mocko Jumbie's role in guarding against hostile spirits. (Plate 31)

Money was more plentiful in the Leeward Islands after World War II, so rather than simply borrowing and modifying a woman's frock, Magnus designed special costumes. These usually consisted of loose blouses made of thick, shiny material, with large ornamental collars and ballooning sleeves, and a knee-length skirt. He often wore a large triangular admiral's hat in colors that matched his costume and turned so that the points were at the front and the back. The void created by Magnus's relocation to New York in the mid-1950s was filled by William Richardson of Anguilla. Richardson retained the can-can petticoats stiffened to flare the skirt of the traditional Mocko Jumbie until he stopped stilt dancing in the early 1970s. Although female attire was common for many years, it was not that of a shemale—that is, it did not involve padding or artificial breasts.

The women's costume was also found on St. Kitts (Alfred M. Williams 1896, 117) and Nevis in the mid-1920s, but Mocko Jumbies on other islands did not invariably wear women's dresses. The "Jumpsa Man" on St. Vincent, for example, wore long striped trousers, and a 1919 photograph of a "Moco Jombie" in Port of Spain, Trinidad, shows a figure dressed as a male in long striped trousers and a matching tailed jacket (Nunley and Bettelheim 1988, 93). From 1960, when twelve-year-old Alli Paul began his performance career wearing long trousers, a woman's dress was no longer considered the quintessential Mocko Jumbie costume in the Virgin Islands. Paul came to represent a new vision, inspiring a new crop of Mocko Jumbies. He started troupes around

Fig. 4.1. Mocko Jumbie dancer William Richardson, Virgin Islands Carnival, St. Thomas, ca. 1963. Note raised skirt revealing petticoats. Courtesy Miles Raymond.

1968 with his younger brothers and his sister. Many of today's senior practitioners of the craft learned directly or indirectly from Paul, including Hugo Moolenaar, John McCleverty, Willard John, Naomi Baylarian, Gerry Cockrell, and Gerard Luz James. (Plate 60)

The Mocko Jumbie has retained its African-derived heritage through the centuries, and although the costume continues to evolve, its design is influenced by certain basic factors—aesthetics, the spiritual nature of the genre, utilitarian considerations, the context of the performance, and cultural authenticity. Local folklore ascribes special power to a Mocko Jumbie, and its height, dance skills, and acrobatic maneuvers are calculated to project an otherworldly presence beyond the realm of normal human capacity. Anonymity has always been an important factor, and the disguise is facilitated by wearing a mask and covering other parts of the body. While many performers wear gloves, others cover their hands with long sleeves. Mocko Jumbies did not wear special masks; rather, they resembled others of the era—wire screen and papier-mâché were standard, while other performers used heavily starched cloth with holes cut for eyes. Most hats are topped by plumes or pennants that add height. In addition to necklaces and bracelets made of different seeds and beads, a Mocko Jumbie often carries a wand or a whip.

In the modern era, various influences have affected Mocko Jumbie costumes, including Gypsy bolero fashions and Creole influences from the Francophone Caribbean, which are exemplified by tight, frilly, long-sleeved shirts with belled cuffs, shirts tied at the waist, matador-type waistcoats, trousers with large colorful ruffles extending down the outside seam, and the like. Caribbean influences are manifested by the use of brightly patterned patchwork textiles, the attaching of small mirrors or ribbons, and the wearing of large straw hats. From the 1970s on, patterned colorful cloth became increasingly available, including African textiles and special carnival textiles imported from Trinidad. With the emergence of female practitioners, new costume features were introduced. Caribbean elements included Market Lady and Bamboula fashions, which involved madras cloth, large earrings, head ties, straw hats, and plumes. Women also exploited glamorous elements such flowers in the hair, tube tops, and feather boas. The Caribbean Carnival has a unique aesthetic dynamic that has recently come to emphasize glitz and glamour, metallic cloth, sequins, and tinsel, and these elements appear as part of modern Mocko Jumbies' costumes. In addition, carnivals have different annual themes that create demands on costume styles. The theme of the 1997 St. Thomas Carnival, for example, was "Let Sapphires Enlighten Your Carnival." One mixed male and female troupe, the St. Thomas Mystical Mocko Jumbies, wore metallic blue costumes with glittery blue Fulani-type hats with plumes as well as more traditional white mesh masks. (Plate 39)

In the face of increasing commercialization, many practitioners strive to maintain cultural authenticity and have studied the history of stilt dancing. The last quarter of the twentieth century saw a re-Africanization of the genre that involves not only the use of Kente and other African textiles but also the reintroduction of the raffia skirt, common in West African stilt masquerading and now widespread in the Leeward Islands. Such grass skirts now may be made of real fiber or a synthetic material dyed in various colors. This trend coincided with and was probably to some extent a reaction to a proliferation of would-be Mocko Jumbies. (Plate 38)

Mocko Jumbie stilt performer Gerard Luz James's costume mirrors the local culture. His tall pointed hat is made of goatskin and is decorated with peacock feathers as well as local flowers, such as those from the Ginger Thomas tree or hibiscus blooms. Around his neck he often wears strings of black and red Jumbie beads (*Abrus*). The textiles he uses might be African prints or cloths considered traditional, such as madras. Small mirrors are sewn onto his costume, and he uses a range of masks, but they are made of more pliable nylon mesh rather than the older medium, safe wire. He may decorate a mask with mirrors, shells, and beads, and he often carries an African fly whisk made of hide and hair (Gerard Luz James, pers. comm., July 9, 1995). (Plate 40)

The possibility that the masquerade might have been considered the "Jumbie of the Moko" has been considered. This is an exotic interpretation, since the early literature portrays the Moko as a more primitive aboriginal African ethnic group. However, the facts do not support the idea that these performances were derived from a Moko prototype; rather, a provenance in the Upper Guinea region seems more plausible than origins in southeastern Nigeria. Evidence suggests that the Mocko Jumbie is derived from Upper Guinea stilt masquerades, which are believed to dispel bad spirits and bring beneficence. Laniboy of the Toma, Guerzé, and Kissien people of Guinea drives sorcerers out of the region. The Gle Gbee of the Dan of Butuo, Ivory Coast, similarly dispels witchcraft and has a faceless fabric mask and a tall conical headdress decorated with cowrie shells. Performers wear blue and white striped "country cloth" shirts and trousers that cover their hands and feet. Similarly, an 1862 description of "De Jumbee" in St. Vincent notes a scarlet cloth mask, cowrie shells, and striped trousers. Laniboy and Gle Gbee represent plausible progenitors for the Mocko Jumbie.

RAFFIA BEAR

Dressed in burlap or raffia and classified here as a bush masquerade, the bear of the Leeward Islands was a blend of different cultures. During Christmas perambulations, the bear sought to provide entertainment and possibly some child discipline in exchange for comestibles or a monetary reward. The Shaggy Bear appeared in Barbados during Crop Over. The bear does not show up in the nineteenth-century literature and is not mentioned in the Danish West Indies (DWI) until 1912, when Elick the Bear appeared at a Carnival (U.S. Virgin Islands, Department of Education 1972). The bear no doubt performed in earlier centuries but was not considered worthy of mention. The animal itself never lived in the Virgin Islands, and Rufus Vanderpool (pers. comm., August 3, 1995) believes that locals' propensity to depict something nonindigenous was remarkable. Such practices indicate cultural diffusion, and perceptible similarities exist among the raffia bears of Europe, Africa, and the Caribbean. Although the character is not called a bear in West Africa, raffia bush masquerades are widespread. They appeared at annual and agricultural-cycle festivals in each of the three regions. The Caribbean bear bestowed good cheer at Crop Over Festivals and at Christmas and New Year's.

Fig. 4.2. Straw Bear performs on Straw Bear Tuesday, Whittlesey, Cambridgeshire, England, January 1988. Note musicians playing big bass drum, melodeon, and saxophone. Photo by Brian Shuel. Courtesy Collections Picture Library (http://www.collectionspicturelibrary.co.uk).

Prior to enslavement, Africans might have participated in performances of raffia masquerades such as Kumpo or Kankuran. Similarly, Irish indentured servants might have played the role of Strawboys before crossing the Atlantic. In this sense, the raffia bear is a creolized blend of different cultures. Bear disguises and straw men were found in various European countries and were included in the 1443 King of Christmas festival held in Norwich, England. The appearance and behavior of the Caribbean bear replicates that of the English Straw Bear in many ways. Migrants from the east of England, such as Cambridgeshire, where the Straw Bear is known, were not as prevalent as those from the West Country. However, no records of raffia masquerades in the latter area have been found (though that does not mean that such masquerades never existed). The mumming of the Strawboys of Ireland in many ways resembled the Straw Bears, and the Irish migrated in substantial numbers to Barbados, Montserrat, and elsewhere in the Caribbean. In Ireland, as many as ten or twenty Strawboys might perform in a team (Gailey 1969, 58), but the West Indies and the Upper Guinea generally only feature one or two at a time; the Sensay of Dominica can appear in troupes. (Plate 44)

Parallels also exist between the bear in the DWI and in Nordic Estonia. The link may be Denmark or Germany, which has a strong Straw Bear tradition.

In the Caribbean, handlers often flogged the bull and the bear, but in Upper Guinea, masquerades were not beaten. In Western Europe, bull masquerades were not beaten, but some bears were, and this similarity among bears in the DWI, the bear in Estonia, and the Straw Bear of England's fenland area catches the attention. In the case of Estonia, the resemblance is more noticeable in the behavior than in the costumes. Because Estonia is cold and people wear furs, costume materials differ, although the overall appearance was similar. Tedre (2007, 414) says that in addition to a mask, the Jõulukaru (Estonian Christmas Bear) "had an inside-out fur coat on. The legs were put in the sleeves, and another fur was put around the body. Then the mittens were worn inside-out and a hat." In contrast, in tropical St. Thomas, the bear's costume was made of straw or rough burlap sacks with a headpiece like a balaclava helmet that left exposed the middle of the face, which was sometimes blackened. Some ears were attached, and he had a little tail. The Estonian bear appeared during the Christmas holidays and visited families, usually with "a rope tied around it, one end of which was in the master's hand" (414). Like Antigua's John Bull, the Estonian bear performer stuffed his back "so the dancing master could hit it with a stick when the bear got angry" (414), in this case, using a pillow or a board rather than dried leaves. Though Estonian bears could frighten children, the main goal of such animal masquerades seems to have been to entertain and play tricks. The Estonian bear might dance alone or with a girl that it caught; it might also chase other people (412). Tedre (2007, 415–16) reports that if the bear "does not play tricks well, then there is this long stick to beat it with. If the dance is over, then the master of each house have to give something to the bear." The St. Thomas bear was similarly a comical, clumsy beast, restrained with a rope around his waist. The bear master would hit him with a whip or stick as part of the theatrics while the bear snarled and growled in anger. The bear had musicians and danced on street corners, in the market square, and at various residences, and people threw coins. Sometimes, the bear captured small children and held them aloft (Philip Rhymer, pers. comm., July 18, 1996).

According to Rufus Vanderpool (pers. comm., August 3, 1995), the Virgin Islands bear's crocus bag costume completely covered him. Charles Turnbull (pers. comm., July 7, 1995) remembers that Koka's costume was made of straw attached to rough brown crocus bags. When Paddy Moore performed as the bear on St. Croix, he wore a two-piece banana shaggy costume (Alma Doward, pers. comm., July 6, 1995). The starting point of the raffia robe was a covering of brown burlap, which might totally obscure the face, resulting in an amorphous haystack appearance. The Straw Bear of England's fenland area has a similar haystack appearance and is leashed by a rope or chain and beaten with a stick by his handler. The day after Plow Monday (the traditional start of the English agricultural year, generally the first Monday after Twelfth Night, January 6) was known as Straw Bear Tuesday or Strawbower Day on the borders of Huntingdonshire and Cambridgeshire, though not elsewhere in England. The oldest reference to "Plow Mundy" comes from Boxford, Cambridgeshire, in 1529 (Cox 1913, 248). A plow was paraded through the streets, accompanied by mummers known as Molly Dancers or Plow Witches, and donations were solicited from householders. On Strawbower Day in Whittlesey, Cambridgeshire, the local plowmen entertained townsfolk in return for gifts of money and food. According to Hole (1978, 287), "In some areas the men who had acted as Plough Witches on the previous day went through the streets dressed from head to foot in straw, and demanded alms from the passers-by." On this day, the Straw Bear was led about the streets on a strong chain by a minder with a stick. According to Gordon Ridgwell (2003, 9), the Whittlesey Straw Bear was first recorded in 1859. Hole describes the costume: "Tightly twisted straw-bands were wound round the Bear's body, with separate bands for his arms and legs. He wore a tail, and a peculiar headdress formed by two sticks fastened to his shoulders, which met in a point above his head, and were covered in straw drawn up to make a kind of cone" (286). Ridgwell points out "the great weight of the Bear's costume, 30 kilos, which is the equivalent of carrying two bales of hay around all day; there are therefore two men who share the duty, switching half way through the procession" (8). An informant from Ramsey Mereside told Hole that the Straw Bear "lumbered about the streets with a band of companions, one of whom led him by a strong chain fastened under his armpits. On arriving at a house, he went down on his hands and knees, groaning and growling as the door was opened, while his attendants pretended to restrain his dangerous ferocity by pulling on his chain and beating him with a stick. The householders were expected to reward him with money-gifts" (286).

Marked similarities existed among customs in different regions. In Barbados, St. Vincent, Trinidad, and elsewhere, gang members vied for the honor of chopping down the final sheaf of sugarcane for the season, and the bear appeared in Barbados during the annual Crop Over celebration, which took place in each mill yard after the last sugarcane was harvested: "Accompanied by his own band the Bear performed his antics. The man who played the part of the bear dressed in a crocus bag around which was wrapped yards and yards of plantain or banana shag. To this were pinned bows upon bows of red cloth or paper. As he capered people danced around him occasionally stopping to pull at his costume and run back as if in fear" (Anonymous 1976, 12). Willock (1996, n.p.) emphasizes the bear's African heritage: "The Shaggy Bear

. . . has been created over the years as a witch-doctor type creature." In Barbados, during Christmas and New Year, the bear conducted perambulations in wassail quête tradition, sometimes accompanying "Scrubbers" musicians or "Tuk Bands" as they made their rounds along with the donkey, Mother Sally, or Tilt-Man (Mocko Jumbie). Such bands are an elaboration of the earlier fife-and-drum combination, on occasion with guitars or mandolins added. As the processions moved from village to village at Christmas or other holidays, "They would stop by some of the houses where they would do a little dance, and the donkey man would give a speech, calling on the 'mistress of the noble cottage' to 'give them something to wet their palates' (rum) and to 'open the seams of their pockets' (money)" (*Barbados Advocate* 1991).

Rufus Vanderpool (pers. comm., August 3, 1995) says that the Virgin Islands bear evolved into a mini-troupe, with the attendant and musicians with the basic fife and drums augmented by other instruments such as a guiro (squash), steel (triangle), and tailpipe (see also Philip Rhymer, pers. comm., July 18, 1996). Children would spot him coming up the street and cry, "Here comes the bear." Some children hid in their houses until he had passed, while others watched out of curiosity. Turnbull (pers. comm., June 19, 1996) confirms that like the devil, the bear would enter houses chasing children and surprising adults, and as with the Mocko Jumbie and bull, the bear was sometimes pressed into service as a parental threat.

Renowned bears in the twentieth-century Virgin Islands were Elick, Koka, and Ezekiel. Elick the Bear performed regularly in the opening decades of the twentieth century and appeared in the 1912 St. Thomas Carnival (held on Valentine's Day). Koka the Bear appeared later, migrating from St. Croix to St. Thomas, with the same performer playing both bear and bull from the 1930s through the 1950s. He traveled back and forth and is equally well remembered in Christiansted and Charlotte Amalie. Many remember his big eyes peering out of the costume. Charles Turnbull (pers. comm., June 19, 1996) recalls that Koka's "mask didn't strictly resemble a bear's face. Authenticity was not a key focus, it was for frolic and fun, and the masquerader was mimicking a bear." Although shaggy, Koka's raffia costume did not directly simulate fur. In this aspect, it differs from the more realistic bear that appears in Carnivals in Pernambuco, Brazil; this character is based on real Italian dancing bears introduced into Brazil by Gypsies in the nineteenth century (Real 2004, 227–29). According to Ruth Moolenaar (pers. comm., August 10, 1995), Koka's depiction became more realistic over time, and the performer ultimately wore a realistic-looking bear's head with a costume of brown or black colored fur, and he was accompanied by a child dressed as a bear cub. Ezekiel the Bear appeared at St. Thomas's Carnivals in both the 1952 and 1953, but by the end of the decade, the bear had died out in the Virgin Islands. (Plate 27) Could it be that with Koka's move to realism, the bear lost the grassroots appeal that the abstraction of the bush masquerade provided?

BULL

Dancing to the music of drums and outfitted with real horns and a dried-leaf costume that acoustically accentuated its movements, the bull masquerade was another popular Christmastime street entertainment. Various bull ensembles existed across the islands, including the Wild Bull and more recently Jam Bull in the Virgin Islands; the Red Bull in St. Kitts–Nevis; the Cowhead Jonkonnu in Jamaica; and Junkanoo in the Bahamas. This entertainment reached its apogee in Antigua as John Bull, who danced to the music of drums and whose cattle horns arced like a crescent moon from his head. The bull's performance was known as running the bull, although children did most of the running. Antigua's Romic Williams, who was born in 1904, indicates (pers. comm., September 22, 1996), "These things are from ancient days, my grandfather and grandmother saw John Bulls in their time." The bull seems to have been the father of all Caribbean masquerades. In Jamaica in 1688, masqueraders tied "cow tails to their rumps and other such things to their bodies" (Sloane 1707, 46). Bovine disguises may go back as much as sixty years earlier, to the beginning of the British colonization of Barbados and the Lesser Antilles, whence Jamaican planters and their slaves migrated. As result of diffusion, the horned Jonkonnu masquerades extended up the North American eastern seaboard, where they were performed by slaves in antebellum North Carolina. The earliest Jonkonnus were bulls, later referred to as cowheads, but the genre mutated and came to appear in diverse nonhorned forms. In West Africa, the wearing of an animal-horned headdress symbolized manhood. In the Eastern Caribbean, the bull played the role of a fearless beast, intimidating but amusing the families of farmers and fishermen and when necessary siding with the rural poor in their disputes.

In Antigua, the bull masquerade tradition encompassed a complex league of powerful men who not only occupied the traditional fraternities of butchers, farmers, cattlemen, coal-kiln workers, and road builders but also represented the preindependence rise of trade unionists—clerks, barge captains, dock operators, stevedores, machine workers, and porters. Antiguan Edgar Lake's play, *The Killing of Arthur Sixteen*, features the bull tradition and centers on the funeral wake of a renowned John Bull masquerader. Lake conceived the idea for the play in 1976 when he and his compatriots in New York heard that Arthur Sixteen had been burned to death while performing in St. John's, Antigua's capital. Occurring as it did during the politically tumultuous days leading up to Antigua's and Barbuda's independence in 1981, the fatality distressed Antiguan expatriates, and Lake began musing about art, life, and contemporary Antiguan society: "Your banana skirt your grass vest, Discolored by orange flames, Amber flashes of movement, Threatening to burn the memory" (Lake 2001a). From afar, he grieved with rural Antiguans over the meager sentence Arthur Sixteen's murderer received: "It was as if the life of a Bull performer and the John Bull itself was worth nothing. The fire largely ended Bull dancing in Antigua and somehow this event became a cipher for the demise of tradition" (Edgar Lake, pers. comm., August 13, 1996). Lake traveled to Arthur Sixteen's gravesite to pay homage to the performer but discovered that "the great Arthur Sixteen was still alive. Another horned masquerader had been fatally set on fire on the Bridge." This irony is captured in the play's wake scene, in which "a group of invited horned masquerades arrive to pay homage to one of their own—until they discover the great Arthur Sixteen standing among them" (Lake 2001b).

The eulogizers at the wake bear the names of legendary Antiguan bull masquerades of the post–World War II era, among them Athanason, a renowned pace bowler who in 1955 was excluded from the Antiguan cricket team when he failed a medical exam as a result of water on the knee. His elimination led to protests because the public felt he was actually debarred because he was from the working classes. As a bull performer, Athanason was known for marathon dances and for affecting a limp for comedic purposes. Other characters who deliver eulogies include Cock Soup, performed by Jim Marrias, who was the "most ferocious Bull on the streets during the 30s and 40s" and is immortalized in a line drawing by Dan Mendes in Antigua Museum literature (in possession of the author); Pharaoh, a Moravian, Bible-reading bull known for terrorizing merchants; Butcher, a bull who was known to be bold and who thrilled children by racing into homes; Friday, a bull known for absorbing whip lashes; and Pelo, a driver who became a bull in penance for a tragedy. Pelo is the most poignant figure. A whip man with a formidable fifteen-foot whip, he became a masquerader to atone for a catastrophic wound inflicted when he accidentally curled the whip around a bull masquerader's leg, injuring his genitalia. Pelo was known as a sorrowful bull beloved by grandmothers and elders (Edgar Lake, pers. comm., August 13, 1996, December 16, 1999).[1] In Lake's play, Arthur Sixteen is characterized as the fiercest bull with the longest horns. A tribute by Lazarus the Griot demonstrates that Arthur Sixteen's stature borders on the mythical:

The finest bovine performer
The Great Arthur Sixteen!
He who personified Terror;
Second only to Everyman's Reaper
Who else could chase us?
Under our grandmothers' skirts
Or scurrying to find refuge
Next to the crab hole
Under the house?
Desasso,[2] face-down,
We learned to stare down
The horned evils of this life. (Lake 2001a)

The Antiguan Labor Union protected workers' rights, organized various rallies, stood up to plantation owners, and led the cane laborers in the general strike of 1951. Masquerades galvanized people around workers' activities and could spearhead protests. As a rural worker, Arthur Sixteen identified with his cohorts. On one occasion, Arthur Sixteen, in his bull garments and with a forked staff, allegedly engaged in a standoff with authorities. Stretching himself across a narrow factory road, he prevented the Antigua Sugar Estates' head, Sir Alexander Moody-Stuart, from driving to town in one of the few cars in Antigua at the time:

PELO: Who else could play dead—on the factory road and not have Sir Moody run over him?
ATHANASON: Who else . . . could lie fearlessly still, still as a rigor mortis corpse and the government not move quickly to bury him?
BUTCHER: Only one! one!
PELO: Only one Bull could stop that heartless knight, Sir Moody, dead in his tracks! Arthur Sixteen, playing the fat Tory, John Bull. (Lake 2001a)

Lake observes, "The writhing and trembling of the John Bull as if in his death throes seemed to symbolize the change of one kind of society to another—the decline of folk culture in the face of modernity but also the decline of the sugar industry."

In Britain, John Arbuthnot coined the term *John Bull* about 1712 to describe rapacious politicians, but the name soon became the personification of England. John Bull's size and apparent gluttony represented prosperity in an age when rosy cheeks and plump faces were signs of good health. Lake's play, Moody rather than Arthur Sixteen might more accurately be seen as playing the role of John Bull.

The extent to which the Caribbean bull masquerades were influenced by Ejumba of Senegambia or the traditional Christmas bull of the British Isles is open to conjecture. Bull disguises appeared during the Christmas season in the Scottish Highlands and during wassailing in England's West Country. Bulls also appeared in Sweden, Denmark, and Germany. Even Russia had bull performers, and Warner (1977, 10) describes a typical bull game at a village winter party at the end of the nineteenth century: "The actor playing the bull wore an earthenware pot on his head with real bull's horns fixed to it. . . . The main aim was for the bull to butt the girls in such a way that this was not only painful but also embarrassing. . . . When the game was over the bull was 'killed,' that is the earthware pot was smashed and the fallen animal carried out." Although the Jola were primarily rice farmers, all of the people of the Casamance associate cattle with wealth (measured by the size of a man's herd). Cattle served as a unit of exchange in the region and could purchase almost anything, including ancestral beneficence. Mark (1992, 50) states, "The primacy accorded to cattle as sacrifice, along with their important roles as images of power in the iconography of initiation rituals, constitutes a distinctive characteristic of the cultures of the northern Upper Guinea Coast. In the nineteenth century, raids for cattle and slaves constituted an important source of wealth for the Jola. . . . To all of these people, cattle stand at the summit of the hierarchy of animals that can be sacrificed in prayers for rain, well-being, and fertility." The *bukut* initiation takes place in the *forêt sacrée* (sacred forest) a patch of primeval bush adjacent to each Jola village. All adult men (i.e., those who have gone through an earlier *bukut*) may attend the initiation retreat; the forest is strictly off-limits for everyone else. The fathers of all initiates who can afford to do so sacrifice bulls, steers, or cows in honor of their sons. Mark (1983, 6) states, "The horned headdress of the Casamance include both horned caps called *usikoi*, which do not cover the face of the wearer, and horned masks that cover the entire head and incorporate a representation of the face. The latter are of two types: *ejumba* and *kebul*." Although the ubiquitous Caribbean gauze masks can claim antecedents in both Europe and West Africa, they are principally a Creole innovation. In contrast, Jola Ejumba masks are finely crafted and durable, representing the height of traditional African aesthetics.

By the twentieth century, a typical Caribbean Bull had cattle horns and wore a screen mask, a fabric mask, or a textile hood. In other cases, his bare face was blackened or painted. Some early Jonkonnu had tusks, though these

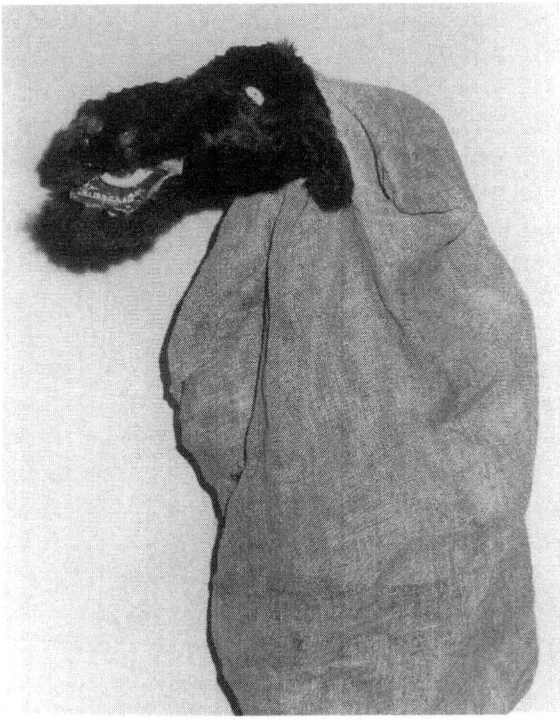

Fig. 4.3. Hobbyhorse head, Newfoundland, Canada, ca. 1966. Newfoundland Hobby horses are of the mast horse variety. The head is carved from wood and covered with moose fur. The ears are commonly moose ears. The jaw is hinged with nails as teeth and controlled by a string hidden beneath the fur operated by the mummer. The head is mounted on a pole with burlap hanging down that covers the performer's torso. Courtesy Memorial University of Newfoundland Folklore and Language Archive (MUNFLA).

features were not reported in the Leeward Islands. The Caribbean Bull masks sometimes covered the whole cranium, but no comparable practice has been discovered in Upper Guinea, however, some Igbo Mgbedike masquerades wear bull's skulls. (Plate 16) In Europe, in Sweden, and in the West Scottish highlands and the Outer Hebrides, a real cow's head was used as a Christmas mask. A complete ox hide including the cranium was worn as part of the ritual of *taghairm* on the Isle of Skye. The Caribbean Bull masks more often involved the horned pate of the skull or simply a calabash cap with the horns attached independently. By the twentieth century, the typical Caribbean Bull costume was constructed of dried banana-leaf raffia; alternatively, burlap costumes could provide a dressed down appearance, as they did for the Tetbury Bull and other Broads of Gloucestershire. Burlap costumes are rare in Upper Guinea, but Samai, a masquerade in the Casamance, wears a burlap costume with a red or white horned wooden mask (Mark 1983, 13). Although bull-hide costumes appeared in early Jamaican reports (Anonymous 1797/1976, 22; Scott 1836/1999, 251), no such instances have been recorded in the Leeward Islands, nor do they appear in reports of bulls in West Africa. However, hide costumes were worn by white Newfoundlanders during their Christmas Janneying, and hide costumes appear to have once been the norm in Britain's West Country—for example, in Evershot, Dorset in 1656.

Reports of palm-leaf raffia and shredded tree bark costumes are common in Upper Guinea. Some Ejumba masquerades wear full-length raffia costumes—for example, at a 1965 initiation in the village of Nioumoune. However, no reports of costumes made of dried banana leaves emerged there. Instances of dried banana-leaf costumes have been found among the Igbo, but only in children's masquerades. In addition to Olu Oguibe, who as a boy wore a masquerade costume of "dry plantain leaves" (Ottenberg and Binkley 2006, 22), an Afikpo Igbo boy wore a costume "constructed of banana leaves, with a metal belt around the waist and a raffia headdress covering the face" (120). A seventeenth-century performance of a bull masquerade whether done by enslaved Mandinkas or Jolas or by British or Scottish indentured servants would have seemed familiar to members of both groups, thereby encouraging the development and spread of the genre. New bull masquerades drew from different elements of Old World exemplars, so that the horns of the Mandinka or Jola masquerades might be coupled with the tusks of Igbo beast masks.

Virgin Islands

Rufus Vanderpool (pers. comm., August 3, 1995) remembers that prior to the Virgin Islands' sale to the United States in 1917, the bull appeared regularly in St. Thomas wearing a crocus or crooter bag costume. A photograph taken in Frederiksted, St. Croix, about 1910 shows a bull-horned masquerade in a shaggy, ankle-length gown. Many elders in St. Croix remembered the bull "running" children during the opening decades of the twentieth century, with a chain dragging on the ground as if it had broken loose from its grapnel (Leroy Arnold, pers. comm., July 8, 1995). The bull died out in the Virgin Islands after World War II. Philip Rhymer (pers. comm., July 18, 1996) remembers Eric Christopher playing the bull in St. Thomas in the 1940s, dressing in brown crocus bags trimmed with red. Unlike some other traditional masquerades, the bull did not make the transition into the annual Virgin Islands Carnival when it reemerged in the 1950s, and in 1952, Christopher played a Zulu. In 2001, the bull was reintroduced into the parade under the name *Jam Bull.* (Plate 36)

Montserrat

The Montserrat bull postured in the conventional way, danced to drums, and chased children. Its costume was the regular crocus sack with dried banana leaves attached. Unlike the Virgin Islands, where the chain drags loose on the ground, Eddie Donoghue (2001, 44) states that in Montserrat, "Controlling the 'animal' from an attached chain was a 'master' who carried a whip. The bull itself carried a forked-stick in its hand." To prevent a threatened assault, the master lengthened or shortened the chain. According to Donoghue, the Montserrat bull died out around 1960.

St. Kitts–Nevis

The Red Bull still performs in a Christmas play in St. Kitts–Nevis. According to Joan McMurray (2001a, 41), the narrative and characters "are based on a local story of a diseased bull whose owner Mr. Arthur Davis, brings in an outside doctor from Montserrat to cure him. The event took place in 1917 and can be verified in the local newspaper." According to Mills, Jones-Hendrickson, and Bertram (1984, 28), Davis owned a sugar plantation, and the play shows "the animal develop[ing] in fierceness and as he made to gore one of the herdsmen, he stabbed it. The bull fell down and thinking it was dead he reported to Mr. Davis, and he brought in a veterinary surgeon who treated it and it survived." The Bull Play follows the format of the British "hero-combat" plays, in which "the victim of [a] supposed killing is brought back to life by a quack doctor" (Cass 2001, 15–16). Although the play is of relatively recent origin, the "doctor's boast" follows a pattern established by 1770 at the Bristol Fair, when a doctor is asked "What can you cure?" and brags, "The cramp, the gout, the pain within and the pain without!" (21). This question and similar responses are found in many mummers' plays. In the Bull Play, however, the doctor is instead asked how far he went to learn his trade. In response, he boasts, "I went to Australia, South America, Africa, Asia, Europe, all over the Caribbean and now I come back to small St. Kitts" (Mills, Jones-Hendrickson, and Bertram 1984, 33). This more closely resembles English versions published in the nineteenth century—for example, in John Wrigley's Peace Egg chapbook (ca. 1832–pre-1852), where he is asked, "How far have you traveled in doctrineship?" and replies, "From Italy, Titaly, High Germany, France, and Spain; and now am returned to cure the diseases in Old England again" (Cass 2001, 214). The Bull Play has eight players or variations thereof: "Bull, Arthur Davis, Sweetie, Oak, Sifter, Dr. Pick-Me-Heel, Backanash the Dog, and a Police Sergeant." Mills, Jones-Hendrickson, and Bertram (1984, 28–29) state, "The bull is usually attired in a bright red suit, and . . . he wears a pair of dangerous looking cattle horns . . . attached to a wire-mesh mask in the shape of an ox's head. [He performs] the gyrations of a sex-crazed animal as he swings his stiffened tail on his backside. Except for the doctor and the sergeant, the others are bedecked in multicolored patterns of dress adorned with bells and mirrors, and each player wields a whip of plaited cattle skin." After Sifter and Sweetie prove powerless to tame the unruly bull, a third brother, Oak, vows to turn the bull into "meat for the butcher's counter. [And] after a series of passes gives the bull a mortal wound" (McMurray 2001a, 44). In the final scene, Davis gives the doctor permission to give the prostrate bull an injection: "Doc scratches a match under the Bull's tail made of wire and some hairs of a real ox. The Bull seemingly springs into life more ferocious than ever as the crowds of onlookers particularly children scamper away in pleasant terror. The Bull however, soon ceases to chase people in order for the troupe to collect as much money as they could from the amused audience" (Mills, Jones-Hendrickson, and Bertram 1984, 34).

Antigua

The John Bull of Antigua was tended by a master but ran free. Austin James (pers. comm., February 19, 1995) saw John Bull masquerades at Christmas in Liberta Village, Antigua, during his childhood in the 1920s. The bull visited between midday and nightfall and stayed just fifteen to twenty minutes at each household. The bull ensemble moved from village to village with a retinue of children in tow. Lornetta Prince (pers. comm., December 26, 1994) remembers household visits by John Bull in Urlins Village during Christmases in the 1960s, when she was a child. No other masquerade troupe visited Urlins at that time. The group consisted of middle-aged men representing John Bull, a "monitor with a clap whip," and drummers. She remembers a bull horn being blown as a bugle in one bull ensemble. Dogs were tied up while the group was invited into the yard. The masquerade wore cow horns and a dried-banana-leaf costume with trousers and shirt. Sam "Miate" Williams customarily played John Bull and blackened his face with soot. Clydie Murrain from John Hughes Village, a local comic known for his tales and stunts, sometimes took on the role of bull and wore a large ring in his nose. (Plate 26) John Bull did a dance, the John Bull Jig. He jumped up and down, turned around, and dipped to get the money thrown to him. On some islands, including Antigua, whipping the bull was part of the entertainment. In Urlins, the monitor with the whip controlled the Bull's behavior. When a coin was thrown on the ground, John Bull would try to pick it up while the whip man hindered him by cracking the whip on the ground or lashing him. The bull eventually grabbed the money.

DONKEY AND HORSE MASQUERADES

The Donkey Man of Barbados is different from the donkey and horse masquerades that performed widely throughout the Eastern Caribbean. Although a tourney horse variety of the donkey also appeared in Barbados, there was also a simple type of Donkey Man that did not use the frame of the complete donkey costume. Instead, the dancer "wore behind him a tail of old rags which he shook as he gyrated using only the lower part of his body" (Anonymous 1976, 12). This seems to be a variation of the dancers that Sloane (1710, 46) saw in Jamaica: They "very often tie cow tails to their rumps and other such things to their bodies."

The donkey/horse masquerade proper is an old and ubiquitous masquerade type. We first learn of them in medieval Europe through the condemnations of early clerics. In addition to costumes, which consisted simply of a cured mare's skin, there are several constructed horse types that can be referred to as hobbyhorses. The stick horse is essentially a decorated broom handle with a carved and painted head. It is a children's toy but has also served as a masquerade. The sieve horse has a large framework and is confined to Europe. The mast horse involves a horse's head that is mounted on a pole and held by a performer who is covered. Some were made from real skulls, and this version appears in Guyana and Jamaica. Other horse masquerades used the stuffed skin of a horse's head or a carved wooden head, possibly with nails for teeth. The horse head masquerades in Guyana and Jamaica are of the mast horse variety, equipped with an articulated jaw. It is painted, eyes are added, and the player is covered with a piece of cloth. An adult horse's skull is heavy, so a smaller mule's skull is commonly used in Jamaica. A Roots Jonkonnu troupe has a varied cast that in addition to the horse head might include a cow head, Pitchy Patchy, the devil, a wild Indian, and others. Technically, the horse head is closest to a British skull-and-pole variety and points to a strong British influence. The Bamana peoples in nuclear Mande country and culturally conterminous areas of Mali used a stick horse masquerade in initiation ceremonies, as did the Dogon of Mali and some Senufo of Ivory Coast. However, stick horses were not among the traditional masquerades that appeared in the Eastern Caribbean, and in West Africa, records of mast or tourney horse masquerades are seemingly nonexistent.

The tourney horse is distinctive because it is designed to give the appearance of a horse and rider; the horse's structure is suspended from the performer's waist. This version appears as the donkey in the Eastern Caribbean—Barbados, Trinidad, the Virgin Islands, and elsewhere. In southern Britain, the tourney horse was common entertainment in the late medieval

Fig. 4.4. Valco horse, St. Stephen's Day, Tammela, Finland, 1928. Photo by Esko Aaltonen. Courtesy Museovirasto, Kuva-arkisto (National Board of Antiquities), Helsinki, Finland.

and early modern periods. Although it declined in England in the middle of the seventeenth century, the tourney horse remained popular in Latin Europe and Spanish America. An alternative name, *burrokeet*, used in Dominica and Trinidad, comes from the Spanish *burroquito* (little donkey) and indicates the Spanish connection. The burrokeet usually had a lightweight frame made of wickerwork, wire, or other light material. An effigy of a donkey's neck and head are attached to the front, and it may have leather ears and glass eyes. An artificial tail is attached to the rear. In the past, the donkey was usually performed by a man, normally a solo performer such as a man called Mr. Phipps who played with musicians in the Virgin Islands in the early twentieth century. His costume was simply a half a barrel split lengthwise, suspended from his waist, and draped with ornate fabric that hung almost to the ground, obscuring his legs. The artificial head was fitted with a bridle and reins that were held as if Phipps was riding the donkey (Lockhart 1979). The donkey later was performed by both males and females. Elmira Espinoza performed the donkey when the Smithsonian Folklife Festival visited St. Croix in 1991, wearing a wire-screen mask with a straw hat. Some masqueraders simply used face paint and possibly a wig. A bright shirt would be worn with a conical hat or a broad-brimmed planter's hat. The donkey danced to a string band and had a distinctive song, "Donkey want water, hold him down." The donkey was mostly a comedian and chased people, kicking up and being rude. Blue Gong and Diana performed as a male and female duo in Frederiksted in the early twentieth century, with romantic interludes giving way to humorous sexually oriented courtship (Eulalie Rivera, pers. comm., July 3, 1995). Asta James (pers. comm., July 3, 1996) remembers a troupe of roughly ten donkeys played by both men and women. In Christiansted in the 1970s and 1980s, Helen Joseph (pers. comm., July 4, 1996) had a donkey troupe, Playing the Ass, that had as many as a hundred donkeys. During the 1997 St. Croix New Year's Festival, Amy Gill had a troupe of half a dozen donkeys. (Plate 30)

In addition to donkey masquerades, real donkeys occasionally appeared at festivals. Riders wore comical costumes, providing a humble contrast to the horses of the equestrian cavalcades. The January 8, 1907, issue of the *St. Thomas Bulletin* reports that Three Kings' Day in Charlotte Amalie, "the donkey parade, which comprised 34 of the long-eared quad, and a single mule all ridden by gaily dressed fellers accompanied by a cartload of music." A donkey parade was featured on the second day of the St. Thomas Carnival held in February 1914. A photograph of such a parade in Christiansted around 1910 appears in Rezende and Walbom (2009, 100).

SENSAY AND PITCHY PATCHY

The Sensay and Pitchy Patchy masquerades are similar in their essentials. While Sensay may dress in raffia shag, its costume can also comprise a voluminous assemblage of multiple ribbons sewn onto a vest and trousers. On some Eastern Caribbean islands, this masquerade is known as Sagwa. Pierrot Grenade, a character in Trinidad's Carnival, is so dressed, and his surname indicates a connection to and perhaps origins in the Grenadine archipelago of the Windward Islands. While using the generic name John Canoe, a Jamaican report that appeared in the *Pennsylvania Freeman* in 1797 describes masquerade costumes that are recognizably Pitchy Patchy, "hung with shreds of various colored cloth dangling like a loose shag." The title *Pitchy Patchy* came to be used in Jamaica and more generally in the Leeward Islands. The costume may envelop the wearer from head to toe, or a mask might be worn. Pitchy Patchy is distinguished by athleticism and a dance that involves turns, cartwheels, and large movements in circular patterns that show off the feathery costume. (Plate 47) Regina Williams (pers. comm., July 11, 1995) recalls that both men and women in the Virgin Islands wore Pitchy Patchy costumes made out of flour bags with colorful cloths stuck on.

Fig. 4.5. Crookham Mummers of Hampshire, England, wear decorated ribbon costumes, 1992. Photo by Brian Shuel. Courtesy Collections Picture Library (http://www.collectionspicturelibrary.co.uk).

Bettelheim (1979, 67–69) refers to Margaret Dean-Smith in proposing that Pitchy Patchy's cloth costume may have evolved from the earlier shaggy vegetal costume. Dean-Smith (1963) suggests that the cloth-strip costumes of British mummers evolved from straw precursors as a result of increasing affluence. Further, the similarities between the cloth-strip Pitchy Patchy costume and the beribboned mummers troupes in Hampshire and Gloucestershire in Britain's West Country are more than coincidental, but the direction of influence cannot be determined. (Plate 28)

Dominicans maintain that Sensay is the oldest masquerade genre in Dominica and that the costume is of West African origin. The Sensay masquerade is also known on neighboring islands. It appears during Dominica's pre-Lenten carnival, Mas Domnik. In addition to the frayed costume, the face is covered by loose raffia, by colored cloth, or by a mask, usually of the wire-screen variety, although commercial rubber masks have recently become popular. Some individuals suggest that Nigerian Egungun masquerades, as are found in Ede, northern Yorubaland, are precursors. These African masquerades also have layered cloth costumes, although the Egungun cloth pieces are considerably larger than ribbons. Like the British mummers, the Egungun dramatis personae include raffia masquerades—for example, to the east of Ede, in neighboring Ekiti—but it is a stretch to say that one evolved from the other. Nevertheless, an African connection is credible.

In Dominica, the original Sensay outfit was made of sisal or "Lange bef," a species of wild agave. The costumes later were made of frayed rope; more recently, colorful cloth strips, paper, and even frayed plastic sacks have been used. (Plate 43) The costume of the Mandinka Kankuran came to correspond with that of Sensay, because when the bark of the *fara* tree became scarce in urban Senegambia, the performers started making costumes out of manufactured materials such as rice sacks. De Jong (2007, 124) states that "the rice-sack clad Kankurangs are called *Sisal*, a name that refers to the material used for their costumes." The title *band mauvais* is applied to Sensay masquerade troupes, and they traditionally appear in La Peau Cabrit parades (goatskin drum parade) in such towns as Soufriere, Pointe Michel, St. Joseph, and Grand Bay. Disguised in their bulky costumes and armed with thick sticks, whips, and batons, the Sensays' movements are erratic and intimidating. (Plate 45) The masquerades were made even more fearful because performers wear wooden clogs studded with metal cleats (later Coca-Cola caps) that clatter loudly in the streets. Sensay remain popular today, and in a true carnival mixture of the real and nonreal, the *bands mauvais* are ready to strike terror when they descend on the towns. One of Dominica's best-known present-day *band mauvais* groups hails from Colihaut.

MONTSERRAT AND ST. KITTS–NEVIS MASQUERADERS, HIGHLANDERS, AND CLOWNS

Montserrat Masqueraders

Howard A. Fergus (1994, 241) shows that Montserrat masquerades conform to Eastern Caribbean norms: "Masquerades are masked, dancing mummers in a colorful costume—a tall head-gear, ribbons, small mirrors, bells and a masque. . . . They danced from house to house, accepting gifts of drink and money." (Plate 53) While the Irish migrated to many Caribbean islands, only in Montserrat were they numerically dominant. A 1678 census lists Montserrat with 1,869 Irish, 761 English, 52 Scots, and 992 slaves. By 1707, the slave population had grown to 3,570, but by the third quarter of the eighteenth-century, that number had reached about 10,000 (Fergus 1975, 16). Even though the Irish were politically disempowered by the British rulers, numerical prevalence means that it is not entirely surprising that the Montserrat masqueraders' headdress was a miter, the tall, peaked hat that is worn by popes and bishops as a mark of office and by St. Patrick in illustrations. According to Eddie Donoghue (2001, 7), Montserrat masqueraders' miters are made from painted cardboard with silver foil decorating the rim. The Montserrat masqueraders also wore decorated wire-screen masks, rosy pink in color and painted with large staring eyes, black eyebrows, and broad mouths. Sometimes a black moustache was added. (Plate 57) The costumes are described as resembling the attire of female house slaves and consist of colorful embroidered bloomers reaching down to the shins and trimmed with lace. Mirrors and numerous long silk ribbons in bright colors hung from the performers' three-quarter-length jackets. According to retired masquerader Reginald Ryan, the mirrors were round and small—about 1.5 inches in diameter. In most cases, four of the mirrors were sewn across the front of the dress just above the breast, and two were sewn at the back, near the shoulder blades (Donoghue 2001, 8). Until the 1960s, the masqueraders wore women's stockings, but they have now been replaced by three-quarter length socks, usually white. Until the 1980s, the dancers had small bells sewn onto their footwear, around their ankles, and attached to their costumes. White gloves completed the disguise. Donna Henry tells an interviewer, "From the jacket or apron hung dozens of silk ribbons in bright colors such as red, green, yellow, blue, as well as a number of mirrors which would light up in the sunshine as they danced. At certain times they would throw back the front of the dress, all the ribbons would fly and it looked really pretty" (Donoghue 2001, 8).

Each Christmas season, several villages had masquerading troupes that toured extensively across the island for several days at a time, dancing for money and food and drink. Fergus (1994, 242) states, "The dancers crack cart whips to make way for themselves, discipline each other and ward off evil spirits." A group seldom had more than a dozen masqueraders (boys and men) and four musicians. According to Fergus, "Music is supplied by the a fife, a kettle drum played with two sticks to give an infectious syncopating rhythm, a boom drum [bass drum], a boom pipe [baha] which emits a 'boom' sound and a *shak-shak* or maracas" (242).

The captain was identified by the ring in the nose of his mask and the whip he wielded as a symbol of his authority (Fergus 1994, 242). The captain is sometimes described as a slave master because the hunter (cart whip) he wields is the same as slave drivers used. He was a hard task master, snapping his whip at the other dancers' rapidly moving feet. The captain could demote bad or misbehaving dancers by using his whip to strip away their ribbons, mirrors, or bells. More commonly, whip strokes were used to orchestrate the troupe's progress—for example, to signal when to cross from one side of the street to the other. The captain also acted as choreographer, and his whip signaled changes from one phase of the dance to another or from one solo dancer to the next. Lashes were sometimes aimed at the mischief, a nine- or ten-year-old masquerader who was attached to each group and who played the role of rascal. He was chosen not only for his dancing ability but also for his toughness and acumen. He ran errands for the adult dancers but was expected to rise through the ranks and ultimately to become a captain. The mischief was sometimes lifted from the ground, twirled around, and carried on the shoulders of an adult masquerade, to the amusement of onlookers (Donoghue 2001, 11). Other officeholders might include a chief mate, a warrior, and sometimes a masquerade queen.

According to Bell Meade, two noteworthy queens of the 1940s were daughters of masquerade captains: "You used to have a queen by the name of Mary Galloway, the daughter of Captain James Galloway. Then Wayne Murraine used to have his daughter, Ionie playing queen in his band" (Donoghue 2001, 27). The captain had to obtain a police permit to perform at certain locations and was valid from December 1 until the following January 1. The masquerades started their tour by dancing in their village before moving on to other locations. On extended tours, the troupe might spend a week on the road, staying with friends and relatives who resided along the route. Galloway was a master masquerader who started as a mischief at the age of ten, around 1921. He recalled that his troupe's "performances took the group to Harris, Trance, Bethel, Brades, Long Ground, Streatham, Dyers, and then to Glendon Hospital near the capital town of Plymouth. On New Year's Day Plymouth would be their venue after having left their home-base in St. John some seven or eight days earlier" (Donoghue 2001, 49). Each masquerader had a money pouch tied to his left wrist in which he would collect coins thrown by onlookers; stamping on a coin that lay on the ground signaled ownership. In addition, the group's treasurer passed a cup (often a chamber pot) in which to collect donations, and troupe members shared the proceeds on a daily basis.

Fergus (1994, 242) maintains that the Montserrat masquerade "blends Europe and Africa with Caribbean colours. The folk religion and drum beat are African, but there are westernized steps in the quadrilles and polkas." The Montserrat masqueraders had choreographed sequences: the march, the introductory curtsy, the concluding bow, and various dances. The groups would use the march as they tramped from one village to another. They commonly moved diagonally from one side of the street to the other with their knees bent and arms outstretched before them. At each stop on the route, the first order of business was a curtsy: Members of a group would line up to face the spectators and bow in unison. The masquerades performed a ring dance and five quadrilles, although those quadrilles bore little resemblance to their European predecessors. Dancers also performed a "heel and toe polka," quickly lifting their feet as if the ground was scalding hot. The dance was known as Chigga-Foot Maya because it supposedly resembled the walk of someone with chiggers in his or her feet. The performance would conclude when the masquerades bowed in unison, went down on one knee, and saluted.

The tradition was severely affected by the 1997 eruption of the volcano at Soufriere Hills that destroyed the island's capital, Plymouth, and led to a forced evacuation. Most masquerade troupes disbanded, and only one major group remains: the Montserrat National Masquerades have adopted the title Hybrid Masqueraders because members include former participants in such discontinued groups as the Streatham Masquerade, Harris Masquerade, Twitts Masquerade, and Long Ground Masquerade. The Hybrid Masqueraders represent Montserrat at arts festivals throughout the Caribbean.

Antiguan Highlanders

Highlanders were the Antiguan equivalent of the Montserrat masqueraders, commemorating Antigua's considerable Scottish legacy. They performed at Christmas and wore wire-mesh masks and used cowhide whips. Their costume originally simulated Scottish military dress, with vestigial kilts, and the players were accompanied by a fife-and-drum band. The costumes were brightly colored and decorated with pieces of cloth, peacock feathers, ribbons, and mirrors. (Plate 54) Highlanders from Old Road toured the southern villages and visited the capital, St. John's. According to Payne (2005), "They would leave close to Christmas Day and wouldn't go back until after New Year's Day. In that time they would travel from St. John's to Willikies and everywhere there was a village."

St. Kitts–Nevis Masquerades

St. Kitts and Nevis have distinctive masquerades. Nevertheless, the two islands are connected by a ferry, and Mills, Jones-Hendrickson, and Bertram (1984, 12) report, "For several decades, the people of St. Kitts awaited the Masquerades of Nevis, particularly those of Gingerland, Nevis. The Masquerades generally attract the largest crowd: bedecked with stunningly beautiful peacock feathers mounted in caps on their head." The St. Kitts–Nevis masquerades are in the same general mode as Montserrat masqueraders and Antiguan Highlanders but evolved from traditional Indians and are distinguished by their tall peacock-feather headgear. (Plate 56) Furthermore, St. Kitts–Nevis masquerades do not wield whips but instead often brandish tomahawks. Although they used to wear wire-mesh masks painted pink, they now wear masks less often. They wear red long-sleeved shirts with colorful ribbons sewn to the backs of their shoulders. The trousers have little bells sewn at the hems: "Overlaying the lower portion is a similarly patterned skirt, which like the shirt is bedecked with ribbons, small mirrors and tinkling bells. Sometimes a cape or mantle trails from the shoulder, and is usually designed from shimmering velvet material" (49–50). Participants previously included people of all ages, but most current masqueraders are teenagers and younger boys. Each masquerade troupe has roughly twelve to fifteen members and is led by an older and more responsible captain. According to Mills, Jones-Hendrickson, and Bertram, Kittitian-Nevisian masqueraders "announce themselves long before they are seen with the thumping boom of their big drum, the rolling sound of the kettle and the piercing fife," and their dancing "is unparalleled in dexterity" (13): "As the tempo of the drum beat develops, with the man on the fife—generally a virtuoso of class—fluting out the traditional 'baile' tune; tomahawks are hurled into the air, to be skillfully caught by the same hand that threw them" (51–52).

Clowns

Although disguise is a common characteristic of masquerading, some costumes do not fit neatly into either the dressing up or dressing down categories. Carnival clowns, for example, are somewhat marginal characters, although their costumes are normally pretty and brightly colored. In many ways, carnival clowns are a modern manifestation of the generic traditional masquerades that have appeared in the Eastern Caribbean throughout the years. Both Antigua and St. Kitts–Nevis have clowns. (Plate 49) According to Mills, Jones-Hendrickson, and Bertram (1984, 53) such performers on the latter islands are "attired in a light multi-coloured material designed in a loose, flabby style to which are fastened several dozen small bells, known as 'clown bells.' Each player carries a plaited cattle-skin whip, and on his head is [a] conical cap topped off with a feather." The troupes can have as many as fifty

Fig. 4.6. Carnival clowns along Main Street, Charlotte Amalie, St. Thomas, ca. 1963. Courtesy Miles Raymond.

performers; unlike the clowns of the European circus, Caribbean clowns wear mesh masks. Some early Virgin Islands clowns more resembled their European forbears, wearing, for example, baggy polka-dot suits; conical caps with pom-poms; ruffles around the neck, wrists, and ankles; and so forth.

Clowns are a long-standing feature of Caribbean masquerading. On April 15, 1903, the *St. Thomas Tidende* reports on clowns in an Easter Monday parade. A clown appears with a bull in a photograph taken in Frederiksted around 1910 (Axel Ovesen Collection, St. Croix Landmarks Society, Frederiksted). This character has the baggy one-piece costume and wire mask identified with carnival clowns. Both Ruth Moolenaar (pers. comm., August 10, 1995) and Rufus Vanderpool (pers. comm., August 3, 1995) recall clowns during the early decades of the twentieth century. They wore tall hats and wire-mesh masks painted with red cheeks and lips and blue eyes, as well as colorful baggy calico costumes with long sleeves and pants and that are decorated with mirrors and little jingle bells.

The clowns of the 1950s–60s sometimes used the conical reels from big spools of thread as horns. The Virgin Islands clowns were significantly influenced by visiting clown troupes in the carnivals of the 1950s. Twenty to twenty-five clowns accompanied the Hell's Gate and Brute Force steel bands from Antigua and the Casablanca steel band from St. Kitts–Nevis, and their performances were emulated in the Virgin Islands. The stocking mask that is now part of the characteristic carnival clown costume became popular soon thereafter, and the white stocking itself now serves as the disguise. Carnival clowns characteristically have long clap whips, which they crack noisily. In the Virgin Islands the whips are made from gwana tail or iguana tail (*Sansevieria*). (Plate 50) These clowns evolved within the carnival context and no longer dance to traditional drums. One troupe, the Tropical Masqueraders, continues to perform in the St. Thomas Carnival in the twenty-first century. They wear wire (or more recently nylon) mesh masks or simply white stockings over their heads. They wear baggy one-piece costumes or robes, often in large check or stripe designs. Many clowns wear hoods as part of their costumes, while others have oversize decorative hats. (Plate 52) The clowns wear white sneakers with jingle bells attached, and most complete the disguise with white gloves. Clowns have to be very lively and are normally performed by adolescent boys, although some teenage girls may be disguised in their midst. (Plate 63) A children's version of the clowns appears in the Children's Parade. (Plate 51)

MAN/WOMAN, WOMAN/MAN

Historically, during festivals, some men dressed as women and women dressed as men. In British ensembles, a man might simply wear a head kerchief or a wig and a women's dress, while in the Caribbean a female mask might be worn with women's attire. Such performances are held to represent the inversion element of Saturnalia. Mills, Jones-Hendrickson, and Bertram (1984, 9) state that the individuals portrayed by the Niega Business troupe in St. Kitts–Nevis often included "a character or two who were men dressed like women, complete with wig, dress, and exaggerated breasts and buttocks." Males wearing female garb, and vice versa, scandalized European clerics during New Year's festivals in sixth-century France, and performances that ridicule the opposite sex have for centuries been ubiquitous in European and Caribbean street theater. Early mummers' troupes in England disallowed females as actors, meaning that female roles were assumed by males, with a few exceptions. Pearson (2007, 124) states that in the plow-jagging gang at Kirton in Lindsey, Lincolnshire, "Old Lame Jane was played by a woman, Mrs. Blades." Similarly, in the words of Mills, Jones-Hendrickson, and Bertram (1984, 9),

"On occasions, groups would make use of natural women that [had exaggerated breasts and buttocks], and despite their shortness and fatness, they would amaze the onlooking crowd with unbelievable gyrations of their rump."

Cross-dressing is relatively rare in traditional West African festivals, but De Jong (2007, 38) reports that when Jola males entered the sacred forest for their initiation rites, "The guardians . . . often dressed up as women or had their faces painted to contribute to the carnivalesque atmosphere of role inversion." Similarly when the novices left the forest after the initiation, some of the guardians "were dressed as transvestites, prolonging the liminality of the ritual process" (43). Moreover, the *diambadong* dance performed when the initiation is completed "is a ritual of inversion since the participants dress in the apparel of the opposite sex. The guardians often wear skirts or long dresses and wigs and make-up. Women, on the other hand, wear trousers and hats. The performance celebrates that liminality characteristic of this stage of rites of passage" (120). Generally, however, cross-dressing is of a different variety in traditional Africa. Most masquerades are danced by men, including Gelede, a "female" masquerade of Yoruba societies that celebrates post-menopausal power. Moreover, similar to the Mbuya masks of the Pende of the Congo Republic, which lampoon female characters such as the flirt or the widow, some Yoruba Egungun male masqueraders parody the bride or the prostitute. Caribbean Creole styles crossed back to coastal West Africa, leading to the appearance of Caribbean-style shemales. The Jolly Masquerade in Freetown, Sierra Leone, is an example (Nunley 2010; Nunley and Bettelheim 1988). Now, however, the appropriation of a female dress to save money is no longer a factor. In costumes such as that of Koo-koo Actor Boy in Jamaica as drawn by Belisario (1837), female representation was taken to a grand level, and costumes are intricate and expensive—Koo-koo's costume cost as much as five doubloons (fifteen pounds sterling), a weighty price tag in the early nineteenth century.

Examples of shemales abound in festivals in the Eastern Caribbean. In some cases, men parodied women with oversize breasts and buttocks (or belly, in the case of Belly Woman) by stuffing their costumes and mincing around, flirting and exaggerating female behavior. One such masquerade, Tanto Liza (Tantalizer) was performed by Albert Halliday in Frederiksted, St. Croix, during Christmases in the early twentieth century. A song accompanied his performance, "Tantalizer gone, gone, he gone to the jailhouse" (Sylvester "Blinky" McIntosh, pers. comm., July 8, 1995). During the 1995 Emancipation Day parade in Frederiksted, Elaine Urgent, a noted cook, did a spoof of store owner Alex Faucett that highlighted a spat between Faucett and his wife,

Ellen. Urgent wore blue pants and shirt, suspenders, a ripped hat, and paint-splattered work boots, and she cut her hair to complete the look. S/he held a little stick and gave a speech about threatening to beat Ellen Faucett (*Daily News*, July 4, 1995). (Plate 29)

Shemale costumes in Europe have another, more esoteric dimension, involving the acquisition of spiritual protection by displaying female clothes, nightwear, undershirts, and clothes worn inside out. Similar practices were perpetuated in the Caribbean, and these ideas carried over into the costumes. Some masquerade costumes were made from the same sacks from which women made their baggy knee-length bloomers, so the costumes connoted underwear. More overtly, the Mocko Jumbie feathered its can-can petticoats to dispel bad spirits. Nevertheless, shemales—Mother Sally, Mother Bessie, Dirty Bet, or Belly Woman—are most often remembered as figures of fun.

FEMALE MASQUERADES

Males dominate in studies of masking and mumming generally as well as in the Caribbean, although some exceptions exist. In Estonia, women and girls organize goose-disguise mumming sorties (Tedre 2007, 410), and Donna Henry (pers. comm., November 18, 2003) confirms that a Miss Goose masquerade was part of the Christmas celebrations in Montserrat. Nevertheless, in traditional Jonkonnu ensembles of the British West Indies, every masked character was played by a male, including female characters, and the same holds true elsewhere. Prior to emancipation in the Danish West Indies, both males and females enhanced themselves in elaborate costumes in queen and mock aristocracy pageants, where the intent was to showcase individuals within prestigious roles. Thus, masquerading research sometimes conveys the impression that Caribbean females did not previously disguise themselves, instead choosing to embrace glamorous roles—for example, the Flower Girls who appeared in Charlotte Amalie at Christmas. Philip Rhymer pers. comm., July 18, 1996) remembers, "The Flower Girls were dressed in white and had a basket of flowers. They would kiss a blossom and fling it after you." Women's costumes, especially modern scanty ones, do not conceal the identity but instead reveal the performer. This apparent earlier paucity of female disguisers has led some authors to proclaim that Caribbean females did not previously wear masks and disguises but dressed up rather than dressed down. However, as is clear from a description of Three Kings' Day 1881 in the *St. Thomas Tidende*, both males and females wore masks: "The general public amusement

. . . being the masquerade . . . the streets were thronged with masques of both sexes" (January 8, 1881). Similarly, in 1903, "Easter Monday was made unusually lively by the appearance in town of a fine cavalcade of maskers dressed as clowns . . . and a number of female maskers followed the procession" (*St. Thomas Tidende*, April 15, 1903). Some women performed in mixed-gender troupes, while other troupes were solely female. Both oral reports and photographs attest to the fact that male and female members of Plait Pole troupes of the early twentieth century were disguised in masks. Today, women maskers are commonplace, disguised as such traditional masquerades as Mocko Jumbies and carnival clowns.

Mother Hubbard

A Mother Hubbard troupe consisted of ten to fifteen adult women dressed in period costumes in the style of the nursery rhyme character, with a bonnet tied by a ribbon under the chin. Each individual wore a brightly colored pink, yellow, or red flared organdy dress with sleeves to the wrist. The dresses were stiff and clean and had ample petticoats. They were tight around the waist and extended below the knee. Sometimes a blouse and a long skirt were worn. Small mirrors, spangles, and little bells often were sewn onto the costume. Members of such troupes wore wire-screen masks, commonly painted light pink with painted eyes and mouth and a shaped nose, though commercial papier-mâché or homemade cardboard masks sometimes were worn. (Plate 32) Mother Hubbards might harass onlookers with their trademark tamarind canes, which were about three feet long and covered with bright cloth or painted to match their attire. A dancer might identify herself to friends in the audience by touching them on the shoulder with her whip and whispering her name (Ethel McIntosh, pers. comm., July 9, 1995). Some dancers might carry a "shek-shek," the seed pod of the flamboyant tree. Eileen Messer (pers. comm., June 7, 1996) reports that Mother Hubbard troupes were dying out when she left St. Croix in 1942, but Elmira Espinoza saw a troupe in about 1944 (pers. comm., July 9, 1995). Various other troupes, loosely termed Party Girl sets, wore wire-mesh masks and period costumes, carried whips, and danced to string band music. For example, members of the Pantalet Troupe were adorned in elaborate frilly knee-length pantalets. In addition, many unmasked women's troupes dressed alike and were identified by the color of their dresses—the Le France Rose Girls, Bluebells, Snow Whites, and Canaries.

Cane Cutters

Prior to the early twentieth century, many Virgin Islands women engaged in hard and dirty work. The Coal Carriers of Charlotte Amalie are a prime example: These robust women in their smutted white dresses featured on early postcards from the Danish West Indies. They were with Bamboula Queen Coziah when she led a September 1892 demonstration to protest working conditions in Charlotte Amalie. Women were also field hands and appeared in masquerades in the guise of sugarcane workers. Despite the fact that they were not particularly fierce or intimidating, the Cane Cutters women's troupe falls into the dressing down category, because members dressed to look like a poorer class of people. Mary Seales (pers. comm., July 5, 1996) says that Nellie Scott had a Cane Cutters troupe that consisted of twenty or thirty adult women. Members of Cane Cutters troupes formerly wore wire-screen masks and usually had madras head ties, over which they wore straw hats. Later, some Cane Cutters did not mask but instead dressed in coarse osnaburg cloth and burlap: Their disguise was their grimy covering and scruffy appearance. Their costume consisted of skirts, printed blouses, and aprons made of common broadcloth. The skirts hung below the knee, sometimes as far as the ankle. The apron was usually white and included a bib. Cane Cutters wore brown stockings rolled below the knee, along with boots and later sneakers. Each Cane Cutter had a rope tied around her waist from which hung a tin cup. A cardboard replica of a bill (billhook) also hung from each woman's waists or was brandished as she danced. Men played the instruments, including drums, guiros, cowbells (metal gongs), fifes, tailpipes (bahas), and banjos. Sometimes children took part, dressing in the same costumes as the adults.

TEA MEETINGS AND VERBAL RECITATION

Tea Meetings

The florescence of British traditions among people of African descent in the Caribbean is little studied, even though it constitutes a considerable part of expressive culture. That the works of William Shakespeare and John Bunyan live on within the Caribbean vernacular tradition is of special interest to scholars of English literature and drama. St. Kitts–Nevis adopted British mumming styles to a greater degree than did other islands, and mummies there are better documented than other masquerades (Abrahams 1967; Fayer

2001b; Millington 1996; Millington and James 2011). The St. George Mummers Play is still performed in England and was performed in Newfoundland, St. Kitts–Nevis, and the Virgin Islands. "Rise up Matty Gru," a Virgin Islands folk song that is still featured in Tea Meetings, is based on an English ballad, "Matty Groves," that documents the murder of a lady's lover by cuckolded Lord Arnold. Hero-combat plays such as *St. George and the Dragon* or *David and Goliath* feature in the mummer-style repertoire, as do other quasi-historical or biblical tableaux such as *Giant Despair*. Even the St. Kitts–Nevis Bull Play incorporates memorized texts, oratory, and a cast of actors. Another hero-combat play, *The Bonaparte and Wellington Masquerade*, was performed by slaves on the Nevisian estate of a man named Jeffery in May 1817. The masquerade depicted the 1815 English victory over the French (McMurray 2001b, 12).

Tea Meetings differ from other masquerade performances because they are enacted in one spot. Mummies and Shakespeare Mas' perform in set locations but move from place to place—between competitions, in the latter case. But while masquerading took place in the streets, usually during the daytime, Tea Meetings could be held at night, indoors in a hall, in a tent built for the purpose, or in a mission chapel similar to the one described by Mrs. Lanaghan (1844) in her account of an 1840 Methodist Tea Meeting in Antigua. Refreshments were served, hence the name. Tea Meetings could be held in the daytime—for example, in the shade of the Grove Place baobab tree in St. Croix. Tea Meetings initially featured Christian-based dramatic materials that evangelical missionaries employed in the chapels of St. Kitts, Nevis, and Antigua to convert the peasant populations, encouraging them to play the roles of characters from the Bible. Joan McMurray (2001b, 5) explains that "two works which were developed into popular folk plays throughout the Anglophone Caribbean were John Bunyan's *Pilgrim's Progress* (1678, later known as *Giant Despair*) and Hannah More's *David and Goliath*." The West Indian Tea Meeting continued to be performed in churches until the late 1800s, but by the twentieth century, they had become all-night social gatherings organized to raise funds and provide entertainment for the laboring classes (5–6). Religious plays were taken over by troupes of male performers who reenacted them in street performances at holidays. Some recent troupes incorporate yellow hard hats into their presentations. According to McMurray, Tea Meetings now "reflect the tastes of their twentieth-century audiences and demonstrate how members of the peasant class modified tradition of the past" (4). She adds, "In Nevis, *Giant Despair* was the property of the villages of Rawlings and Gingerland; in St. Kitts *David and Goliath* belonged to Sandy Point" (13). *David and Goliath* also came to be performed on street corners in St. Croix.

In addition to Christian-based folk plays, Abrahams (1970, 247) points out, "On Nevis and St. Kitts . . . the tea meeting became an occasion not only for speechmaking, but also for . . . Elizabethan-type jigs." Kings and queens presided over Virgin Islands Tea Meetings; these figures were not masked but dressed regally and wore crowns. The program consisted of humorous skits and speeches on high-flown topics such as physiology and astrology, and individuals took turns speaking, singing, and trying to outdance each other. According to Soule (1992), "Performers—or even audience members—may interrupt to recite a rhyme or riddle. Set speeches are often interspersed with improvised ones; each speech is followed by a call for music and vigorous dancing." Lekis (1960, 183) states, "The jig dance takes hours to perform and sometimes is never finished, for the dancers become exhausted before completing their stories[, which are] never repeated in exactly the same way." Tea Meetings often incorporated the King George play, which includes assorted characters, among them the Turkish Knight, the Bold Slasher, Saladin, Count Valentine, the Dragon, Matty Gru, and Show Boy. Their costumes were not elaborate, and the actors did not mask but sometimes decorated their faces with paint. Show Boy dressed in bright colors with either short or long pants. He had a cardboard sword and made the first speech. The Dragon was covered with a mantle and had horns. Eileen Messer remembers a Christiansted "Jig" (Tea Meeting) with King George and Count Valentine singing songs and making speeches about fighting each other. According to Lekis (1960, 184), Count Valentine traditionally wore a crown of lighted candles, precariously balanced, and the king was required to snuff them out when he dueled with the count. Mary Seales (pers. comm., July 5, 1996) recounts that Willie Carroll, who was known as a caller at quadrille dances, was also a great Tea Meeting man. Tea Meetings declined in the early decades of the twentieth century, although they are occasionally revived. For example, a reenactment of a Tea Meeting was held at Fort Frederick on July 4, 1995.

Giant Despair

In Nevis, performances of *Giant Despair* took place at Christmas in yards along the island roads and are now part of Culturama, Nevis's premier festival, held in August to celebrate emancipation (Fayer and McMurray 1999, 71–72). A group of male performers recites a set text taken from *Pilgrim's Progress*, by John Bunyan (1678). The heroes, Christian and Hopeful, are captured by Giant Despair and imprisoned in Doubting Castle: "The plot is the Christians' journey to the Celestial City and concludes with the mock death of Despair. The players then threaten and chase spectators, especially the children. A string band accompanies the performances" (72). According to McMurray (2001b, 18), "The words, the sentences, the texts have rhythmic and auditory appeal which has nothing to do with meaning. Responding to modern creole performances doesn't entail understanding the words."

David and Goliath

David and Goliath was street theater popular in St. Kitts–Nevis, Tobago, Barbados, and Saba and was probably introduced into the Virgin Islands by laborers from the British West Indies. It is a hero-combat play based on the Old Testament story of the Philistine giant who was slain by the Israelite David. (Dialogue for a *David and Goliath* play in Nevis is found in Abrahams 1973, 120–31; for St. Kitts, see Mills, Jones-Hendrickson, and Bertram 1984, 35–45). Each troupe included ten or twelve men, and the roles included King Saul and Abner as well as the two title characters. The players wore costumes but not masks. According to McMurray (2001b, 12), "Costumes were created to fit the roles of the characters—shepherds' attire for David and Jesse, soldiers' dress for Abner and the troops, kingly robes and a crown for Saul." Goliath was dressed like a warrior and often wore a bulky galvanized belt from which a sword hung. A tall sheepskin cylinder on his head extended his height. He carried a staff. David was usually played by a boy and was dressed simply as a shepherd with a slingshot in his hand. The soldiers wore short skirts to make them look like people of olden times. Frank Charles played the kettle drum and bass drum for *David and Goliath.* A full band of musicians would include a flute and a squash, and the troupe would march down the street with music playing, stopping to stand in a circle at appropriate locations and reenact the play. Extended dialogue led up to the confrontation. The band would play again following the performance, and Goliath would brandish his long stick and make the soldiers dance around in circles (Frank Charles, pers. comm., July 1, 1996). *David and Goliath* groups are documented by Richard Schrader (1989, 67), who recalls, "The play was performed all over St. Croix. Mr. Willie Carroll, a robust man over 6 feet tall, weighing more than 200 pounds, played the role of Goliath. He was dressed like a warrior with a sheepskin wrapped like a tora on his head, and he carried a sword on his side and a large pole in his right hand. . . . A young boy named Ira Giddings played David. He was dressed like a shepherd and had only a sling shot in his hand." William Richardson recalls appearing as Goliath in Elmo Roebuck's troupe during the Carnivals in St. Thomas of the

1950s. He strode up and down, flourishing his stick, and roared, "I sent for a man to fight me and you send me a little boy. I'm going to feed your bones to the beasts of the field and the fowls of the air." In response, according to Richardson, "People would run; even David would run" (pers. comm., July 15, 1996).

Mummies

The mummies of St. Kitts–Nevis derive directly from British mummers' hero-combat plays and include recitation and lengthy monologues. Mummies' plays were frequently performed in St. Kitts and Nevis during Christmas celebrations in the early twentieth century. McMurray (2000, 3) points out, "Most lines are in strongly accented 'dog trot' rhythms, tetrameter or pentameter with irregular rhymes in couplets or triplets." Millington (1996) attempts to debunk the supposed antiquity of mummies by showing that the two mummies plays of St. Kitts–Nevis discussed by Abrahams (1967) were linked to Peace Egg plays published by Juliana Horatia Ewing (1871) in the second half of the nineteenth century. In McMurray's (2000, 1–2) words, "Mummies is meant to be performed in a characteristic perambulator style of the Mummers' genre. Amateur performers costumed to represent the traditional Mummers' characters parade down a street to the music of a fife and drum. Once the performers attract an interested audience, they begin to enact a typical Mummers' plot with a formal presentation and a series of disputes. The introductory matter includes music, a dance routine, and participation by the audience."

The plots conform to the British model: Champions from England, Ireland, Wales, and Scotland defeat their foreign adversaries, and their victories reaffirm their status as champions of Christianity. Christian figures representing St. George, St. Patrick, St. Andrew, and St. David slay adversaries such as "Dragon, Black Prince of 'Paradine' [Palestine], Hector, Bold Slasher, Turkish Knight, and Giant" (McMurray 2000, 4–5). With the exception of the Black Prince, the deaths are temporary, and a doctor is called on to resurrect the characters. According to McMurray, the St. Kitts version is closest to the British model, while the Nevision text underwent two significant alterations: "St. George lost in his fight with the Giant and his defeat destroys the heroic status of England's patron saint and, secondly, the romantic union between the Christian hero and the lady becomes a comic episode in which an angry St. George—determined to proclaim his masculinity—refuses to be matched with a crossed-dressed boy actor" (11).

Shakespeare Mas'

The Shakespeare Mas' of Carriacou is a type of verbal dueling between two players to determine who can recite the most speeches in a competitive exchange. On Shrove Tuesday, as part of Carnival, groups of men compete both verbally and physically in their recitations of Shakespeare's *Julius Caesar*. Poor or inaccurate recitations result in a whipping by the opponent and a challenge by another player. Fayer and McMurray (1999, 59) explain, "Signifiers are combined in the Shakespeare Mas' where English literary text, verbal combat, costumes, and dance-like movement intersect to create a Caribbean Creole artifact." Carriacou is the largest of the Grenadine islands, and its cultural expressions are especially interesting because as a consequence of its isolation, African aesthetics have been more thoroughly perpetuated: "In Carriacou slaves were a high percentage of the population. In 1833, just before emancipation, there were 3,200 slaves in the total population of about four thousand. After emancipation, European planters departed" (59). The conjunction of Africanized aesthetics with Shakespearean drama creates a fascinating blend. Fayer and McMurray (1999, 59) report that "one of the oldest residents remembers mas' performances at the end of the [nineteenth] century." They continue, "During the rehearsal period the group selects a king and peacemaker or peacemakers; the king is generally an experienced mas' player. . . . The peacemaker is another performer who knows the speeches as well as the 'unwritten' rules of performance. He is able to control the players on the frequent occasions when players from both side get out of hand" (65). Typical headwear consists of a crown made by pasting colorful fabric onto bags that originally held cement; the crown extends down the back of the player: "The base of the crown is a cotta woven from the fibrous air roots of a ficus [Jumbie] tree, which supports the crown and is tied around the head and under the chin" (65; a cotta is normally used to support pots carried on the head). The wire-screen mask, painted white, provides some protection from the whip blows: "One experienced mas' player said that the masks used to be 'pretty' but now are 'Grenadian' screen wire painted with crude drawings of human or animal faces" (65). "A player wears baggy trousers, a petticoat, tennis shoes or leather boots, and a loose fitting, colorful shirt that has overlapping rows of fabric cut in triangles with a large black heart and mirrors on the front; he also carries a whip. Some players wear gloves and carry a bell. Trousers are tucked into the tops of socks. (Plate 55) The design and colors of the fabric of the shirt and crown are different for each player" (65). A player carries a whip made of telephone wire wrapped in plastic tape. Hard blows are delivered, and the fighting frequently becomes fierce. According to Fayer and McMurray, the schedule normally begins with an early morning warm-up mas' at Top Hill and another in Bogles. The mas' players then proceed to the first major encounter, at Mt. Royal, a second in Six Roads, and a third in Brunswick: "Then the players and the crowd move on to Hillsborough for freer, less structured recitations—simply for the fun of it—and much drinking of beer and Jack Iron, a very strong rum" (66).

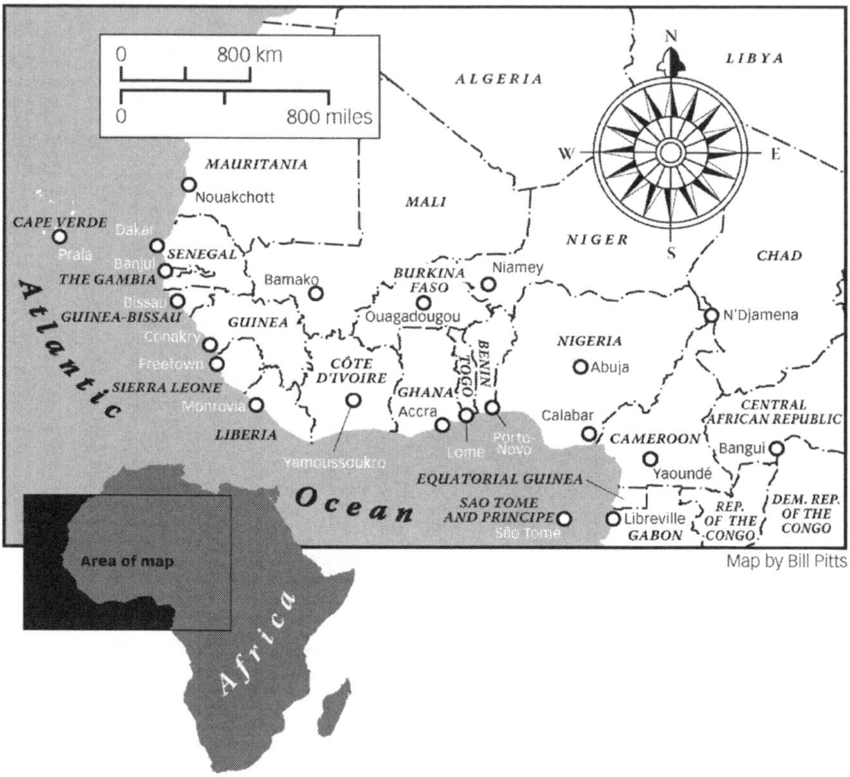

Map by Bill Pitts

West Africa

Chapter 5

MASQUERADE PROTOTYPES IN WEST AFRICA

VARIETIES OF MASQUERADE

Bush Masquerades

Masquerades in West Africa include animal disguises and bush masquerades made of vegetal material. As an animal, the bear is not indigenous to Africa; therefore, one would not expect masquerades to be so named. Raffia masquerades are widespread, however—for example, the costumes of ancestral Egungun masquerades from the northeastern region of Yorubaland are made entirely from shredded plant fibers. The bulky raffia contributes to its appearance of hugeness, while bold, exaggerated gestures similarly add to its "bush monster" appearance. Figures clad in raffia fiber of one kind or another are among the oldest masquerades found in Upper Guinea and were documented in the late eighteenth century. The umbrella term *bush masquerade* covers a variety of costume types: Both the Kumpo and the Kankuran wear dried fiber costumes, though their appearances differ. The Kumpo, like the British Straw Bear, resembles a mobile haystack, although its long palm strands hang in a more orderly fashion. The covering extends to the legs and feet, but the mass of the bulky costume envelops head and torso. The Kankuran, conversely, is not as colossal and is dressed in sections, with separate raffia leggings and sleeves that have enlarged tufts covering the hands and feet. The main part of the costume covers the neck and upper body and is tied around the waist, with a raffia skirt that hangs down below the knees. The masker's face is concealed with a textile hood, but it is largely hidden by the large tufts of raffia that envelop the head.

Kumpo

The Kumpo masquerade is found from Gambia through the Casamance and south into Guinea Bissau. In Senegambia, the Kumpo masquerade appears among both the Bainunk and the Jola. According to De Jong (2007, 160),

Kumpo likely originated among the Bainunk ethnic group and spread to the Jola, probably in the 1930s. Yet De Jong also points out, "To attribute distinct cultural features to either Bainunk or Jola is a haphazard enterprise considering they have a shared history of more than four centuries" (160). However, "while the Kumpo mask performance is considered the 'cultural heritage' of the Bainunk ethnic group in Senegal, it has recently acquired the status of a national heritage in the Gambia" (169). Kumpo's costume is made of ronier palm fibers and covers the dancer's body and head. The ronier fan palm (*Borassus aethiopum*) is also used to weave mats and baskets. Kumpo's draped costume consists of multiple layers that radiate outward when he spins, and the entire rustling form is topped by a stick several feet long (Mark 1983, 12). De Jong (2007, 156) describes a performance by a Kumpo masquerade of the Jola: "Kumpo is normally performed in the village square. . . . At nightfall the young women gather and line up at the central square. They then begin to sing and dance, using old spades for rhythmical accompaniment, and are later joined by the young men. After some time Kumpo appears stalking around and frightening the children. Three drummers then heat their drums at a bonfire and start playing, encouraging the young men and women to dance. . . . Kumpo admonishes the youths to take the dance seriously, participating in the dance himself. He sticks his pole in the ground and whirls in circles around it, displaying great speed and agility." Kumpo's dance, like that of Sengko, simulates the disruptive whirlwinds: "When the Kumpo dances, the swirling raffia tumbles and cascades in the moonlight. He becomes the visual embodiment of electrical energy" (Mark 1983, 13).

Samai and Jarimamma

Kumpo is often accompanied by a companion termed *Samai* by Peter Mark and *Jarimamma* by De Jong. Samai is a burlap-covered masquerade that wears a horned mask painted red or white, often with a goat's hair beard (Mark 1983, 13). De Jong (2007, 165) includes a black and white photo of Jarimamma, guarding Kumpo in Diatock village. De Jong does not describe Jarimamma, but the photo shows him in a simple dark fabric shirt-and-pants costume with long ribbons embellishing the shirt. The wooden mask is styled after an antelope and has wooden fluted horns. Like Samai, it has a white goat's hair beard.

Sengko

The Sengko masquerade was important in the former kingdom of Wuli in eastern Gambia and central Senegal. According to Peter Weil (1988, 153), "The *sengko* was central to the *barrango*, one of three female ritual initiation stages which preceded marriage." The last barrango in Wuli was held in the Gambian community in about 1971. Sengko differs from other raffia masquerades in that it has an internal cane frame (comparable to the London Jack in the Green). It is constructed of two materials, shredded bark from the *fara* tree and bamboo (161). The masquerade is constructed of an external covering of the dark reddish-brown bark over an internal frame shaped somewhat like a traditional hut (159). The bark is attached to the top of the frame and hangs down to the performer's ankles. The masker holds a short sorghum or millet stalk baton that sticks out of the costume and resembles a tongue protruding from Sengko's mouth. In performances, the tongue is used to threaten or hit the audience or initiates.

Mumbo Jumbo

One of the earliest descriptions of a bulky masquerade in shredded tree bark raffia is provided by Francis Moore during his travels along the Gambia River in 1732: "On the 6th of May at night, I was visited by a Mumbo Jumbo, an idol, which among the Mandingoes is a kind of cunning mystery. It is dressed in a long coat made of the bark of trees, with a tuft of fine straw on top of it, and when the person wears it, it is about 8 or 9 feet tall" (1738). Moore's name, *Mumbo Jumbo*, is not dissimilar to *mama jumbo*, which among the Mandinka describes a category of senior, powerful masks (along with *mamakortro* and simply *mamo*). Weil (1988, 153) notes, "All of these terms share the root '*mamo*' which means 'ancestor' or 'great ancestor.'"

Kankuran

Moore's "cunning mystery" is comparable to several masquerades that are modifications of Kankuran (Kankurang/Kangkurang/Kankouran). Kankuran refers to a family of figures covered from head to midcalf by leaves, whether green or dried (*fita*), or shredded tree bark (*fara*). Kankuran was documented under the name *Mumbo Jumbo* in the late eighteenth century by both Francis Moore (1738) and Mungo Park (1799/1983), and it is one of the oldest masquerades found among the Mandinka. A French Catholic missionary, Doutremépuich (1939, 490), describes a Kankuran masquerade in an initiation camp: "A masked figure completely hidden in an ochre-coloured fibre costume, makes several gestures. His hands are completely covered, as well as his legs and feet. His face is hidden by a tuft of fibres that hang down from the top of his head. He holds in every hand a machete, a sort of cutlass, which makes his appearance even more terrifying. . . . [H]e jumps advances and retreats, and strikes the ground with his cutlasses, either in front of him or in between the children" (490). De Jong (2007, 129) states, "The Kankurang does not wear

Fig. 5.1. Kankurang in the rice fields on the outskirts of Ziguinchor, Casamance, Senegal, 1991. Courtesy Ferdinand de Jong.

a wooden face mask, but a costume of multiple pieces of bark fixed in such a way as to render the identification of the masked individual impossible. . . . When the mask is brought out, it is usually accompanied by around ten young men who are fifteen to thirty years old. They carry sticks and threaten to beat the numerous spectators." (Plate 8)

The bark of the *fara* tree is believed to be imbued with special beneficent qualities and able to combat malevolent forces. In urban areas, where the bark of the *fara* tree is increasingly hard to find, masked performers have started using manufactured material for the costume: "The masks are increasingly made of materials that do not originate in the bush. Performers used rice sacks that are sewn into the costumes and dyed with industrial paint. In addition to the ochre-coloured masks clad in bark, artificially coloured masks have emerged in fancy colours such as purple. The rice-sack clad Kankurangs are called *Sisal* a name that refers to the material used for their costumes" (De Jong 2007, 124). These new masks are considered mystically less dangerous, and the "real" Kankurang is supposed to wield powers his urban counterpart does not possess, because power is no longer obtained in the bush but is purchased in the market (144–45). The ways in which the Kankurangs are named, dressed, and perform suggests that their occult function—the fighting of witches—is now considered less important (124).

Horned Masquerades

In West Africa, the use of real horns on headdresses is much less frequent than the use of carved wooden horns on masks. Examples of wooden horned headdresses appear in Upper Guinea among the Tussian and Siemu peoples of Burkina Faso. Some are complex artistic configurations including a second pair of horns within the larger constellation (Petridis 2008). Horned headdresses, both masks and caps, with pairs of real horns (as opposed to a cluster) are found from Senegambia, to Guinea Bissau and the Bissagos Islands, to Guinea, Sierra Leone, and the northwestern Ivory Coast. Such horn-wearing groups as the Mandinka, Jola, Bainunk, Bagnun, Balanta, and Baga and Temne were transported to the Americas in significant numbers. A historical relationship exists between cattle and slavery, and Mark (1992, 124) maintains that a horned mask such as the Mandinka Red Spear "contains a symbolic reference to the slave trade" because slaves were purchased or ransomed in the region using cattle as currency. Baum (2010, 145) explains that among the Jola of Esulala, relatives had to pay a sum of cattle equivalent to the mourning period: "A standard ransom of six cattle for a woman and seven for a man was linked to the mourning period of six days for a woman and seven for a man."

Judith Bettelheim (1979, 52–53) posits that cattle-horn headdresses in the Caribbean are derived from a similar West African type that is today "found among West Atlantic, Manding and Voltaic groups." She refers to the Endyambi (Ejumba) headdress of the Diola (Jola); the "cow-horned headdress" of the Bijugo (Bijogo/Bidjogo) of the Bissagos Islands; and the Fanaden (Fanada) circumcision headdress of the Balante (Balanta) in Guinea Bissau. She also refers to the "horned helmet mask" of the Bamana of Mali documented by Gray and Dochard (1825) in Kaarta State, which was previously used for circumcision ceremonies but has subsequently died out. Notably, it included tusks, like the early Jonkonnu Bull. Gray and Dochard provide an illustration that Bettelheim (1979, 57) suggests "may in fact be a bit fanciful": "The only solid ethnographic evidence it provides is that the mask was worn over the head, extending to the shoulders, representing the neck and head of an animal who had horns and tusks and was snouted." The illustration shows what appear to be antelope horns on the head and very long upward-pointing tusks that rival the horns in length. The Fanada initiation headdresses of the Balanta are dissimilar to the Caribbean Bull because Balanta helmet masks consist of gigantic baskets topped by one or more pairs of cattle horns (see Mark 1992, figs. 29–32).

Among the inhabitants of the Bissagos Islands off the coast of Guinea Bissau, cattle assume a central role in visual imagery of wealth and power and have done so for at least four hundred years. The Bijogos take bovine imagery to a level of realism not found in mainland African groups or in the Leeward Islands, and elegantly carved cattle heads formerly adorned the prows of war canoes (Mark 1992, 50). Bijogo helmet masks consist of life-sized replicas of whole bull heads. Moreover, unlike in mainland groups, the masquerader sometimes adopts a quadrupedal stance. Other horned masquerades such as the Bamana secret society masquerade, Komo, whose headdress, *komo kun*, includes antelope horns, are excluded from consideration here because the horns are backswept rather than lateral (see Diamitani 2008, 20). Bipedal masquerades with a pair of lateral horns among the Mandinka and Jola include the Ejumba, Kebul, and Red Spear, which are often used within the male initiation process. Horned headdresses appear in the historical records of François Froger (1698) and Jean Labat (1728) in Gambia, while Louis Binger (1892) documents a horned headdress at a funeral ceremony in southern Mali. Labat includes a 1685 description of a bull-horned headdress at the commercial center of Geregia in the Casamance: "We encountered a griot who had a headdress made more or less like the head of an ox, completely covered with certain little seeds the color of fire, with a pair of the most beautiful horns placed in such a manner that they seemed to grow out of his head" (5:32–33; Mark [1992, 88 n. 2] says the passage has since been attributed to Sieur de la Courbes; the seeds are doubtless *Abrus* seeds).

Kebul

François Froger (1698, 98) published another early description of a Mandinka bull-horned headdress in the town of Barra on the north bank of the Gambia River, where it was worn by both the king and male initiates: "The King of Barra appeared . . . dressed in a small red shirt covered with the tails of wild animals and charms; upon his head he wore the headdress of an official decorated with several strands of coral and two cattle horns." Froger's account is illustrated by an engraving, *Habillement de Circoncis* (Dress of the Circumicised), that shows a semihorizontal horned mask revealing the lower part of the wearer's face. The mask is practically identical in form to that of Kebul in the twentieth century (see Mark 1992, 5). Kebul masks have a simpler form than the Ejumba and are found in the northwestern Casamance and in adjacent southwestern Gambia. They are wedge-shaped and woven with broader strips of fan palm leaves (also used for the raffia costume of Kumpo of the Mandinka). Kebul masks lack the Ejumba's protuberant eyes, merely having eye holes cut through the fiber. However, Kebul masks include many of the decorative elements of the Ejumba, including *Abrus* seeds. Although made of perishable materials, a surprising number of horned masks from the

Casamance and Lower Gambia have been preserved in museums and private collections. Mark (1992) refers to forty-four different pieces.

Ejumba

The Ejumba masks of the Jola are woven from palm fronds to form a basket-like helmet. The cattle horns are attached to the crown of a cone-shaped head. The apex of the crown is usually mirrored by a downward pointing triangular chin. The face has a pair of projecting tubular eyes through which the dancer looks out. The mask is covered with a resinous material and decorated with *Abrus* seeds and cowrie shells. (Plate 13) An Ejumba mask is worn by the spiritual leader of the graduates, and the tubular eyes are associated with clairvoyance and the ability to perceive invisible supernatural forces. An extended fringe of tree bark fibers, up to two or three feet long, hangs from the base of an Ejumba mask, helping to hide the dancer's identity. Mark (1983, 7) includes photographs of Ejumba masquerades at an initiation with full-body raffia costumes and states that the photographs are of "a costume and masque that were danced together in 1965 in the village of Nioumoune" (pers. comm., October 25, 2008). (Plate 11) In West Africa, wearing an animal-horned headdress symbolized manhood. For the Jola and others in the Upper Guinea region, transitioning to manhood involved becoming "a bull," dancing in a horned mask and generally embodying masculine values, which are instilled in the initiates. Mark (1983, 40) describes a preinitiation dance by the youths of Badiam village where "twenty-seven usikoi danced together." During the dance, "The youths tossed their heads wildly about in a manner that called to mind the untamed energy of a ferocious bull." For Mark, the initiation ceremony today preserves and forges a Jola identity (24).

Red Spear

The prototype for the Mandinka Red Spear masquerade is more than two hundred years old. Red Spear is distinguished by a red woven fiber mask (recently red flannel) with facial features outlined in cowrie shells and topped by bull horns. Like the Ejumba mask of the Jola, it has a broad, triangular forehead and narrows to a pointed chin. (Plate 12) The horned mask is combined with a vegetal dress, but the costume is now usually made from green rather than dried leaves. The costume of fresh leaves, *fita*, can be distinguished from one made of shredded bark, *fara* (Weil 1971, 279–81). The Red Spears of the Kiang Districts currently use leaf costumes, which replaced bark costumes at the end of the nineteenth century. Thus, during the Atlantic slave-trade era, the Red Spear or its precursor probably wore raffia costumes of bark.

Sörsörnë

Frederick Lamp (pers. comm., February 15, 1998) affirms that the Temne of northern Sierra Leone have cow-horn headdresses and that the Baga, who occupy a narrow strip of marshy lowland along the coast of the Republic of Guinea, have cow-horn headdresses that are affiliated with secret societies. As with the Jola, cattle-horned headdresses and sacred forests are part of Baga initiations. Simo, a magistrate, organizes the ceremonies, as Caillié reports (1830, 153–55): "The ceremony is accompanied by a great feast [that] lasts sometimes for several days; after it is over, the Simo withdraws to the woods, and takes with him the boys who have been initiated. On the festival day, the Simo again announces his approach by frightful howlings, which are imitated by his pupils with cows' horns. They are all armed with whips, in token of their authority."

Figure 198 in Lamp's (1996) report on the Baga of Guinea shows a tall masquerade, Sörsörnë, with large bull horns atop a head area that is draped with a dark cloth set on a billowing raffia dress that reaches the ground. The Sörsörnë is a towering bull, atypical because it extends its height during a performance. The name is derived from *sörnë*, meaning "to heighten" (205). Furthermore, the example depicted also diverges from the standard because Sörsörnë is usually surmounted by a carved wooden headdress "in the form of a female bust with short vertical horns" (205).

Trophy Caps in Northeastern Ghana

The horned helmet is found in the arid northeastern region of Ghana among hunters and warriors of such groups as the Konkomba, Navropio, Bulsa (Builsa), Kassena, Moba, and Frafra, all of whom used the horns of antelope and buffalo as ceremonial headdresses (Kyerematen 1964; Cole and Ross 1977; Fred T. Smith 1987). Although these groups were prey to slavers, most were carried to the north to the Sahara and beyond rather than to the Atlantic coast, as Fred T. Smith (pers. comm., May 20, 2011) confirms: "From my evidence, the major slave raiding into the Frafra and related areas and related trade was to the North, dating back to the 15th century." Research conducted by Der (1998) suggests the region was not solicited by the transatlantic slave trade until the early nineteenth century, when the trade was coming to a close. Thus, whether northern Ghanaian groups were brought to the Caribbean early enough to influence horned masquerades is not clear.

The Builsa people of Ghana view the wild bull or buffalo as part of their ancestry and the bull's horns as symbolizing manhood. In the past, a young man was not deemed marriageable until he had hunted and killed a wild buffalo and collected the horns as a trophy. According to Soulay Ousman (pers.

comm., March 20, 2003), a male who had proved his manhood in this way could wear the horns on his head and join the circle of hunters during special dances that invoked the spirits of the ancestors. Fred T. Smith (1987) describes the Frafra tradition and includes a picture of a Frafra horned headdress. (Plate 9) Smith describes hunters' and warriors' costumes in the context of dances performed at funerals and explains that horned helmets are also worn by both the Dagomba and the Konkomba peoples. Dagomba warriors wore calabash helmets with horns in battle; accordingly, the horns are short—no more than six inches—and they are now seen primarily at Dagomba funerals. Konkomba horns are 2.5 feet long, and the helmet is not battle headwear but for ritual dancing. The skullcap is embroidered with cowries, and from it hang chains of cowries of up to four feet long. Gehrts (1915, ii) describes a Konkomba headdress: "The helmet is a calabash, elaborately ornamented with cowrie shells, and surmounted by a fine pair of roan antelope horns. Other less lucky warriors or less clever hunters, content themselves with the smaller horns of the commoner puku antelope."

At Frafra funerals, men dance in military formation adorned in prestigious attire, including horned headdresses. For a male, being selected to dance and especially to lead a formation is a singular personal and family honor. According to Fred T. Smith (1987, 51), "In the past horned helmets were much more numerous among the Frafra and the owners had to compete in order to lead a formation. Today they are still viewed as symbolic of both individual achievement and clan strength, in fact the horns of an important deceased person may be attached to the peak of a thatched roof in a compound that is celebrating a funeral." Like the caps of the Builsa, Frafra helmets are comprised of calabash or basketry bases that fit like skullcaps and are covered with leather, fabric, and/or cowrie shells and adorned by animal horns: "The helmet with horns (*nugo illa*) can be worn only by a hunter who has killed a large bush animal with a bow and arrow. The prized animals are antelope or bush cow. The skull and horns are kept by the hunter in a special shrine in his sleeping room until he decides to make a *nugo illa*" (51). Because the horns are hunting trophies, only horns from wild game are used, and not the horns of domestic cattle; instead, the Frafra emphasize the importance of domestic animals for sacrificial use. On this point, Mark (1992, 120) concedes, "Mandinka masks that incorporate materials associated with the 'deep bush' are considered to possess greater power than masks associated with the village and with domesticated animals." He suggests that antelope horns attached to Ejumba masks in old museum pieces probably refer to "the initiate's skill as a hunter" (13).

Kyerematen (1964, 81–82) describes horned helmets known as *yugongo* by the Navropio of the northern region of Ghana: "They are made of sliced halves of calabashes and are decorated with cowries and skins. They have tops made of the horns of certain animals such as the cow, buffalo and waterbuck. They were originally worn by the ruler and his men on the battlefield but are now chiefly worn by his bodyguard and musicians." Kyerematen's description does not specify whether "cow horns" refers to domestic cattle or the bush cow, which is a wild animal like the buffalo and waterbuck. Since there is no other mention of the horns of domestic animals in the northeastern region, it is probably bush cow. In contrast, the power of the horns of the Ejumba mask is derived from the use of domestic cattle as sacrificial beasts.

Igbo Horned Masks

Groups in southeast Nigeria such as the Igede and Igbo do not conduct age-set initiation rituals involving seclusion of a cohort group in a bush school like the Mande and Jola of Upper Guinea and those run by the Poro Society in Liberia and adjacent countries. Instead, individual adolescents are considered adult when they are initiated into the lower ranks of local masquerade societies or their equivalent. Amid the diversity of Igbo mask types, some categorization is necessary. There are several distinct masking genres in Igboland in southeast Nigeria. A genre is a group of different types of masks that operate as an institution, and each genre is recognized and named as an entity by its members (Eli Bentor, pers. comm., February 12, 2012). Within a genre, there may be several types of masks. Each type has a specific appearance, costume, dance, drum rhythms and music, and rules of behavior. Mmanwu is a dominant genre in Anambra and in adjacent areas of northern Imo and Enugu states and is often identified as the typical Igbo masking tradition. It is mostly found in north-central Igboland in Anambra and northern Imo. Mmanwu includes Mgbedike, Oji Onu, Nwa Abuja, and the well-known maiden spirit masks (Eli Bentor, pers. comm., February 11, 2012). Unlike Okoroshi (Okorosia), Mmanwu does not have the "Beauty and the Beast" dichotomy, although some white-faced female Okoroshi masks bear some resemblance to Mmanwu's maiden-spirit masks. According to Bentor (pers. comm., February 12, 2012), "Okorosia, Owu, Okonko, Ekeleke, Ekpo, and Mma are separate masking genres distinct from Mmanwu. Okorosia is found mainly in northwestern Imo state in the area of Ihialla and Mgbidi between Orlu and the Niger. Some communities in that area have both Okorosia and Mmanwu." Some of the Mmanwu masks documented by Bentor are equipped with real cow horns, though the examples here are not identified specifically as either bulls or bush cows. Those masks referred to by the Igbo as bush cow masks are made of wood and sport carved horns that resemble the broad horns of a buffalo. For example, the Atu Ejeogu that appeared in the Enugu Mmanwu Festival is part of the Mma genre. *Atu* is the Igbo name for bush cow, and *Atu Ejeogu* means "fighting bull." Other giant full-body Mmanwu bull masquerades occasionally perform. These large structures are rather realistic bovine replicas and somewhat resemble the European pantomime horse. Other quadruped bulls with short stilts attached to both legs and arms are called Mmanwu Hawusa (Hausa) and have artificial heads and horns.

A bull-horned masquerade from the Njima Club of Arondizuogu danced in a shaggy costume and a checkered apron at Oror, Arochukwu, on January 5, 1988, during the burial ceremony of the Eze Aro, the traditional ruler of Arochukwu (Plate 15). Arondizuogu is the largest and most prosperous of the Aro people's settlements and is located in northern Imo, while Oror is one of the nineteen villages that make up Arochukwu (sometimes referred to as Arochuku, or Aro-Okigbo), the homeland of the Aro people, an Igbo-speaking group in southern Abia State on the border with Akwa-Ibom State. The Njima masquerade club was established in 1972 to restore the masking culture of Arondizuogu following the Nigerian civil war. Many Njima members are employed outside Arondizuogu for most of the year, and the club's largest and most active branch is based in the commercial city of Aba, in Abia. Their members wear uniforms of George cloth, with black singlets and black and red caps. They tend to be older and more established members of the community than the younger men who masquerade at the village level, and Njima does not roam the local roads the way most masquerades do. In the 1980s and 1990s, Njima members were invited to perform at different functions throughout Nigeria. Performers often were paid by local patrons to accompany them as part of their entourages at major events. The Njima club once performed for President Shehu Shagari at the opening of a large hotel owned by an Arondizuogu man in Abuja; club members also performed at the burial of Muslim politician Shehu Aminu Kano in Kano in 1983. During Arondizuogu's annual Ikeji Festival, Njima is often invited to perform at the houses of wealthy patrons (Eli Bentor, pers. comm., February 11, 2012).

In addition to dancing and promenading, the activities of the bull-horned Njima masquerade included paying homage to an ofo tree (*Detarium senegalense/elastica*). Although ofo trees are not particularly large or impressive, they often serve as shrines, including one for the Aro Clan Council whose members are comprised of the Aka-ji-ofo (the hand that holds the ofo). The ofo refers to an emblematic dowel made from the ofo tree, although in Oguta and Asaba, they are also cast in bronze. The ofo is used in sacrifices among the Igbo as a mark of righteousness and authority (Eli Bentor, pers. comm., July 19, 2004). The Mmanwu genre exists at Arondizuogu but not in Arochukwu, and only those initiated into Mmanwu can join Njima. However, Njima functions as a separate organization, and its masks are somewhat unusual and do not correspond to the regular Mmanwu types. Njima masks are usually large and spectacular in appearance.

Another masquerade in the Mmanwu genre is the Mgbedike, performed at the New Yam Festival (known locally as the Afo Festival) in the village of Umuokwara, in the Akokwa area just to the west of Arondizuogu (Plate 16). Not all Mgbedike have masks; however, some (for example the Ndikelionwu masquerade of Anambra) have carved wooden masks surmounted by a complex superstructure that includes horns. Such masks often have large teeth, and the performers carry machetes, appear formidable, and must be restrained by handlers. Mgbedike masquerades are not accompanied by musicians but often have clappers made out of dried pods tied to various places on their costumes, resulting in a rattling sound when the performers move. Some Mgbedikes use the skull and horns of a bull instead of a face mask. Mgbedike masquerades usually use warm colors—reds, browns, and yellows, so the red Islamic prayer mat on the back of the Mgbedike depicted in this book is in accordance with this color scheme (Eli Bentor, pers. comm., February 7, 2012). (Plate 17)

Another masking genre, Okonko (Plate 18), differs from Mmanwu in that the Mmanwu costume must cover all parts of the body, while Okonko often leaves the hands and legs bare. Okonko masquerades are often adorned with horns, and the heads of some, like the masquerades documented by Boston (1960) in northwest Igboland, are topped by multiple animal horns. Tufts of raffia adorn the wrists and ankles. Some Okonko masquerades wear bulky raffia costumes topped by antelope horns and a semiconcealed cloth mask with the eyes and nose outlined with cowrie shells (Plate 19). The Okonko festival of Umuowa is celebrated in several stages. On the first day, the masqueraders will circle the market five times. During the next seven days, masquerades perform in their villages. On the ninth day, the villagers will return to the main market for dancing but without masquerades. Eight days later, a particularly secretive masquerade will come out during the night and walk along the boundaries of the community to mark the end of the festival (Eli Bentor, pers. comm., February 26, 2012).

Horse Masquerades

Rather unusual horse masquerades appear in Mali among the Bamana and among the Dogon peoples in the form of a stick hobbyhorse that is used as part of male initiation ceremonies. Although various forms of horse or donkey masquerades appear in Western Europe and the West Indies, they are either of the tourney horse or the mast horse variety. In Europe, stick horses are relegated to the status of a child's toy because they are essentially decorated broom handles. In his studies of the Dogon of Mali, Marcel Griaule (1938, fig. 150) includes an illustration of a Pullo (Fulani) masquerader in Sanga that is reproduced by Dieterlen (1989). The performer wields a lance and holds a wooden stick horse between his legs. He wears a tunic with an overshirt of long knee-length fibers. According to Dieterlen (1989, 36), Pullo costumes are worn "by very young men who have just joined the society of masks after leaving the retreat that follows circumcision." The Pullo is identified as Dyobi, "the runner," which "is the first mask to appear after the drum call. He does not dance, but rather runs here and there in disorder" as he enacts a Dogon celestial myth. It seems odd that that this form of masquerade appears in the hinterland of West Africa. It could be a case of parallel evolution; if cultural diffusion from Europe played a role, it could be that North Africa was integral to the process. Although this volume focuses on maritime diffusion across the Atlantic, a two-way movement of European and African traits also occurred across the Mediterranean Sea. Fourth-century church literature contains references to stag masquerades in Spain, and stag and horse masquerades appear in North Africa when Saint Augustine of Hippo Regius, Algeria (A.D. 354–430), preached against dressing up as these animals. Bordering the Sahara Desert, Mali had access to the North African trade as well as cultural ideas; indeed, Islam became established in Upper Guinea through this interaction.

Bettelheim (1988, 55) discusses horse costumes that appear among the male initiation masquerades "in nuclear Mande country and culturally contiguous areas of Mali." The graduating classes of the Poro society use such costumes: "The honor graduates have the right to perform on a sculpted hobbyhorse in dances held in their honor during the dry season following their graduation" (202 n. 47). A horse costume and mask are also used in the *duga* class of the *kore* society among the Bamana peoples. When the initiates dress as the *kore duga*, they masquerade as horses: "Each brotherhood within the *kore* owns two or three horses and they go from village to village, clowning, begging, and eating food continuously. The *kore duga* represents a summation of the universe, incorporating intelligence, initiation, the spirit of life, and the wisdom of the creator. As the initiate plays his role, he holds the horse stick between his legs, grasps a sword in his right hand and wears a horse mask. His dancing consists of jumps, kicks, and runs, interpreted as an enactment of man's struggle and search for a life without end. During his ride, the initiate receives gifts and food" (55).

According to Zahan (1960), who conducted research on Bamana initiation societies, the masquerader is at the same time a clown and an incarnation of the struggles and accomplishments of *kore* members. Zahan reports that in their roles as clowns, the *kore duga* went to the town of Segou, where they attended certain festivals and entertained groups of Europeans.

Stilt Masquerades

Evidence suggests that the West Indian Mocko Jumbie was influenced by the Mandinka, Mende, and related groups in the Upper Guinea region. However, with a tribal designation of "Moko," the possibility of influences from southeastern Nigeria must be considered, an idea reinforced by Day's (1852) report of an early Igbo practitioner. More likely, however, his description represents an example of a Mandinka prototype that was adopted and modified by Igbos. Whatever the case, the southeastern Nigeria connection is strengthened by interpreting "Mocko" to refer to the Moko (Efik/Ibibio) ethnic group. (See appendix 4.) However, considering the plethora of masquerades in Igboland, there are surprisingly few reports of stilt masquerades, and they generally describe short stilts that raise the performers' feet between twenty and thirty inches above the ground. These include reports from the western rim of Igboland among the Nri-Akwa clans in the northwest corner of Igbo territory, where J. S. Boston (1960, 61) reports on the Ezaga masquerade of the Ayamelum and Umueri area: "A single performer, disguised by a white suit, gives a straightforward display of stilt walking." Boston does not report on the height of the stilts, but they are probably short, since they are in a comic play he also describes. Boston believes that comic masquerades do not have a long history in the area.

Rich in masking, the eastern rim of Igboland is sparse in reports of stilt masquerades. Afikpo is in southeastern Igboland, bordering groups such as Yako and Mbembe in Cross River territory. Simon Ottenberg (pers. comm., December 19, 1997) has been studying the Afikpo since the 1950s, and to the best of his knowledge, there are no stilt masquerades in Afikpo and the surrounding region. Keith Nicklin traveled throughout the Cross River region and has studied Efik, Ekoi, Yako, and Iyala masks. He occasionally saw stilt masquerades among the Ekoi and northern Cross River groups. These performances were essentially playful and youth-oriented, intended for entertainment rather than ritual purposes. The stilts were short—three feet or less. Masks occasionally were worn, with raffia skirts more frequently but not always present. Nicklin (pers. comm., April 22, 1997) speculates that taller stilts might be found further east among the Ejagham of the Cameroon borderland as well as further west toward the Niger Delta. He suggests that the Moko were essentially Ibibio and accordingly that the northern Ibibio region might yield tall stilt masquerades. However, in G. I. Jones's (1984, 148) surveys of the masquerades of Nigeria's eastern region, including the Cross River, Niger Delta, and Igboland, the only stilt masquerade mentioned is Ekeleke.

Ekeleke are stilt masquerades from the southwestern section of the Igbo region among the western Igbo of the Kwale area and among nearby southern Edo communities. As described by Cole and Aniakor (1984, 204–10), Ekeleke masquerades perform choreographed unison dances, competitive solo dances, and a dramatic playlet involving several nonstilted masquerades. They wear long-sleeved white shirts and gloves cover their heads with white lace shawls while long-necked effigy headdresses rise about thirty inches over their heads. Philip Peek (1980, 59) has documented "Ikelike" stilt masquerades among the Isoko of the Edo of the northwestern Niger Delta fringe, and some of these performers dance on tall stilts. The Ekeleke masquerade of the Western Urhobo communities of the Niger Delta has been documented by Wilson Perkins Foss (1976). Also known as Ikenike, this masquerade wears a slender effigy headdress and an opaque veil similar to the Ekeleke of Kwale, but unlike the Kwale version, it uses stilts up to nine feet long and generally performs alone. According to Foss, among the Urhobo, costumed dances are performed for water spirits, earth spirits, and spirits of the air (*ejdo enu*), who are recipients of elaborate and daring displays of acrobatic skills by stilt masquerades. The stilts place the performer as near to the *ejdo enu* as possible because "Ikenike dancers are entertaining not only their mortal audience, they are also performing for the spirits which exist in the air" (193). (Plate 23)

Stilt masquerades are found in other areas of Urhoboland, but those of the Ughienvwe clan towns of Oto-Edo and Usiefru that Foss studied are renowned. A major spectacle consists of a high-wire performance in which the dancer swings with his stilts entwined in a rope suspended from two tall poles. Although the Ughienvwe masquerades' primary purpose is to honor the spirits of their own communities, they travel widely throughout Urhoboland. In 1956, they performed in Lagos to celebrate a visit by Queen Elizabeth II.

The Igede, an Idoma subgroup, have a tall stilt masquerade known as Ebuwo. Igede territory adjoins the Cross River region at Ogoja, and the Igede are northerly neighbors to the Igbo. The Ebuwo hails from the Uwokwu District, bordering the territory of the Ezza and Izzi Igbo. A photograph of an Ebuwo shows the performer wearing a horizontally striped body-stocking costume that covers his face and torso, a voluminous raffia skirt over raffia leggings that extend well below the performer's feet, and a broad-brimmed hat surmounted by many tall plumes. The masquerade was measured at sixteen feet, nine inches tall. (Plate 20) None of these masquerades seems to represent a prototype for the Mocko Jumbie, but further research is needed in this area.

A provenance for the Mocko Jumbie in the Upper Guinea region seems more plausible. The observation that the St. Vincent Mocko Jumbie is derived from the Mandinka (Young 1807) is echoed by Visby-Petersen (1917, 26) in St. Thomas more than a century later. The Mande encompass a broad swath of ethnic groups in the Upper Guinea. The Dan (or Yacuba) of western Ivory Coast and adjacent portions of Liberia are noted stilt masqueraders. M. C. Jedrej (1986, 78) discusses the possibility that the Mende and the Dan share a common historical origin. He includes a photograph of a Mende stilt dancer whose feet are about five feet from the ground (fig. 6). Doris Green (1996, 25) discusses the Chakaba stilt masquerade, which exists in Senegal, Gambia, Guinea, and Mali. Michel Huet (1978, 26) uses the term *triple border region* to refer to the territory where southeast Guinea meets northern Liberia and northwestern Ivory Coast. He says that the region's stilt masquerades originated in the Kono area of Guinea and spread to the Toma (a Southwestern Mande people) on the Liberian border and to the Dan in Liberia and Ivory Coast. Huet discusses Kono and Dan masks as a single entity, and his photographs show the similarity between their stilt masquerades: The most noticeable difference is that the Kono masquerade wears white rather than striped trousers. In both cases, the shirt cuffs are sewn shut to conceal the hands, the dancer wears a raffia skirt, and his feet are about six feet from the ground. The trousers end just below the dancer's feet, and the stilts are covered in cloth. Both masks are made of a net of palm-tree fiber and are black and featureless apart from a braided "tail" that dangles from the mouth region. Both wear "a conical-shaped hat with cowries, grains, leather and cloth rags [ribbons] surmounted by a tuft of white ram's hair" (27). According to Huet, the preparation of the costume must take place at the outskirts of the village. He describes the *kwuya* dance as an "escape from the gravitational forces of the earth" and states that "this breaking through the barriers, shows that man has the power to thwart the traps that are constantly being set for him by the 'witches.'" The sounds uttered by the "long mask" are high-pitched and grating.

The ritual functions of the stilt masquerades of the Toma, Guerzé, and Kissien people of Guinea are described by Beatrice Appia (1943). These masquerades include Yana and Laniboy of Ninibou village, in the area of Macenta. Yana wears a black veil decorated with small shells, a long braided "beard," and a tall bonnet with birds' feathers and small bells at the tip. He performs at biannual festivals in Macenta. Laniboy, the Great Niamou, is a secret society masquerade that dispels sorcerers from the region during ritual ceremonies. Like Yana, his feet are about six feet from the ground, while the peak of his hat is more than twelve feet high. The wooden stilts are bound in red cloth and have pads on the ends. His mask is a black net with an animal's tail attached. His bonnet is decorated with small shells and circular pieces of cut glass. He wears a short raffia skirt over blue and white striped trousers that cover his feet. The long sleeves of his blue shirt cover his hands, and a cape decorated with patches of panther, calf, and antelope skin hangs from his shoulders. He holds a cow-tail fly whisk, a sword, or a whip, with which he keeps inquisitive onlookers at bay. Laniboy is accompanied by two instrumentalists playing hourglass drums and an attendant with a pot of water in which medicinal herbs are crumbled. Using a horse-tail whisk, this mixture is sprinkled on the ground in front of Laniboy while incantations are recited. Laniboy executes a skillful dance in which he twists and turns, moves backward, shakes his hips, throws a leg in the air, and dances on one leg. It is believed that as a result of these actions, all local witchcraft gathers in front of Laniboy, where it is symbolically trampled underfoot and negated. The attendant interprets the high-pitched sounds that Laniboy makes and informs villagers of his demands.

Like Laniboy, the Gle Gbee of the Dan of Butuo, Ivory Coast, performs for entertainment and to dispel witchcraft. As one stilt dancer states, "When the gle gbee are in town there is no witchcraft, for the witches are afraid—gle gbee sometimes kills them" (Robert Farris Thompson 1974, 166). The Gle Gbee described by Thompson wears a faceless mask with a long fiber tail dangling from its center and a tall conical headdress trimmed with leather strips, animal fur, and cowrie shells. He wears a blue and white striped "country cloth" shirt and trousers that cover the hands and feet, a short raffia skirt, and a belt of bells. As he dances, he crosses his stilts before his body, sits in the air with his posterior below his knees, twists his body at the waist and swings his legs, jumps backward seven times, and at one point conspires to fall safely into the arms of his retinue. Green (1996, 25–26) calls the stilt masquerade of the Dan "Gue Gblin" and says that in Ivory Coast, they can be found in the regions of Dan, Man, Mahou, Karadjan, Danane, Biankouma, Touba, and Seguela. (Plate 22) A photograph in the Elisofon Archives, National Museum of African Art, Smithsonian Institution, shows a Dan stilt masquerade in a dark costume, raffia skirt, and a featureless black mask with a "tail" dangling from the area of the mouth.

Freetown, Sierra Leone, has a tall stilt masquerade, Mamabara, that is described as a "stilt 'devil'" and is a society masquerade that fulfils ritual purposes that dictate when it will appear (Nunley 1985, 48). Frederick Lamp (pers. comm., February 15, 1998) reports that the Temne of northern Sierra Leone have a stilt masquerader, Ya Mama. Guinea might well serve as a cultural corridor, since it borders on Senegal to the north, Mali to the northeast, Ivory Coast to the east, and Sierra Leone and Liberia to the southwest. A postcard of a street parade in Guinea around 1995 shows a tall stilt masquerade wearing a dark featureless mask and a large decorated bonnet, gloves, a pink and red shirt decorated with cowrie shells, a short blue raffia skirt, and long, brightly colored pants made of horizontal bands of different cloth stitched together. The masquerade bears a marked resemblance to present-day Mocko Jumbies in the Leeward Islands. (Plate 21)

Ebuwo, Chakaba, Laniboy, Gle Gbee, Nyon Kwouya, Ya Mama, and others share the practice of wearing raffia skirts. Considering the incidence of Mocko Jumbies in women's attire in the Leeward Islands, one might be tempted to equate grass skirts with female dress. However, West African men, even warriors, wore grass skirts, and they are often associated with priests and priestesses. All of these African masqueraders are male, and their costumes appear male or genderless. In contrast, the Fulani Woman stilt masquerade of the Dogon of Sangha, Mali, is danced by a male who impersonates a female. The mask is large and black with a coiffure or crest on top. The eyes are circled with rings of cowrie shells, and a large flap decorated with cowrie shells dangles from the lower portion of the mask's face. Shaggy ruffs of red raffia adorn the dancer's elbows and wrists, and he wears a red raffia skirt. The dancer's torso is bare except for artificial breasts in a dark brassiere decorated with cowrie shells. The Dogon live on remote plateaus amid easily defensible rock outcrops in the hinterland of Mali and Burkina Faso and were not affected by the Atlantic slave trade to any great extent.

AFRICAN MASQUERADES AND SOCIAL REGULATION

Mandinka Initiation

In Upper Guinea, masquerades play important roles in rituals that commemorate life transformations such as funerals and male initiations. They officiated at initiation ceremonies, both of males and females, and protected the ritual against sorcery. In the early seventeenth century, Richard Jobson (1623/1968, 105) published an account of a Mandinka male initiation. The young men were circumcised in the bush and then kept in seclusion in a lodge and guarded by previous initiates. Drums were played in the lodge, and the circumcised boys were protected by "a devil" (masquerade): "At night 'their Devvil' called *Ho-re* frightened people with its loud roarings," probably a bull roarer. De Jong (2007, 110) reports on a Mandinka initiation in Ziguinchor town in the 1990s that was organized during the dry season and lasted from February to April, after which the boys acquired the moral status of adult men. Circumcision was performed on the first day, and the novices remained in the initiation camp for weeks thereafter. The ritual was organized by the male elders, but the day-to-day supervision was delegated to the guardians. The novices were taught esoteric lore and instructed in the secret sign language. The end of their retreat was marked by a ritual bath in the river. A festive dance marked their reentry into society. The Kankuran played various roles during the seclusion of the novices and reinforced their enculturation: "The Kankurang's most important role was to protect the novices against the evil forces of witches. . . . While offering mystical protection to the novices, the mask ensured their submission. . . . During the performance, every now and then the mask ordered the guardians to lie down on the ground and the mask then danced on their backs" (111–12).

The masquerade's role as an instrument of social regulation included controlling the novices' behavior and chastising them when necessary. However, licentious behavior has customarily been part of the initiation ritual, and Mandinka novices are awarded a lot of latitude in this area. This is true today as it was in the seventeenth century, when Jobson (1623/1968, 146) observed that Mandinka novices were licensed to steal: "There is unto these youthes allowed a certaine licentious liberty, whereas they may steale and take away peoples hennes, or poultry; nay from the Fulbies [Fulani], a biefe or cattle to eat and banquet themselves without any offence to the lawes."

Jola Initiation

Among the Jola, Mark (1992, 50) explains that cattle sacrifice was reserved for significant occasions, such as funerals, initiations, marriages, and ratifying solemn treaties. Cattle are also sacrificed to mark secular celebrations, such as the visit of a government minister (27). Jola men were traditionally not permitted to marry prior to their initiation, which marked the accession to adulthood of an entire generation of young men. Although circumcision was once part of initiation, the two events have become separate in recent years. Initiations are marked by their secrecy and their long duration. In the latter part of the twentieth century, each Jola village celebrates an initiation approximately once every twenty-five years. De Jong (2007, 35) documents a July 1994 male initiation in the town of Thionck Essyl that was the first one held since 1962; the one before that was in 1940. During initiation, novices take up residence in the local sacred forest, which contains the community's principal shrines. Males and females have separate sacred forests.

De Jong (2007, 39) reports that in 1994, within a series of preliminary exercises, the "guardians" (initiated in 1962) taught the novices the initiation dances and ostentatiously rebuked and humbled them. Behind the scenes, the cohort of men initiated in 1940 secretly directed the ritual preparations. The procession to the sacred forest is headed by the elders, followed by the novices, who are surrounded and protected by their guardians. The day of entry into the forest "started with the killing of bulls. Every lineage killed as many bulls as it needed to feed the members of the family and their guests."

Mark (1992) describes age-grade initiation ceremonies (*bukut*) where the horns of sacrificed cattle are used for the headdress of an Ejumba or Kebul masquerade. Large numbers of cattle might be killed for the initiation. In 1965 at Niomoun, Louis-Vincent Thomas (1965) counted two hundred head of cattle being slaughtered. One of Mark's (1992, 50) informants, Nazaire Diatta, recalls that in earlier initiations, "Immediately before the actual circumcision, a black bull was sacrificed in the forest. The initiates . . . then stepped in the animal's blood." This association between the bull and the initiate helps explain the pervasive bovine symbolism of the *bukut*. After the animals have been sacrificed, the initiates' fathers fashion headgear using the horns of the consecrated cattle. The horns may come from a cow or steer; there is no requirement that they come from a bull. Mark states, "Bukut actually comprises two distinct parts: public ceremonies preceding the period in the forest [and] the circumcision or scarification and the liminal period that follow, [which] are centered in the forest" (38). Within the initiation camps of the Jola, the horned Ejumba masquerades served as sentinels and protected the initiates from supernatural threats. In their role as authority figures, they were feared and respected.

Like the Mandinka, Jola novices enjoyed some license following their initiation, comparable to an Antiguan John Bull at Christmastime. François Froger (1698, 98) explains that in Barra, Gambia, the male initiates' horned headdresses authorize "them to carry out all imaginable misdeeds, without anyone daring to complain." Leo Frobenius (1898, 146) made a similar observation: "Along the Gambia, newly circumcised youths wear for a time a remarkable costume, a peaked cap of wonderful form with a pair of ox horns attached. Dressed in this manner, those who live in remote areas cause great disorder, extort money, and take liberties. Jannequin says that Senegambian youths have a month after their circumcision to steal." Similar license existed among the Bamana of Mali. The horned headdress of the Bamana documented by

Gray and Dochard (1825, 383) was worn by a "Mohometan Prince" just before circumcision, and he danced with it for one month, when the masker and his musicians toured neighboring towns for handouts: The "young men visited several towns for the purpose of levying contributions on the provisions and purses of the inhabitants . . . or during (the prince's) exhibitions in public, be seizing on some of the spectators, whom he held fast and pretended to goad with the horn attached to the wooden figure [mask] on his head."

Masquerades and Social Control

Africans have commonly used masquerades as vehicles for behavior modification. In the equatorial part of the continent, Bakwele elders employed masked dancers representing the Gon spirit cult whenever they encountered difficulty enforcing law and order (Siroto 1969, 256–58). In West Africa, prior to colonialism, powerful masked spirits, deputized by councils of elders, often had broad governmental authority, policing, fining, judging, and sometimes executing criminals. Many of these roles were assumed by colonial authorities and eventually by national governments. The degree to which masquerades penetrated the actual governance of local communities varied among ethnic groups. Kasfir (1988, 7) states, "In the Dan country of Liberia and Ivory Coast . . . the mask system penetrated the social system, rather than remaining its symbolic counterpart. Masks personified and carried out real political roles from the judgment of criminals to the settlement of land disputes. This also happened in southeastern Nigeria and Cameroon."

During an "Egbo [Ekpe] ceremonial" in Calabar, in mid-nineteenth-century Nigeria, a missionary, Hope Masterton Waddell (1863/1970, 265) describes the harsh character of the masked and straw-clad "Egbo runners" who roamed the streets on "Grand Egbo day," keeping the streets clear for the procession: "Egbo runners disguised with black masks and wild dresses of dry grass and sheep skins scoured the streets in all directions, each wielding, however, only a long rod instead of the terrible cow-skin whip, and without striking anyone. [However] one rash fellow tried to cross [the street] but was so hunted down by three runners who followed him closely . . . till he reached the very beach and plunged into the river."

For the acephalous Igbo, masquerades were most often attached to men's societies, and some masquerades had regulatory functions, implementing sanctions against individuals who violated communal norms. Many masks still radiate an aura of power and still serve effective regulatory roles. Simon Ottenberg (1989, 58) confirms that masquerades of the Afikpo Igbo such as *okpa* can still wield coercive power: "A devout Christian, annoyed by an *okpa* playing in front of his house, violated secret-society rules by trying to drag the masquerader away. The next day dozens of *okpa* from all over Afikpo tore the man's house down (and those of neighbors as well) and killed his animals. . . . The police took no action."

Among the Mandinka, De Jong (2007, 134) documents a fatality resulting from masquerade infringement. In 1987, Solo Thiouda, a noninitiate and an outsider who belonged to the Manodi, a Balanta subcategory, attempted to challenge a Kankuran masquerade and was killed the following day by a crowd of outraged masquerade guardians: "Solo encountered this Kankurang when he was walking down the street in Marsassoum. No one knows why, but the two came to blows and Solo, who was a strong man, partially undressed the mask. . . . The next morning, the guardians came to Solo's compound. Each one was armed with a club and the young men were accompanied by two Kankurangs. . . . Solo and his uncle were both beaten to death. Solo's corpse was subsequently burned." The matter went to trial nine years later, but the public was solidly in favor of the release of the suspects as defenders of Mandinka culture, and all were given suspended sentences or found innocent.

Francis Moore (1738) alludes to the eighteenth-century Mumbo Jumbo's role in social control: "This is a thing invented by the men to keep their wives in awe, who are so ignorant (or at least are obliged to pretend to be so) as to take it for a wild man. . . . Whenever the men have any dispute with the women this Mumbo Jumbo is sent for to determine it. . . . When the women hear it coming they run away and hide. . . . He will send the people for them and then whip them. . . . There are very few towns of note but what have got one of these coats."

Park (1799/1983, 29) confirms the Mumbo Jumbo's function: "This is a strange bugbear, common to all the Mandingo towns and much employed by the pagan natives in keeping their women in subjection." More recently, the Sengko masquerade also had a baton and "would beat any initiated female he found on the paths" rather than assembled in the village square (Weil 1988, 172). Sengko was central to the *barrango*, women's initiation ceremonies, and "when the *barrango* was still performed, the masker might substitute a sword for the 'tongue,'" or baton (159). Kumpo masquerades also helped to maintain social cohesion and traditionally worked to mete out discipline, particularly to women and uninitiated boys (Mark 1983, 12).

These reports emphasize the use of masquerades to control women's behavior, but Weil (1988, 288) shows that masquerades also apply rules "to male behavior, particularly that requiring cooperation for a public purpose."

As initiation masquerades, Kankuran and Sengko assisted in the discipline of both initiates and the uninitiated. By enforcing respect for authority, the masquerades reinforced the norms of social conduct. Weil (1971, 285) outlines the "rule-application" function of Mandinka masquerades: They apply rules created at villagewide meetings and punish "malingerers, adulterous women, sorcerers, gossips, and the like." The masked figure and its secret association offer this age grade a mechanism for establishing its credibility. Furthermore, during communal rituals, "respect for the authority of the masked figure is to be expressed by obedience, cooperation, and generosity" in terms of music, dance, and food (288). Children generally fall beyond the purview of masquerades but are nevertheless scared of being chased by adult maskers: "This fear is symbolized in the manner in which adult masquerades sometimes swoop down on children, chasing them, threatening to thrash them, and even to capture them" (Ottenberg and Binkley 2006, 25).

SPIRITUAL FUNCTIONS OF AFRICAN MASQUERADES

Upper Guinea masquerades predate the importation of Islam or Christianity to the area. According to oral traditions, the Sengko is about five hundred years old (Weil 1988, 160). Kankuran is also one of the oldest masquerades found among the Mandinka. Its presence was documented in the late eighteenth century by Francis Moore (1738) and Park (1799/1983), and it is doubtless much older. The same is true of the Mandinka Kumpo, with written descriptions of the masquerade dating from as early as the 1730s. In 1720–21, John Atkins (1737, 56) traveled to Gambia and Sierra Leone and asserted, "The Religion here, if it may be called such, is their Veneration to Gregries," or gris-gris. Gris-gris are various types of spiritually charged objects, including shrines, masquerades, and amulets, that can be manipulated for practical ends. Although Islam has been making inroads into Upper Guinea for centuries, indigenous shrines retain ritual importance for many communities. According to Jola traditional beliefs, Emitai, the supreme being, created the *ukine*, spirit shrines (singular *boekine*) to establish specific ways for individuals, families, and communities to seek help in the resolution of their problems.[1] An important group of entities associated with the *ukine* were the spirits of benevolent ancestors. Baum (1999, 96) explains, "They were summoned to the shrine of the dead, Kouhouloung, during all funeral rites and memorial rites and during the periodic greetings of the Kouhouloung shrine. They also assisted at the rites of the family shrine, Hupila, and the various lineage-related shrines." Moreover, "These ancestors served as intermediaries between the place of the dead (*kahoeka*) and their living descendants. They were also sources of various types of information that they revealed through their appearance in dreams. They gave advice and warnings to their descendants among the living" (46).

Sacred forests constitute the traditional locus of Jola political and spiritual authority, and Jola warriors received symbolic protection by wearing roots from trees noted for their strength and endurance. Sometimes, earth from a shrine altar is placed in a goat or antelope's horn and then sealed, creating a gris-gris and thereby invoking the power of a particular *boekine* wherever the item is carried (Baum 1999, 97).

Among the Jola and others in the Casamance, cattle could be used to purchase spiritual beneficence. Cattle are sacrificed in large numbers only on two occasions: the *bukut* initiation and funerals (Mark 1992, 93). After nineteenth-century funerals, horns of sacrificed animals were used to decorate the housing compound of the deceased. Funerals are profound occasions that celebrate an elder joining the ancestors, and the presence of masquerades is considered crucial. At the interment of a Jola elder, horned Ejumba offer kinetic testimony to the stature of the deceased. As a further homage, the funeral bier might be decorated with cattle horns. A typical Jola bier consists of a low frame structure with a solid base and cowlstaffs (lateral poles for the bearers); the body, wrapped in burial cloths, is placed in the bier. Behind the corpse's head is a latticework shelf that holds seven sets of cow horns (see Thomas 1958, appendix, plate 32). At funerals, cattle horns were also associated with finding individuals who harbored ill intent against the deceased and who may in some way have contributed to his demise. Mark (1992, 93) states, "The funeral bier, decorated with horns, was carried around the village while the pallbearers asked the corpse whether the death was caused by unnatural means. If the actions of the *kussay* [witches] were suspected, either because the deceased had been killed by witchcraft or because his death was retribution for the fact that he or someone in his family had been an *assay* [witch], the corpse would so indicate by the route along which it led the pall bearers."

For African art historian Robert Farris Thompson (1974, 184), raffia signifies danger and mystery. Raffia masquerades are thought to embody the bush; through them, humans are seen to be able to manipulate the power of the wild for the community's benefit. Thompson points to raffia masquerades such as the Yoruba Egungun as making full use of this property. The Kankuran family of figures are similarly covered from head to midcalf by green or dried leaves (*fita*) or by shredded tree bark (*fara*). The *fita* masquerades use leaves from

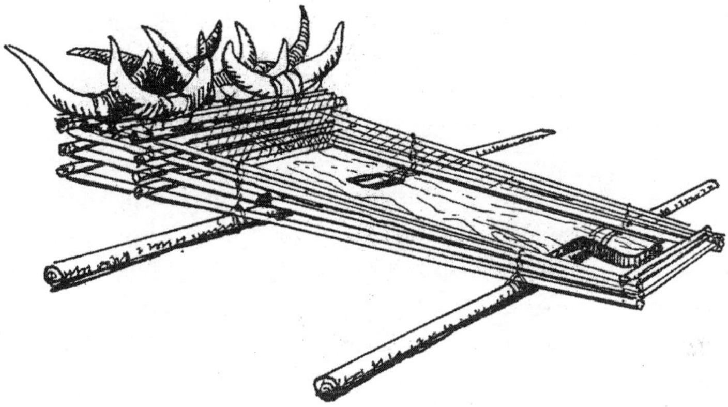

Fig. 5.2. A Jola funeral bier for a respected adult male, Ziguinchor, Basse Casamance, Senegal, ca. 1950. Behind the corpse's head is a latticework shelf that holds seven sets of cow horns. From Louis-Vincent Thomas, *Les Diola* (1958).

the talo tree (*Detarium senegalense*; the ofo tree of the Igbo) whose spiritual qualities are spread by means of dances (Weil 1971, 282). West African ethnic groups share an abiding concern with the actions of antisocial beings that use supernatural means to bring misfortune on members of society. Witchcraft generated by such covetous individuals was a constant concern, and masquerades such as Kankuran and Kumpo were used to undo hexes and identify sorcerers, and intermittently cleanse the community with healing rituals. The *fara* masquerades use the shredded bark of the *fara* tree (*Piliostigma thonningii*) as a means to generate righteousness. The *fara* tree grows in low-lying savannah and is believed to possess an intrinsic goodness that combats wickedness; consequently, where possible, it is "often planted in the household compounds to protect the compounds from evil forces. Pieces of the bark are also chewed to gain similar protection" (Weil 1971, 161–62). In addition to the Sengko masquerade, whose framework superstructure is draped with dark reddish-brown *fara* bark, "Four other [Kankuran] masquerades . . . are primarily or exclusively constructed of the bark: the *kangkurang wulengo*; the *kangkurang mumuneyo*; the *jamba-kangkurang* and the *finso*" (161). In Sengko, Weil explains, "The fara bark is symbolically categorized, in turn, as fire and wind" (177). He continues, "The *sengko* masquerade is . . . a social mechanism to encapsulate and control the forces of nature, to harness them . . . to help the community fight the community's antithesis, the evil powers of nature resident in the bush and females, with the only forces thought to be powerful enough to accomplish the task, other evil natural forces, the strategy is to literally and figuratively, to fight fire with fire" (175). Weil further explains, "The Mandinka perceive everyday whirlwinds as being djinns or devils (*sey-tano*).... Among the Mande Bambara, whirlwinds are directly associated with femaleness. Whirlwinds are disruptive, can stir up dust that blinds" (168). In fighting fire with fire, the Sengko's dance becomes a whirlwind.

The Balanta use the term *afara* to denote "a person who, driven by jealousy or envy, uses supernatural means to gain personal advantage at the expense of others while causing them direct harm" (Mark 1992, 30). For the Balanta, "an important form of protection against sorcery was the *jambacoss*, a combination of healer and clairvoyant who worked to detect and disable the *afara*" (31). Among the Jola, the *bukan bujak* (literally "good people") served similar purposes, often while wearing the horned Ejumba mask. The good people are a group of individuals gifted in wizardry and with the ability to locate and nullify witches. The *bukan bujak* are pitted against antisocial and jealous *kussay* or witches (26; singular, *assay*). Both the *kussay* and *bukan bujak* were feared because of the awesome and dangerous power they possess, but the latter use their invisible powers to combat evildoers. Among the northern Jola, only men who have demonstrated their clairvoyance in detecting evil intent are allowed to wear the horned Ejumba masks; "they, and perhaps they alone, would have access to esoteric information about the masks' meaning" (119). According to Mark, "Clairvoyance was usually inherited. Thus, the son of a man who had worn an *ejumba* mask was likely to be selected to dance with the mask himself. To be selected one had to be an excellent dancer. To provide him with added strength and endurance, he was given special medications" (108).

The Ejumba masquerades are adorned with small mirrors, which are believed to unmask and reveal witches, who, seeing their true nefarious nature reflected in the glass, must either flee or die (Mark 1992, 104). The mirrors are reminiscent of those worn by warriors wore to repel bullets and arrows (Baum 1999, 97). Thus, the masquerades served as a safeguard against disease and against attacks by *kussay*. They were the physical embodiment of *bukan bujak*. The authority of masquerades as an instrument of social regulation was buttressed by their recognized spiritual power and their ability to guard against malevolence. Both the Ejumba of the Jola and the Mandinka raffia masquerades protected initiation rites and generally combated sorcery that can spread discord in the community and harm people.

Senegambia today is predominantly Muslim. Islam was embraced by some Mandinka as early as the seventeenth century, and most of the caste of Mandinka leatherworkers at Wuli converted to Islam before the nineteenth century.

Weil (1988, 157) maintains that "the Mandinka of Wuli practice a syncretic form of Islam which combines elements of pre-Islamic religion with Islamic elements." Many of the Jola did not convert until the end of the nineteenth century, but the religion spread rapidly during the first quarter of the twentieth century. According to Mark (1983, 5), Islam adversely affected the Jola's annual rain ceremony, which involved the sacrifice of a black bull (black being the color of the clouds that that bring rain). Because traditional religion was aimed at practical outcomes, Islamic elements were incorporated in the region if they were considered functional. Masquerades such as Kumpo were used to undo hexes and identify sorcerers. In time, Muslim amulets and Koranic charms came to be viewed as valuable in this area. Moreover, Francis Moore (1738) reports that in the eighteenth century, oaths were taken on the bark-costumed Kankuran (117, appendix I, p. iv). This no longer occurs; instead, Mark (1983, 9) explains, this function has been taken over by the Muslim ulema (clerics), while Weil (1971, 290) reports that various suras of the Koran are used for this purpose.

AFRICAN MASQUERADE INSTRUMENTS

Jola Initiation Dances

When I studied the masquerades, music, and dance of the Igede people of Nigeria, I discovered that the primary drums included an all-wooden hollowed-log slit drum that was beaten with sticks and a set of three drums, each played by a different drummer, who squats over his drum and beats it with his bare hands. *Ubah* is the generic Igede name for drum, and it is a wooden cylinder with skin covering one end. *Ubah* is also the name of the lowest-pitched of a set of three instruments. *Egbong*, a long baritone drum, and *okpirih*, a short tenor drum, complete the set. Parallel instruments appear in Upper Guinea. The Jola have a slit drum used in initiations, while the Mandinka have a three-drum ensemble that consists of a lead drum (*sabaro*) with two accompanying drums (*kutirindingo* and *kutiriba*) (Charry 2000, 195). The Mandinka drums resemble those used by their Wolof neighbors and are beaten with a short stick in the right hand and a bare left hand.

Al-Bakrî (1068/1981, 80), a Spanish geographer, saw a slit drum in the eleventh century in the ancient Upper Guinea city of Ghana, where the royal meeting "is announced by the beating of a drum which they call *duba*, made from a long hollow log." Regarding Jola sacred forests where initiations take place, De Jong (2007, 35) states, "A particular lineage is said to be the 'owner' of the forest and also 'owns' the drums to be used during the initiation ritual. Every sub-ward has a pair of drums (*emumbi*, a wooden slit drum, and *fujundum*, a huge wooden cylindrical drum with a leather drumhead). Both of the drums are considered sacred."

Slit drums are venerated in most societies that have them. In the western Ivory Coast, Dan acrobatic dances in which prepubescent girls are thrown into the air are accompanied by the two-toned slit drum. For the Igbo, the slit drum is known as *ekwe*, while the Igede call it *ogirigboh*. It is traditionally a signal instrument and has two lips that are beaten with sticks to reproduce the local language's tonal structure. Among the Igede, the *ogirigboh* is considered the voice of the ancestors, and a chicken is sacrificed on it to improve its sonority; blood and feathers remain stuck to it.

While the slit drum is sacred and reserved for special use, the standard Jola instruments used for dancing include a set of three or four drums (*bugarabu*, *bugarab*, or *bugareb*) played by a single person (Charry 2000, 22). Because of the secrecy surrounding male initiations held in Jola sacred forests, De Jong (2007) is unable to provide much information about the dances performed. More information is available, however, about the dances associated with female initiation in Thionck Essyl, which had strong Mandinka overtones:

> At midnight the women started a procession through the ward accompanied by three drummers playing the *kutiring* (Mandinko drums). . . . The next morning all the girls were led into the female sacred forest. The drummers played a variety of rhythms, some of which were typical of Thionck's fertility dances (*enyalenay*), others of Jola dances (*bugarabu*), others again of Mandinko initiation rites (*diambadong*): the selection of rhythms was rather eclectic. The women and novices . . . spent the day at their sacred forest and the night in their hut at the ward's central square. . . . At night, the beating of the drums in the hut could be heard throughout the ward. After a week of seclusion, the novices left the sacred forest. . . . Led by the "queen of initiation" (*kuya mansa*), the initiates then danced the *eking* (from Mandinko, *kin*), the appropriate dance for the closing of Mandinko initiations. (47–48)

Mandinka and Maninka Initiation Dances

Drums are an essential component of Mandinka and Maninka circumcision and excision ceremonies, both prior to the ceremony itself and when the young people return to their homes. Charry (2000, 205) states, "In the days and nights leading up to the operation there is drumming and dancing culminating on the eve of the operation when *soli si* takes place, an all-night event with singing and dancing. The exhausting dancing might have an anesthetic effect on the children and is intended to give them courage." Moreover, at night, while the initiates are confined within the sacred forest, "the beating of drums in the forest could be heard" (De Jong 2007, 40). At this time, the Kankurang figure will dance to the accompaniment of the *kutirindingo*, *kutiriba*, and *sabaro*, and the masquerade may be brought out during the healing period to combat any problems. According to Charry (2000, 205), "The return from the bush is marked by a celebration involving drumming, dancing, and singing called *boloko dennu don bo* in Maninka or *ngansing jenjengo* in Mandinka. . . . The main Maninka drum rhythm and dance associated with circumcision and excision is called *Soli* (in Guinea) or *Suku* (in Mali). . . . In the Senegambia boys dance *Chingo* and girls dance *Lenjengo* (which is more of a recreational dance). Their mothers may dance *Nyaka julo* on this occasion." De Jong (2007, 118) quotes a Bambara informant living in Ziguinchor as stating, "When the circumcised boys had recovered they left the bush and for days and nights at a stretch people danced the dance of the leaves (*diambadong*)." Charry (2000, 237) points out, "Both the name and the shape of the Mandinka sabaro and the Wolof sabar drums are very similar . . . but in contrast to the Mandinka ensemble, fixed at three drums and rarely augmented, Wolof sabar-based ensembles consist of more drums and can accommodate large numbers of players. In the case of celebrations with many participants, the Mandinka ensemble is still not augmented, rather, many ensembles play for smaller groups within the larger crowd." Charry also describes the return of newly circumcised boys from the bush: "Different families hired their own drummers who escorted them through the village, meeting up in the large town square, where separate circles formed" (237 n. 37). De Jong (2007, 120, 122) describes the male novices' exit from the sacred forest beginning with a ritual bath:

> Each group that has come to wash the novices has usually managed to get the materials required for the fabrication of a Kankurang, which is dressed on the spot. The river shore is crowded with the masked figures each shouting and slapping their machetes. With the drummers playing the rhythm of *diamadong*, the groups of novices go home one by one in festive processions. When they enter town, the drumming attracts women and girls who start to participate in the procession dancing the special steps of the *diambadong* rhythm. . . . Every now and then the girls and women have to flee the

> masquerade and hide in nearby compounds. But the performance is not meant to send them away and women actually enjoy the play. . . .
>
> After a meal the novices and guardians are allowed to rest. . . . [Later] in the afternoon the passage of the novices to their new status is formally concluded. While the men are seated in easy chairs . . . the women gather in the courtyard where the drummers play the various rhythms. One particular rhythm is considered appropriate for this special occasion: *kindongo*. The new initiates, wearing a new colorful caftan, are . . . led one by one into the circle of women. They then dance the *kin* [*kindongo*].

Igbo Masquerades: Musical Dimensions

The type of music used with Igbo masquerades differs from genre to genre and by type of mask within each genre. Igbo drums are many and varied, but the Igbo do not use a double-ended drum slung from the neck of a musician (like the Mande dundun), and the hourglass drum does not traditionally appear south of the River Benue and east of the Niger. Instead, open-ended skin drums are ubiquitous; the drummer may place the drum on the ground and squat on it, or he may hold it between his knees. The term *Igbo drum* is used in the Caribbean to describe drums of this kind. Cynric A. Williams (1826, 22), for example, distinguishes between a "gombay" drum and an "ebo drum," describing the latter as "made of a hollow tree with a piece of sheepskin stretched over it." Such drums, often played in sets of three by three drummers, accompany Igbo horned masquerades. Sets of three or more open-ended drums sometimes are mounted in frames and played by a single drummer. *Ekwe* slit drums, either played alone or in pairs, are beaten with sticks to provide the heavy beats for the masquerade's dance. Metal gongs and basketwork maracas normally round out masquerade ensembles, enabling the creation of the various rhythms for different types of masquerades. At festivals, Bentor (pers. comm., February 26, 2012) often saw "a central orchestra seated under one of the market canopies that provided music for all masks at that event." The Igbo masquerades that roam the village streets are customarily accompanied by a hand-carried talking slit gong (see Nicholls 1993, 250). In the photograph included in this book, the Mgbedike masquerade (Plate 16) is accompanied by an Oji Onu masquerade with a small slit gong and an Oja talking flute. The flute is particularly associated with the Oji Onu masquerade, which speaks in squeaky sounds through a voice disguiser; Oji Onu can only understand the language of the flute. Mgbedike masquerades are not customarily accompanied by musicians but have clappers made out of dry pods attached to their costumes. Such rattles and other accoutrements, including relatively large brass bells, are often parts of a masquerade's regalia and add to the acoustic quality of the performance.

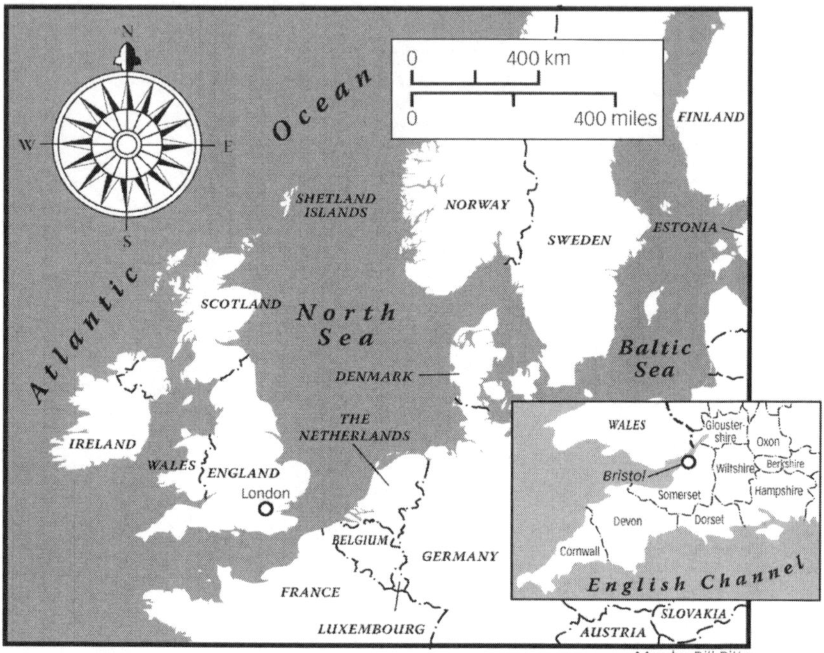

Map by Bill Pitts

Western Europe

Plate 1. Straw masquerade, New Year's parade, Styrian Salzkammergut, Austria, 1989. The tall pole makes it resemble a besom (an old-fashioned broom). Courtesy Eva and Michael T. Criss.

Plate 2. Bull mask, New Year's parade, Styrian Salzkammergut, Austria, 1989. Courtesy Eva and Michael T. Criss.

Plate 3. St. Nicholas and Knecht Rupprecht, New Year's parade, Styrian Salzkammergut, Austria, 1989. Courtesy Eva and Michael T. Criss.

Plate 4. Mannequin with straw mask and skirt displayed in County Hall, Enniskillen, County Fermanagh, Ireland, June 2003. Courtesy Molly Carter.

Plate 5. Robert Collins's painting of Waterley Bottom Mummers at the Hunters' Hall, Kingscote, Gloucestershire, England, 2010. Courtesy Robert Collins. www.rcollinsart.com

Plate 6. The ox skull Broad of the Waterley Bottom Mummers appears at Robert Collins's art exhibition, Francis Kyle Gallery, London, May 10, 2011. Courtesy Richard P. Chidlaw.

Plate 7. The shaggy Onyunwunyu masquerade dances during the New Yam Festival of the Igede people of Nigeria's Benue State, 1978. Photo by Robert Nicholls.

Plate 8. Kankurang pair, Banjul, Gambia, December 26, 1970. Their green-leaf costumes are adorned with the shredded red bark of the *fara* tree. Courtesy Roderic Knight.

Plate 9. Frafra "hunter/warrior" from northeastern Ghana wearing the *nugo illa* helmet with antelope horns, ca. 1973. Courtesy Fred T. Smith.

Plate 10. Horned Makalo dancers, Banjul, Gambia, December 26, 1970. Courtesy Roderic Knight.

Plate 11. Ejumba *bukut* initiation mask, Niomoun, Casamance, Senegal, 1965. Courtesy Museum Haus Völker und Kulturen, Sankt Augustin, Germany.

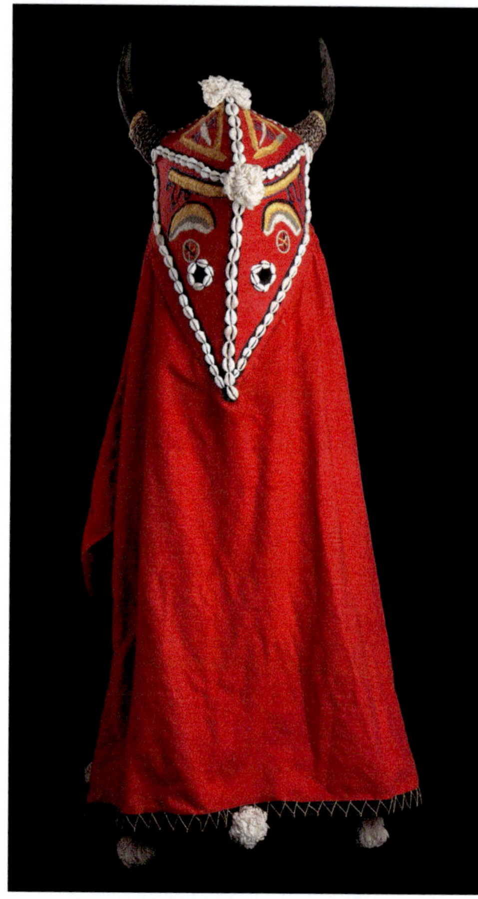

Plate 12. Red Spear mask, 1967. Artist: Lang Kuta Demba. Mandinka, Gambia; Kiang Central Division; Bumari. Collector Peter M. Weil. Photo by Mark Craig. © President and Fellows of Harvard College, Peabody Museum of Archaeology and Ethnology, 993-18-50/12824.

Plate 13. Ejumba mask from Casamance, Senegal, acquired in 1886 by the Berlin Museum. Note the bajumbi beads used as decoration. Photo by Claudia Obrocki. Courtesy Staatliche Museen zu Berlin, Preußischer Kulturbesitz, Ethnologisches Museum.

Plate 14. Igbo Okoroshi Ojo mask from Mgbala Agwa, southeast Nigeria, carved in wood by Anozie, ca. 1948. Its local name, *Death Has No Friend*, is taken from a proverb. Nigerian National Museum at Lagos. Courtesy Herbert Cole.

Plate 15. Bull-horned Mmanwu masquerade of Njima Club, Arondizuogu, dancing at Oror village, Arochukwu, Abia, Nigeria, during the funeral of the Eze Aro, the paramount Aro chief, January 1988. This mask is atypical and may be an elaboration of the Mgbedike type. Courtesy Eli Bentor.

Plate 16. Mgbedike masquerade from Akokwa, Imo, Nigeria, with a bull's skull and horns, January 14, 1988. The lower part of the costume is natural raffia. Two eagle feathers, a common status symbol, are attached to the skull. The white fiber around the head is produced by combing out the woven plastic bags used for cement and fertilizer. On the back of the head is a cluster of *mkpiri* seedpods, which rattle when the masquerade dances and jumps. The mask on the left is called Odudu, and the one on the right is Oji Onu. The musician at front right is playing a small slit gong, while another is blowing an Oja, the ubiquitous talking flute of the Igbo. Courtesy Eli Bentor.

Plate 17. Back of the Mgbedike masquerade adorned by an Islamic prayer rug used as a shawl, Akokwa, Imo, Nigeria, January 14, 1988. The rug is for adornment only, and no Islamic connection is intended. Courtesy Eli Bentor.

Plate 18. Horned mask from Umodim village, Umuowa, Imo, Nigeria, March 12, 1988. This mask, one of many used at the Okonko Festival, appeared on the festival's first day (Eke of the Igbo four-day week), when the five villages of Umuowa sent their masquerades to the main market. The antelope horns show a connection to hunting. The masquerade wears a woven body stocking costume with raffia apron, white gloves, and a pair of sashes across the chest. Two members of the entourage are holding cow horns; these are not bugles but are used for drinking palm wine. Courtesy Eli Bentor.

Plate 19. Okokonko masquerade, Umuowa, Imo, Nigeria, March 12, 1988. The masquerade wears a bulky raffia costume topped by a pair of antelope horns as well as a semiconcealed cloth mask with the eyes and nose outlined with cowry shells. His bared hand carries a machete, and he is jousting with another machete-wielding masquerade. Courtesy Eli Bentor.

Plate 20. Ebuwo stilt masquerade of the Igede, Uwokwu, Nigeria, 1981. Courtesy Gabriel Idikwu.

Plate 21. Dan stilt dancers, Ivory Coast, 1982. Courtesy M. and A. Kirtley/ANA.

Plate 22. Stilt dancer (possibly Gue Gblin masquerade) watched by villagers, Ivory Coast, ca. 1970. Courtesy Robert Harding World Imagery.

Plate 23. Stilt masquerade of the Urhobo people, northwestern Niger River Delta, Nigeria, 1976. The shadows reveal that the masquerade is jumping. Courtesy Perkins Foss.

Plate 24. Fancy Dress pair known as Kakabotofo, Fante, Elmina, Ghana, 1974. Courtesy Herbert Cole.

Plate 25. Fancy Dress or Kakabotofo with bitonal face, Fante, Elmina, Ghana, 1973. Note the similarity to the Sensay mask in Plate 42. Courtesy Herbert Cole.

Plate 26. Clydie Murrain wearing a horned headdress, John Hughes Village, Antigua, December 1994. Courtesy Lornetta Prince.

Plate 27. Raffia masquerade in Frederiksted, St. Croix, ca. 1980. The full-bodied costume of the raffia bear of the past finds an echo in the scanty costume of this performer. Courtesy *St. Croix Avis*.

Plate 28. Pitchy Patchy during Emancipation Day parade, Frederiksted, St. Croix, July 3, 1995. Photo by Robert Nicholls.

Plate 29. Elaine Urgent performs a spoof of Alex Faucett, a store owner, during Emancipation Day parade, Frederiksted, St. Croix, July 3, 1995. Photo by Robert Nicholls.

Plate 30. Donkey mas' during St. Croix Festival, Frederiksted, 1997. Courtesy Estelle McIntosh.

Plate 31. Magnus the Mocko Jumbie performs, St. Thomas, ca. 1950. Courtesy Don Toschi.

Plate 32. Fiesta de Santiago de Apóstol, Loiza Aldea, Puerto Rico, July 1997. The mask evokes the defunct Mother Hubbard masquerade of the Virgin Islands. Photo by Robert Nicholls.

Chapter 6

MASQUERADE PROTOTYPES IN WESTERN EUROPE

VARIETIES OF MASQUERADE

Bush Masquerades: Straw Bear, Straw Staffan, Strawboys

Acknowledging that customs from diverse societies migrated into the Caribbean, this exposition draws broadly from rural masquerades across Western Europe. Bear disguises made of straw or burlap were found in England, Russia, Czechoslovakia, Estonia, and Germany, and raffia masquerades were also found in Sweden, Denmark, and Norway. Gunnell (1995, 105) establishes that straw figures must have been known in southern Scandinavia before 1300. In Russia, the bear masquerade smeared soot on his face, and his costume was constructed of withered pea stalks, which were "quite effective as a disguise when bound neatly around the arms, legs, and body of the mummer" (Warner 1977, 15). In Czechoslovakia, such a pea stalk costume was worn by a farm laborer, and "a straw tail was stuck on and a bell hung around the neck" (15). The choice of costume material was often guided by pragmatic concerns: "In the North Atlantic and elsewhere in Scandinavia people tended to use to use materials that were closest at hand, and if skins were not available then they would use something more practical. In the Faroes it would seem that this material was often seaweed" (Gunnell 2007, 302). Territories on the periphery of Western Europe, such as the Faroe Islands, sometimes provide cultural fossils by maintaining customs that have diminished in other areas less isolated from cultural crosscurrents. The Faroes had a tradition of Shrovetide mumming associated with the festival; the character was known as Lengeføsta (Long Fast) and was either "a personification of the festival" or "a bugbear used to frighten children at Lent; a costumed figure" (Svabo 1966, 290, 291). According to an 1821 account, Langeføsten had "a large coat of seaweed which dragged behind her like a tail, and a rusty black hook in each hand" (Gunnell 2007, 303). In accordance with the idea of using materials that were easily available, mummers in Finland used "fur coats turned inside out and animal-like masks made of birch-bark" (Kulmanen 2007, 609). Furthermore, a 1602 account reports that Irish mummers "enter in this order. First a boy with a lighted torch, then two [men] beating drums, then the maskers themselves, two by two, then another torch. . . . They were dressed in shirts with ivy leaves sewed on, thickly in some places, and thinly in others, and over their faces they had masks made of rabbit skin, with holes to see out of" (Ó Catháin 2007, 745).

Animal impersonations and masquerades in leaf costumes are ancient disguises in Europe and seem to be somewhat interchangeable. Leaf-clad mummers, *Wilde Mäanner undwilde Weiber*, were standing figures in the Nuremberg *Schembartlauf* (processions), which existed from about the middle of the fourteenth century (Rudwin 1920, 33), while "in parts of Sweden, the name 'julbock' was applied to the living yuletide figure wrapped in straw" (Gunnell 1995, 107). Better known as Halm-Staffan, a masquerade resembling a sheaf of corn was associated with farm visiting on St. Stephen's Day (December 26). According to Terry Gunnell (1995, 101), "The farm visits were led by a figure completely wrapped in straw or corn, and was sometimes known as *Halm-Staffan* ('Straw Staffan'). According to an account from Uppland, the performer himself 'was tall and well built but dressed in the straw costume he became so large that he could hardly squeeze through the doors of the building where the singing was going to take place.'" In another Uppland area, the party comprised "several variously costumed figures including a *staffansbock* ('Staffan's goat') and three or four *staffansgossar* ('Staffan's lads') who were so completely wrapped in straw that their faces were rendered indistinguishable. In parts of Dalsland, the same costume was worn by a figure known as the *julegoppa*," a birdlike character (102).

Equivalent raffia masquerades are found in Ireland, the Shetland Isles, and Austria. In the fen lands of England, on Straw Bear Tuesday or Strawbower Day (the day after Plow Monday in January), the Straw Bear was led through the streets on a strong chain by a group of farmhands. On January 16, 1886, England's *Peterborough Advertiser* reported, "The 'straw bear' also favoured us with a visit, capering to a dulcet accompaniment on the concertina." It also appeared in Whittlesey, Cambridgeshire, in 1911, but had died out by 1914. It was revived in 1979 and continues into the present.

In Killesher, one Irish raffia masquerade is known as Jack Straw. The character "was clothed completely in straw, with a tall conical mask of the same material rising almost from shoulder level to a point" (Gailey 1969, 57). Elsewhere in Ireland, straw-covered masquerades are known as Strawboys, and in the Shetland Islands, they are known as Skeklars. In Ireland, woven barley was used for the conical hats, while in the Shetlands, the material was oat straw (Gunnell 2007, 303). An account by R. Menzies Fergusson (1884, 303)

Fig. 6.1. Skeklars at Brough Lodge, Fetlar, Shetland, Scotland, ca. 1900. Photo by Sir Arthur Nicholson. Courtesy Shetland Museum, Scotland.

first published in the *Orcadian* in 1857 includes a description of straw-clad Shetland mummers at Halloween: "Eyes, mouths, or noses, they had none, nor the least trace of countenance. . . . They were all veiled, and their head dresses or caps were about eighteen inches in height, and made of straw twisted and plaited. Each cap terminated in three or four cones of a crescent shape, all pointing backwards and downwards, with bunches of ribbons of every colour waving from the points of the cones."

In 1977, Venetia Newall (1993, 62) saw Skeklars dance a reel: They "were dressed in leggings, skirts and capes of woven straw; tall hats from the same material were drawn up and back into three peaks, decorated with three ribbons." According to Newall's informant, Tom Anderson, the practice "goes back hundreds of years: they did it for weddings" (61). The garb of the Irish Strawboys also included pointed hats and ribbons. In some parts of Ireland, they sallied out on All Hallows Eve, while they appeared at wakes in County Kerry and elsewhere; however, in County Kerry, as in the Shetland Islands, "Strawboys were most commonly associated with weddings" (MacDonogh 1983, 19). (Plate 4)

Gunnell (2007, 324) points out that "as with the other Shetland traditions, this custom of mumming at weddings offers a potential bridge between Irish traditions and traditions from western Norway and Sweden." A band of Strawboys could number as many as ten or even twenty, and they had a recognized leader who was distinguishable by having a larger, more elaborate crown placed at the top of his conical straw mask. In Austria at New Year's, various masquerades parade the streets, including a raffia masquerade with a tall pole extending vertically from the top of the head that resembles a besom, an old-fashioned broom. (Plates 1 and 2)

Horned Masquerades

In Bavaria, in southern Germany, there are still "young fellows who dress as if for Carnival. With blacked faces and terrifying masks adorned with cows' horns they rush, dance, or dawdle through the villages. Housewives gladly give them something so as to get these scary figures away from their frightened children" (Ruland 1978, 23). In medieval Europe, the bull had strong competition from the stag and appeared alongside likenesses of other animals. In contrast to rural masquerades further north, miniatures of Romans in Alexandria wearing animal heads in the mid–fourteenth century show them neatly dressed in small capes and culottes (E. K. Chambers 1903/1967, 1:frontispiece). The *Schembartlauf* procession in Nuremberg, Germany, featured the bear, wolf, goat, stag, and other masquerades: "The day preceding Shrove Tuesday, is called in the Rhineland *Hirsmonntag* (Stag Monday), as the speaker is masked as a *Hirsch* (stag)" (Rudwin 1920, 34). Mare-skin masquerades performing in "Gadding" revels were well-known in the Channel Islands in the 1620s–30s (Ogier 1998, 55). On South Uist, an island in the Scottish Hebrides where Margaret Fay Shaw (1955, 14) lived between 1929 and 1935, "Hallowe'en was a night of much jollity, when the house was invaded by visitors in the ugliest disguises they could contrive of sheepskin and unraveled rope." Bull, calf, horse, bear, and goat masquerades made farm visits during Christmas in sixteenth-century Scandinavia. Sweden and Denmark had stag disguises: Notes Gunnell (1995, 121), "Both horses' and bulls' heads are reported to have been used as masks in certain area of Boohulsen, in Sweden." Describing Shrovetide masking, Olaus Magnus (1555/1972, bk. 13, chap. 42, p. 463) refers to people wearing bulls' or goats' heads and making the appropriate animal sounds. Accounts from both Bø Telemark and Forsand Rogaland in Norway mention the use of the head skin or skull of a calf's or cow's head for a mask (Weiser-Aall 1954, 25–26). Descriptions of quêtes by Yule Goats demonstrate both customary and risqué behavior: "The *julebukk* used to pay visits on farms, stopping to receive a near compulsory offering of food and drink, and sometimes to dance" (Gunnell 1995, 112). An account from South Trøndelag tells how the Julebukks "were usually furious so they butted people, and the first one each goat butted (lit. 'stabbed') was supposed to become his wife" (Lid 1928, 42).

Fig. 6.2. Halloween disguise, Uist, Outer Hebrides, Scotland, ca. 1930s. Photo from Margaret Fay Shaw, *Folksongs and Folklore of South Uist* (1955). Courtesy Routledge Taylor and Francis, London.

Female masqueraders apparently were actively engaged: According to Tedre (2007, 410) in some places, the Estonian Jõuluhani (Christmas Goose) "tended to be carried out by women and girls." Like the goat figure, the goose was seen as bringing good luck and peace and as giving health and strength (411).

In England's medieval West Country, Twelfth Night celebrations included an ox-horn dance performed by "six people wearing horned headdresses . . . around a wassail tree. [An] oxhorn cake . . . was placed on the head of one of the dancers." According to Lambdin and Lambdin (2000, 190) the purpose of the dance was "to awaken the spirit of the earth in order to assure the coming of spring." In 1687, John Aubrey (1881, 40) who lived near Malmesbury, Wiltshire, just a few miles from Tetbury, wrote of "cakes at Twelfetyd [Twelfth Night] when they wassell [wassail] the oxen." At that time, a song was sung to the oxen in the ox house. According to Cawte (1978, 83), "There are six principal areas [in Britain] of animal disguise, horses in Kent, South Wales, Cheshire, and North Lincolnshire. Horse and sheep south of Sheffield, horses and bulls in Gloucestershire and a few deviations such as the hobby horse with the Horn dancers at Abbots Bromley," in Staffordshire. Cawte explains Christmas Bulls also toured districts in South Wales and Monmouthshire just after the turn of the nineteenth century (94). Edmonds (1858, 277) shows

Fig. 6.3. Tapanipukki goat, Tammela, Finland, 1928. The costume is made from a fur coat and goat's horns. Photo by Esko Aaltonen. Courtesy Museovirasto, Kuva-arkisto (National Board of Antiquities), Helsinki, Finland.

that in the early nineteenth century, during the twelve days of Christmas in Penzance, Cornwall, some "'guise dancers' occasionally masked themselves with the skins and heads of bullocks, having the horns on." Furthermore, Alan Gailey (1969, 89) states that bull-hide costumes were also worn in the eighteenth and nineteenth centuries in the Scottish Highlands: "In parts of the west Highlands of Scotland and in the Outer Hebrides . . . a group of lads used to go around the township at night, and one of their number was enveloped in the cured hide of a bull, to which the horns and hooves still attached. When the group came to a dwelling . . . they ran around sun wise, the man in the hide shaking the horns and hooves, while the other beat on the hide with sticks."

The "Horn Fair" held at Charlton, London, in the eighteenth century was an annual carnival of cuckoldry in which participants wore antlers and horns from cows, rams, and goats. In Dorset and Wiltshire, according to Christina Hole (1978, 65), the Christmas Bull performer's body was "concealed in some cases by the animal's hide, with the tail hanging down from behind, and in others by rough sacking." She continues, "The Christmas Bull was a man wearing, or supporting on a pole above his own head so that he seemed to be

Fig. 6.4. Tetbury Bull, Gloucestershire, England, 1975. The bull has bottle-top eyes, and the wooden face is covered with whitewashed hide. It is considered to display England's national colors because the boss (rosette) on top is blue and its ribbon red. The head of the bull is mounted on a pole held by the performer, who is concealed by three feet of Hessian sackcloth. Photo by Hector Paroussi. Courtesy Richard P. Chidlaw.

wearing, a hollowed-out bull's head, complete with horns and glaring eyes of bottle-glass. . . . The Bull went around the parish at Christmas time. . . . None knew when he might or might not appear" (65).

The bull mask apparently disappeared from the market town of Tetbury, Gloucestershire, sometime after 1975, when it was photographed. Reg Wilkins said that the Tetbury Bull had been with the Wilkins family since his great-grandfather's day—at least 170 years ago. By the late nineteenth and early twentieth centuries, the tradition was waning, and the Tetbury Bull last performed with the Gloucestershire Wassailers in the 1930s. During the 1975 photo session, it was examined by Richard Chidlaw as part of his ongoing research on West Country Broad masquerades and the accompanying wassailing songs. The Tetbury Bull had real horns that spanned twenty-seven inches. They were yellowed with age and had black tips. Its wooden head was covered with whitewashed hide with the bases of black wine bottles for eyes. The head was mounted on a pole, and the whole structure stood four feet high. Brown sackcloth hung about three feet from the lower part of the face to conceal the performer's body. The bull evidently had to be visible on a dark winter's night: its face was white, the boss between the horns, which supports the rosette, was blue, and the ribbon red—that is, it bore the English national colors. Reg Wilkins told Chidlaw that the bull represented "beef," and for the members of the Wilkins family, the goal of mumming and wassailing was to collect a little extra money at Christmastime. Consequently, the Wilkinses jealously guarded the bull. The gentry in the local big houses welcomed the performances and exchanged food, drink, and money for visits. Some wassailers carried two wassailing bowls, one for drink, the other for collections. Affixed to their bowl, the Wilkins wassailers also carried a small tree decorated with tinsel and ribbons. The mask was referred to locally as the Tetbury Broad.

A broad was an imitation ox or bull that appeared, usually with wassailers, at Christmas in some villages of the South Cotswolds/Wiltshire border. In the villages of Horton and Kingscote, the broad was known for chasing girls and children and making them scream. The literature indicates that it was known by the 1830s and probably earlier (Ditchfield 1896, 29; Maylam 1909, 70). The Ooser of Melbury Osmond of Dorset performed until the 1890s (Oates and Wood 1998, 42). The Ooser had a bull-horned mask that was made of painted wood and worn with a cow skin. An ox is a castrated bull, and *Broad* is actually a familiar name for an ox, perhaps signifying its girth. Chidlaw states that "'broad' was a name that a farmer might call his ox, like Buttercup or Daisy for a cow. I have found it used in wills from the 16th to 18th century" (pers. comm., July 15, 2010). Teams of powerful oxen were used as draft animals to plow the fields for barley, wheat, and oats grown in the thin soil of the Cotswold Hills. As many as six paired oxen might be yoked to the plow. A popular local wassailing song involved multiple references to the ox: "Here's to the Ox/Broad and to his right eye/ear/long horn/tail/hind leg," etc. Another wassailing (pronounced "walsailing") song that mentioned the ox was sung at Leighterton in the 1870s and was collected by Chidlaw from Alice and Florence Frankcom and Sally Dickenson in July 1969:

We'll sail, we'll sail all over the town,
The bread it is white and our ale it is brown,
Our bowl it is made of the malpaling [maple] tree,
With the walsailing bowl, I'll drink unto thee.

Chorus
Drink unto thee, Drink unto thee,
With the walsailing bowl, I'll drink unto thee.

Here's to the ox, and to his long tail,
May God send our master a fine keg of ale,
A fine keg of ale, as we may all see,
With the walsailing bowl, I'll drink unto thee.

Chorus

Now here's to the ox, and to his hind leg,
May God send our master a fine Christmas peg [pig],
etc.

Now here's to the ox, and to his long horn,
May God send our master a good crop of corn,
etc.

Now here's to the ox, and to his right eye,
May God send our master a nice Christmas pie,
etc.

Now here's to the ox, and to his right ear,
May God send our master a happy new year,
etc.
(Cawte 1978, 146)

When interviewed by Chidlaw in July 1970, a man named Hatherell who lived in Wickwar remembered the Horton Bull: "Lads of 14–22 years of age would come round to the lawn in front of the house (Little Sodbury Manor) and they'd have the Horton Bull. . . . The bull would roar and go at the girls and make them scream. They had a bowl with decorations up over it, ribbons and garlands of evergreen. They'd drink and pass it round. It was made of white wood. There were 6 or 7 chaps" (Richard Chidlaw, pers. comm., August 12, 2010). Two Gloucestershire folklorists and singers, Gwilym and Carol Davies, made a Tetbury-style bull with red flashing eyes around 1995 and periodically bring it out at Christmas in conjunction with a version of the Gloucestershire Wassail (Gwilym Davies, pers. comm., August 3, 2010).

At Christmas 1969, in the market town of Dursley, Gloucestershire, Chidlaw and others started the Waterley Bottom Mummers, a group that still appears. It is based on the traditions of several local villages as recalled by elderly people and incorporates the Wassail Song from Tresham. In addition to

Fig. 6.5. Waterley Bottom Mummers outside Dursley Church, Gloucestershire, England, December 24, 1972. From left to right: King George, Niddy Noddy (with wassailing bowl), Boney Part, Father Christmas, Bellsy Bob (with dripping pan for money), the Doctor, Jack Vinney (the doctor's assistant), Saucy Jack, the Dragon, the Broad (ox skull on a pole). Photo by *Dursley Gazette*. Courtesy Richard P. Chidlaw.

a horned broad made from the skull of an ox (mounted on a pole with its jaw attached by elastic so it can clack its teeth at people), the group includes King George, Niddy Noddy (with wassailing bowl), Boney Part, Father Christmas, Bellsy Bob (with dripping pan for money), the Doctor, Jack Vinney (the doctor's assistant), Saucy Jack, and a dragon. Chidlaw (pers. comm., December 13, 2011) says that none of the Waterley Bottom Mummers wear reversed jackets, but "Father Christmas and Boney Part have hats covered in all sorts of 'tat' including plastic flowers, flashing Christmas lights, feathers, birds' wings, etc." He adds, "This is as much due to the person who made and wore the costume as to any tradition."

Artist Robert Collins produced a painting of the Waterley Bottom Mummers in 2010 after observing a Christmas performance at the Hunters' Hall, Kingscote, Gloucestershire, in 2008 (Plate 5). According to Chidlaw, the painting illustrates "the first fight. The second is King George and Boney Part. The doctor only cures the second death. The Dragon gets driven out and dies outside the door to general cries from other mummers (yet to enter). . . . Mary Tinker is the character wearing women's clothing. The words are:

In comes I, Mary Tinker, ale, wine and cider drinker
I told the landlord to his face, his chimney corner was the place, where I sat and blacked my face, when Jones's ale was new.
Me mother, me mother, she killed a fat hog and that you can plainly see
She gave me the gut the bladder to blow
And left me a hurdy-gurdee."

The Waterley Bottom Mummers, replete with Broad, attended the opening of Collins's exhibition on May 10, 2011, at the Francis Kyle Gallery in London. (Plate 6)

An interesting variant of the bull masquerade, the Old Tup, is performed at Christmas and New Year's in the Chesterfield area near Sheffield, England. It uses a ram's head with a cloth draped over the performer and is constructed like a mast horse, but the head is not a skull. The Old Tup is sometimes made of wood, but at Worksop "a dried ram's head" was used, and similar preserved heads were used in Brimingtonn Clowne, Ecclesfield, and Stavely (Cawte 1978, 112). Boys who could not procure real heads might use burlap sacks instead: For example, "At Upperthorpe the corners of the sack were tied to represent horns" (112). Tup was accompanied by a team of players who often blackened their faces. The characters included a butcher with a leather apron and a knife, an old man and woman, and sometimes a player "who carried a bowl to catch the tup's blood" (113). Other players might include a doctor (to revive the stabbed creature), and a mumming-style recitation was enacted. Ian Russell (1979) recorded forty-one Old Tup groups from fourteen villages in the northeast Derbyshire area from 1975 to 1978. He points out that a popular folk song, "The Derby Ram," is derived from the Old Tup play, and he maintains that "the Tup is arguably as active today as it ever has been" (401). Contemporary Tups utilize modern features: The Harthill Tup in South Yorkshire, for example, incorporates flashing lights for eyes. In this instance, according to Russell, "a large head, based on a cardboard box with a moving jaw was covered in simulated white sheepskin with black horns modeled from papier-mâché and wire, and mounted on a stick with a black cover" (422).

Horse Masquerades

The horse disguise is an old and ubiquitous masquerade type. As with other animal disguises, they are first known in medieval Europe through the condemnations of clerics. In addition to costumes that consisted simply of a cured mare's skin, there are several constructed horse types, all of which can be referred to as hobbyhorses. The stick horse is essentially a decorated broom handle with a carved and painted head. They are children's toys but have served as masquerades in Mali. The sieve horse has a large framework and is confined to Europe. The tourney horse is distinctive because it is designed to give the appearance of a horse and rider; the horse's superstructure is suspended from the performer's waist. In southern Britain, the tourney horse was common entertainment in the late medieval and early modern periods and was regularly associated with the morris dance. Stubbes (1583, 189) decried them as "hobby horses and other monsters" that were part of the Lord of Misrule processions that defiled the church and churchyard. The one depicted in England's Betley stained-glass window (ca. 1509–36) shows the basic costume makeup. The hobbyhorse received a few mentions in the fourteenth and fifteenth centuries but became prominent in municipal parades and midsummer pageants in London and elsewhere in the sixteenth century, when churches sometimes used them to collect money for candles and repairs (Cawte 1978, 23). In England, the tourney horse declined in the middle of the seventeenth century. In the words of Cawte (1978, 82), "The records are less frequent after 1625, and after 1641 there is no evidence that the tourney horse existed, except as an isolated survivor at Abbots' Bromley, and Chester, and Salisbury." A version of the tourney horse appears as the donkey in the Leeward Islands, but there it seems to have evolved from the *burroquito* (little donkey) of the Spanish islands.

The mast horse comprises a horse's head mounted on a pole and held by a covered performer. Some were made of a real skull, but an adult horse's skull is heavy, and smaller skulls may substitute. According to Cawte (1978, 127), Dick the Wild Horse of the Antrobus Soul Cakers of Cheshire, England, used a blackened and varnished donkey's skull. The stuffed skin of a horse's head or a carved wooden head, possibly with nails for teeth, might also be used. A mast horse was recorded in 1736 in Kent, England (83–87), 1793 in Ireland, and 1798 in Wales. In England, various records of the skull-and-pole variety of horse masquerade exist from the early nineteenth century, including Old Ball the Easter Horse in Lancashire, who chased people and held them for money (140), and Dick the Wild Horse, who appeared in a Souling Play performed primarily around All Souls' Day. At Frodsham and Higher Whitley, the skull was secretly buried from one year to the next and exhumed for the next season (126). The Mari Lwyd (Gray Mare) of South Wales consists of a horse's skull on a pole with a white sheet to cover the skull and the carrier. The head was decorated with colored ribbons and taken wassailing during the Christmas period. When the members of the party gained admission to a house, they received food and drink, the horse chased people, and performers danced (94–102). Mummers in Dorset normally had a horse of the mast variety, such as Tommy the Pony in Symondsbury and Evershot, but it had a wooden head (148–49). A description of the Hooden Horse of Kent, England, states, "The horse was made with a wooden head on a pole about four feet long, the jaw was hinged and moved by a string, the hoodener was covered with a dark cloth. The head was decorated with horse brasses or rosettes, and ribbons and caddis [coarse worsted cloth] for a mane. . . . The team consisted of four to eight men [with a] fiddle, tambourine, triangle, or melodeon" (Cawte 1978, 86–87). The Lair Bhan (White Mare) of Ireland involved a sieve horse with a frame that could be up to eight feet long. It appeared, for example, in Kerry on May Day 1846. It also appeared on All Saints' Eve and went about at Christmas with the Wren Boys, when it "reared and kicked at those who refused money" (153–56). An 1819 account from West Glamorgan states, "The most conspicuous figure is the *Aderyn Bee y llwyd* bird, with a grey beak; this is formed by the skeleton bones of a horse's head, furnished with artificial eyes and ears, and highly decorated with ribbons and coloured paper; it is borne by a man whose person is concealed beneath a long cloth; his part is to imitate the amblings, curvetings, startings, and kicking of the horse; he is attended by a groom, whose business it is to sooth his affected angers and fears, and keep him within proper bounds" (94).

North Lincolnshire is historically significant for hobbyhorses, which accompanied plow-jagging gangs. Documented by Mike Pearson (2007), plow jagging was a way for farmworkers to obtain alms on Plow Monday. Nongivers risked having their front path "jagged" (torn up) by the plow. The practice is recorded as early as 1597, when ten men in costume plowed an illegal furrow across a churchyard (88). However, few plows were seen in plow plays after 1875. In an 1898 photo of a West Halton gang, the twenty-two figures consist of two hobbyhorses and two horn blowers as well as black-faced females, tribal warriors, soldiers in uniform, and four men in tall decorated hats (190). North Lincolnshire hobbyhorses evolved from the tourney horse, but they were unusual because they were made from the outer rim of a large farm sieve that hung on two straps from the performer's shoulders. A small wooden horse's head was attached to the front, and man and sieve were draped in a long cloth. Moreover, by the beginning of the twentieth century, sieve horses and riders began to mutate: The rider wore a cloth horse mask and became one with the steed. In place of horse/rider, there is a horse/horse—or, rather, an apparition. As the masquerade evolved, the mask's similarity to a horse decreased, and the animals came to "resemble cows or dogs or polar bears or ghosts" (193). Although the performers carried whips, with which they kept the line together, there was now no rider left to goad the horse; whips instead were turned on innocent bystanders. Such creatures usually presented a frightening appearance, and in Scunthorpe it was reported that they "run after folks an' scare 'em nigh ter dead!" (95). Hobbyhorse performers were usually tall men and were expected to fight the horses from other teams. Fights took place between rival villages on the opposite side of the Trent, and the Burringham and Burton gangs regularly came to blows. The hobbyhorses would try to knock each other over, with the winner declared "Cock of the North," champions for that year (193).

Mummers

Mumming troupes historically appear throughout rural Britain, but those in the West Country are of special interest because the costumes they wear bear some similarity to Caribbean masquerades such as Pitchy Patchy. Mumming was customary Christmas entertainment, and according to the perambulation mode, they performed on the street or were invited into residential parlors or pubs. Mummers utilize memorized text and recitation and often include monologues of some length. In Britain, the term *mummers* (mommers) was used in the sixteenth century in a dramatized work by Ben Jonson, whose masques were written in concurrence with James I's preference for the antimasque, a lowbrow spectacle. Jonson's *Christmas, His Masque* (1616) describes a visit by Christmas mummers: "Old Christmas leads in the ten entertainers who include personifications of Misrule and Mumming—the latter dressed in a masquing pied suit with a visor [mask], his torchbearer carrying the box and ringing it" (Billington 1984, 104). Billington (1984, 113, citing Sandys 1852) includes a description of a "mock play" performed at Christmas in Cornwall: "The leading Fool figure, dressed as the devil, was Old Father Christmas, personified as a grotesque old man, wearing a large mask and a wig, with a huge club in his hand. A second comic character was the doctor and his dress was a cross between a mountebank and white-faced clown. They called him 'a sort of Merry Andrew to the piece,' is dressed in some ridiculous way, with a three-cornered hat and painted face. Finally there was a female character, played by a woman; she dressed in the costume of her great-grandmother."

Sandys (1852) maintains that some of the properties of the fool in mumming plays of yore were carried by Old Father Christmas, who resembled the medieval devil Beelzebub, with calf skin, grotesque face, and club. Animal disguises transitioned into the persona of the fool—for example, in a rapper-dance performance that William Henderson recorded in Durham in 1866, the leading fool, Tommy, wore an animal head and skin and was accompanied by a man/woman, Bessy (Billington 1984, 114). Mummers readily appropriated the fool's accoutrements—for example, the bladder on a stick. At a Whit Ale

Fig. 6.6. Marshfield Paper Boys of Gloucestershire, England, perform the King William play, December 26, 1986. Photo by Brian Shuel. Courtesy Collections Picture Library (http://www.collectionspicturelibrary.co.uk).

morris dance at Kirtlington in 1858, the fool carried a staff with a bladder and cow's tail at opposite ends: "His duties were to belabor the bystanders and to clear the ring for the dancers who followed him" (Howkins 1974, 5). In a report on Newfoundland Janneys, Caroline Carver (1975, 66) similarly states, "The mummers—also called janneys or fools—wore elaborate costumes. They sometimes carry 'swabs,' codfish bladders blown up like a balloon and filled with pebbles to make them rattle. Attached to sticks, these were used to beat the passerby." Billington (1984, 52) argues that "the entertaining Fool kept his coat and changed his name. Three names appear most frequently and by the end of the eighteenth-century were interchangeable: Zany—the Italian equivalent of Johnny—, Merry Andrew, Jack Pudding. . . . also the Antick." *Zany* had already become current usage for the fool by 1637, when D'Avenant's Masque, *Brittania Triumphant*, contained an antimasque that included "a mountebank, a grave doctor, a zany, a harlequin, an old lame charwoman, and two pale wenches." "The Venetian *montebanc* was an offshoot of *Commedia Dell'Arte*" (Billington 1984, 58), an Italian theatrical form that flourished in Europe from the sixteenth through the eighteenth centuries. Commedia dell'arte doubtless influenced urban masquerading, as seen, for example, in the modern Venice Carnival, where masqueraders disguise themselves in elegant Harlequinesque costumes, often with tall or elaborate headwear. To a degree, commedia dell'arte also influenced Carnival masquerading in the West Indies. (See Plate 50)

By the time the play texts of British mummers were documented in the second half of the eighteenth century, they were well established as an oral tradition. Mummers combined costumes with the enactment of folk plays, usually of the hero-combat genre—typically, St. George fighting the Dragon—and often include a death-resurrection scene. Alex Helm (1981, 27) states, "In a combat of champions, one is killed and revived by a doctor. Occasionally the combats are multiplied. Characteristic performers include St. George, Turkish Knight or Black Prince, 'Female,' Doctor, Jack Finney, Devil Doubt, Big Head. These names, however, are subject to endless local variations." Billington (1984, 112) maintains that the centuries-old *St. George and the Fiery Dragon* "seems to have been based more on Fool-Droll than combat drama."

Some mumming troupes in England's West Country wear shredded cloth costumes similar to the Caribbean Pitchy Patchy. Mummers troupes with ribboned and fringed costumes in England's West Country include Hackwood Park, Overton, Minstead, Nettley Abbey Mummers, and the Marshfield Paper Boys of Gloucestershire, who substitute strips of paper for cloth and who perform King William plays, as on Boxing Day 1986. Crookham mummers have highly decorated ribboned costumes, as do other troupes in Hampshire. Those worn in Uttoxeter, Staffordshire, are equally colorful, as are those in Symonsbury in Dorset.

EUROPEAN MASQUERADES AND SOCIAL REGULATION

Europe's peasant culture has long been subjugated by the church and feudalism, but vestiges of egalitarian sociopolitical control models nevertheless can be recognized within skimmingtons, while inversion rites such as the Lord of Misrule games and yearly pageants of transition such as carnivals also served as agents of sociopolitical transaction and sometimes transformation. Such communal "taking care of business" represents an ancestral form of social coercion, akin to West African models. However, agrarian communities were fighting a rearguard action against the incoming feudal and church-imposed social organization. The decentralized and segmentary clan systems of earlier times were overwhelmed by a centralized administration, while Christian doctrine encroached on traditional customs.

During the Reformation, guising was treated harshly: According to Hayward (1992, 11), "Branding was a punishment for beggars in sixteenth-century Scotland and more appositely for guising, the Kirk Session in Elgin in 1597 ordained that for any traditional celebration of Yule, or 'enormiteis,' 'disorder or baudice' in the 'obseruation of superstitious dayis and vaniteis thairof,' the punishment was to be the 'burnyng of thame on the cheik.'"

The records of the Royal Court in the Channel Islands show that on September 25, 1624, three men were arrested "for having by night gadded under the form of an artificially re-skinned mare." On April 3, 1630, five individuals were charged with having been "disguised by night under a most hideous and shocking form" (Ogier 1998, 55). British courts often found their January dockets crowded with Christmastime offenders. On January 18, 1702, Scotland's Falkirk Court Sessions rebuked seven men who "confessed that upon the last night of December last they went about in disguise in an unseemly manner" (Hayward 1992, 163). Following the Civil War and revolution of the 1640s, the Reformation had a chilling affect on masquerading in Britain, but on play days or "daft days," the laboring classes fought back. An account from Evershot, Dorset, reports that in 1656, "Thomas Hurlston . . . wrapt in a bull's hide, came among the rabble to the meeting-house door, and threw in an horn, with which he struck off part of the Preacher's lip" (Besse 1753, 231). The schism between laboring-class mummers and civil and parish authorities remained in evidence at least until the middle of the twentieth century. The use of masquerades for social regulation was more radical and activist in medieval Europe than was the case in West Africa. Alford (1978, 59) maintains that the horned masquerade known as the Ooser of Melbury Osmond in Dorset could be "brought out for the punishment of village wrongdoers in a Skimmington or Rough Music."

Skimmingtons

"Rough music" or "charivari" survived until the end of the nineteenth century and demonstrates how masquerades once played a role in behavior modification. In England, such ritualized humiliation was generally known as a skimmington or, according to E. P. Thompson (1991, plate 15), as "Riding the Stang" in the North of England and "Cool Staffing" in the West Country. It was administered to people who offended village morals in some way, such as engaging in marital violence or infidelity. The word *skimmington* is derived from the skimming ladle used by West Country women for making cheese—and for assaulting their husbands. The name "Mrs. Skimmington" denoted a husband-beating spouse. Natalie Zemon Davis (1971, 100) states, "Husbands beaten by their wives were led by a noisy, masked and costumed throng through the town facing backwards on an ass." A "stang" or "cowlstaff" sometimes replaced the ass. The demonstration was usually led by unmarried youths, singing and wielding "hand-bells, gongs, cow horns, whistles, tin kettles, rattles, bones, frying pans" (E. P. Thompson 1991, 506). Animal horns were often paraded: "Where the reputed infidelity of the wife was the occasion, a petticoat or shift would be carried in the procession, along with horns, brewing grains and other symbols of cuckoldry" (477). (To this day in the Eastern Caribbean, "He's been horned" refers to a cuckolded husband.) This symbolism reached its peak with the "Horn Fair" held at Charlton (north of Blackheath): By the seventeenth century, this annual carnival of cuckoldry was held on St. Luke's Day, with "a riotous mob [meeting] at Cuckold's point near Deptford, and march[ing] from thence in procession . . . to Charlton, with horns of different kinds upon their heads" (Grose 1788/1931, 193). A "Horn Fair" poster from that period shows antlers, cow horns, ram horns, and goat horns sprouting from participants' hats (E. P. Thompson 1991, plate 24). Horns were not only used to signal adultery but were a general skimmington artifact. They were used against a wife beater in Southeast England around 1840, when "a procession was formed. First came two men with cow horns; then another with a large old fish-kettle round his neck. . . . Then came the orator of the party, then a motley assembly (Thompson 1991, 506). In 1782, when a butcher at Newport, on the Isle of Wight, married "an elderly maiden of good fortune," he was greeted by such an assembly, "each with a pair of rams' horns fixed on their heads and a drummer which they had hired" (483). Horns were also used in cases of petty theft. For example, "in 1691 in a Warwickshire village two offenders were musicked by the smith (dressed as an old woman) and a farmer (wearing buck horns) at the head of a hundred others" (516). Like Kankuran, the license enjoyed by the horned figure legitimized this means of community enforcement. The Christmas Bulls of Dorset and Wiltshire were "given the freedom of every house and allowed to penetrate into any room" (Hole 1978, 65).

Bringéus (2007, 692) makes the case that the purpose of Knut mumming with straw effigies in southern Sweden was social control, citing the Christmas 1910 edition of the *Hallands-Posten*, which recalled, "When Knut was on the move . . . [h]e punished misers, idlers, weaklings, hypocrites, thieves, arrogant rascals of both sexes, gossips, envious wretches and so on." According to Bringéus, "Before literacy became widespread . . . social criticism was formulated not in words but in actions. This way of communicating is part of an ancient tradition. . . . It was thus a custom among the common people to make fun of objectionable individuals by means of effigies" (696). Hanging up a straw man from the roof truss when the builders were not treated to topping-up beer occurred in Sweden and Denmark. In 1962, in northern Skåne, two men were acquitted of this crime "because they were following a generally known and accepted custom which could not cause offense to the general public" (695). Another aspect of human interaction with straw effigies is that of the scapegoat, used to punish foes and unpopular figures: "Burning a human effigy on a Lenten bonfire was a widespread custom in Switzerland" (696). In the mid-twentieth century in North London, children annually constructed Guy Fawkes dummies stuffed with hay, leaves, cloth, and newspaper and burned them on a bonfire each November 5. Straw figures have featured in combat genres and pageants going back to the Renaissance. In Denmark, a Shrovetide festival, Fastelavn, was held in preparation for Lent. During Fastelavn, jousting competitions were held in which young men tilted at straw effigies: "In the afternoon around 3–4 P.M. the Strawman was placed in a suitable place in the village and the riders now enjoyed themselves for an hour or so by lifting it off its foundation with a lance" (Bregenhøj and Larsen 2007, 261).

Children's Culture

Christine Eike (2007a, 509) points to the role that the Julebukk has played in controlling children's behavior: "The oldest known Norwegian record dealing with this figure states that the *raageit* (pole-goat) was a mask used to frighten children. Furthermore, it was often said that such a fear was a good thing because it . . . made them obey: it was an early form of pedagogy."

As is often the case, children's culture perpetuates old practices and sometimes contains cultural fossils, as is evidenced by the use of masquerades for social regulation at Christmas. Similarly, the "trick or treat" aspect of Halloween, formerly the Celtic New Year, includes the idea of rewards and punishment. At these times, cultural norms were on display, and ancestors were appeased to circumvent any ill will against the living as a consequence of their transgressions. Christmas is a time of goodwill as well as a time when errant individuals traditionally came under scrutiny and behavior modification applied. In Britain, "good" children found gifts in their stockings, while "naughty" children (hypothetically, at least) got coal or ashes. The disciplinary aspect was also pronounced in parts of Germany, where this reward-punishment dualism was personified by a compassionate St. Nicholas, whose authoritarian side was embodied by a baleful alter ego known as Black Peter or Knecht Rupprecht, "a mysterious character . . . dressed in skins, or straw, and [looking] very fierce" (Hole 1978, 70). (Plate 3) He often carries a bunch of switches to distribute to parents, and while "good children get cakes for saying their prayers; the bad ones are beaten with ash-bags" (Alford 1978, 116). The Rupprecht figure has a host of names and manifestations, depending on the region: "In Southern Germany it is known as the Krampus . . . in Silesia as

Bartel or the Wild Bear" (Ruland 1978, 17). Krampus is shaggy, has a goat mask and horns, and brandishes a bundle of birch twigs (Bruce 1958). In Styria (eastern Austria), Krampus goes around the village with St. Nicholas, and they are sometimes accompanied by men wearing straw mantles and wearing antlers (Cawte 1978, 201).

In Britain, E. P. Thompson (1991, plate 26) indicates that the "diabolical mask" of the horned Ooser of Melbury Osmond had a hinged lower jaw and that it was supposedly used to frighten unruly children. In the Dorset village of Symondsbury, England, a hobbyhorse, Tommy the Pony, sought out offenders at Christmastime by psychic means. Cawte (1978, 149) reports on the performers' dialogue:

> Now Tommy, you go round and tell me the little boy that pinches his mother's sugar.
>
> Now Tommy, you go round and find out the little girl who throws the bedclothes off in the morning whilst dreaming about her sweetheart.

A description of the chained British Straw Bear growling and straining against his tether on household doorsteps suggests that it could have been used as a parental threat, although this is not explicitly stated. However, Gailey's (1969, 14) description indicates that Irish Strawboys may not have been used for child discipline: "They were seldom turned away from any door in the country side. . . . Exceptions occurred only at houses where there were small children who might too easily have been frightened by the strangely-garbed, gruff-voiced visitors."

SPIRITUAL FUNCTIONS OF EUROPEAN MASQUERADES

Masquerading in Europe is very ancient, seemingly extending back to the decentralized clan systems in place prior to the implementation of Christianity and feudalism. In Scandinavia, Gunnell (1995, 105) explains, there is a "good reason to believe that the figure of the straw man *Halm-Staffan* probably goes back to pagan times." However, the use of terms such as *pagan* is controversial because it implies religious content. The term *pre-Christian* is less provocative and simply refers to a time that predates Christianity. *Traditional* or *non-Christian* might be even more appropriate because there was no neat cutoff between the pre-Christian and Christian eras, and traditional ideas and practices lingered in out-of-the-way rural areas.

Straw Effigies

Gailey (1969, 75) maintains that the practice of mummers carrying straw effigies when visiting homes in southwestern Scotland, Ireland, Belgium, and Holland was intended to personify vegetation and the bounty of nature. Sweden and Denmark had a harvest custom of making a dummy in human form. In Skåne in Sweden, "The last sheaf at the end of the harvest was called *stådare* (beggar) or *käring* (old woman), typically disparaging anthropomorphic names. . . . In south-west Skåne [such] sheaves were given disparaging names such as . . . 'lazybones' or 'dawdler.' . . . Similar customs were known in Denmark. . . . As a means of making fun of the person who finished the harvesting last, people in Skåne could also place a straw man outside his home" (Bringéus 2007, 695).

In Denmark, harvest festivals with straw effigies included dances with straw dolls to fiddle tunes. An informant born around 1865 remembers that young men rode around with a straw maiden and then danced with it in the big hall (Bregenhøj and Larsen 2007, 261). The practice of creating life-size straw dolls was fully articulated in Sweden and occurred in Switzerland and Austria. For Sweden and Finland, neighbors across the Baltic Sea, the day after Epiphany is known as St. Knut's Day, January 7 (sometimes also January 13). In his research on "mumming in effigy in Southern Sweden and the custom of perambulating with stuffed straw dummies," Bringéus has discovered that "straw was an ideal, easily available material for making these human-sized effigies. With a few old garments (a coat, trousers, and a hat or headscarf), it was not a problem making a dummy known as a *Knutsgabbe* (Knut man) or *Knutskäring* (Knut woman) because St. Knut's Day marks the end of Christmas in many Nordic countries" (2007, 685). St. Knut symbolically drives out the sweetness and lightness of Christmas, and on St. Knut's Eve, a hideous straw dummy would be secreted into someone's home with mocking or joking intent: "Effigies were normally placed in stealth under cover of darkness, in front of a farmhouse door" (688). From there, the dummy was taken from farm to farm: "Anyone who kept the man could be given a straw woman the next evening, the idea being that she was supposedly out searching for her husband, or vice versa" (692). One year, a Knut man equipped with an oversized stuffed penis was passed to various households—in four villages over three weeks—of wives with absentee husbands (691). Some Knut men were provided with "Knut passports," letters or notices crudely spelling out alleged infractions. According to one of Bringéus's informants, "They would put a man like that in the privy. . . . If you needed to pee you just had to wait" (692).

In some cases, the straw effigies satisfied the people's need for religiosity. Gailey (1969, 85) includes a reference to an inanimate Irish straw figure with religious overtones at Inishere in the Aran Islands, Galway: "Old women got some straw and clothing and made up an effigy which they took from house to house, saying a prayer as they crossed each threshold. Every person in the houses they visited took a straw from the effigy to make a cross which was then nailed to a roof timber for the duration of the following year."

Although no discussion of a spiritual dimension to the British Straw Bear has emerged in recent literature, Gunnell (1995, 104) observes that in Scandinavia, the "revered straw man" was regarded as a household idol and that "straw figures, both inanimate and enacted, seem to have carried considerable weight as objects of superstitious belief." He continues by pointing out that the "inanimate man-sized straw figures that used to be well known in Denmark or Sweden . . . had positions of reverence in the farmhouse over the Christmas period. This is well demonstrated by the account of the *Lussebrud* doll from Eda in Varmland which was clad in a dress, pullover, hat, and bright ribbon, and placed in the centre of the dance-floor where the ensuing *Lusse* dance took place around it" (103).

According to Gunnell (1995, 104), it is likely that "enacted straw figures" (masquerades) "have very early roots, possibly related to seasonal fertility customs of some kind." In such instances, Gunnell suggests some links between straw figures and Freyr, the Norse god of crops, fruitfulness, and prosperity (101).

Taghairm

One of the more uncanny instances of the wearing of a bull's hide involves the Scottish ritual of *taghairm*. In this ancient form of divination, an individual sewn into an ox hide was deemed to have the gift of prophecy. In Gaelic, *taghairm* means a spiritual "echo." According to Pennant (1776, 360), "A wild species of magic was practiced in the district of Trotternish. . . . A family [member] who pretended to oracular knowledge . . . was sewed up in the hide of an ox." Wrapped in this "cloak of knowledge," the individual was left on a precipice by a lonely waterfall, where the roaring of the waters was thought to amplify the portentousness of the moment. Sir Walter Scott (1810, 314) discusses *taghairm* in a footnote to his *Lady of the Lake*: "Whatever was impressed upon him by his exalted imagination, passed for the inspiration of the disembodied spirits, who haunt these desolate recesses." Thomas Pennant (1776, 360; see also Dwelly 1977) states, "The question is put, and the person in the hide delivers his answer. And so ends this species of divination styled *taghairm*."

Esoteric Roots

For more insight on the spiritual roles that European guisers once played, it is useful to look at the historical record of Nordic mummers because their arcane roots survived long enough to be documented. For example, in Estonia, which is east of the Baltic Sea and south of Finland, Tedre (2007, 416) suggests that it is possible to detect an early religious background in the fact that the bear guiser was said by some to cure infertility: "The bear was taken into the cow shed and stable to deter bad spirits and help with the growth of animals." In Norway and elsewhere, animistic beliefs prevailed, including a belief in Nisse, a house- and farm-protecting spirit who around 1843–60 would be "served porridge with butter at Christmas" (Bregenhøj and Larsen 2007, 222 n. 60). Both Denmark and Norway had legends and beliefs relating to groups of wild spirits that visited farmhouses at Christmas: "In Denmark they were called the *Den vilde Jagt* (Wild Hunt) which was often connected with the god Odin" (222 n. 59). Icelandic mummers wore costumes utilizing straw and visited "on either New Year's Eve or Twelfth Night, times when according to Icelandic folk belief, the *álfar* (elves) and *huldufólk* (hidden people) are on the move" (Davíðsdóttir 2007, 646). Both these terms are used interchangeably for nature spirits. At the close of Christmas, "it was a firmly established custom to talk of *álfar* going back home after visiting the human world during the Christmas season and need some provisions for the road" (647).

Formerly in Norway, the terms *Julebukk* and *Julegeit* were applied to certain supernatural spirits that could be represented by the familiar horned goat, while in Denmark, as in Sweden, the name could refer to either the masked figure or a figure wrapped in straw. Norwegians believed the invisible Julebukk spirit started to appear before Christmas, and by Christmas Eve, the Julegeit spirit "would come into the cellars to taste the beer" (Eike 2007b, 69). Older records show that Julebukk mummers "acted as if they were spirits, talking with distorted voices, saying that they came from a far off place, from the mountains or the forest, for instance" (76). To children, these creatures appeared ghostly and frightening, were noisy, and seemed to be able to grow taller when the performer raised the pole holding the mask toward the ceiling. In the Shetland Islands, the house-visiting mummers were seen as representing something inhuman or supernatural, even animal-like. They tended to make animal noises and instead of talking normally used inverse speech;

they "would often talk of coming from a long way off, for example, from the mountains (in the Faroes) . . . or from an inaccessible beach" (Gunnell 2007, 304). Similarly, during Icelandic Vikivaki dance games, "all the masked figures come from 'outside' the dance room indeed the 'Fingálpn' [the horse] from 1644 is supposed to live . . . on the heaths and in the woods" (289).

Certain times of the year were particularly identified with ancestral visits. In the early eighth century in northeast England, the Venerable Bede, a Northumbrian monk, records that February was known as Sol-monath (Soul Month) because cakes were offered to the gods (probably ancestors) during that month. In both ancient Greece and Rome, food was prepared for returned souls in February, and when the dangerous days were over, they were symbolically swept out. In Cheshire, England, songs survive from "Souling" celebrations, when soul cakes were baked as a symbolic offering to the ancestors around All Souls' Day, the time for remembering dead relatives. The Wild Horse disguise appeared as part of a Souling Play performed in Cheshire.

For Estonians, an annual "soul period" was considered sacrosanct and "was the time at which the spirits of forefathers were expected to visit those who were living" (Tedre 2007, 434). It began around St. Michael's Day, September 29, and ended before St. Martin's Day, November 10, a period that encompassed Halloween, All Saints' Day, and All Souls' Day. The Estonian *hingesandid* (soul mummers) dressed in white, recalling shrouds, while performers representing evil spirits were dressed in black. During their homestead visits, they are said to have whimpered in thin voices and even to have screamed demands for food. They danced and jumped and hit residents with thin twigs to bestow health. At the end of the soul period, Estonians bid the *hingesandid* farewell and drove the spirits away.

Good Luck Bestowal

By the time British guising and mumming caught historians' attention, the practice's earlier spiritual significance was no longer overtly articulated. Instead, historians have speculated about residues of defunct belief systems. Nineteenth-century authors Sir Edward Tylor and Sir James Frazer theorized that pagan notions of fecundity originally lay at the core of seasonal mumming and disguising. This "myth/ritual" interpretation of mumming is spelled out in Alex Helm's (1981, 6) definition of the mummer's play as "a men's seasonal ritual intended to promote fertility, expressed basically in terms of an action of revitalization." By the end of the twentieth century, some British folklorists—especially Ronald Hutton (1997, 93) but also Eddie Cass (2001) and Tom Pettit (1995)—challenged the idea of continuity between ancient guising practices and those documented in the nineteenth century as a consequence of "the lack of any sustainable historical support for the theory" (Cass 2001, 4). It was suggested that the Reformation had severed any links, and the hard-liners applied rigorous new standards to the discipline. Cass (2001, 4) argues that the myth/ritual interpretation of mumming filled a public need that emerged as a consequence of the Industrial Revolution: "The resultant social change engendered a fear of instability . . . which led to a yearning for a more stable, but mythologized, period of the past."

Hard-line folklorists resist spiritual interpretations of masquerading and are reluctant to entertain notions of mummers bringing good luck because it is analogous to the idea of bestowing a blessing. Cass (2001, 25) maintains that historically, the primary rationale for mumming was "the need of working men to raise money at times of seasonal festivals." Although mumming is fun and sustains communal fortitude, Cass sees these as subsidiary factors: "The play was a 'begging custom,' the 'legitimized wealth transfer transaction' of the social historian. Other functions of the mumming play have been identified, the bonding or validating of a community, for example, but . . . the major purpose was to raise money for the players" (25).

Nevertheless, an interesting variant of the quête appears in Czechoslovakia, where straw masquerades danced with farmers' daughters to bring good crops (Warner 1977, 15). As in the Shetland Islands, in Fermanagh, Cavan, and Leitrim in Ireland, mummers visited marriage parties simply to wish the newlyweds health and prosperity. Gailey (1969, 92) states, "Strawboys differed from the performers of the other customs because they did not set out to collect either money or food. Their intention was, and is, to bring luck and happiness to the newly-weds, to wish them health and prosperity. If they are admitted to the wedding-house they dance or sing asking the bride in particular to join them. . . . It was the leader's privilege to dance with the bride." Gailey continues, "The collection of money is really a reversal of the original reason for the custom. In fact, one may still find traditions that the mummers went out to take luck around the houses of the community and that it was incidental if they were rewarded with money or food. Of the Ballybrennan mummers in county Wexford in the early nineteenth century, Patrick Kennedy said that they would not stoop to make a collection" (14). The idea that beneficence is being distributed is included in the rhymes of some plays in western County Tyrone:

We come not to your door to beg nor to borrow.
We come to your door to drive away all sorrow.
(Gailey 1969, 14)

Discussing Galoshins in southern Scotland, Thomas Wilkie (1815; in Hayward 1992, 30) states, "Tradition says that it is very unlucky to let the gysarts [guisers] go out of the house . . . without giving them some money to drink to the success of the family." Nordic mumming traditions provide unambiguous illustrations of good luck visits, and Bregenhøj and Larsen (2007, 208) assert that Danish mummers "go to friends' homes simply for the immaterial purpose of making them happy." By this means, "social ties are maintained without having to be negotiated in the open" (208); "the importance of such visits lies in the way they confirm social affiliations, the avoidance of a visit then marking the understanding of a lack of affiliation" (211). Comparable to the Scottish tradition of "First Footing," the Estonian Nääripoisid (New Year Boys), "aimed at being the first guests of the New Year and also good luck wishers" (Tedre 2007, 388). They were costumed but not necessarily disguised, although some wore headdresses made of straw with straw dresses. A spell-like wish might be sung to the family: "Good morning, New Year morning, good luck next year! Girls to marry, hens to lay eggs, horses to have mouse-dun colts, sheep to have white-headed lambs, cows to have cream-coloured calves, pigs to have seven pigs. Spinsters against a northern wind!" (392). The term *New Year Boys* indicates "the belief that the good-luck wisher would be more influential if the wisher was a young male being" (390). Earlier folk beliefs stipulated that "if the first visitor was female she brought bad luck or spoiled the house's fortune, and that the older the woman was, the bigger the misfortune" (388). In such cases, it was advised, men's trousers should be thrown at the female visitor's neck in the doorway to avoid the bad luck (390). Reminiscent of the St. Martin's Eve mummers who used to hit family members with a twig to bestow health, Nääripoisid carried straw knouts "with which they would hit family members especially the sleepers." The purpose of hitting them was supposedly to "liven them up" and make them hardworking and alert (391).

The Nääripoisid sometimes were identified with visits by goat masquerades, and "in general, the goat [disguise] was seen as a bringer of good luck" (Tedre 2007, 404). This was literally true in the sense that if a household was missed, people would say that those families were considered bad. Once inside a residence, the goats had a partiality for butting people until they received what they wanted. Although spreading good luck was the explicit purpose, a form of reciprocal barter usually took place to seal the deal: "Certain gifts have roots in more archaic, ritual tradition, as with a special cake . . . and beer . . . or vodka. . . . [T]his was necessary to guarantee the 'realisation' of the wish-congratulation" (395). In the Saaremaa area, the tradition was that mittens, socks, garters, or stockings were "tied to the goat's horns. [However,]

Fig. 6.7. Julbock and Julget (Christmas goats, male and female), Vemdalen, Harjedalen, Sweden, 1919. Photo by Nils Keyland. Courtesy Nordiska Museet.

only the very first goat was given mittens and socks, while those who came later were only offered beer" (407). Tedre states, "It was also believed by some that if the goat(s) were not offered anything, they would take away the luck of the household" (405). In Estonia, "if the *mardid* [St. Martin's Eve mummers] were not let in, they would leave with evil sayings. . . . If they received nothing for their performance, they would curse the fields, the cattle, the children and the entire family" (439). Similarly, if Finland's St. Stephen's Day mummers "were refused admission or the refreshments were not to their liking they would sing a song wishing the host bad luck or perform some other kind of mischief" (Vento 2007, 348).

Palpable links existed between masquerading and fertility customs because the context of visits emphasized life giving, increase, and abundance. In Tedre's (2007, 440, 447) words, "It is clear that some mumming was related to a greater fertility rite"; "its earliest function seems to have been to bring luck (in the form of fertility) to those households visited." This reinforces the idea that pre-Christian notions of fecundity originally lay at the core of such folk expressions, though that idea recently has been called into question by hardline folklorists.

EUROPEAN MASQUERADE INSTRUMENTS

Musical accompaniment involving one or more drums has been a staple for masquerades throughout history in the three regions under consideration. In 1583 in Britain, Philip Stubbes (1583, 189) condemned the "baudy Pipers and thundering drummers" associated with the "Hobby-horses, Dragons and other Antiques." In 1782, when a butcher on the Isle of Wight was mocked by individuals wearing rams' horns, the party included a drummer (E. P. Thompson 1991, 483). The pipe and tabor are often mentioned in relation to both the costumed morris dancers with jingle bells on their legs and the tourney-style hobbyhorse. In olden times, the pipe and tabor were paired, with a three-hole pipe (two in front, one in back) played with one hand and a portable drum played with the other. The tabor was suspended by a strap from the performer's left forearm, and his right hand would beat the drum with a stick, while his left hand would play the pipe with the thumb and the first two fingers. A tabor has a cylindrical wooden shell and two skin heads tensioned by ropes and a leather strap. One head has an adjustable gut snare. Historically, the tabor is played with just one stick, which usually strikes the snare head. The width and depth of tabors vary, although medieval pictures of pipe and tabor usually display a large shallow drum similar in shape to the bodhran.[1] Stephen Rowley (pers. comm., August 9, 2010) reports, "In Gloucester Folk Museum there is an important tabor, owned by the last traditional Morris taborer, Joe Powell of Bucknell, from the beginning of the twentieth century. This instrument shows clear pattern of wear indicating a double-ended technique. The tabor is small and the wear shows that the butt of the stick was hitting the tension hoop of the tabor." Having a stick hitting the rim of the tabor would add a sharp rat-a-tat-tat sound.

Unlike fiddles, which have an established history, melodeons and concertinas were not in existence until the early to mid–nineteenth century. In times of yore, fiddles were used for country dances but were relatively fragile and costly compared to the more commonplace drums and pipes. Nevertheless, a fiddle was played along with a tambourine, triangle, or melodeon for performances of the Hooden Horse in Kent (Cawte 1978, 86–87). Fiddles regularly appear in reports of masquerading in northern Scotland and the Nordic countries. Mummers in the Shetland Islands often included a fiddler to accompany singing and dancing during their New Year's visits (Gunnell 2007, 316). In Finland on St. Knut's Day, parties of visiting straw-clad Nuutti figures and fur-clad Pukki goats included a drummer (*rumpali*) and a fiddler (*viuluniekka*) (Vento 2007, 353). In Norway, mock wedding plays held on St. John's Eve, June 21, to coincide with the summer solstice included a fiddler and a

Fig. 6.8. Hobbyhorse dance, from Francis Douce, *Illustrations of Shakespeare* (1839). Note the pipe and tabor player, hobbyhorse, and morris dancer and partner, all led by a Motley Fool/Merry Andrew with a ladle and bladder. Courtesy English Folk Dance and Song Society, London.

drummer, and fiddlers led processions of guisers on farm visits at Easter and other times (Eike 2007b, 93; Eike 2007a, 519). In Denmark, harvest festivals with straw effigies of men and maidens included dances to fiddle tunes (Bregenhøj and Larsen 2007, 260–61). During Christmas in Estonia, Jõulupoisid "used to go around in groups from farm to farm. . . . They had accordions and . . . they stopped the everyday work of the household and started to dance" (Tedre 2007, 386–87). St. Thomas Day mummers in Estonia dressed in white and were sometimes disguised with blackened faces or big beards. Accoutrements included a cowlstaff or yoke that was "used to mark the rhythm during the dancing that took place during the visit" (381). Fergusson's (1884, 160) account includes a description of staves used to keep time among straw-clad Shetland mummers at Halloween: "They kept up an incessant grunt, grunt, grunt, or a noise partly resembling swine and partly turkey cocks. . . . The spirits, for such they appeared to be, had long staves which they kept rapping on the floor. . . . Immediately upon our entering the kitchen they formed themselves into pairs and commenced hobbling and dancing." In Britain, a photograph of a "hoodening" with a horse disguise, taken about 1908 at Saint Nichols-at-Wade in Kent, shows musicians with a triangle, a tambourine, and a melodeon (Cawte 1978, 86). Some texts of mumming plays in Gloucestershire end with the words, "They sing a wassail, then dance the Morris," implying the presence of a musician. Wassailers in Gloucestershire often sang in unison without accompaniment, but Richard Chidlaw (pers. comm., August

12, 2010) reports that a concertina was played by wassailers at Hillesley. In July 1970, a man named Hatherell, of Wickwar, told Chidlaw that wassailers with the Horton Bull at Little Sodbury would sing the wassailing song and play "ribs of beef" (bones played in one hand for rhythm) as well as "a tambourine, Jews harp and a mouth organ." Among North Lincolnshire hobbyhorse plow gangs, music was provided by drum and melodeons and included horn blowers (Nicholls 2010, 110). The large sailor's horse masquerades use drums to celebrate May Day in Padstow and Minehead on the north coast of Cornwall and Somerset, respectively. At Padstow, May Day songs are sung, among them, "Oh Where Is Saint George?" and "Where Are the French?" (Cawte 1978, 162–63). Cawte (1978, 211) includes a copy of an engraving made about 1835 that shows the Padstow Horse accompanied by a fife and a large bass drum beaten with a stick, while other individuals fire guns into the air. The Minehead horse is accompanied by a drum and melodeons that play a variant of "Soldier's Joy" and other tunes (170). In the late 1970s, Stephen Rowley (pers. comm., August 9, 2010) played for the Red Oss at Padstow: "Charlie Bate was the main musician, he played melodeon. The most significant instruments were the drums one was a Napoleonic drum from a ship, the rhythm is very distinctive." Brian Shuel's photo of the Whittlesey Straw Bear taken in the 1980s shows the animal escorted by musicians with a big bass drum worn perpendicular to the ground, a melodeon, and a saxophone. The Irish Strawboys might add tin whistles and even mouth organs to the melodeon and drums they commonly played.

THE AMERICAS

John Kuner in North Carolina

Although the Bahamas are especially identified with Junkanoo, these Christmastime masquerades dispersed along North America's eastern seaboard in the form of the John Canoe of slaves in the antebellum Carolinas, belsnickeling in Virginia and Nova Scotia, and mummering or Janneying in Newfoundland. There are a number of reports of Jonkonnu in North Carolina in the vicinity of Cape Fear. Edward Warren (1855, 53) visited the Josiah Collins plantation in Washington County, North Carolina, and described a Christmas "John Koonering" performance by Collins's slaves: "The leading character is the 'rag-man' whose get up consists [of] two great ox horns, attached to the skin of a raccoon, which is drawn over the head and face leaving apertures only for the eyes and mouth." Escaped slave Harriet Jacobs described the "Johnkannaus" of the early 1800s in Chowan County, North Carolina: "Cows tails are fastened to their backs and their heads are decorated with horns" (Brent 1973, 121). Wilmington, Edenton, and Hillsborough, North Carolina, were also areas that celebrated the "John Kuner" tradition (Louis T. Moore 1946, 7). Rebecca Cameron (1891/1913, 8) recalls that at Christmas 1848, when she was a child at Buchoi, her family's rice plantation near Durham, North Carolina, the "John Coonahs" paraded to the great house from the slaves' quarters, and "a gigantic pair of branching deer horns decorated [the leader's] head" (see also Fenn 1988). The performers danced to the music of a banjo, bones, triangles, castanets, a fife, and drums. Considering the use of stag headdresses in medieval Europe and their probable use during the Horn Fair at Charlton, London, in the eighteenth century, the antlers are a notable feature of this account.

Belsnickels in Virginia

The belsnickeling mumming tradition is a form of Christmas and New Year's entertainment that was introduced into the United States by German and Dutch immigrants and parallels Christmas Saturnalias in the Caribbean. Belsnickels often included the inquisitors Black Peter and St. Nicholas and were found in nineteenth-century Virginia and Pennsylvania (Halpert 1969, 43). Barney Moss (1982, 153) cites belsnickeling as among the influences for Newfoundland's Janneying. In a report on late-nineteenth-century Christmas and New Year belsnickels in Virginia's Shenandoah Valley, Ruth Cline (1958, 164) recounts historian John W. Wayland's description of the custom: "Belsnickles, when I was a boy, would go around wearing false faces and perhaps other disguises, and would make it a point to frighten children, if they could. If admitted to the house, they would sometimes throw candy or other sweets on the floor, and then cut with long switches they carried anyone who would stoop to pick up the candy." Cline explains, "The first White settlers in the Shenandoah Valley were Germans. . . . I should imagine that these settlers brought the custom with them from the German territories" (165). She juxtaposes the Shenandoah customs with Helen Creighton's (1950) account of New Year's belsnickeling as it existed in Lunenberg County, Nova Scotia, where "men dressed in hides and sometimes used the tails of the hides to whip children." Again, Cline notes, the participants are "largely descended from an original German stock" (1958, 165).

Janneying in Newfoundland

As part of the Atlantic Rim, Newfoundland is subject to the crosscurrents of cultural ideas. The mumming of white Newfoundlanders provides an example

Fig. 6.9. Janneys, Newfoundland, Canada, ca. 1995. Photo by W. Calvin Barbour. Courtesy Paul Smith, Memorial University of Newfoundland.

of British-style masquerading dispersed to an island of the northwest Atlantic Rim where African influences were probably not significant factors, although the Caribbean House Jonkonnu may have influenced Newfoundland maskers, who wore cocked hats surmounted with paper models of ships in the mid-1800s. Some Newfoundland mummers performed their Christmas Janneying in moose antlers, but "more frequently the head of a bull, cow, or calf was used" (Widdowson and Halpert 1969, 153). In Shallop Cove, "Sometimes a mummer would put the dried head of the bull or cow over his own head and wrap himself in the hide" (154). In Fortune Harbour, "They used to use horns [and] skin a lamb or a ram or something. . . . They looked ugly looking" (154). Halpert and Story (1969) refer to but do not fully flesh out the practice's British origins. In the past, the St. George play and other mummers' plays were performed, and various costumes were worn. By the 1980s, costumes often consisted simply of cross-dressing, and the majority of visits were to friends, neighbors, and peers (Powers 1988). Christmas Janneying still continues in Newfoundland, with rudimentary masks or simply textiles covering the face and onlookers attempting primarily to guess the maskers' identities.

Chapter 7

OLD WORLD–NEW WORLD COMPARISONS

SPIRITUAL COMPARISONS

Some West African spiritual ideas crossed the Atlantic. Regarding the use of charms to protect property, Baum (1999, 165) states that among the Jola, special "medicines made of palm fibers consecrated at the Gilaite [blacksmith's] shrine were placed near valuable goods to keep them from being stolen." In the Eastern Caribbean, a Bapoo, or "Jumbee in a bottle," was placed on fruit trees to keep thieves away (Valls 1981, 7).

Funerals

African funerals do not simply mourn a death but celebrate the deceased's life. Masquerade dancers are disguised because they represent ancestral spirits welcoming the deceased's soul into their ranks. Expensive burial cloths are found among many groups, including the Igede of Nigeria, where the deceased's kinfolk dance wearing distinctive textiles identified as burial shrouds. Slave funerals in the Eastern Caribbean took place on the plantations but are not well documented because they were out of sight of the white literati, often under a tree at some distance from the Great House. Samuel Smith declares, "We dare not disturb massa. We at Jonas use to make our music at an old tamarind tree, north of where Freeman's Villa was. That use to be about a mile from Jonas" (Keithlyn B. Smith and Smith 1988, 39). Descriptions from the Virgin Islands in the 1700s tell primarily of drumming and dancing. Johan Christian Schmidt, manager of La Grande Princess Plantation on St. Croix during the 1780s, states that "the bosals [African-born slaves] bury their dead in the manner they were used to on the [African] coast. They have a memorial dance over them with strange gestures" (in Tyson and Highfield 1994, 120). Discussing a funeral in the mid–eighteenth century in St. Thomas, Oldendorp (1770/1987, 264) states, "There is dancing, accompanied by a raging noise, sometimes sustained by the drunken assembly through the entire night." Whether masks were worn is not documented, but Carstens (1997, 79), a planter on St. Thomas in the early 1700s, echoes the idea of burial clothes doubling as performance costumes: "The small children sing several songs of lamentation over the dead. They cover them all over with the same fine cotton linen with which they have wrapped the body."

Traditional lore in the Eastern Caribbean holds that coffins en route to the cemetery can lead pallbearers to persons who may have contributed to the death or with whom the deceased had unresolved issues, a practice that recalls similar activities by Jola funeral biers. Oldendorp (1770/1987, 264) describes an Antiguan funeral with "a great many Negroes following the coffin, engaged in continuous singing and dancing accompanied by drums and calabashes. . . . As the procession approached the gravesite, the pall bearers moved as if the deceased had no desire to be buried there. To all appearances . . . they were pulled from the route against their will. . . . Then they shot ahead again so rapidly that they almost fell. . . . At other times . . . the deceased apparently wished to proceed no further."

Spirit Comestibles

As in Barbados, remembering those who have died with liquor, soup, or foodstuffs was once fairly widespread in the Eastern Caribbean and is a common ancestral observance in West Africa. In Montserrat on Christmas Eve, a Jumbie Table would be set up inside a house and stocked with black pudding, rum, cheese, and water as treats for the Jumbies. The table is taken down next morning (Donna Henry, pers. comm., November 18, 2003). A parallel is found in Norway around 1843–60: Nisse, a homestead spirit, was served porridge with butter at Christmas (Bregenhøj and Larsen 2007, 222). In Cheshire, England, "Souling" celebrations were held, with cakes baked as a symbolic offering to the ancestors around All Souls' Day.

Good Luck Bestowal

In West Africa, bush masquerades have been linked to annual-cycle rituals—for example, the Jola Rain Ceremony and Igede New Yam Festival. In Europe, masquerades have been linked to Halloween, Christmas, New Year's, and Strawbower Day (the beginning of the agricultural year). In Barbados, such masquerades are associated with the end of harvest in the Crop Over festival. Raffia and bull masquerades in Upper Guinea also appeared at initiations and funerals and are thus associated with life-cycle rituals. Mummers in Norway, like the Irish Strawboys and the straw-clad mummers of the Shetland

Fig. 7.1. Wedding mummers, Stardalen, Jølster, Norway, ca. 1900–1950. Photo by Anton Oygard. Courtesy Sunnfjord Museum, Movika, Norway.

Islands, similarly solemnized life-cycle events such as weddings and wakes. In the Eastern Caribbean, masquerades primarily provided entertainment at Christmastime, much in the same manner as Swedish and Danish Julebukks and Irish Strawboys. Masquerades continue to provide beneficence by entertaining hospital patients during Carnival in the Eastern Caribbean, while the Mocko Jumbie stilt dancer's presence at a housewarming or a new venture is still considered a good omen. Although spiritual notions have become diluted over time, the Mocko Jumbie, a kind of supernatural scarecrow, has retained its authority more than most such figures and, like Sensay, is believed to interact with spirits. Whether from Africa or Europe, ancestral notions of the proletariat were perpetuated in the Caribbean to some degree, and practitioners believe that masquerading benefits society. In the vein of keeping the culture alive, Caribbean islanders are proud of their masquerading performances and the enjoyment and aesthetic stimulation they provide.

Spirits in Disguise

There is some continuity between the Old World and Eastern Caribbean masquerades regarding the extent of disguise sought by covering the body, an especially important factor in West Africa. To maintain the illusion that the masquerade is a spirit, societies in Upper Guinea hide the identity of the costume wearer, who both dresses and undresses out of public view. Although distinguished by the rather unique use of female costume wearers, the Sande society of the Vai of Liberia demonstrates this secrecy. The Vai term *nyana* means "spirit" and is used to describe the Zooba masquerade. It is imperative that the mask wearer not be identified or any part of the body revealed. A companion carries a rolled-up mat to cover the dancer should the costume come apart during the vigorous dancing (Monts 1984, 56).

In Western Europe, disguise was important, though to a lesser extent. In some places, part of the fun of mumming involved guessing the performers' identity, a trait that carried over to Newfoundland. Janneys not only cover every part of the body (a prudent practice because of the Christmastime cold) but also adopt other disguises, as Powers (1988, 655) explains: "Mummers try to change their gait and if possible, their entire physical appearance, for example, by stooping or by adding stuffing inside their boots to make themselves appear taller. Most importantly, they disguise their voices in what is known as 'mummer talk,' a quick and garbled way of speaking at a high pitch while holding one's breath." Other Janneys talk while inhaling rather than exhaling—that is, using inverse speech—a technique also employed by mummers in the Shetland Islands. If or when a mummer's identity is exposed, the pretense is no longer maintained.

In the Eastern Caribbean, masqueraders sought to impersonate spirits by disguising themselves with masks and covering all other body parts. Accordingly, the disguises of the carnival clown and Mocko Jumbie are total. This extensive covering not only hid the individual performer but also concealed that he or she had a human identity. Mystery was important, and spectators generally did not know a performer's identity, though they sometimes tried to guess. George Farrell (pers. comm., November 13, 2002) reports that someone would ask in Creole, "For who he? The man have on mask so me wan' to know who he. Me no know who he." The intensely curious might wait for the performer to raise his mask to drink. Eventually, however, the need for secrecy receded, and disguise for the purpose of making merry in anonymity took precedence, with the illusion maintained only during the performance. Within a festival, the disguise factor was often followed by the revelation of the wearer's identity, as Turnbull (pers. comm., June 19, 1996) points out: "People wore masks because you were not supposed to see the real person, although after a performance they might raise the mask and reveal themselves. People would say 'Oh my goodness it's so and so.' Sometimes people you wouldn't suspect—conservative types would cause quite a stir when they revealed themselves. But by this means, people would show their other side." In the modern era, many individuals no longer take disguise seriously and masks may be raised or abandoned during performance.

SECULAR COMPARISONS

Black Disguises

The ebony nakedness of those devils akin to Jab Jab Molasses of the Windward Islands is noted below. Moreover, Antiguan John Bull performers Sam Williams and John Jude blackened their faces with soot rather than wearing masks, while in St. Thomas the opening in the bear's balaclava helmet often revealed a blackened countenance. However, although painted and soot-smeared faces emerged as a form of disguise among animal performers in the Leeward Islands, no reports emerged of British bulls blackening their faces rather than masking, despite the fact that the players accompanying the Old Tup ram often blackened their faces. As noted earlier, an exception combining cow horns and blackened faces occurs in Bavaria. Black makeup was, however, commonplace among British mummers: Alex Helm (1981, 40) notes that the faces of the "Toms" at Sleights "were blackened, either wholly or partially." Gailey (1969, 82) reports, "In Roscommon the wrenboys' leader had his face blackened and he wore a suit of straw," while William Tydeman (1978, 10) states, "Black-faced 'Moggies' still appear in Maytime festivities in Ickwell Green, Bedfordshire." The plow-jagging gangs of North Lincolnshire even include black-faced females (Pearson 2007, 190). Similarly mummers of the St. Kitts–Nevis Neagar Business troupe often included individuals with faces covered with soot and locomotive grease, while the members of the Virgin Islands Down South troupe were essentially minstrels in blackface. Although color symbolism is not widespread it does appear in Estonia whereby the soul mummers were dressed in white, while performers representing evil spirits were dressed in black (Tedre 2007, 434). Similarly, the black beast masks of the Igbo Okoroshi (Okorosia) are overtly fierce and grotesque and distinguished from the white-faced "beautiful" Oma masks. Conversely, a "black is beautiful" interpretation is provided by the female Dea masks of the Poro Society of Liberia. Ndege and Nicholls (1990, 26) point out that the Dea female mask has a "smooth black surface and a calm demeanor [and] the Dan consider it beautiful." The masquerade appears at initiation ceremonies, and "its main function is to keep the initiates happy."

Quêtes

Caribbean masquerade groups toured villages and households and engaged in quêtes. Although the begging factor is not emphasized among adult masquerades in West Africa, quêtes are a feature of European mumming that carried over to the Caribbean. Nevertheless, African masquerades can impose fines, and reciprocal exchanges provide remuneration for performance. Sometimes gifts are given, and Weil (1988, 172–73) provides examples received by the Sengko raffia masquerade at a Mandinka girls' initiation: The mothers and female relatives give presents "of cloth and other wealth," while the initiates' fiancés "brought gifts, including liquor." During Sengko's performance in the village square, assistants collect gifts from the audience and "inform the masker in whispers of the names of those who have given gifts so that the masker can include their names in his songs" (169). Held every twenty years or so, the Jola male initiation ceremony is known as a time of largesse, essentially a potlatch. Mark (1992, 53) states, "The memory of how much meat was consumed after these sacrifices became the stuff of legend." Gift giving among West Africa children's masquerades undoubtedly resembles European quêtes (Ottenberg and Binkley 2006). In Nigeria, "in Orlu, Imo State, about 1976, I witnessed two different Igbo boy's masks called by the generic term Agaba. They toured family compounds with a troupe of boy dancers during the Christmas season and danced in return for gifts" (Nicholls 2006a, 129). Modernity brings change, and De Jong (2007, 143, 144) describes the "transformation" of Kankuran as it came to provide "young maskers . . . a means to earn pocket money": "The Kankurang himself has started begging [and] the people of Ziguinchor considered the behaviour of the mask performers evidence of the masquerade's 'degeneration.'" Moreover, although the Kumpo masquerade has become commodified or folklorized, it remains "authentic" to traditional audiences. It not only performs in Jola villages but also dances for tourists in modern settings for remuneration. In De Jong's words, "In the village context it emerges from the sacred forest, while in the hotel setting it comes out of the swimming pool changing room" (168).

Perambulations

In Antigua, the days between Christmas and the New Year were touring season for masquerades. The John Bull perambulation cycle and that of the Montserrat masquerades, wandering from homestead to homestead, mirrored British and Irish mumming tours. Glassie (1975, 78) illustrates the time frame of the Ballymenone Strawboys mummers' excursion in Ireland: "Boxing Day, the second day of Christmas, was a major marker for mummers. . . . They might begin then [and] the more they mummed, the more ambitious they became. . . . P. Flanagan recalls: 'That time we went out thirteen rounds; twelve nights and one day. Thirteen trips altogether. Our last day was New Year's Day, and we went out all day long.'" Thus, by the twentieth century, a marked concurrence exists between the Caribbean Christmas perambulation cycle and mumming in Britain and Ireland. In contrast, West African masquerades might go around a village to provide ancestral oversight and beneficence or perform in another village, but in most cases they perform in one specific location as part of agricultural, life-cycle, or curative rituals. Such locations include the sacred forest, the initiation ground, the dance arena, and often the village square—the *ojiya* playground of the Igede—where people gather to participate in a performance. An exception exists among the Yoruba of Ede township: According to Beier (1969), the annual Shango festival concludes with a procession in which a pot of fire is carried to all quarters of the town to bring blessings from Shango, the god of lightning. This ritual is equivalent to "Beating the Bounds" in Britain, which aims at dispelling misfortune and bringing luck within a circumscribed area.

Whipping

In the Caribbean, whips and masquerading often coincide. The whippings received by the John Bulls in Antigua and John Canoes in Jamaica and elsewhere bear a marked similarity to the beatings with sticks received by the bull in the Scottish Highlands. It is generally true that if whippings were to be meted out in West Africa, the masquerades or their handlers were the perpetrators rather than the recipients. For example, among the Mandinka, the raffia Mumbo Jumbo whipped miscreants, and Sengko carried a baton and beat any initiated female he found on the paths instead of assembled in the village square (Weil 1988, 172). The masked Egbo [Ekpe] runners who roamed the streets of Calabar pursued bystanders with a "terrible cow-skin whip" or a "long rod" (Waddell 1863/1970, 265). The cow-skin whip probably resembles the hunter whip of Montserrat, which is made out of plaited cow skin and used by the bull masquerade minder. The whipping of opponents is an important feature of Shakespeare Mas' in Carriacou. Caribbean masquerade whippings would seem to be an echo of the slavery era and refer to the harshness of those times. They are not replicated in Western Europe or West Africa, where bulls were not whipped or beaten, although bears are in some locations in Europe.

Straw Surrogates

An aspect of European mumming in effigy that is reflected in the Eastern Caribbean is the substitution of a straw doll for a foe or unpopular figure as a form of scapegoat that can be symbolically punished in a socially acceptable form. For example, during the Danish Shrovetide festival, Fastelavn, jousting competitions were held in which young men tilted at a straw effigy. These ideas are reflected in the treatment afforded "Mr. Harding" in Barbados. During the Crop Over festival, an inanimate straw effigy by that name held court: According to Flora Spencer (1974, 3), "The procession of carts bringing in the last loads of canes signalled the beginning of the festivities. . . . One cart carried an effigy of 'Mr. Harding.' Mr. Harding who symbolised hard time and represented all cruel gang-drivers was made of sugar-cane trash and dressed in an old black coat, a top hat and wore a mask." John Chester Greville (1869, 82) adds, "The proceedings are varied by the introduction of a 'trash man,' a figure, i.e. stuffed with cane trash and tied on the back of the mule, which, being finally let loose, galloped about with his incongruous burden to the delight of the spectators." Following various dances performed by the attendees, the Crop Over festival concluded with the effigy "burnt to the singing of the song 'Hold fast, old Ned at the door' Ned being the personification of lean and difficult times ahead for the labourers before the next crop season" (Spencer 1974, 4). Sweden and Denmark had a harvest custom of making life-size straw dolls in human form, and similar practices were known in Switzerland, Austria, and Finland. In Skåne, Sweden, the last sheaf at the end of the harvest was called by disparaging anthropomorphic names. Burning a human effigy on a Lenten bonfire was a widespread custom in Switzerland. In the former Danish West Indies, straw effigies were used in fairground-type games during holidays. In St. Thomas, "John Hog" was made out of crocus bags stuffed with straw and dressed in a suit and shoes. He seems to have been based on a real person, possibly John Swilo. A band of musicians would carry the effigy from place to place and put a stick behind him, and members of the public threw missiles at him to try to knock him down and win a nickel (Philip Rhymer, pers. comm., July 18, 1996). According to Crucian Eulalie Rivera (pers. comm., July 3, 1995), two effigies made of bags stuffed with straw were known as Farass and Marass. During holidays, they were set up at Faster Field (Two Brothers Estate) at the head of King Street in Frederiksted. They were part of a competitive game in which people threw sticks at them. By this means people could vent their annoyance at certain individuals.

Cow's Tails

The use of cow's tails as prestigious dance accoutrements occurred in West Africa. Baum (1999, 169) states that for the Jola, "cow's tails are symbols of wealth" and that dancers carry "cow's tails they stir in rhythm and jump." Writing in the Virgin Islands in the eighteenth century, Oldendorp (1770/1987, 190) found that the Amina (from Ghana) believed that a consecrated cow tail had protective qualities. Because the killing of cattle is no longer done at the village level in the Eastern Caribbean but takes place in abattoirs, cow's tails are now rare as costume elements. They previously were featured more prominently, and one of the earliest reports of animal disguises, that of Hans Sloane (1707, 46), tells of dancers in Jamaica who "very often tie cow tails to their rumps." Moreover, Harriet Jacobs's (1861/1987, 118) description of North Carolina slaves' "Johnkannaus" states, "Cow's tails are fastened to their backs, and their heads are decorated with horns." Only a couple of reports of the use of natural tails in the Leeward Islands have been found. One was in a description of a Christmas Bull in Nevis in the mid-1920s: The performer had his face painted red, wore a plain orange-colored cloth costume with a wide silver waistband, and sported a "real brown tail from the slaughter house" (Simeon Roper, pers. comm., August 2, 1995). The Montserrat Bull also apparently wore a real tail. Although later bulls were tailless, the bulls of the early twentieth century often wore fake tails of cloth or stuffed burlap, as did the bear and devil masquerades. Around 1910, Romic Williams (pers. comm., September 22, 1996) remembers seeing John Bull masquerades with artificial tails in Urlins Village, Antigua, that were made from a plantain or banana fruit stalk and attached to a standard plantain flag costume. Bold children might tease the character and try and pull his tail. Austin James (pers. comm., February 19, 1995) saw a John Bull in Liberta Village, Antigua, in the 1920s wearing a full-length gown made of brown sugar bags with a cloth tail with a tuft at the end. The Red Bull of St. Kitts–Nevis had an artificial cloth tail stiffened with wire; however, some hairs of a real ox were attached to the end (Mills, Jones-Hendrickson, and Bertram 1984, 34).

Whifflers

Reflecting Western European traditions, sometimes players with brooms who make sweeping motions appear as advance parties for masquerades in the Eastern Caribbean. For example, Asta Williams and another revivalist masquerader impersonated sweepers with brooms when they appeared in the 1995 St. Croix Emancipation Day parade. Sweepers belong to a broad category of masquerade companions who serve as heralds who clear the way, both physically in terms of crowd control but also symbolically in terms of dispelling bad spirits or disruptive influences. In Britain, they are known as whifflers, harbingers who wave objects such as staves, swords, or inflated animal bladders on sticks or make sweeping gestures with brooms. Alford (1978, 130) describes a whiffler in the Austrian Alps: "Their leader is dressed in red.... He carries a long broom, swinging it from side to side, for he is the whiffler. His duty is to whiffle away the spirits of Winter and to clear the way for the entrance of Spring." African masquerades also have attendants with switches of foliage who serve as guards and guides for the performer. Among the Igede, the *ojiya* dancing round is prepared for a performance. The masquerade's attendants sprinkle "holy water" from a calabash around the performance arena prior to the masquerades' appearance to drive out ill intent and prevent missteps and mishaps (Nicholls 1998).

License

Some concurrence exists between West African and Caribbean practices in the sphere of licentious behavior. Licentious behavior within masked performance customarily followed male initiation in Upper Guinea rituals, and Mandinka novices are still awarded a lot of latitude in this area, as was the case in the seventeenth century, when Jobson (1623/1968, 146) observed them. Jola novices also enjoyed a large degree of license. Froger (1698, 98) found that in Barra, Gambia, the male initiates' horned headdresses "authorize them to carry out all imaginable misdeeds." Similar freedom existed among the Bamana of Mali when the initiates wore the horned headdress (Gray and Dochard 1825). The Christmas Bulls of Dorset and Wiltshire in England's West Country were "given the freedom of every house and allowed to penetrate into any room" (Hole 1978, 65). Within their perambulations, and depending on the genre, masquerades in the Eastern Caribbean were allowed a degree of excess, and John Bull masquerades, for example, could help themselves to food and even money from street vendors. According to George Farrell (pers. comm., November 13, 2002), "You could go and lift up this towel, see what you see in this tray that you need, you could take it out.... Food, you take out what you want.... They will be happy, over it.... Some of them does have a big round crock or thing with their money, and open it and if you want you take out a dollar ... and go about your business." The latitude extended to bulls during their perambulations extended to commercial establishments such as convenience stores. Farrell states, "When you step into the shop everybody run out you know, everybody gone, gone with speed, it was good.... Any village you there, you could even walk into a shop and stretch your hand over the counter like that and the fellow will put money in your hand and you do a little shake up in the shop." Rather than taking umbrage, proprietors were glad to have renowned bull performers such as Arthur Sixteen and Silver Horn in the neighborhood. Masquerading was a Christmas tradition; it livened up the village and probably increased clientele.

SOCIAL REGULATION

The Caribbean Bulls' dancing with comedic and aggressive butting and goring served as a vehicle for parents' cautionary threats and the behavior modification of young people. There is some concurrence between Old World and Caribbean observances. Masquerades have been shown to have both spiritual and social roles, the latter in terms of discouraging anomalies. These roles are not mutually exclusive but overlap. Thora Visby-Petersen (1917, 26) reports on a "bogeyman," a "traditional 'Mumbo-Jumbo' or Mukka Jumbe" in St. Thomas around 1892 who did "an insane dance on tall stilts." Visby-Petersen's description shows the connection between the spiritual and social roles. While the term *Mumbo Jumbo* refers to arcane functions of dispelling bad spirits and attracting good ones, her reference to the figure as a "bogeyman" points to the more pragmatic function of social regulation. This emphasizes that beliefs in masquerades' intrinsic spiritual nature undergirded their authority in the secular realm and made them effective tools of social regulation. Leona Watson (pers. comm., August 9, 1996) admits that she wet herself at the age of eight when she first saw Marshall the Mocko Jumbie in St. Croix. Her grandfather had told her that masquerades are "the spirits of our ancestors," while her mother had threatened, "If you don't behave, I'll bring Marshall the Mocko Jumbie."

Caregivers capitalized on children's trepidation, using the threat of the masquerade as a disciplinary tool. The threat alone was often enough. Helen Joseph (pers. comm., August 13, 1996) confirms that merely telling a child, "Be good or the ghost will come to get you," was usually enough to obtain obedience. Charles Turnbull (pers. comm., June 19, 1996) also remembers parents cautioning children, "You had better behave or else Koka the Bear will come for you." He confirms that bears and devils would enter houses, chasing children and surprising adults: "Who wouldn't be startled, if unexpectedly you look up and there's the devil coming at you from the other side of the table with a roar?" Paddy Moore (1979) remembers performing the dragon and frightening adults. Wearing horns and burning candles on his headdress, the dragon would appear with King George at Tea Meetings. Moore says, "I walked in on my hands and knees like a dog, with a light and things on my head, and I've got a chain hanging from me. [I stood up] making noise like cattle, hooo hooo. Let me tell you, people ran out of that place!" William Richardson (pers. comm., July 15, 1996) says that when he performed as a Mocko Jumbie, parents sometimes asked him to chase naughty children and that adults also ran. He remembers performing in Guadeloupe while a church procession was taking place: When he appeared on his stilts, "the procession broke up [and] they all ran, including the priest."

Masquerades traditionally were agents of social regulation in both Africa and Europe. West African masquerades were often attached to men's societies, some of which had regulatory functions, implementing sanctions against individuals who violated communal norms. The Caribbean mirrored regulatory Old World functions to some extent, and the formidable appearance of some masquerades and larger-than-life personas lent themselves to use as a vehicle to correct behavior, particularly of children. A review of adults' conduct also occurred at Christmas, and troupes such as Niega Business focused on social commentary. However, critiques of adults occurred primarily within the lyrics of annual songs such as cariso (the precursor of calypso) or songs of Bamboula dances that drew attention to and sought to remedy socially unacceptable behavior. Masquerades would visit various homesteads and be told to run any child who had been naughty; bed wetters were prime targets. The bull had permission to enter houses and pull children from under beds if necessary. He would seize the child and in a disguised voice ask, "Gonna pee your bed again?" The terrified child would answer, "No." According to Farrell (pers. comm., November 13, 2002), scaling a tree did not put a child beyond the clutch of Arthur Sixteen: "He does climb tree too you know, he does go up in tree." The bull served as a deterrent: "You have a child disobedient, you wait, you say, 'Wait until Christmas man, you know, you wait until Christmas and I'll see Arthur Sixteen, I'll go put him 'pon you.' You start to count your fingers and them hope for Christmas is there, and you gone rude still because Christmas still there far. You know when Christmas come you're a nice boy. Sixteen, the man Arthur Sixteen, come here at your place, he say, 'Hold that boy there? Carry him away for me.'" Arthur Sixteen, who was also known as "Graveller" because of his propensity to kick up dust, was not above lecturing children on good behavior: "He will . . . hold his hand and carry him out a little way and ask him, 'Why you so rude to your parents?' 'I not do um again sir.' 'Are you going to change?' 'Yes, Yes.' . . . 'Yes sir, no sir' and all this thing, and he'll let him go." By modern standards, concerns about the level of child trauma might be raised, but Eulalie Rivera (1992) challenges this apprehension. Rivera met the devil in Frederiksted during the early 1920s, when she was a child, and "he had two horns on his head; his face was painted black and red. . . . [H]e hit me one lash!" But, Rivera concludes proudly, "That was masquerading!"

Nineteenth-century chroniclers occasionally named Caribbean masquerades but rarely described their costumes. The January 3, 1866, *St. Thomas Tidende* reported, "It would be difficult to . . . describe the innumerable costumes, grotesque exhibitions . . . that comprised" the recent Christmas masquerades, although "Satan" was among "this motley whole." Fierceness is apparent in Visby-Petersen's (1917, 26) description of horned masquerades in a St. Thomas Christmas parade near the end of the nineteenth century: "Two devils . . . form part of the tradition on these occasions. The devils have to act as violent as possible. The pitch black negroes are quite naked except for a loincloth to which the devil's tail is fastened. Big horns are attached to their foreheads and long talons to their wrists. A strong rope, held by a muscular negro, is fastened to the waist of each devil, so that he will not endanger the crowd."

The behavior of these and other ferocious masquerades clearly resembles G. I. Jones's (1984, 60) description of a masquerade performance in the Northern Igbo village of Amobia: "The fierce characters had ropes or chains around their waists which were held by burly attendants to prevent them from attacking the crowd." However, the blackened nakedness of the performers is not so much typical of the Leeward Islands but more akin to the Jab Jab Molasses of Trinidad and Grenada, who daub their bodies with grease or molasses and threaten to smear onlookers, supposedly converting them to become as they are (Myron Jackson, pers. comm., July 20, 1995). Day (1852, 314) recalls "gangs" of "maskers" who paraded the streets of Trinidad in the mid–nineteenth century: "The primitives were negroes, as nearly naked as might be, bedaubed with a black varnish. One of this gang had a long chain and padlock attached to his leg, which chain the others pulled. . . . As the chained one was occasionally thrown down on the ground, and treated with a mock bastinadoing it probably represented slavery."

Reports of marginal or fierce characters become more plentiful in the twentieth century. On January 8, 1907, the *St. Thomas Bulletin* reports that on Three Kings' Day, "at evening . . . . 'Death' stalked about and scared many." Accounts from other islands indicate that Death is likely to have worn a death's head mask, depicting a skull, with a white skeleton imprinted on a black costume, as is reported in Trinidad in the mid–nineteenth century: "One personation of Death, having what was understood to be a skeleton painted on a coal-black shape, stalked about with part of a horse's vertebra attached to him, and a horse's thigh bone in his hand" (Day 1852, 315). Similarly dressed

Fig. 7.2. Death's head masquerades, Virgin Islands Carnival, St. Thomas, ca. 1963. Courtesy Miles Raymond.

maskers appeared in the St. Thomas Carnival in the early 1960s. Pirates and other renegades appeared periodically among the masquerades, stereotypically wearing boots, matelot vests, eye patches, and pirates' hats. Helen Joseph (pers. comm., August 13, 1996) remembers the ghost performing in Christiansted: He "would swoop down on you. He was tall and dressed all in white. His hands were covered in a white sheet. A skull face adorned his face."

Long Ghosts/Long Tom

Standing about twelve feet high, the top section of the costume of the Long Ghosts of Antigua was a cylindrical mask with cuts for eyes and nose and a grotesque configuration of teeth illuminated by an internal candle. The mask was inscribed on both front and back, providing a Janus effect. The Long Ghosts roamed the streets at Christmas in search of donations; if money was not forthcoming, a string inside the costume was pulled, making the arms wave and adding a sinister effect. In Tortola, in the British Virgin Islands,

Eadie (1931, 68–69) remembers Long Tom, "a ghostly figure about ten feet high, wearing a mask, with two fiery orbs for eyes. Beneath his long white robes emerged a pair of enormous flat feet. His antics invariably strike terror into the hearts of the picnees and even the dusky youths and maidens flee if he pursues them. All night long he parades from one cabin to another accompanied by dancers, players, and minstrels." A more advanced form of tall masquerade is known as Egunugu in Freetown, Sierra Leone, or Igunugu in Nigeria. The main difference between Long Tom and Egunugu is that the latter can telescope from relatively small to as tall as twenty feet high (Nunley 1987, 201).

The Devil

The devil had horns, a tail, and a long chain. But whereas the bull's horns were broad and spreading, the devil's were small and pointed, possibly from a goat or a younger bull. Evelyn Richardson (1984, 147) remembers a devil in Frederiksted, St. Croix, during her childhood in the first decade of the nineteenth century: "He was dressed in a black robe with bull horns lashed onto his head and an iron chain around his waist with a handbell. He had quite a following of children though most of us were afraid of him. His face was painted red and he gave out a loud roar as he came near you!"

Frank Charles (pers. comm., July 1, 1996) remembers the Wild Devil with horns in Enfield Green, St. Croix, about 1912. He wore a ragged shirt and old blue drill pants, and his feet were bare. Ethel McIntosh (pers. comm., July 9, 1995) saw a devil with cow horns and a tail. The costume was made of burlap and retained its tan color. The tail was a burlap cylinder with paper or cloth inside it to make it stiff. He carried a whip because children tried to pull his tail. The devil might wear a wire mask or he might decorate his face with chalk and paint. Leroy Arnold (pers. comm., July 8, 1995) remembers a devil's costume made from a large red and green piece of cloth put together by a seamstress; he wore a safe-wire mask painted to look fierce. The devil also performed in the St. Thomas Carnival parade in the 1950s. According to Charles Turnbull (pers. comm., June 19, 1996), the performer donned a black costume with a black cotton mask with openings for the eyes. His horns were sometimes real and sometimes artificial. On some occasions, the devil was accompanied by imps—children dressed in black with little horns and little whips. One Easter Monday in Christiansted, Maurice Thomas (pers. comm., July 7, 1995) saw "Lucifer," dressed in red with horns, a tail, and a pitchfork. He had an open face, with no paint or mask.

The Bull

Many elders in the Virgin Islands remember the bull chasing children with its chain dragging on the ground as if it had broken loose from its grapnel. Asta O'Bryan James (pers. comm., July 3, 1996) remembers a chain hanging from the bull's waist in St. Croix: "No chain could hold him as he represented a fierce and powerful creature." Richard Schrader (1989, 64) remembers seeing Smokey Joe from Bethlehem play the bull on St. Croix in the 1930s, again with his chain dragging along the ground: "This character was most feared by us children. He acted so crazy and mean; he ran after us as though he wanted to gore us with his horns."

Mother Hubbard

What constitutes a marginal or deviant character is not always obvious. As a consequence of the mutable quality of many masks, a well-defined, clean-cut mask can degenerate during an outing and become increasingly grotesque. Even the relatively innocuous Mother Hubbard played a role in social regulation. Each Mother Hubbard carried a tamarind cane, and according to Ethel McIntosh (pers. comm., July 9, 1995), the performers were prepared to use their canes on mischievous children. Schrader (1989, 2) remembers one Mother Hubbard masquerader in particular, Mrs. Langley, who "wore one of the ugliest masks I have seen as a child. . . . Just the mention of her name gave me the creeps and brought immediate silence in the Children's Home. . . . She was our cooler and we feared her."

Decrease in Symbolic Distance, Fire Hazard

Over time, the respect shown for masquerades in the Caribbean has waned, reducing their effectiveness as an agent of social control. The dry shaggy vegetal costume proved to be a fire hazard. Sensay masquerades were barred from the Dominican Carnival in 1963 after arson occurred on King George Street in the capital, Roseau, and three costumed individuals—Eddie Martin, George James, and Eric Shillingford—lost their lives. A reality was thus exposed: The bush costumes that had previously inspired awe had an Achilles' heel (Honychurch [2004b]). This vulnerability was demonstrated several times in the Lesser Antilles in the twentieth century—for example, in 1976 in St. John's, Antigua, when a John Bull burned to death. On July 4, 1933, in Frederiksted, St. Croix, Paddy Moore's bulrush costume was set on fire by a thrown cigarette. Moore was known as an agile dancer with finely tuned reflexes and rapid movements, and onlookers assumed the gyrations were part of his act until he set off running. Stanley Jacobs (pers. comm., June 30, 1996) maintains that Moore's speed probably saved his life, enabling him to reach the sea to douse the flames. Schrader (1996, 115) says that "according to one source, the man who threw the lighted cigarette on Paddy, said that Paddy was 'plehin' de devil. An' if de devil deh ah hell he must gah fire 'round he rass."

Such events are not mentioned in literature from the nineteenth century or earlier, and this outcome may thus reflect an erosion of respect as the symbolic and physical distance between players and bystanders decreased over time, leaving masquerades vulnerable. In the past, traditional Mandinka bush masquerades received considerable respect and secrecy that aided in their protection: "When the [Kankurang] roamed the streets at night, cooking fires were extinguished, lights were switched off, and women would close their doors and hide" (De Jong 2007, 143). Samai, a Jola masquerade in the Casamance region, explicitly addresses the issue: Fires must not be lit in his presence (Mark 1983, 13). Samai is a burlap-covered figure with a wooden horned mask who is a companion to the Kumpo masquerade, who wears a bushy costume made of the dry, highly flammable fibers of the fan palm, though Samai's burlap costume is less at risk. The Jarimamma masquerade similarly guards Kumpo in Diatock village in the Casamance, and masks with similar functions have been described among the Dan. They likely originated as "policemen" to ensure that cooking fires were extinguished after use in the dry season (Mark 1983, 13). In Dominica, the ban on Sensay was lifted in 1993 with precise entry regulations imposed (Honychurch [1982]; Honychurch [2004b]).

CHRISTMAS SATURNALIA

Prior to emancipation, Christmas and New Year's were the high point of the slaves' year in the West Indies, and with resources invested in the celebrations, they were actively involved in the festivities. In the mid-1840s in the Virgin Islands, according to Victor Schoelcher, "The Negroes have three days of freedom, three days of unlimited independence, over which their masters have nothing to say." Thus, he concludes, Christmas "might be properly considered the Saturnalia of modern slavery" (Tyson 1995, 7). In Barbados, Trelawny Wentworth (1834, 2:37), a member of the white elite, recalled, "For three days, all business or control over [the slaves], and all distinctions of rank cease, so far, at least, as they do what they please, within the bounds of justifiable liberty and hilarity." There was also a notable "spirit of rebellion on the part of the negroes, which too frequently has manifest at this particular season. [It was] deemed expedient to put martial law in force during the holidays" (39). As the holidays drew near, whites took steps to ensure their safety and protect their properties. Those residing in towns hurried to their estates, while others mobilized as militia to stand guard against anticipated attacks. In St. Croix, it was "considered sufficient to consign the troops, to keep arms at the ready and to maintain the horse of the cavalry and artillery saddled in a state of readiness in their stables" (Tyson 1995, 7). Janet J. Schaw (1939, 108) spent Christmas 1774 in Antigua, where "at this Season the crack of the inhuman whip must not be heard" and "it is necessary . . . to keep a look out during this season of unbounded freedom; and every man on the island is in arms, and patrols go all round the different plantations as well as keep guard in the town. They are an excellent disciplined Militia." Amid the glittering spectacle of the slaves' Saturnalia, many planters felt ill at ease because "Christmas meant setting aside the very premise of inequality upon which relations normally rested and replacing it with a cordial and sportive, if at times somewhat tense egalitarianism" (Dirks 1987, ix). Whites feared that slaves' withdrawal from their usual servile roles engendered a capacity for real violence and insurrection. Schoelcher observes, "The job of the miserable helots is frightening for their masters and it is always to be feared that a rebellion might occur as a result of it all" (Tyson 1995, 7). Dirks (1987, 189) states, "If those who ran the estates were not fully committed to the spirit of the bacchanal, at least they were aware of having to deal with an 'overheated boiler' and were prepared to bend every effort toward making sure it did not explode."

Christmas thus was a tense time for the white administrators and planters, and their anxiety was not without grounds. Dirks (1987, 168) has reckoned that nearly one-third of the rebellions in the British Caribbean were planned and executed during the festive month. In December 1759, a Christmastime plot was uncovered on St. Croix: "When the whites began their Christmas celebration in earnest, and thought of nothing but a good time, "the insurgents, who included both free blacks and slaves, planned to "go out and shoot white-headed pigeons" (Westergaard 1926, 53). The rebellion was exposed, and more than a dozen conspirators were executed. During Christmas week 1839–40 in St. Croix, Alexander Wilde recalled half a century later, "No matter how much excitement nothing disturbing would occur, but the authorities were always pleased to see men of war nearby" (translated in Colby Papers, Whim Museum Research Library, St. Croix). Slaves would not be denied their celebrations, which they viewed as rightfully theirs. In 1701, Major Samuel Martin of Antigua made the mistake of denying his laborers the Christmas holiday: In response, on December 27 they butchered him (Dirks 1987, 163).

Joseph Tuckerman (1837, 25) describes the 1836–37 St. Croix holiday festivities as a "complete Saturnalia": One man was "alternatively serving his guests with cake and wine, and, although he was seventy-three years of age, joining with them in their dances." Emphasizing the merely temporary inversion of social distinctions, however, Tuckerman concludes, "But their liberty expired with the day. They slept, and were again slaves." Saturnalia enabled common people in the Eastern Caribbean briefly to exert a power they did not possess in their everyday lives and to make sociopolitical statements intended to redress social ills.

Compared to Gombay and Bamboula songs, masquerading was viewed as relatively innocuous, and the administration appeared to tacitly endorse it. Toward the final years of the nineteenth century, pressure to quell boisterous music and dance in the Virgin Islands increased, but the repression was aimed more at African drum dances with their biting song texts than at masquerading. The perambulatory aspect of the masquerades' parades probably rendered them more transitory and less disturbing to the elites than drum dances, which remained in one spot for days and nights at a time. The establishment sometimes appeared at times to encourage masquerading, apparently believing it to be the lesser of the two evils. The practice may have been less alien to European sensibilities since it bore some resemblances to European Christmas mumming; alternatively, officials may have taken a gradual approach toward extinguishing perceived remnants of African culture. On January 7, 1865, the *St. Thomas Tidende* discussed the pros and cons of masquerading: "Groups of persons dressed in masquerade have paraded the streets, and would seem to have afforded much pleasure both to themselves and their numerous beholders. To the children and nurses, it no doubt proved an excellent substitute for our bygone Militia [parades], and could there . . . be imparted to it some method . . . it could oftener be indulged in as a source of public amusement." The editorial offers only an aesthetic critique but clearly indicates that masquerading had establishment support, while drum dances did not. This seems to have been adopted as policy, for in 1872, S. B. Haynes (1872, 201) reports, "The Danish governor, who understood the material he had to deal with, this year permitted the privilege of masquerading, wisely concluding that this gratification of vanity would prevent the riot of drunkenness of former occasions." However, masqueraders often danced to the music of songs that extolled the virtues of anti-establishment figures such as Queen Mary, a leader of the 1878 Fireburn.

Public ridicule performed as a masquerade caricature was used as a behavior modification technique in West Africa. In his discussion of the Igbo, Victor Uchendu (1965) outlines a notion he describes as "transparent living"—that

Fig. 7.3. Masquerades parade in Christiansted, St. Croix, ca. 1900. Note flute and drum players to the rear. Photo by Alfred Paludan-Müller. Courtesy Royal Library, Copenhagen, Department of Maps, Prints, and Photographs.

is, rendering invisible behaviors visible, a technique that can lead to irreverence and mockery. Ottenberg and Binkley (2006, 120) describes the popular Okumkpa masquerade of the Afikpo Igbo of Nigeria: "A variety of masqueraders sang and acted out humorous and scurrilous events that had occurred in the community within the past year. The masqueraders impersonated and named individuals, ridiculing them, often making moral comments on their behavior." The technique was used in the Eastern Caribbean to instigate change, with errant individuals ridiculed in masquerade or shamed in song. Writing of the early Trinidad Carnival, James Edward Alexander (1833, 206–7) conjures up the Greek god Momus, god of mockery, blame, ridicule, fault finding, and censure: "At the period when the people give loose their gaiety, at the Carnival, every house in Port of Spain is thrown open and the authority of Momus universally acknowledged. Groups of masks perambulate the streets at all hours, and as much life and spirit are then shown, as there is listlessness during the previous period of the year."

The busiest time for lampooning in the British West Indies was Christmas and New Year. An account from Jamaica in the early nineteenth century shows how recognizable personages might be caricaturized in masquerade: "The John Canoe, who was the workhouse driver, was dressed up in lawyer's cast-off gown and bands, black silk breeches, no stockings or shoes, but with sandals of bullock's hide strapped on his . . . feet, a small cocked hat on his head, to which were appended a large cauliflower wig, and the usual white false face, bearing a very laughable resemblance to Chief-Justice S——, with whom I happened to be personally acquainted" (Scott 1836/1999, 253).

To guard against negative repercussions from planters and administrators, messages were encoded or rendered obliquely to keep outsiders in the dark. Earnest social commentators often had to disguise themselves as comedians. Cynthia Oliver (1995, 74) states, "Under the guise of the silly[, entertainers] communicated important messages of either highly personal nature or that which the slave public at large needed to hear." Discussing the Niega Business troupe, whose sole purpose is to lampoon higher-ups, Mills, Jones-Hendrickson, and Bertram (1984, 10) state, "If the West Indian is known in general for hyperbole in speech when he resorts to the vernacular, it reaches its zenith in this sport." Masquerades that parodied such authority figures as gendarmes, admirals, and clerics were relatively common, and texts making fun of elites and administrators that would not have been permitted at other times appeared in festival songs and comical speeches. In the Virgin Islands in the early twentieth century, Albert Halliday portrayed a pompous cleric, Parson Darknight, who read from a ledger that was an upside-down Sears, Roebuck catalog, including profound perspectives within otherwise nonsensical diatribes (Nicholls 1998, 35). Although much of his oratory was humorous, Halliday often included satirical insights into the operations and thought patterns of the white establishment, known as buckra: "Thanks to 'Buddo,' ahwee bruck slavery chain long ahgoh. Ahwee one, happy, free people. Bu' buckra seh ahwee choopid. And only good foh sing, dance, cut cane and grass. Bu' lil do buckra knoh, ah deh same choopid Nega sah cut buckra rass. Ha! Ha! Ha! MUSIC!" (Schrader 1989, 64).

Masquerade performances enjoyed a special kind of license and served as a vehicle for otherwise prohibited or inappropriate criticism, joking, or aggression. Turnbull (pers. comm., June 19, 1996) suggests that some of the deeper levels of communication may not have been fully understood by the participants themselves. He cites the David and Goliath troupes who dramatized the biblical confrontation. The idea that a righteous little person could overcome a larger bully was inspirational and appealed to a subjugated population; however, that symbolism and psychological aspect can be appreciated in retrospect but were probably not expressed explicitly at that time. In Antigua, the people co-opted the name of England's national symbol, John Bull, for their principal animal masquerade, representing him as fearsome, but at the same time they turned the tables by subjecting him to a flogging. In this way, the Antiguans remodeled their negative experience of oppression and resentment against the colonizers in a perceptible but camouflaged form.

Plate 33. John Bulls square off during New Year's festival, St. John's, Antigua, 1994. Note big drum on left. Photo by Skip's. Courtesy Chinwe Osaze.

Plate 34. John Bull of the Vitus Mas' group, Antigua, Christmas 1999. Photo by Robert Nicholls. Courtesy Keva Margetson, director of Vitus Mas'.

Plate 35. Jam Bull with drummers, Main Street, during Virgin Islands Carnival, Charlotte Amalie, St. Thomas, 2001. Gassau Peltier on bass drum, Huntley Heywood on kettle drum, and Lassington Jackson on steel (triangle). Photo by Blake. Courtesy Jam Bull Cultural Productions.

Plate 36. George "Pope" Farrell as Jam Bull, on stage at Lionel Roberts Stadium, Virgin Islands Carnival, Charlotte Amalie, St. Thomas, April 28, 2001. Photo by Robert Nicholls.

Plate 37. Glenn "Trini" Pierre as Jam Bull in ankle-length costume with a rubber mask, accompanied by whip man Austin Burnett, Virgin Islands Carnival, Charlotte Amalie, St. Thomas, April 28, 2001. Photo by Blake. Courtesy Jam Bull Cultural Productions.

Plate 38. Mocko Jumbie on Main Street, Virgin Islands Carnival, Charlotte Amalie, St. Thomas, ca. 2002. Photo by Robert Nicholls.

Plate 39. Mystical Mocko Jumbies, Virgin Islands Carnival, Charlotte Amalie, St. Thomas, April 26, 1997. Photo by Robert Nicholls.

Plate 40. Mocko Jumbie dancer Gerard Luz James II follows a Pitchy Patchy masquerade worn by Amy Gill, Emancipation Day parade, Frederiksted, St. Croix, July 3, 1995. Photo by Robert Nicholls.

Plate 41. Stilt dancer in the Moko Jumbi 'n' Fren Dem troupe, Reichhold Center for the Arts, St. Thomas, 1996. Courtesy Naomi Baylarian.

Plate 42. Sensay in Dominica with bitonal mask, ca. 1998. Courtesy Joseph Jones.

Plate 43. Sensay at Carnival, South City, Dominica, 2010. Photo by Edona Jno Baptiste. Courtesy Kneath Warrington.

Plate 44. Parade of Sensay masquerades in burlap costumes at Carnival, South City, Dominica, 2010. Photo by Edona Jno Baptiste. Courtesy Kneath Warrington.

Plate 46. Horned Sensay of Waseen Dominica Association, Virgin Islands Carnival, Lionel Roberts Stadium, Charlotte Amalie, St. Thomas, 2009. Photo by Robert Nicholls.

Plate 45. Sensay of Waseen Dominica Association in burlap costume, Virgin Islands Carnival, Lionel Roberts Stadium, Charlotte Amalie, St. Thomas, 2009. Photo by Robert Nicholls.

Plate 47. Sensay (Pitchy Patchy) with the Vitus Mas' group, Antigua, Christmas 1999. Photo by Robert Nicholls. Courtesy Keva Margetson, director of Vitus Mas'.

Plate 48. Carnival clowns with stocking masks, thread spools as horns, and whips, Charlotte Amalie, St. Thomas, ca. 1963. Courtesy Miles Raymond.

Plate 49. Clown with the Vitus Mas' group, Antigua, Christmas 1999. Photo by Robert Nicholls. Courtesy Keva Margetson, director of Vitus Mas'.

Plate 50. Heraldic clown with clap whip, Virgin Islands Carnival, Charlotte Amalie, St. Thomas, April 26, 1997. Photo by Robert Nicholls.

Plate 52. Carnival clown with featureless black mask, Virgin Islands Carnival, Charlotte Amalie, St. Thomas, April 26, 1997. Photo by Robert Nicholls.

Plate 51. Clown twins of the Tropical Masqueraders troupe, Children's Parade, St. Thomas, April 25, 1997. Photo by Robert Nicholls.

Plate 53. Montserrat masqueraders perform at Antiguan Festival, St. John's, 1994. Courtesy Richard A. Schrader.

Plate 54. Highlanders with the Vitus Mas' group, Antigua, Christmas 1999. Photo by Robert Nicholls. Courtesy Keva Margetson, director of Vitus Mas'.

Plate 55. Carriacou Shakespeare Mas' player Albert "Donkey" Duncan, Top Hill, Carriacou, March 29, 2007. Courtesy Joan Fayer and Joan McMurray.

Plate 56. Kittitian wire-screen mask with peacock feathers, St. Thomas, ca. 1996. Photo by Robert Nicholls. Courtesy Wendy Warner.

Plate 57. Montserrat masquerade mask, Plymouth, Montserrat, 1995. Photo by Robert Smith. Courtesy *Caribbean Week*.

Plate 58. Mystical Mocko Jumbie mask, Virgin Islands Carnival, Charlotte Amalie, St. Thomas, April 26, 1997. Photo by Robert Nicholls.

Plate 59. Aboriginal Mocko Jumbie masquerade with faceless black mask, Virgin Islands Carnival, Charlotte Amalie, St. Thomas, April 26, 1997. Photo by Robert Nicholls.

Plate 60. Mocko Jumbie performer Alvin "Alli" Paul in a fine gauze mask and Fulani-style hat, Virgin Islands Carnival, Charlotte Amalie, St. Thomas, April 26, 1997. Photo by Robert Nicholls.

Plate 61. Naomi Baylarian of Moko Jumbi 'n' Fren Dem troupe, wearing a net mask, St. Thomas, 1996. Photo by Robert Nicholls.

Plate 62. Moko Jumbi 'n' Fren Dem cloth mask with noodle design made by Naomi Baylarian, 1996. Photo by Robert Nicholls.

Plate 63. Tropical Masqueraders member donning her costume, Virgin Islands Carnival, Charlotte Amalie, St. Thomas, April 26, 1997. Spectators would assume that this performer is male. Photo by Robert Nicholls.

Plate 64. Jester troupe member, Virgin Islands Carnival, Charlotte Amalie, St. Thomas, ca. 2002. The performer's painted face serves as a disguise. Photo by Robert Nicholls.

Plate 65. Promenader with exposed torso and beaded costume, Virgin Islands Carnival, Charlotte Amalie, St. Thomas, ca. 2002. Photo by Robert Nicholls.

CONCLUSION

THE IMPACT OF RELIGIOUS CENSURE

Both Islam and Christianity are Abrahamic religions that have generally discouraged traditional masquerading in its various forms and often actively eradicated it. Throughout the centuries, Christians' criticism of the practice has been relentless, and masquerading has been accused of preserving heathenism. In many ways, traditional African religions and the animistic religions of pre-Christian Europe are similar. Both focused on local sources of spiritual power and pragmatic outcomes. The list of prohibitions embedded in the Ecclesiastical Canons of King Edgar in A.D. 959 reveal some European pre-Christian beliefs: "Well worshipings . . . divinations, and enchantments, and . . . various spells, and with 'frithsplots' (estuaries) and with elders [elder tree, *Sambucus nigra*], and also with various other trees, and with stones." Trees were central to both Western European and West African belief systems. In Nordic areas, the ash tree (*Fraxinus excelsior*) was favored, while the Celtic Druids believed the oak (*Quercus robur*) was divine. In Upper Guinea, baobabs (*Adansonia digitata*) were known as palaver trees, while the Jola's *forêt sacrée* was the habitat of the sacred silk cotton tree (*Ceiba pentandra*). Christianity in Britain developed both as a reaction against and in accommodation to the paganism of the inhabitants, and its final form was conditioned by the old religion. That is why the Sabbath is the Sun Day and the days of week denote Anglo-Saxon deities. Saint Augustine II (d. A.D. 604) was a Roman monk sent to convert the English to Christianity. Established traditions were accommodated (for a while), churches were built on or near existing temples, and holy days (Christmas and Easter) were timed to coincide with pagan feast days.

The clash between missionaries and indigenous religion in Africa is well documented. Unlike England, where the new beliefs were grafted onto preexisting customs, Christianity in Africa obligated a cultural tabula rasa whereby traditional religious practices need be razed. Discussing Church Mission Society missionaries of African origin at the Niger-Benue confluence in the

1860s, Femi Kolapo (2000, 94) states, "At Lokoja, the mission party was responsible for cutting down two trees that were sacred to the local people to make way for a road under construction." Missionary James Thomas "took the opportunity to speak with [a village head] in [concerning] the third Chapter [of the] 'Lamentation of Jeremiah' about the futility of pleading with a tree" (94). During the building of Abuja, the new federal capital of Nigeria, in the 1980s, most of the local Gwari people had to relocate. Many were bitter, not only because they received inadequate compensation but because their sacred groves and tree shrines had been leveled to make way for the new construction while the federal government had allocated twelve million dollars each for the building of a mosque and a cathedral, monuments to religions that the Gwari saw as essentially non-African (Shekwo 1984).

In Upper Guinea in 1939, Father Doutremépuich and a Kankuran "nearly came to blows" when the Catholic priest tried to "'rescue' members of his congregation from their two month seclusion in the sacred forest" (Mark 1983, 9). The priest had no trouble identifying the masks as "the Devil, or at least a son of the Devil" (Doutremépuich 1939). In this respect, there was mutual agreement between Doutremépuich and the guardians who referred to the Kankuran as a demon (*seytané*, or Satan) (De Jong 2007, 109), which attests to the penetration of Islamic terminology (and perceptions) into the local parlance. Nunley (1987, 13) documents an 1843 altercation in Sierra Leone between the Reverend R. Amos and an Egungun Hunting Society devil in "one of the many liberated African villages surrounding Freetown." When Amos "warned the masked procession that the devil was in the image of Satan, they replied: 'It has nothing to do with the white man, it was their country-fashion and to that they must keep.'" Then, the reverend recorded, "They shouted pooh! pooh! and struck the tomtoms with redoubling fury, their hellish appearance and infernal gesticulations harrowed up my feelings'" (13).

Censure in Islam

In African areas that became Muslim, Islamic theology significantly affected traditional culture, art, and masquerade traditions. Mary Smith (1981, 286) observes, "The adherents of different explanatory principles (spirits, medicine and the will of Allah) carry on competition between these principles on a practical plane." Muslims viewed masquerades as agents of supernatural power: In the case of the Sengko masquerade, for example, "the masker becomes the *djinn*" (Weil 1988, 166). Moreover, "the *sengko* is regarded as a 'bush thing' that is empowered by a spirit that is, under Islam, categorized as a *djinn* or *gino*. . . The *ginos* . . . have become regarded as competitive with Allah and the achievement of sacred goals" (160). Accordingly, Muslims regard the vital forces derived from nature that are believed to animate masquerades as adversative to Islam. Weil states, "Pre-Islamic positive vital forces tended to be redefined in the Mandinka conception of Islam as inherently evil and antithetical to human society and to life as a true Muslim. . . . The linkage of those forces with specific masquerades and their related rituals has resulted in the masquerades and rituals being either only minimally tolerated or eliminated in community life by Muslims who are increasingly strong and numerous" (158).

According to De Jong (2007, 123), most Muslims among the Jola of Ziguinchor "tolerate traditions as long as they remain compatible with Muslim obligations. Initiation has thus been incorporated into the local Islamic discourse as a 'tradition,' as has the Kankurang masquerade. Although some Muslims prefer to define the Kankurang as a Devil opposed to Allah's powers, the mask is now always understood in Muslim categories. The Kankurang mask is no longer perceived as the transformation of an elder but as a *jino* subordinate to Allah."

Islam includes strictures against figurative representations of humans or animals because such representations are believed to encourage idolatry. Accordingly, Mark (1992, 143) noticed that Muslims were more tolerant of *usikoi* initiates who simply wear a horned cap than of Ejumba masquerades that wear horns plus a face mask, concluding that a "significant factor affecting the masks' acceptance by Muslims would appear to be the presence or absence of a face." As a consequence, raffia masquerades fare better because a face mask is absent. This supposition is borne out by the Jola's adoption of Kankuran at the end of the nineteenth century. Mark (1983, 9) states, "The introduction of Kankuran among the Diola [Jola] appears to have been directly associated with the spread of Islam. . . . Today, in Muslim Diola communities, Kankuran plays a role in the 'bukut' [initiation], where it helps to enforce discipline." Finally, however, Weil (1971) believes that the decline of traditional masquerades in Upper Guinea has less to do with the adoption of Islam than with the increasing secularization of tradition in the face of modernity-induced changes in the economic and social structure. Bilby depicts the increasing secularization of the Jonkonnu masquerade as a rearguard action and a defensive maneuver that is less than positive.

Censure in Christianity

Since Christianity was introduced to Europe, a restriction of masquerading has been the modus operandi, and Christian prohibition in fact provides a primary source of information about Christmas guising. Edgar's canons reflect the spirit of the mission. He enjoined "that every priest zealously promote Christianity, and totally extinguish every heathenism, [and] on feast days heathen songs and devil's games be abstained from." Nearly five hundred years earlier, around A.D. 500, Bishop Caesarius of Arles angrily reported that at New Year's celebrations, even baptized women disguised themselves as deer or bitches, covered themselves with the skins of animals, or put on animal heads. In A.D. 578, the Council of Auxerre forbade dressing up as a stag of calf on the "kalends of January," while in Britain between the years 1000 and 1002, Wulfstan, archbishop of York, forbade pagan songs and games on Christian feast days (Hutton 1991, 298). In medieval Europe, the practice of masquerading continued to be viewed with disfavor by those in power. In 1333, the Bishop of Exeter started a thirty-year campaign to prevent masking and mimes at Christmas (Hutton 1997, 99). Orders of the city of London in 1334, 1393, and 1405 forbade wearing false faces (masks) in the streets at Christmas. In 1417, "mummying" was included in the prohibitions, and in 1418 a proclamation banned the wearing of "peyntid visers and diffourmyd or colourid visages." A 1511 act of Parliament forbade house visits by "persons with Vysoures . . . disguised or apparelde as Mommers" (E. K. Chambers 1903/1967, 1:394). Puritan Philip Stubbes (1583, 189) condemned the Lord of Misrule parades with "hobby-horses, Dragons and other Antiques [and] dancing . . . like devils incarnate." As a result of the Puritan revolution, even the seemingly innocuous Maypole was suppressed, and around 1640, the wardens of Wandsworth in Surrey dug up the village Maypole (Hutton 1994, 201). Appropriately, "maypoles formed gathering-points for popular uprisings in May 1648 at Bury St. Edmunds in Suffolk and in Kent" (210). Lowe (1957, 76) records that in 1655, a case was brought to the Staffordshire quarter sessions involving Lapley morris dancers—nine men and four women, "mostly husbandmen and papists," who were charged with "dancing promiscuously"; one was even accused of having "danced in woman's apparel." By 1647, Christmas, Easter, Whitsun, and all other church feasts were abolished by both secular and ecclesiastical ruling (Hutton 1994, 212). The censure extended to the New World. Nissenbaum (1996, 1) points out that because of Christmas's pagan roots and unruly public displays, Puritan Massachusetts outlawed the celebration of the holiday from 1659 to 1681. In 1687, Norway enacted a law that banned Julebukks: "All frivolous and contemptible games at Christmas or other times and the Lenten races, are strictly prohibited, and offenders must be seriously punished." Denmark had already forbidden the Julebukk nineteen years earlier, and Sweden soon followed suit. Although the Julebukk disappeared from Danish soil, it continued in Norway and large parts of Sweden because church pressure and state laws were less easy to enforce than was the case in Denmark.

Fig. 8.1. Julegetta (Christmas goat) mask with clacking jaws from Fredrikstad, Norway, ca. 1920. Courtesy Fredrikstad Museum, Old Town, Fredrikstad, Norway.

Composer Percy Grainger attended the North Lincolnshire Musical Competition Festival in England in 1905 and documented more than fifty songs by local singers. Pearson (2007) laments the fact that just at the time when rural performances in Lincolnshire came under the scrutiny of an emerging generation of folklore collectors such as Grainger, such performances were at the point of disappearance. The situation resulted in part from rural depopulation as a consequence of agricultural depression; soon thereafter, World War I killed and demoralized many other carriers of tradition. Pearson also points out that the demise of such mumming was presaged by opposition in the press: As early as 1821, publishers were applauding magistrates who "visit with exemplary severity the misconduct of persons who appear as Morris-dancers, or Plough Bullocks, or under the names of similar character" (123). J. G. Frazer and G. C. Moore Smith (1909, 202) report that in 1909, the police in Whittlesey, Cambridgeshire, England, prevented performers from taking around the plow on Plow Monday because they saw it as a form of cadging. This action led to the cessation of the Straw Bear perambulation, which was part of plow play activities. It is a testament both to the resilience of masquerades and the need for masquerading in human lives that the Straw Bear survived the early-twentieth-century bans, was revived in 1979 by Brian Kell, and now regularly attracts visitors to the town (Ridgwell 2003, 9).

Censure in the Caribbean

Honychurch ([2004a]) explains that in Dominica, African religions and beliefs were outlawed from the earliest days of plantation slavery, not merely because they were seen to be pagan, primitive, and generally un-Christian but more because the plantocracy feared that these practices provided a cover for revolt. In Jamaica in 1842, "several Negroes residing on an estate near Montego Bay gave themselves out to be Myal men; and in St. James, Westmoreland, and Trewlawney, thousands of deluded people became their followers." The ritual activities of such large number of people attracted the censure of the establishment, and "it became necessary at last to swear in several hundreds of special constables, and punish numbers of these deluded people for disturbing the peace" (Joseph J. Williams 1932, 148–49). According to Bilby (2010, 183), myalism was part of Jonkonnu practices in Coker, Jamaica, and religious or spiritual meanings were lost or become submerged over time through a process of cultural erosion supported by hegemonic colonial ideologies that stigmatized any visible traces of the African past. Bilby points to role of Christian evangelizing in this process, especially on Cat Island, with its "long history of intensive Christian missionization, of Western theological principles" (195). Within performances in the Bahamas, Jamaica, and Belize, Jonkonnu was "eventually overtaken by a gradual process of actual secularization (or partial secularization), it then survived as an 'icon' of the African spirituality it had once both embodied and concealed" (215).

Bilby's (2010, 211) major findings were centered in the Jonkonnu tradition of Coker, Jamaica, with their manifest spirituality, but even there a tension exists between Jonkonnu practitioners and Christian evangelical churches, and "the final outcome of this contentious encounter is not yet known." By balancing the cloaked public face and the inside private significance, performers previously forestalled a clash of worldviews in which the balance of power (both material and ideological) was clearly not in their favor (211). However, "such a clash finally became unavoidable in the latter half of the twentieth century, when a number of Christian evangelical churches (and, more importantly, their local proxies) penetrated the 'inside' spaces of Coker and became active right in the heart of the community, where the ancestral presence surviving under the 'mask' of Jankunu could not be concealed" (211). The result is a situation in which "the continuing existence of Coker's Jankunu tradition is likely to depend on its increasing 'secularization' via the ongoing incorporation of younger performers into touristic performance venues outside the community, official government-sponsored festivals, and the like—a process that has already begun" (211).

Bilby (2010, 211) argues that changes in the larger society that favored the dissimulation of an absence of spirit made the actual embodying of spirit increasingly untenable. He concludes, "Whether, and how, the kinds of spiritual meanings embodied in the ancestors' version of Jankunu will survive this process in Coker remains to be seen."

This discussion illuminates a situation that exists elsewhere in the Caribbean, including the Leeward Islands. In St. Thomas, one man has for years regularly submitted letters to the editor of the *Daily News* berating Carnival. A typical letter, printed on November 13, 1997, appeared under the title "All Souls' Practices Are Evil"; includes the words *satanic*, *witchcraft*, and *voodoo*; and invokes Christ as a panacea. The U.S. Virgin Islands have done better than the British Virgin Islands and neighboring St. Martin in preserving culture. Joan McMurray (2001b, 5) saw cultural erosion in Nevis and refers to the "historical irony" that marks the secularization of *Giant Despair* and *David and Goliath*: The church originally installed these plays but has come to reject them as immoral and has even condemned them as a "travesty on religion" (Alfred M. Williams 1896, 120). Writes McMurray, "Associating performances with sinful activity is apparently common in Nevis. In an interview with a [onetime] dancer in a Masquerade troupe I was told that his commitment to religion (Seventh-Day Adventist) was in conflict with his participation in Christmas Sports" (9n). Another man, Teddy Tross, "had been an active member of the Giant Despair troupe in Gingerland; but when he was 'called' to the pulpit of one of the evangelical churches, he promised to leave active membership in the troupe. [And] even talking about his 'secular' experiences with the troupe would be condemned by his church" (9n).

PAST, PRESENT, AND FUTURE

The idea of heteroglossia (multiple voices) reinforces the fact that masquerading can work on different levels and that more than one function may pertain. Bilby (2010, 217) maintains, "For its creators and early practitioners Jankunu was not simply the temporary 'rite of rebellion,' it appears to have been more important than this, it was an expression of an alternative worldview maintained through an ongoing dialogue with the ancestors." Limited interpretations do not consider the many complexities, and Bilby warns against considering only the views of "present-day scholars who filter the past solely through historical documents written by uncomprehending European observers" (217). Instead, he argues, "there is every reason to believe that Jankunu performances in the past, as in the present, contained complex, multiple layers of meaning [that can] come into play at different points and in different contexts, or even simultaneously" (195 n. 21). For Bilby, the spiritual significance of Caribbean masquerades has been routinely overlooked.

Historically, masquerading has been considered as a thing of pride, "of the ancestors," an artistic display that celebrated the essential character of Afro-Creoleness and what it means to be Caribbean. In the words of Bahamian Arlene Nash Ferguson (2000, 2), "The mere mention of the word 'Junkanoo' evokes strange and inexplicable emotions and compulsions. At the very core of your being, your 'Bahamianness,' the rhythm of a drum begins to pulsate, the beat vibrating through every pore of your body." Ultimately, the title of this book refers not only to the physical site of the performance arena but also to the milieu in which the masquerade operates, the social drama that is enacted, the aesthetics and spiritual values portrayed, and the impact of all of these factors on the community.

Even contemporary varieties of masquerade with purely secular performances arouse in some participants at least a vague and sometimes a powerful sense of the spiritual. Bilby (2010, 212, 213) makes the case that some Garifuna Jonkonnu performers in Belize claim that "the performance of Jankunu itself has the power to attract the spirit of the ancestors." In his study of the Ode-Lay societies of Sierra Leone, Nunley (1987, 12) points out that whereas "the European mind contemplated religious expression within walled space, the African mind found its expression of spirituality in music and dance, which themselves defined the sacred space." For Nunley, this "sense of kinesthesia" meant that Africans newly freed in Sierra Leone could take their rituals to spaces outside the reach of the church (20). Bilby (2010, 213) remarks, "this close connection between music and spirit, in fact, is present throughout the African Diaspora, where generations of scholars working in different areas have repeatedly encountered music, song, dances, and legends that have the power to attract, convey, dispel, honor, and celebrate the sacred energies of nature and the spirit worlds." In today's Caribbean, despite the drum machines and electronics, the Afro-Creole cultural spirit lives on in performances of modern soca bands such as Antigua's Burning Flames, the Virgin Islands' Jam Band, Barbados's Krosfyah, and Dominica's WCK. After all, many twenty-first-century carnival masquerades dance to this music. Robert Farris Thompson (1984, 118) invokes the idea of the flash of the spirit: When witnessing a masked Mocko Jumbie dancing to high-quality soca music, the flash and arrest of the spirit become palpable.

Various masquerade traditions have waxed and waned in the Eastern Caribbean. Caribbean masquerades have a potential advantage over British wassailers and other Old World masquerades in that the New World events are viewed through the lens of modern Carnival, which remains a vibrant force despite being less Saturnalian and more commercial than in previous times. Although often discussed disparagingly in the nineteenth-century newspapers, Caribbean animal disguises and other traditional masquerades survived into the twentieth century before declining, mostly as a result of the depression and the world wars. In the twenty-first century, the disguise element is less central and masks are less prevalent, with the exceptions of the Mocko Jumbie, Sensay, and carnival clowns, which continue to evolve as masquerade genres. Although the donkey occasionally performs, the bear is defunct, and Mother Hubbard seldom appears. Some masquerades have been resurrected within the carnival setting, but the context has changed, and traditional quêtes and perambulations for the purpose of greeting and bestowing good wishes are hardly maintained. Moreover, local respect for traditional masquerades is waning. Anthony Richards (pers. comm., March 15, 2012) remembers the fierceness of the bull in Antigua: "Once the whip started to crack, the bull would become enraged and charge at an unsuspecting group of children. Many soiled themselves, rooted to the spot." Richards also observes that the masqueraders no longer garner such awe, "and, dem blasted kids—dem aint 'fraid o nutten now." Moreover, the requirement for total disguise is often disregarded, and many performers do not bother to wear masks. Richards states (pers. comm., March 16, 2012), "I feel personally affronted when I see moko jumbies strapping on their stilts in full public view. I know that some other masquerade dancers feel the same way." The bull masquerade had virtually become extinct outside of Dominica and St. Kitts–Nevis, but it has recently reappeared in the Virgin Islands Carnival in St. Thomas.[1] (Plate 37)

Major differences between the mas' of yesteryear and current Carnival processions are to be expected, since economic factors are paramount: Carnival is a tourist attraction. Modern carnivals are substantially larger and grander than previous events, involving government sponsorship. Parades are consequently less spontaneous and more regimented, and participation requires registering as an official entrant or being part of a recognized troupe. The negative effects of overstructured and overregulated parades have been noted in the Bahamas: "Back in those days you could 'jump in.' In those days coming out meant coming out with a uniform on . . . then nobody knows you and that was the beauty of it. These days they all come out in big groups, but no masks" (A. B. Malcolm, interview, October 27, 1976, in Bettelheim 1979, 213). Myron Jackson (pers. comm., July 20, 1995) argues that in the Virgin Islands, Carnival appropriated masquerading traditions, and ownership moved from individual performers, families, and various neighborhoods to Carnival committees.

Rather than shunning recognition, modern troupe members flaunt themselves, and Carnival parades are comprised mostly of enhanced promenaders rather than disguised masqueraders. Nowadays, skimpy costumes and naked arms and legs are common, while faces and torsos are commonly exposed. The unencumbered flesh of modern Carnival is often equated to glitz and glamour. (Plate 65) Large troupes wearing elaborate helmets, colorful costumes, and face and body paint are the norm. The drums and acoustic instruments of former times are less in evidence; instead, amplified bands on trucks provide the music, and lascivious dances with sexually explicit themes are on show. Nevertheless, continuities exist; the festive atmosphere of mas' remains contagious, and Eastern Caribbean communities are still nourished and sustained by Carnival culture, with its costuming, parading, music, dance, and merriment. The credo of Willard John (pers. comm., September 13, 1995), director of the Guardians of Culture Mocko Jumbie troupe, is that "the best way to preserve culture is to live it." A twenty-first-century aesthetic renaissance is needed to counterbalance the advancement of ultrarational high tech, with more expressive affective experience not only in the Americas but globally. In the Caribbean, there is a need to recommit to time-honored customs, and because evangelical Christianity is pervasive in the Leeward Islands, there is a need for better accommodation between Christianity and traditional culture if the latter is to survive. An overarching goal should be educating local youngsters, who will be the eventual custodians of masquerading. Perhaps masquerading will find a niche in the business sector, as proposed by the Bahamian Festival in the Workplace initiative, which seeks to use the transforming agencies of festival and ritual to increase productivity and humanize the workplace.

There is a need for further interdisciplinary research in the international dimension of cultural interchange, especially the investigation of cultural transfers between European and African descendants in the Caribbean. As nourishing fare for the soul, traditional masquerades have tremendous strength and value and can be fascinating and multifarious artworks when the human imagination is given free rein rather than straitjacketed by convergent, antipantheistic schema. We need a new crop of researchers, a generation of clear thinkers who see the inherent worth of traditions that have buoyed humanity for millennia and who can bridge the divide between recording traditions and conserving them.

APPENDIXES

1. INFORMANTS IN THE VIRGIN ISLANDS

Leroy Arnold
Naomi Baylarian
Bertha Boschulte
Violet Aggie Bough
Lithia Brady
Irvin Brown
Leona Bryant
Frank Charles
Bradley Christian
Mary Ann Christopher
William Cissel
Anne Marie Danet
Alma Doward
Elmira Espinoza
Rudy Farrell
Amelia Gill
Arnold Golden
Veronica Gordon
Clacia Hendrickson
Naomi Jacobs
Stanley Jacobs
Asta O'Bryan James
Austin James
Gerard Luz James
Willard John
Helen Joseph
Alfred Lockhart
Cain Magras
Charles Matthew
Hortencia McIntosh
Estelle McIntosh
Ethel McIntosh
Sylvester McIntosh
Gertrude Melchior
Eileen Messer
Ruth Moolenaar
Ayesha Morris
Wilford Pedro
Alexander Petersen
Lornetta Prince
Philip Rhymer
William Richardson
Eulalie Rivera
Elmo Roebuck
Lena Schulterbrand
Mary Seales
Elroy Sprauve
Maurice Thomas
Elaine Urgent
Rufus Vanderpool
Tracy Warner
Leona Watson
Celestino White
Asta Williams
Regina Williams

2. DIASPORA IN REVERSE

The Caribbean has been depicted as a recipient of Old World ideas, and the basis of this research, as with other research on Afro-Creole culture, is that traits inherited from the Old World took root in the Caribbean. However, it is a mistake to view the Caribbean and

African diaspora as merely recipients of customs originating elsewhere (see Blyden 2000). Transatlantic exchanges occurred in both directions; indeed, Atlantic Rim studies suggest that Creolisms can emerge in any of the countries that border the Atlantic, and Caribbean Creolisms were exported back to West African coastal areas. While this process is easily visible in the twentieth century, with reggae influencing music in Britain as well as in West and South Africa and Caribbean carnivals having similar effects, Creole ideas have crossed back over the Atlantic and emerged in West African coastal areas at least since 1800, possibly earlier.

The extent that masquerading traits may have crossed back to Britain is less clear. It has been speculated that the similarity between the cloth-strip costume of Pitchy Patchy and the beribboned mummers troupes in Hampshire and Gloucestershire in Britain's West Country is more than coincidental, but the question of the direction of influence is open to conjecture. The same applies to the Christmas Bull. According to Hutton's rationale (1997, 93), the scarcity of British reports in seventeenth and early eighteenth centuries seems to indicate that in Britain, bull masquerading declined following the Reformation, only to reemerge in the late eighteenth and early nineteenth centuries, particularly among those West Country populations from whom many Middle Passage sailors were drawn. This resurgence in Britain corresponded with an upsurge in animal disguises during Caribbean colonization, and it is unlikely that this dual escalation is coincidental. Could it be that a dormant folk memory was reawakened within the home communities of British sailors as a result of witnessing Caribbean performances during transatlantic expeditions?

The return of the expressive culture of the diaspora to Africa occurred in the eighteenth and nineteenth centuries, and Jamaican Maroons, African-based West Indian colonial regiments, and the Krio of Sierra Leone's Freetown were instrumental in the cross-fertilization process. Both Bettelheim (1985) and Nunley (1985) provide examples of "pan-Afro-Caribbean" traditions that exist in the Lantern Festivals in Senegambia and Sierra Leone, and again, the Upper Guinea area is seen to be instrumental in the migration of cultural ideas. Gombay drums and dances were introduced into Sierra Leone by repatriated Jamaican Maroons. John Collins (2001) explores the beginning of this process with the arrival of 550 freed Jamaicans in Freetown on October 1, 1800. John Storm Roberts (1972, 248) concedes that "Sierra Leone . . . like Liberia, founded in 1792 as the capital of a colony specifically for freed slaves, [was] a Euro/Afro/African American nexus from the start." Roberts points to the Mandinka and Temne and especially the Krio as historical players in the Creolization process and argues that the presence of the West Indian garrison in Freetown was influential. While Sierra Leone was still a young colony, people arrived from other areas, including African Americans from Nova Scotia who had sided with the British in the American Revolution, poor blacks from London, and Jamaican Maroons. According to Nunley (2010, 45), "Later, with the establishment of a British Administration, black West Indian regiments from Jamaica and Trinidad and Tobago were transferred to the colony to maintain order." He continues, "After 1807 the British declared transatlantic slavery illegal; and as a result intercepted slave ships destined for the New World and 'liberated' their black cargo in Freetown, hence the name." The July 1820 general census of Sierra Leone "included 943 Africans liberated from slave vessels, 85 persons from Barbados and Honduras, and 1,030 discharged soldiers and families of the second and fourth West India Regiments and Royal African Corps" (Nunley 1987, 19).

A Fante informant told John Kedjanyi (1967, 51) that masquerading was brought to Ghana by Sierra Leoneans: "From 1822 Sir Charles M'Carthy as Governor of the Gold Coast and

Sierra Leone, brought over companies of West Indian troops then stationed in Sierra Leone into this country [Ghana] to help check Ashanti invasions of the South." The movement of troops from Sierra Leone to the Gold Coast continued until the sacking of the Ashanti capital, Kumasi, in 1874. The West Indian Regiment recruited 2,000 soldiers from Sierra Leone, with 1,660 of them going to the West Indies (Buckley 1979, 131). Kedjanyi (1967, 52) contends that "everything points in the direction of the West Indian troops.... In any case the fact remains that masquerading as it is today was not known or practiced in . . . southern Ghana in pre-colonial times." The British West Indian Regiments were disbanded primarily in both Sierra Leone and Trinidad. Moreover, African, European, and Caribbean seafarers—specifically, the Kru sailors of Liberia and the Fante sailors of Ghana—facilitated the spread of Creole masquerade types along the coast of West Africa. As a result of this cultural interchange, various Caribbean Creole masquerades became established in West African coastal towns.

The Kru originally derived from several ethnic groups in Liberia that were recruited into the British merchant marine fleets and industries along the West African coast (Martin 1982, 19). The Kru even plied their trade in the Caribbean, thereby reinforcing their role as cultural intermediaries. Writing about his experiences in Guyana in the latter half of the nineteenth century, Henry Kirke (1898, 171) remembers Kru oarsmen: "My crew on the river was composed of Kroomen from Africa; they were splendid men, with filed teeth and tattooed on their noses and cheeks. . . . [T]hey roused the spirits by chanting wild Kroo songs, which marked time to the measured beat of the oars." The "wild Kroo songs" may well simply have been sea chanties, because James Edward Alexander (1833, 131) in Guyana fifty or more years earlier, remembers a canoe trip where "the negroes merrily plied the paddles, and we brushed past the overhanging trees to their favorite song of 'Velly well, yankee, velly well oh'!" The words to this song show it to be a chanty that appears on Tom Sullivan's *Salt Atlantic Chanties* (1980), but *negar* replaces the word *sailor* in the Guyanese version.

De bottley oh! de bottley oh!
De neger like de bottley oh!
Right early in the morning, de neger like de bottley oh!
A bottle o' rum, loaf a bread
make the negar dandy oh!
Right early in de morning, de neger like de bottley oh!

Many Kru migrated from Liberia to Ghana, Sierra Leone, and Togo and performed masquerades at Christmas in these new locations. The migrants wore gowns called *mufti* and cardboard masks that represented animals or depicted characters in fairy tales (Nunley 2010, 60). Nunley (2010, 68 n. 8) comments, "That the Kru found jobs in the Caribbean provides a tantalizing historical link between the entertainment masquerades of both sides of the Atlantic." Bettelheim (1979, 75) discusses urban, secular festivals in Africa that are "fully creolized," citing the Fancy Dress of Ghana, the Eri Devil Societies of Sierra Leone, and the secular masquerades of Sao Tomé and adding that "the possible Caribbean influence on the African Creole festivals must be considered."

In Elmina and other coastal cities in Ghana, the Christmas and New Year's masquerades use wire-mesh and papier-mâché masks similar to those used in the Caribbean. The conical hats decorated with crepe paper are typically West Indian. In Accra, the masquerades that appear in the Christmas parade are known as A-mass or more generally as Kakamotobi. The Fante call them Fancy Dress or Kakabotofo. (Plates 24 and 25) A stilt dancer, Sakrabudul, is often featured in the seasonal festivals held in Elmina (Cole and Ross 1977, 179). In his field notes, Herbert Cole observes that Fancy Dress troupes are composed of young adults, male children, and some females. Anonymity is important, and some performers carry sticks and whip people who reveal masqueraders' identities or nonmembers who join in without paying the required fee. The Dutch controlled Elmina for about two hundred years, and Fancy Dress was probably established before 1872, when they left Ghana. However, Herbert Cole (pers. comm., July 1, 2003) states, "There is nothing specifically Dutch about Fancy Dress[; instead,] much about it reminds one of both Italian Comedy and Caribbean Carnival." Cole concludes, "It seems that in Fancy Dress we have another significant component in the trans- or pan-Atlantic artistic interchange." Kedjanyi (1967, 52) describes Fante masquerade societies in Ghana that parade "at the principal feasts of the Christian year—Christmas and Easter. . . . The turn-out is a procession through the streets of a city, town or village by members." His drawings of costumes and his text reveal the Caribbean carnival influence.

> Members dress up as one of the following three kinds of characters: (1) imitation or caricature of particular people, (2) animals, or (3) nondescript human faces. An example of caricature was a double-life-size likeness of Neville Chamberlain (the pre-war Prime Minister of Britain) towering head and shoulders over the procession with a top hat and a high collar. An example of the animal masks which I once saw was a huge cockerel as big as a small car, who used to career up and down the procession. . . . There was also a frightful gorilla. . . . The nondescript and expressionless human-face masks form a majority of masks at the turn-out. The faces are usually painted pink. . . . There are occasional attempts by members to be creative: A horseless cowboy, a Roman Soldier . . . or a fetish priest. (53)

The human-face masks are of two types, cast papier-mâché, usually imported, and wire net (54). Kedjanyi also describes a Fante stilt dancer: "High above the whole turn-out often is the stilt-walker 'Sakrabudu.' He walks or rather dances on stilts. . . . His mask is always a plain pale-face one" (54). Kedjanyi's drawing resembles stilt masquerades of the Caribbean rather than the those of Upper Guinea. The dancer wears fitted leggings that do not cover the stilts. His shirt is gathered at the waist to form a short skirt. Although the shirt is long-sleeved, gloved hands are revealed, and the performer holds a fly whisk (55). The Ga of Ghana and the Guro and Baule of Ivory Coast also have stilt dancers based on Creole rather than on traditional African models.

3. ST. CROIX GOMBAY CONFRONTATION OF 1852 AND THE DECLINE OF THE BAMBOULA

During the nineteenth century, the potential for political upheaval in the Danish West Indies lay just beneath the surface. Major events in St. Croix include the emancipation uprising of July 1848, the Gombay dancers' confrontation with the militia during Christmas 1852, and the Labor Revolt (Fireburn) led by Queen Mary in October 1878. In St. Thomas, the Coal Workers' dispute of September 1892 led by Bamboula dancer Queen Coziah is notable. On December

24, 1852, in Christiansted, St. Croix, a stationary Gombay group kindled an altercation between "Gumbee dancers" and the militia that led to bloodshed and loss of human life. The revelers had stoned the police who tried to disperse them, and three militia brigades were mobilized. When the soldiers fired on the crowd, three civilians were killed and others wounded. During the tumult, two militia drummers begun to roll their drums, providing an ironic juxtaposition between the drums of the Gombay dancers beating African rhythms before being disabled by the police and the drums of the militia vested with governmental authority beating drum rolls to indicate attack. On December 25, to prevent repercussions from aggrieved laborers, Governor Birch disbanded the militia on St. Croix, and it was not reestablished until 1907. On December 30, 1852, Birch wrote a letter of explanation to the Danish Colonial Office about the confrontation in which he differentiated between street parades and the stationary Gombay bands: "The lower part of the population in the towns is accustomed to spend Christmas and New Year's Eve with amusements consisting partly of street parades accompanied with boisterous music and singing; partly in dancing to the sound of an instrument called the Gumbee, a peculiar kind of drum presumed to be of African origin. . . . On St. Thomas . . . the drumming has in recent years been directed to the outskirts of town" (Nicholls 1998, 77, 207). Under the new policy, the drum dances did not fare well, and subsequent demands to quell them increased. Although the *St. Thomas Tidende* pointed out on November 22, 1890, that the satirical songs of the Bamboula were as likely to praise individuals as lambaste them, the editors roundly condemned the songs: "It is not a rule, however, that individuals . . . are ridiculed or scandalized; in many cases it is just the other way, but whether the nature of the song be emulative or derogatory, it [is] an unwarrantable license that people's names be handled with such levity." The paper pondered "whether dragging an individual's name and character into sing song and holding them up to public obloquy is a tolerable or harmless, kind of amusement." By the end of the nineteenth century, the island establishment applied pressure against the street revels and particularly against Gombay's successor, Bamboula, with its overt African characteristics. Bamboula dances were energetic and viewed by Europeans as overtly sexual, with offensive and ribald lyrics. The establishment clamped down, and the Bamboula dwindled as a viable African-style folk expression early in the twentieth century. Miss Clara and the Southside Bamboula Dancers kept the genre alive until the St. Thomas Carnivals of the 1950s. By this time, however, it was more a form of adult parade entertainment than a viable folk form. In recent years, Mary Ann Christopher and Ayesha Morris have been active in reviving the Bamboula, and 2009 through 2012 saw reenactments of Queen Coziah's historic march through Charlotte Amalie.

4. THE MOKO AND CARRIACOU NATION DANCES

The word *Mocko* in Mocko Jumbie can be interpreted in different ways: as a mocker, as a sorcerer, or as relating to the Moko ethnic group of southeastern Nigeria. Historical reports and the existence of a now-defunct ethnic designation, Moko, requires that the ethnic group interpretation must be considered. However unlikely, construing Mocko Jumbie to mean the Jumbie of the Moko is an intriguing interpretation. The Moko were present in the Virgin Islands in the eighteenth century, and Moravian missionary C. G. A. Oldendorp (1770/1987, 203–5) documented their language, which can now be identified as Efik, the language of Ibibio groups in the Calabar region of southern Nigeria, where numerous minor ethnicities are located. The Ibibio provided an unduly large proportion of the slaves shipped from the Bight of Biafra in the eighteenth century (Jones 1984, 174). Territory labeled Moko appears on the map in Baikie's *Narrative of an Exploring Voyage* (1856). It is some fifty miles northeast of Calabar in the area occupied today by various Ekoi groups, who are Ibibio-related. It is conceivable that the Moko were "Ekoi (Yako) and, taken as slaves from Calabar may have included Ogoni and Okrika" (Douglas Chambers, pers. comm., May 19, 1997). Little is known of the Moko and their masquerades; however, the area is not known today for stilt masquerades. Nevertheless, the Ekpe leopard society masquerade of the Efik and Ejagham has taken root in Cuba under the name *Abakuá* (Miller 2009).

Although the designation is no longer used in West Africa, Moko leaves a legacy in the Caribbean within the African nation dances of Carriacou. Such dances occurred throughout the Caribbean but gradually died out as the slave population became indigenized. Because of its remote location, small size, and high proportion of blacks, Carriacou maintained nation dances longer than did other islands. These dances were performed in Big Drum rituals in the twentieth century and were recorded by musicologist Alan Lomax in 1962. They continue in a tourist-diluted form into the twenty-first century. The names of the African nations indicate the regions in West Africa from which Carriacou people trace their ancestry. McDaniel (1998, 38) has documented these names:

Nation	*Region*	*Modern Country*
Cromanti	Gold Coast	Ghana
Igbo	Bight of Biafra	Nigeria
Manding	Senegambia, Mali	Senegambia, Mali
Temne	Sierra Leone	Sierra Leone, Liberia
Kongo	Congo, Central Africa	Republic of Congo
Chamba	Bight of Biafra	Nigeria
Moko	Bight of Biafra	Nigeria, Cameroon
Arada	Ardra, Dahomey	Benin Republic
Banda	Possibly Gold Coast or Congo	Possibly Ghana/Central Africa

A Moko song, "C'est Mwe, Nani Moko" (I Am Nani Moko), is sung in patois on *Tombstone Feast: Funerary Music of Carriacou* (2001). The song belongs to the Moko Yegéyéyé nation. The Moko of Carriacou split into two groups. The Moko Bangé became sophisticated townspeople, while the Moko Yegéyéyé remained country folk and thus more African (*Big Drum Dance* 1956). Historically, the Moko seem to have been considered deeply African and did not secure a favorable reputation among whites. In the eighteenth century, Bryan Edwards (1793, 75) writes that the "tribe which are distinguished by the name of Mocoes . . . in general appear to be the most wretched of all the nations of Africa." The *Mocko* of Mocko Jumbie could refer to the Moko in a symbolic rather than actual sense—that is, to their Africanness.

NOTES

INTRODUCTION

1. The USVI comprise four islands—St. Thomas, St. Croix, St. John, and Water Island—situated among the Leeward Islands at the northern end of the Lesser Antilles in the Eastern Caribbean. Puerto Rico lies to the west, and the British Virgin Islands are to the east. The United States purchased what were then known as the Danish West Indies for $25 million in 1917 for strategic reasons. The islands are now a U.S. territory. St. Croix is located forty miles south of St. Thomas, which is the site of the territory's capital, Charlotte Amalie. St. Croix has two major towns, Frederiksted at the island's west end and Christiansted toward the east.

I refer to inhabitants of the various islands by the terms used locally: A person from St. Thomas is a St. Thomian, from St. Croix a Crucian, from Barbados a Barbadian or Bajan, from Antigua an Antiguan, from Anguilla an Anguillan, from Montserrat a Montserratian, from St. Kitts a Kittitian, from Nevis a Nevision, from the Bahamas a Bahamian, and so forth.

2. The premise of studies of Atlantic Rim performance arts as outlined by John Nunley is that Creole culture started "on the boat." Thus, the Atlantic is pivotal to the diffusion of cultural elements among West Africa, Western Europe, the West Indies, some regions in Central and South America, and the North American eastern seaboard as far north as Nova Scotia and Newfoundland in Canada. I worked with Nunley to organize a series of panels that explored the diffusion of art and culture among Atlantic Rim nations at the 1998, 2001, 2004, and 2007 Triennial Symposiums of the Arts Council of the African Studies Association. The 2001 symposium was hosted by the University of the Virgin Islands in St. Thomas and was timed to coincide with the Virgin Islands Carnival.

CHAPTER 1

1. Kwabena Nketia (1974, 244) emphasizes that in Africa, "musical performances are generally multi-dimensional in character, for it is customary to integrate music with other arts, with dance and drama, as well as with various forms of visual display such as masks."

2. Commencing in 1978, while at Ahmadu Bello University in Nigeria, I conducted field research on the expressive culture of the Igede people of Benue State. I studied their music and dance, subsequently published articles on Igede music and masquerading, and produced an audio CD of traditional music, *The Igede of Nigeria* (1991). My doctoral dissertation was "Music and Dance Associations of the Igede of Nigeria: The Relevance of Indigenous Communication Learning Systems to Rural Education in Africa" (1992).

3. From 1995 to 1998, I received two grants from the Virgin Island Humanities Council that facilitated research on masquerading in the U.S. Virgin Islands and led to a report (Nicholls

1998). I observed various masquerades; interviewed performers, culture-bearers, senior citizens, and experts; and conducted an extensive review of the literature. I subsequently expanded the scope of the study and gathered information about Leeward Islands masquerades from firsthand observation, interviews, and a review of the historical literature. This volume juxtaposes these studies with my African research, consultation with scholars and specialists, and an examination of the literature about Western European and West African masquerades.

4. *Saturnalia* was the term of choice for the preemancipation literati in the Eastern Caribbean. Reports dating from between 1800 and 1848 contain at least five uses of *Saturnalia* to describe the Christmas festivities in the Danish West Indies, while a sixth document uses the term *Bacchanalian Revel.* Some of the earliest references to *Carnival* include S. B. Haynes 1872; an editorial in the January 4, 1873, *St. Croix Avis*; and Visby-Petersen (1917) (describing St. Thomas Christmas festivals around 1892). In Rome, Saturnalia comprised a symbolic reversal of power relations. According to E. O. James (1961, 176), "All social distinctions and public business [are] in abeyance during the festival. . . . The community gave itself up to feasting . . . and the reversal of the established order of society. Slaves were served by their masters and sat at the table with them . . . clad in their masters' clothes. . . . Senators laid aside their togas and assumed an undress garment. . . . Lots were cast for a mock king who was to exercise his rule . . . during the festival [by] issuing comic injunctions." Saturnalian revels occurred throughout the English-speaking West Indies, and Wentworth (1834, 37) ponders how the enslaved population learned about this convention: "By whatever means [the Negroes] have acquired a knowledge of the privileges which the Saturnalia conferred upon the Roman slaves, or whether it be from the deduction of reason that they imagine themselves entitled to them, they do not fail to practice as much impudent vivacity in 'paying their respects' to their masters, as marked the conduct of the Roman bondsmen in doing honour to the Pagan deity."

5. Crucian Veronica Gordon (pers. comm., August 6, 2001) recalls that when her father opened a bottle of brandy, he poured a little on the ground, calling out his father's and grandfather's names and saying, "This is for you." In special cases, holy water (fresh rainwater caught directly in a calabash or a bowl without having touched the roof or the eaves of a house) would be used as an offering. Jumbies could be harnessed for the protection of the homestead. In Antigua, Jumbie beads were put in a bottle and hung from a tree or a shrub in an orchard as a charm to protect the area from thieves (Lornetta Prince, pers. comm., May 21, 1997). Charles Kingsley (1877, 292) describes the Jumbie dance in Montserrat, which is designed to communicate with spirits and which, like the Bamboula, is an African-style drum dance that leads to spirit possession and trance. The instrumentation for Jumbie dances includes large and small tambourines and a metal triangle. "The large tambourine is called a 'jumbie drum' and the small one a 'babala.' . . . Both instruments closely resemble the Irish bodhran" (Messenger 1973, 56). When the Jumbie drum is rubbed with the moistened forefinger, it produces an eerie moaning sound calculated to summon "good ghosts" (57).

6. Parallel inspiration theories are supported by Jungian notions of symbolic archetypes and Freudian notions of an archaic heritage. Psychologist Carl Gustav Jung (1964, 107) believed that some of the symbols that appear in dreams are derived from the collective unconsciousness, which is "the part of the psyche that retains and transmits the psychological inheritance of mankind." Jung's sojourn in East Africa no doubt influenced the development of his ideas, and his notion of a collective unconscious equates in some ways to the African

ancestors. Psychoanalyst Sigmund Freud's notion of an archaic heritage—symbolic archetypes inherited from the human psychic history—coincides with these ideas.

7. J. B. Smith's (2010, 8) informant in Britain said, "If you are in a field or any place and cannot find the entrance out you are pisky-laid; then turn your jacket or apron inside out and put it on so, and then you will find where you are." These agents of spirit protection appear regularly in costumes worn by British mummers. Descriptions of Lancashire pace eggers demonstrate that they often "went about with their coats turned inside out. . . . In the Bury play this tradition is carried on. . . . [S]ome of the characters, the Fool, Little Johnny Jack, for example, and the musician, who wear jackets, turn them inside out" (Cass 2001, 51). In Scotland, the mummers known as Galoshins did the same, especially the character known as Johnny Funny or Mickey Funny. Bickerton (1988, 20) describes house visits by guisers during Halloween: "They wore cocked hats, turned their jackets inside out, blacked their faces and carried mock swords." A similar spectacle occurred in 1890 in Hawick in the Scottish borders region: "The boys wore men's jackets turned inside out, and either blacked their faces or wore 'false faces'" (Robert Wood quoted in Hayward 1992, 203).

8. The debate over the serious versus lighthearted nature of masquerades took on national importance in the Virgin Islands in the early 1990s, when officials proposed placing a statue to represent justice at the door of the federal courthouse in St. Croix. It was important to islanders that the statue "evoke the Virgin Islands' ties to African history and the struggles for freedom by enslaved Africans" (Resnik and Curtis 2010, 121). The artist, Jan Mitchell, initially proposed a bronze figure of a nine-foot-tall Mocko Jumbie on stilts. This might be considered appropriate because folklore holds that Mocko Jumbies' height enabled them to oversee villages and "act as mediators between the world of the living and the spiritual world of the ancestors, . . . ask for special favors [and] mediate disputes among the living when all else has failed" (Green 1996, 25). According to Resnik and Curtis (2010, 122), "Moco Jumbies sometimes sport mirrors [and] like the Renaissance Virtue Prudence who was regularly shown with a mirror and at times a second face looking backwards, Moco Jumbies can metaphorically see what is happening in the past, present, and future." However, members of the "District Court family" thought that using a statue of a Mocko Jumbie was unsuitable. Although it was "definitely Caribbean," it was considered "a jester of sorts," associated with mockery, and the courthouse is "hardly a place for clowning and jesting" (Clerk of the District Court of the VI quoted in Resnik and Curtis 2010, 122). Supporters protested that the rejection was a display of ignorance about local culture. On July 11, 1991, under the headline "Moko Jumbie: No Mockery of Justice," the *St. Croix Avis* published a letter arguing that jesting was but one of the roles of the character, who also could transform into a "village ancestor" with the power of judgment to "reprimand those who violated the laws." Moreover, "an editorial in the *Virgin Islands Business Journal* went further, insisting that use of the Moko Jumbie figure would be an antidote to the oppressive conditions that had reduced its historical significance to that of a carnival figure. . . . Supporting the project, the newspaper argued that using the figure would be a 'reclamation by the oppressed of a measure of justice'" (Resnik and Curtis 2010, 122–23). A bronze figure, Market Woman, was finally chosen to bring dark-skinned justice into view in a federal courthouse. Mitchell describes it as a modern-day version of Themis shown as a local resident of St. Croix. The Market Woman, now renamed Lady of Justice, holds the scales of justice but is dressed in a headscarf, an open shirt, a knee-length skirt, and sandals. Her informal attire underscores the "civil responsibility that every citizen has in maintaining a

democratic society" (121). Resnik and Curtis suggest that unlike other proposals that provocatively engaged histories of injustice, this image was safe and comfortable (Judith Resnik, pers. comm., July 15, 2010).

9. Other popular masquerades that were developed in situ are not discussed in this treatise. These include the Wild Indians and the Zulus who might be depicted as "Third World soldiers" active in the nineteenth century—for example, when the Plains Indians were still battling American military forces as depicted in the penny dreadfuls. It is difficult to determine whether the original Caribs and Tainos exerted marginal influences on masquerade styles, although Nunley and Bettelheim (1988) explore this issue. In St. Thomas, on Easter Monday 1883, "Cetewayo, Zulu Chief," was among the characters represented in masquerade (*St. Thomas Tidende*, March 28, 1883). Four years earlier, Cetewayo and an army of ten thousand men had inflicted a crushing defeat on the British at Isandlwana in Zululand. The portrayal of this celebrated African must have been a source of pride for West Indians. Today's performing Indians and Zulus do not represent Old World influences; rather, they were developed in the New World.

10. A similar process occurred with the songs and dances of Gombay and Bamboula. Most scholars posit that the precursor of these drum dances was established by the first wave of slaves from Angola and Congo early in the colonial era. The drum dances are quintessentially African and would have seemed familiar to later-arriving slaves, including the Igbo, whose "Igbo drum," along with the frame drum, became a trademark of Gombay (see Nicholls forthcoming).

11. Unlike raffia masquerades, which use dried leaves, the Jack in the Green is adorned with a canopy of fresh leaves and is historically associated with the chimney sweeps' parades in London (Judge 1979, 19). Strutt (1801/1876, 461) describes its construction: "The Jack-in-the-Green is a piece of pageantry consisting of a hollow frame of wood or wicker work . . . sufficiently large and high to receive a man. The frame is covered with green leaves and bunches of flowers interwoven with each other so that the man within may be completely concealed, who dances with his companions."

12. Abrahams (1967, 461) assumes that the St. George Mummers Play was performed prior to emancipation in 1833. However, the antiquity of such plays has been called into question. Millington (1996) shows that the two "mummies" plays of St. Kitts–Nevis published by Abrahams were linked to plays published by Juliana Horatia Ewing (1871) in the second half of the nineteenth century. Moreover, chapbooks containing texts of mummers' plays printed in Britain were widely available during the nineteenth century (Brody 1969, 7). Nevertheless, the fact that enslaved people in Jamaica performed "court plays" is evinced by Lady Maria Nugent (1966, 66), who tells of 1801 performances of "Johnny Canoes" in Jamaica accompanied by "actors" including a man dressed as "Henry the 4th of France." Fayer and McMurray (1999, 42–43) report that the earliest reference to Shakespeare's plays in Jamaican folk performances is in H. T. De La Beche's 1825 account: "Some of the negroes go about at Christmas and Easter attended by drums, &c., and perform much in the same manners as our Mummers. [Some were] fantastically dressed to represent kings and warriors; one of them wore a white mask on his face, and part of the representation had evidently some reference to the play of Richard the Third; for the man in the white mask exclaimed, 'A horse, a horse, my kingdom for a horse!'" These examples suggest that the St. George play might have been performed prior to emancipation in the BWI.

13. On November 13, 2002, I interviewed George Farrell under the auspices of the Documenting Living Treasures program of the Center for Black Music Research, Columbia College, Chicago. Known as Pope because of his regal style, Farrell later painted the tips of his horns silver and adopted the name Silver Horn. Farrell is an authentic practitioner and a protégé of Arthur Sixteen. Farrell prefers the name *Jam Bull* rather than the more old school *John Bull* because it connotes "jamming. . . . We play the wild side of this thing."

CHAPTER 2

1. Taino shamans also used rattles when treating sick persons: "He lighted a torch and sang, accompanying himself with a rattle, then approached the patient and pretended to suck an object from the latter's body" (Rouse 1992, 14). The Caribs who lived in the Windward Islands do not appear to have had slit drums, but they used rattles as a shaman's accoutrement as well as for dancing (Stephan T. Lenik, pers. comm., July 23, 2005).

2. The upper part of the jembe's body is shaped like a bowl, while the lower part is a narrower cylinder that is customarily gripped between the knees. The jembe's escalation into international prominence is contemporaneous with its widespread use in national ballet companies of Upper Guinea countries.

3. Pinckard (1806, 127) describes stationary drums used during Sunday afternoon recreational dances in the Virgin Islands, providing an early record of the banjo and the use of katta sticks (two sticks rapped independently on the side of the drum): "While one negro strikes the Banjar, another shakes the rattle with great force of arm, and a third sitting on the body of the drum, as it lies lengthwise upon the ground, beats . . . the sheep skin . . . with his hands and heels, and a fourth sitting upon the ground at the other end . . . beats upon the wooden sides of it with two sticks. . . . Numbers of the party of both sexes bawl forth their . . . song." Earl Leaf (1948, 140–41) describes the Virgin Islands' bamboula drum played in this manner as the "ka drum," quoting Lafcadio Hearn, who studied it in Martinique in 1878: "The skilful player straddles the drum and plays upon it with the finger-tips of both hands simultaneously. Occasionally the heel of the naked foot is pressed lightly or vigorously against the skin at one end so as to produce changes of tone. . . . Meanwhile a boy keeps striking the drum at the uncovered end with sticks so as to produce a dry, clattering accompaniment. The sound of the drum itself, well played, has a wild power that makes and masters all the excitement of the dance, a complicated double roll with a peculiar bellowy rising and falling." Using the heel of the foot to produce changes of tone is a West African technique, used, for example, by the Igede of Nigeria. "A drummer straddles each drum, beating it with both hands, and sometimes pressing the drum skin with the heel of his foot to muffle or vary the pitch" (Nicholls 1988, 206). The concept of a "complicated double roll" might equate to the "broken rhythm" that Lekis (1960, 178) maintains is characteristic of Virgin Islands music: "Typical in the music is a broken rhythm quality, meaning simply the ability to produce and maintain highly polyrhythmic structures." The reference to "a boy" playing katta sticks may be a paternalistic use of the diminutive, because according to Gerda Benjamin (1979), the katta rhythm is more essential than the drum rhythm: "The katta stick is like the leading part, and the drum is just keeping the beat to suit the katta stick; and if you knocking the drum and the katta man find you making bad notes, he knock you, he tap your behind." On January 6, 1816, in Jamaica, Lewis (1834/1999, 80) saw a mixed-gender dance group accompanied by instruments that

"consisted of Gambys (Eboe drums), Shaky-shekies [maracas] and kitty-katties," which are "a flat piece of board" beaten with two sticks. It can be compared to the katta sticks, although in this case a separate piece of board is beaten rather than the side of the drum. In Puerto Rico, where the Bamboula is perpetuated in the form of Bomba, drum ensembles include a cylindrical wooden instrument that is rapped with sticks to produce the distinctive Bomba rhythm.

CHAPTER 3

1. Easter is the first Sunday after the full moon following the Northern Hemisphere's vernal equinox. Ecclesiastically, the equinox is reckoned to be on March 21 (regardless of the astronomically correct date), and the full moon also is not necessarily the astronomically correct date. The date of Easter varies between March 22 and April 25. Lent begins on Ash Wednesday, which is forty days prior to Easter, not counting Sundays. Whitsun coincides with Pentecost, seven weeks after Easter Sunday.

CHAPTER 4

1. Antiguan disenchantment with British symbols is indicated in the text of the play: "Now that Big Ben's chime has changed, Its two hands rotting off, Churchill's reciting a West Indian's poem" (Lake 2001a).

2. *Desasso* (dey-seh-so, i.e., "They say so") is a Creole phrase used by the older generation of Antiguans as an emphasis: "At this moment in time, without question!"

CHAPTER 5

1. Senegambia today has a Muslim majority, although a few communities are Catholic. However, indigenous shrines retain great ritual importance for many people. Many shrines are located in the sacred forest, which consists of huge trees overgrown with lianas and virtually impenetrable as a consequence of the thick undergrowth: "The centre of the forest usually consists of a huge silk cotton tree [*Ceiba pentandra*] planted many generations ago" (De Jong 2007, 34). Baum (1999, 39) explains that the Jola believe in a supreme being, Emitai, that can communicate with humans through dreams and visions: "Such revelations were seen as inspiring the introduction of Bukut, the male circumcision ritual, and of Kasila, the rain shrine of Alinesitoue." Thus, Kasila was used to address problems of drought, Ehugna for fertility, and Cabai for war (42). In some cases, the appearance of the shrines seems to hold little importance: "The most powerful often appeared to be nothing more than a hole in the ground or a forked stick, whereas less important shrines might be more elaborate" (43). According to Baum, "Almost every activity of the community has a *boekine* associated with it be it palm wine tapping, fishing, blacksmithing, or farming. Other shrines were important for healing, either as diagnostic shrines or for treating specific disorders. Others were connected with perennial problems of rain, crop fertility, and the fertility of women. There were several shrines associated with war, the well-being of the community, and township governance. Finally, there were *ukine* associated with the extended family and the lineage. This multiplicity of shrines . . . encouraged broad access to religious authority; with so many *ukine* in a small

community, chances were excellent that any given individual would become an elder or priest of at least one shrine" (43).

CHAPTER 6

1. William Kemp (1600/1840, 8), a morris dancer who completed a marathon dance from London to Norwich in 1599, was escorted by Thomas Slye, who provided music on a large tabor, possibly twenty-four inches deep, hung from his left arm, and a pipe. In *The Witch of Edmonton* (1621), a stage drama by William Rowley, Thomas Dekker, and John Ford (1958), a morris dance was essential to the plot. The script mentions a pipe and tabor, but when the dancers perform, they have a fiddler who would have played "The Flowers of May" if his fiddle had not been bewitched.

CONCLUSION

1. This revival has resulted from an April 27, 2001, performance of a scene from the play *The Killing of Arthur Sixteen* by Antiguan author Edgar Lake at the University of the Virgin Islands' Reichhold Center before an international array of scholars attending the Triennial Symposium on African Art sponsored by the Arts Council of the African Studies Association. *The Killing of Arthur Sixteen* features the bull tradition and centers on the funeral wake of a renowned John Bull masquerader. The following day, the Carnival's Adult Parade included a Jam Bull troupe featuring George "Pope" Farrell and Glen Pierre in bull costumes, with Austin Burnett as the whip man, Clement Gassau Peltier playing bass drum, Lassington Jackson playing the steel (triangle), and Huntley Heywood playing kettle drum. Jam Bull paraded again the following year and has since become a relatively stable Carnival fixture.

REFERENCES

Abrahams, Roger D. 1967. "The Shaping of Folklore Traditions in the British West Indies." *Journal of Inter-American Studies* 9(3): 456–80.

———. 1970. "British West Indian Folk Drama and the 'Life Cycle' Problem." *Folklore*, 81:241–65.

———. 1973. "Behold the Foe: Christmas Mumming on Nevis, West Indies." *North Carolina Folklore*, 21:120–31.

———. 1983. *The Man-of-Words in the West Indies: Performance and the Emergence of Creole Culture*. Baltimore: Johns Hopkins University Press.

Abrahams, Roger D., and John F. Szwed. 1983. *After Africa: Extracts from British Travel Accounts and Journals of the Seventeenth, Eighteenth, and Nineteenth Centuries Concerning the Slaves, Their Manners, and Customs in the British West Indies*. New Haven: Yale University Press.

Adams, Monni Jeanne. 1989. "African Visual Arts from an Art Historical Perspective." *African Studies Review* 32(2): 55–103.

———. 2010. "Locating the Mano Mask." *African Arts* 43(2): 16–37.

Ahuwan, Abashiya Magaji. 1992. "Clay as a Creative Media: A Survey of the Kimkim Musical Instrument from South Kaduna." In *Diversity of Creativity in Nigeria: A Critical Selection from the Proceedings of the 1st International Conference on the Diversity of Creativity in Nigeria*, ed. Bolaji Campbell, 143–52. Ile-Ife, Nigeria: Department of Fine Arts, Obafemi Awolowo University.

al-Bakrî. 1068/1981. *Kitâb al-Masâlik wa-'l-Mamâlik* (The Book of Routes and Realms). In *Corpus of Early Arabic Sources for West African History*, trans. J. F. P. Hopkins, ed. N. Levtzion and J. F. P. Hopkins, 62–87. Cambridge: Cambridge University Press.

Alexander, James Edward. 1833. *Transatlantic Sketches*. Vol. 1. London: Bentley.

Alford, Violet. 1978. *The Hobby Horse and Other Animal Masks*. London: Merlin.

Ames, D. W., and K. A. Gourlay. 1978. "Kimkim: A Women's Musical Pot." *African Arts* 11(2): 56–64.

Andreas, Maude. 1979, 1980. Interview by Mary Jane Soule. T055, T056, T070, T095, and T114, Soule Archive of St. Croix and St. Thomas Song and Dance, First Half of the Twentieth Century. Library of Congress, American Folklife Center and Von Scholten Collection, Enid M. Baa Library, St. Thomas, Virgin Islands.

Anonymous. 1797/1976. *Characteristic Traits of the Creolian and African Negroes in Jamaica*. Ed. Barry Higman. Mona, Jamaica: Caldwell.

———. 1976. "An Old Plantation Festival: The Truth about the Origins of the Crop Over Festivities." *The Bajan*, June, 12–13.

Antigua, Ministry of Education, Culture, Sports, and Youth Affairs. N.d. *Christmas to Carnival*. N.p.

Appia, Beatrice. 1943. "Masques de Guinée Française et de Casamance." *Journal de la Société des Africanistes* 13:153–82.

Arnold, Leroy, Sr. 1979. Interview by Mary Jane Soule. T028, Soule Archive of St. Croix and St. Thomas Song and Dance, First Half of the Twentieth Century. Library of Congress, American Folklife Center and Von Scholten Collection, Enid M. Baa Library, St. Thomas, Virgin Islands.

Atkins, John. 1737. *A Voyage to Guinea, Brasil, and the West-Indies in His Majesty's Ships the Swallow and Weymouth*. London: Ward and Chandler.

Aubrey, John. 1881. *Remaines of Gentilisme and Judaisme*. Ed. James Britten. London: Satchell, Peyton.

Baikie, W. B. 1856. *Narrative of an Exploring Voyage up the Rivers Kwora and Binue in 1854*. London: Murray.

Bakhtin, Mikhail. 1984. *Rabelais and His World*. Bloomington: Indiana University Press.

Barbados Advocate. 1991. "Scrubbers No Longer Around." December 25.

Barringer, Tim, Gillian Forrester, and Barbaro Martinez Ruiz, eds. 2007. *Art and Emancipation in Jamaica: Isaac Mendes Belisario and His Worlds*. New Haven: Yale University Press.

Baum, Robert M. 1999. *Shrines of the Slave Trade: Diola Religion and Society in Precolonial Senegambia*. New York: Oxford University Press.

———. 2010. "Secrecy, Shrines, and Memory: Diola Oral Traditions and the Slave Trade in Senegal." In *Activating the Past: History and Memory in the Black Atlantic World*, ed. Andrew Apter and Lauren Derby, 139–56. Newcastle: Cambridge Scholars.

Bayley, F. W. N. 1830. *Four Years Residence in the West Indies*. London: Kidd.

Beckford, William. 1790. *Remarks on the Situation of the Negroes in Jamaica: Impartially Made from a Local Experience of Nearly Thirteen Years in That Island*. London: Egerton.

Beier, Ulli. 1969. *A Year of Sacred Festivals in One Yoruba Town*. Lagos: Nigeria Magazine.

Belisario, Isaac Mendes. 1837. *Sketches of Character in Illustration of the Habits of the Negro Population of Jamaica*. Kingston: Belisario.

Bell, Hesketh J. 1889/1970. *Obeah: Witchcraft in the West Indies*. Westport, Conn.: Negro Universities Press.

Benjamin, Gerda. 1979. Interview by Mary Jane Soule. T109, T126, T127, T193, T194, Soule Archive of St. Croix and St. Thomas Song and Dance, First Half of the Twentieth Century. Library of Congress, American Folklife Center and Von Scholten Collection, Enid M. Baa Library, St. Thomas, Virgin Islands.

Bentor, Eli. 2002. "Spatial Continuities: Masks and Cultural Interactions between the Delta and Southeastern Nigeria." *African Arts* 35 (1): 26–41, 93.

Berry, Jason. 2004. "Mardi Gras in New Orleans, USA: Annals of a Queen." In *Carnaval!*, ed. Barbara Mauldin, 299–334. Seattle: University of Washington Press.

Besse, Joseph. 1753. *A Collection of the Sufferings of the People Called Quakers*. Vol. 1. London: Hinde.

Bethel, Clement. 1977. "The Origin and Growth of Junkanoo." In *Final Report to the National Endowment for the Humanities*, 3:10–13. Washington, D.C.: Howard University, Center for Ethnic Music.

Bettelheim, Judith. 1979. "Afro-Jamaican Junkanoo Festival: Playing the Forces and Operating the Cloth." Ph.D. diss., Yale University.

———. 1985. "The Lantern Festival in Senegambia." *African Arts* 17(2): 50–53, 95, 103.

———. 1988. "Jonkonnu and Other Christmas Masquerades." In *Caribbean Festival Arts: Each and Every Bit of Difference*, ed. John Nunley and Judith Bettelheim, 39–83. Seattle: St. Louis Art Museum and University of Washington Press.

———. 1991. "Negotiations of Power in Carnaval Culture in Santiago de Cuba." *African Arts* 24(2): 66–75, 91.

———. 1998. "Women in Masquerade and Performance." *African Arts* 31(2): 68–70.

Bickerton, Helen. 1988. "The Goloshans." *Traditional Drama Studies* 2:24–27.

Biebuyck, Daniel P. 1979. "The Frog and Other Animals in Lega Art and Initiation." *Africa-Tervuren* 25(3): 76–84.

The Big Drum Dance of Carriacou. 1956. Folkways Records FW04011.

Bilby, Kenneth M. 1985. "The Caribbean as a Musical Region." In *Caribbean Contours*, ed. Sidney W. Mintz and Sally Price, 181–218. Baltimore: Johns Hopkins University Press.

———. 1998. "Jonkonnu, Gumbay, and the Afro-Creole Spirit." Paper presented at the Triennial Symposium of African Art, New Orleans, April.

———. 1999. "Gumbay, Myal, and the Great House: New Evidence on the Religious Background of Jonkonnu in Jamaica." *ACIJ Research Review* 4:47–70.

———. 2010. "Surviving Secularization: Masking the Spirit in the Jankunu (John Canoe) Festivals of the Caribbean." *New West Indian Guide* 84(3–4): 179–223.

———. 2011. "Africa's Creole Drum: The Gumbe as Vector and Signifier of Trans-African Creolization." In *Creolization as Cultural Creativity*, ed. Robert Baron and Ana C. Cara, 137–77. Jackson: University Press of Mississippi.

Billington, Sandra. 1984. *A Social History of the Fool*. New York: St. Martin's.

Binger, Louis Gustave. 1892. *Du Niger au Golfe du Guinée*. Paris: Hachette.

Blyden, Nemata Amelia. 2000. *West Indians in West Africa: The African Diaspora in Reverse*. Rochester: University of Rochester Press.

Borgatti, J. M. 1988. "Anogori: Okpella's Masked Festival Heralds." In *West African Masks and Cultural Systems*, ed. Sidney L. Kasfir, 65–84. Tervuren, Belgium: Musée Royal de l'Afrique.

Bolton, H. Carrington. 1890. "Gombay: A Festival Rite of Bermudian Negroes." *Journal of American Folklore* 3(10): 222–26.

Boston, J. S. 1960. "Some Northern Ibo Masquerades." *Journal of the Royal Anthropological Institute* 90(1): 54–65.

Brady, Lieutenant. 1829. *Observations on the State of Negro Slavery in the Island of St. Croix*. London: Simpkin and Marshall.

Bravmann, René A. 1979. "Gur and Manding Masquerades in Ghana." *African Arts* 13(1): 44–51, 98.

Bregenhøj, Carsten, and Hanne Pico Larsen. 2007. "Masks and Mumming Traditions in Denmark: A Survey." In *Masks and Mumming in the Nordic Area*, ed. Terry Gunnell, 189–274. Uppsala, Sweden: Royal Gustavus Adolphus Academy for Swedish Folk Culture.

Brenneker, Paul. 1977. "Sambumbu: Volskunde van Curacao, Aruba, en Bonaire." In *Final Report to the National Endowment for the Humanities*, 3:61–66. Washington, D.C.: Howard University, Center for Ethnic Music.

Brent, Linda [pseud.]. 1973. *Incidents in the Life of a Slave Girl*. Ed. L. Maria Child. New York: Harcourt Brace.

Bringéus, Nils-Arvid. 2007. "Mumming in Effigy around St. Knut's Day in Southern Sweden: An Example of the Popular Exercise of Justice." In *Masks and Mumming in the Nordic Area*, ed. Terry Gunnell, 685–704. Uppsala, Sweden: Royal Gustavus Adolphus Academy for Swedish Folk Culture.

Brody, Alan. 1969. *The English Mummers and Their Plays*. Philadelphia: University of Pennsylvania Press.

Bruce, Maurice. 1958. "The Krampus in Styria." *Folklore* 69:45–47.

Buckley, Roger N. 1979. *Slaves in Red Coats: The British West Indian Regiments, 1795–1815*. New Haven: Yale University Press.

Buhnen, Stephan. 1993. "Ethnic Origins of Peruvian Slaves (1548–1650): Figures for Upper Guinea." *Paideuma* 39:57–110.

Burton, Richard D. E. 1997. *Afro Creole: Power, Opposition, and Play in the Caribbean*. Ithaca: Cornell University Press.

Caillié, René. 1830. *Travels through Central Africa to Timbuctoo and across the Great Desert to Morocco, Performed in the Years 1824–1828*. Vol. 1. London: Colborn and Bentley.

Cameron, Rebecca. 1891/1913. "Christmas at Buchoi, a North Carolina Rice Plantation." *North Carolina Booklet* 13(1): 3–10.

Carmichael, Mrs. A. C. 1834. *Domestic Manners and Social Conditions of the White, Coloured, and Negro Population of the West Indies*. Vol. 1. London: Whittaker.

Carstens, Johan Lorentz. 1997. *St. Thomas in Early Danish Times: A General Description of All the Danish, American, and West Indian Islands (ca. 1730–1739)*. Trans. Arnold Highfield. St. Croix: Virgin Islands Humanities Council.

Carver, Caroline. 1975. *Canadian Christmas Handbook: A Handset from Our Victorian Past*. Toronto: Collins.

Cass, Eddie. 2001. *The Lancashire Pace-Egg Play: A Social History*. London: Folklore Society.

Cass, Eddie, and Steve Roud. 2002. *Room, Room, Ladies and Gentlemen . . . : An Introduction to the English Mummers' Play*. London: English Folk Dance and Song Society.

Cassidy, Frederic G. 1967. "Some New Light on Old Jamaicanisms." *American Speech* 42(3): 190–201.

Cawte, E. C. 1978. *Ritual Animal Disguise*. London: Brewer and Rowman and Littlefield for the Folklore Society.

Chambers, Douglas B. 2001. "Ethnicity in the Diaspora: The Slave-Trade and the Creation of African 'Nations' in the Americas." *Slavery and Abolition* 22(3): 25–39.

Chambers, E. K. 1903/1967. *The Mediaeval Stage*. London: Oxford University Press.

Charry, Eric S. 2000. *Mande Music: Traditional and Modern Music of the Maninka and Mandinka*. Chicago: University of Chicago Press.

Cline, Ruth H. 1958. "Belsnickles and Shanghais." *Journal of American Folklore* 71(280): 164–65.

Coffin, Tristram Potter. 1973. *The Book of Christmas Folklore*. New York: Seabury.

Cole, Herbert M., and Chike C. Aniakor. 1984. *Igbo Arts: Community and Cosmos*. Los Angeles: Museum of Cultural History, University of California.

Cole, Herbert M., and Doran H. Ross. 1977. *The Arts of Ghana*. Los Angeles: Museum of Cultural History, University of California.

Collins, John. 2001. "Gumbay Drums of Jamaica in Sierra Leone." Paper presented at the Triennial Symposium on African Art, St. Thomas, April.

Conniff, Michael L., and Thomas J. Davis. 1994. *Africans in the Americas: A History of the Black Diaspora*. New York: St. Martin's.

Conway, Cecelia. 1995. *African Banjo: Echoes in Appalachia*. Knoxville: University of Tennessee Press.

Coolen, Michael Theodore. 1984. "Senegambian Archetypes for the American Folk Banjo." *Western Folklore* 43(2): 117–32.

Cooper, Vincent O. 1992. "The Origins of the St. Kitts–Nevis Masquerade Tradition." *University of the Virgin Islands Humanities Bulletin*, 2–4.

———. 1999. "St. Kitts: The Launching Pad for Leeward Island Creoles." In *St. Kitts and the Atlantic Creoles: The Texts of Samuel Augustus Matthews in Perspective*, ed. Philip Baker and Adrienne Bruyn, 379–86. London: University of Westminster Press.

Cox, J. C. 1913. *Churchwardens' Accounts from the Fourteenth Century to the Close of the Seventeenth Century*. London: Methuen.

Crahan, Margaret E., and Franklin W. Knight. 1979. *Africa and the Caribbean: The Legacies of a Link*. Baltimore: Johns Hopkins University Press.

Creighton, Helen. 1950. "Folklore of Lunenberg County, Nova Scotia." *National Museum of Canada Bulletin* 171:58–60.

Crowley, Daniel J. 1956. "Traditional Masques of Carnival." *Caribbean Quarterly* 4(3–4): 42–90.

Curtin, Philip D. 1969. *The Atlantic Slave Trade: A Census*. Madison: University of Wisconsin Press.

———. 1975. *Economic Change in Precolonial Africa: Senegambia in the Era of the Slave Trade*. 2 vols. Madison: University of Wisconsin Press.

Davíðsdóttir, Vilborg. 2007. "Elves on the Move: Midwinter Mumming and House-Visiting Traditions in Iceland." In *Masks and Mumming in the Nordic Area*, ed. Terry Gunnell, 643–66. Uppsala, Sweden: Royal Gustavus Adolphus Academy for Swedish Folk Culture.

Davis, Natalie Zemon. 1971. *Society and Culture in Early Modern France*. Cambridge: Polity.

Day, Charles William. 1852. *Five Years' Residence in the West Indies*. Vol. 1. London: Colburn.

Dean-Smith, Margaret. 1963. "Disguise in English Folk Drama." *Folklife: A Journal of Ethnological Studies* 1:97–101.

De Jong, Ferdinand. 2007. *Masquerades of Modernity: Power and Secrecy in Casamance, Senegal*. Bloomington: Indiana University Press.

De la Beche, Henry T. 1825. *Notes on the Present Condition of the Negroes in Jamaica*. London: Cadell.

Der, Benedict G. 1998. *The Slave Trade in Northern Ghana*. Accra: Woeli.

Diamitani, Boureima Tiekoroni. 2008. "Observing Komo among Tagwa People in Burkina Faso." *African Arts* 41(3): 14–25.

Dieterlen, Germaine. 1989. "Masks and Mythology among the Dogon." *African Arts* 22(3): 34–43.

Dirks, Robert. 1987. *The Black Saturnalia: Conflict and Ritual Expression on British West Indian Slave Plantations*. Gainesville: University of Florida Press.

Ditchfield, P. H. 1896. *Old English Customs*. London: Redway.

Donoghue, Eddie. 2001. "Montserrat Masquerade: Cultural Preservation in the Modern World." Paper presented at the Triennial Symposium on African Art, St. Thomas, April.

Dookhan, Isaac. 1974. *History of the Virgin Islands of the United States*. Epping: Caribbean Universities Press.

Doutremépuich, E. 1939. "Visit á un 'Camp' de Circonis en Casamance." *Les Missions Catholiques* 72:474–77, 486–92.

Dwelly, Edward. 1977. *The Illustrated Gaelic-English Dictionary*. Glasgow: Gairm.

Eadie, Hazel Balance. 1931. *Lagooned in the Virgin Islands*. London: Routledge.

Edmonds, Richard. 1858. "The Celtic and Other Antiquities of the Land's End District of Cornwall." *Archaeologia Cambrensis* 4:66–75.

Edwards, Bryan. 1794. *The History, Civil and Commercial, of the British Colonies in the West Indies*. Vol. 2. London: Stockdale.

Eike, Christine. 2007a. "Disguise as Ritualised Humour in Norway, Past and Present." In *Masks and Mumming in the Nordic Area*, ed. Terry Gunnell, 497–530. Uppsala, Sweden: Royal Gustavus Adolphus Academy for Swedish Folk Culture.

———. 2007b. "Masks and Mumming Traditions in Norway: A Survey." In *Masks and Mumming in the Nordic Area*, ed. Terry Gunnell, 47–106. Uppsala, Sweden: Royal Gustavus Adolphus Academy for Swedish Folk Culture.

Elder, J. D. 1988. *African Survivals in Trinidad and Tobago*. London: Karia.

Eltis, David. 2000. *The Rise of African Slavery in the Americas*. Cambridge: Cambridge University Press.

Emerick, Reverend Abraham J. 1916. *Jamaican Mialism*. Woodstock, Mich.: privately printed.

Eru, Peter Oibe. 1988. "Proverbs as Expression of Igede People's Wisdom." In *Igede Gedegede*, ed. Ogwona Oboh, Ogaga Agocha, Isaac Ode, John Adima, and John Aja, 59–61. Oju, Nigeria: Oju Local Government Council.

Ewing, Juliana Horatia. 1871. "The Peace Egg: A Christmas Tale." *Aunty Judy's Magazine* 10(69): 98–117.

Eyo, Ekpo. [1980]. *Guide to the Nigerian Museum in Lagos*. Lagos: Associated Press of Nigeria.

Falola, Toyin, and Matt Childs. 2004. *The Yoruba Diaspora in the Atlantic World*. Bloomington: Indiana University Press.

Fayer, Joan M. 2001a. "The Carriacou Shakespeare Mas': A Preliminary Analysis of the African Influences." *La Torre: Revista de la Universidad de Puerto Rico* 6(19): 65–73.

———. 2001b. "Neagar Business: A Christmas Folk Play Performance in Nevis." *La Torre: Revista de la Universidad de Puerto Rico* 6(19): 51–64.

Fayer, Joan M., and Joan F. McMurray. 1999. "The Carriacou Mas' as 'Syncretic Artifact.'" *Journal of American Folklore* 112(443): 58–73.

Fenn, Elizabeth A. 1988. "'A Perfect Equality Seemed to Reign': Slave Society and Jonkonnu." *North Carolina Historical Review* 65(2): 127–53.

Fergus, Howard A. 1975. *History of Alliouagana: A Short History of Montserrat*. Montserrat: Montserrat University Center.

———. 1994. *Montserrat: History of a Caribbean Colony*. London: Macmillan Caribbean.

Ferguson, Arlene Nash. 2000. *I Come to Get Me!: An Inside Look at the Junkanoo Festival*. Nassau, Bahamas: Doongalik Studios.

Fergusson, R. Menzies. 1884. *Rambles in the Far North*. Paisley: Gardner.

Flannigan, Mrs. 1844. *Antigua and the Antiguans*. 2 vols. London: Saunders and Otley.

Flax, Patricia. 2004. "Childhood Memories of Christmas Time in Antigua." http://silvertorch.com/c-christmas-readers.html#Patricia.

Foss, Wilson Perkins. 1976. "The Arts of the Urhobo Peoples of Southern Nigeria." Ph.D. diss., Yale University.

Franco, Pamela R. 1998. "Dressing Up and Looking Good." *African Arts* 31(2): 62–67.

Frazer, J. G., and G. C. Moore Smith. 1909. "Straw-Bear Tuesday." *Folklore* 20(2): 202–3.

Frett, Amos. 1979. Interview by Mary Jane Soule. T126 and T127, Soule Archive of St. Croix and St. Thomas Song and Dance, First Half of the Twentieth Century. Library of Congress, American Folklife Center and Von Scholten Collection, Enid M. Baa Library, St. Thomas, Virgin Islands.

Frobenius, Leo. 1898. *Die Masken und Geheimbunde Afrikas*. Halle: Kaiserl. Leop.-Carol. Deutschen Akademie der Naturforscher.

Froger, François. 1698. *Relation d'un Voyage Fait en 1695, 1696, et 1697 aux Côtes d'Afrique*. Paris: Quay de l'Horloge.

Gailey, Alan. 1969. *Irish Folk Drama*. Cork, Ireland: Mercier.

Gardner, W. J. 1873. *A History of Jamaica*. London: Cass.

Gehrts, M. 1915. *A Camera Actress in the Wilds of Togoland*. London: Seeley.

Glassie, Henry. 1975. *All Silver and No Brass: An Irish Christmas Mumming*. Bloomington: Indiana University Press.

Granger, Mary. 1940. *Drums and Shadows: Survival Studies among the Georgia Coastal Negroes*. Athens: University of Georgia Press.

Gray, Major William, and Staff Surgeon Dochard. 1825. *Travels in Western Africa in the Years 1818, 1819, 1820, and 1821*. London: Murray.

Green, Doris. 1996. "Traditional Dance in Africa." In *African Dance: An Artistic, Historical, and Philosophical Inquiry*, ed. Kariamu Welsh Asante, 13–28. Trenton, N.J.: Africa World.

Greville, John Chester. 1869. *Transatlantic Sketches in the West Indies, South America, Canada, and the United States*. London: Smith, Elder.

Griaule, Marcel. 1938. *Masques Dogons*. Paris: Institut d'Ethnologie.

Grose, Francis. 1788/1931. *A Classical Dictionary of the Vulgar Tongue*. 2nd ed. Knoxville, Ill.: Beard.

Gunnell, Terry. 1995. *The Origins of Drama in Scandinavia*. London: Brewer.

———. 2007. "Masks and Mumming Traditions in the North Atlantic: A Survey." In *Masks and Mumming in the Nordic Area*, ed. Terry Gunnell, 275–366. Uppsala, Sweden: Royal Gustavus Adolphus Academy for Swedish Folk Culture.

Gurney, Joseph John. 1840. *A Winter in the West Indies: Described in Familiar Letters to Henry Clay, of Kentucky*. London: Murray.

Haagensen, Reimert. 1758. *Description of the Island of St. Croix in America in the West Indies*. Trans. Arnold R. Highfield. St. Croix: Virgin Islands Humanities Council.

Hall, D. 1989. *In Miserable Slavery: Thomas Thistlewood in Jamaica, 1750–1786*. New York: Macmillan.

Hall, Gwendolyn Midlo. 1992. *Africans in Colonial Louisiana: The Development of Afro-Creole Culture in the Eighteenth Century*. Baton Rouge: Louisiana State University Press.

Halpert, Herbert. 1969. "A Typology of Mumming." In *Christmas Mumming in Newfoundland*, ed. Herbert Halpert and G. M. Story, 34–61. Toronto: University of Toronto Press.

Halpert, Herbert, and G. M. Story, eds. 1969. *Christmas Mumming in Newfoundland*. Toronto: University of Toronto Press.

Handler, Jerome C., and Charlotte J. Frisbie. 1972. "Aspects of Slave Life in Barbados: Music and Its Cultural Context." *Caribbean Quarterly* 11(4): 5–46.

Hayes, Edward. 1589/1958. "A Report of the Voyage and Success Thereof, Attempted in the Year of Our Lord 1583 by Sir Humphrey Gilbert Knight." In Richard Hakluyt, *Voyages and Documents*, ed. Janet Hampden, 236–82. London: Oxford University Press.

Haynes, Robert. 1934. *The Barbadian Diary of Gen. Robert Haynes, 1787–1836*. Ed. M. W. Cracknell. Medstead, Hampshire: Azania.

Haynes, S. B. 1872. "The Danish West Indies." *Harpers New Monthly Magazine*, January, 200–202.

Hayward, Brian. 1992. *Galoshins: The Scottish Folk Play*. Edinburgh: Edinburgh University Press.

Heaney, Michael. 1987. "New Evidence for the Abbots Bromley Hobby-Horse." *Folk Music Journal* 5(3): 359–60.

Helm, Alex. 1981. *The English Mummers' Play*. Woodbridge, Suffolk: Brewer for the Folklore Society.

Herskovits, Melville J. 1958. *The Myth of the Negro Past*. Boston: Beacon.

Herskovits, Melville J., and Frances S. Herskovits. 1938. *Dahomey: An Ancient West African Kingdom*. 2 vols. New York: Augustin.

Heuman, Gad J., and James Walvin, eds. 2003. *The Slavery Reader*. London: Routledge.

Hole, Christina. 1978. *A Dictionary of British Folk Customs*. London: Paladin Grafton.

Honychurch, Lennox. [1982.] *Our Island Culture*. Roseau: Tropical Printers for the Dominica Cultural Council.

———. [2004a]. "African Influences in Dominica." http://www.lennoxhonychurch.com/africa-dominica.cfm.

———. [2004b]. "Mas Dominique: A History of Carnival." http://www.lennoxhonychurch.com/article.cfm?id=380.

Horton, Robin. 1971. "Stateless Societies in the History of West Africa." In *History of West Africa*, ed. J. F. A. Ajayi and M. Crowder, 1:78–119. London: Longmans.

Hovey, Sylvester. 1838. *Letters from the West Indies*. New York: Gould and Newman.

Howkins, Alun. 1974. *Whitsun in Nineteenth Century Oxfordshire*. Oxford: History Workshop.

Huet, Michel. 1978. *The Dance, Art, and Ritual of Africa*. New York: Pantheon.

Hurston, Zora Neale. 1995. *The Complete Stories*. Intro. Henry Louis Gates Jr. and Sieglinde Lemke. New York: HarperCollins Perennial.

Hutton, Ronald. 1991. *The Pagan Religions of the Ancient British Isles: Their Nature and Legacy*. Oxford: Blackwell.

———. 1994. *The Rise and Fall of Merry England: The Ritual Year, 1400–1700*. New York: Oxford University Press.

———. 1997. *The Stations of the Sun: A History of the Ritual Year in Britain*. New York: Oxford University Press.

Iaconetti, Joan. 1997. "Tobago: Folk Tales." *Latitudes* (American Eagle Airline) 7(1): 42–47.

The Igede of Nigeria: Drumming, Chanting, and Exotic Percussion. 1991. Liner notes by Robert Nicholls. Music of the World, CDT-117.

Ikoni, John O. 1988. "Igede Indigenous Religion." In *Igede Gedegede*, ed. Ogwona Oboh, Ogaga Agocha, Isaac Ode, John Adima, and John Aja, 27–33. Oju, Nigeria: Oju Local Government Council.

Illiffe, John. 1983. *The Emergence of African Capitalism*. Minneapolis: University of Minnesota Press.

Jacobs, Harriet. 1861/1987. *Incidents in the Life of a Slave Girl*. Cambridge: Harvard University Press.

James, E. O. 1961. *Seasonal Feasts and Festivals*. New York: Barnes and Noble.

Jedrej, M. C. 1986. "Dan and Mende Masks: A Structural Comparison." *Africa* 56(1): 71–79.

Jobson, Richard. 1623/1968. *The Golden Trade*. New York: Da Capo.

Jones, G. I. 1984. *The Art of Eastern Nigeria*. New York: Cambridge University Press.

Judge, Roy. 1979. *The Jack-in-the Green: A May Day Custom*. Woodbridge, Suffolk: Brewer for the Folklore Society.

Jung, Carl Gustav. 1964. *Man and His Symbols*. London: Aldous.

Kaivola-Bregenhøj, Annikki. 2007. "Eros in Disguise: Eroticism in Mumming Interaction." In *Masks and Mumming in the Nordic Area*, ed. Terry Gunnell, 531–47. Uppsala, Sweden: Royal Gustavus Adolphus Academy for Swedish Folk Culture.

Kandinsky, Wassily. 2006. *Concerning the Spiritual in Art*. London: Tate.

Kasfir, Sidney L. 1982. "Anjenu: Sculpture for Idoma Spirits." *African Arts* 15(4): 47–51.

———. 1988. "Masquerading as a Cultural System." In *West African Masks and Cultural Systems*, ed. Sidney L. Kasfir, 1–16. Tervuren, Belgium: Musée Royal de l'Afrique.

———. 1989. "Remembering Ojiji: Portrait of an Idoma Artist." *African Arts* 22(4): 41–51, 86–87.

Kedjanyi, John. 1967. "Masquerade Societies in Ghana." *Research Review* (University of Ghana, Institute of African Studies) 3(2): 51–57.

Kelly, James. 1838. *Voyage to Jamaica*. Belfast: Wilson.

Kemp, William. 1600/1840. *Kemp's Nine Days Wonder*. Intro. Alexander Dyce. London: Camden Society.

Kingsley, Charles. 1877. *At Last: A Christmas in the West Indies*. London: Macmillan.

Kinser, Samuel. 1990. *Carnival American Style: Mardi Gras at New Orleans and Mobile*. Chicago: University of Chicago Press.

Kirke, Henry, 1898. *Twenty-Five Years in British Guiana*. London: Sampson, Low, Marston.

Kolapo, Femi J. 2000. "CMS Missionaries of African Origin and Extra-Religious Encounters at the Niger-Benue Confluence, 1858–1880." *African Studies Review* 43(2): 87–115.

Kubik, Gerhard. 1999. *Africa and the Blues*. Jackson: University Press of Mississippi.

Kulmanen, Mari. 2007. "Changes in the St. Knut's Day Mumming in Äetsä, Finland." In *Masks and Mumming in the Nordic Area*, ed. Terry Gunnell, 603–20. Uppsala, Sweden: Royal Gustavus Adolphus Academy for Swedish Folk Culture.

Kyerematen, A. A. Y. 1964. *Panoply of Ghana: Ornamental Art in Ghanaian Tradition and Culture*. New York: Praeger.

Labat, Jean-Baptiste. 1728. *Nouvelle Relation de l'Afrique Occidentale*. Paris: Cavelier.

Lake, Edgar. 2001a. "The Killing of Arthur Sixteen." Script of drama performed at Triennial Symposium on African Art, St. Thomas, April. Melville Herskovits Collection, Northwestern University.

———. 2001b. Program for "The Killing of Arthur Sixteen," performed at Triennial Symposium on African Art, St. Thomas, April. Melville Herskovits Collection, Northwestern University.

Lambdin, Robert T., and Laura C. Lambdin. 2000. *Encyclopedia of Medieval Literature.* Westport, Conn.: Greenwood.

Lamp, Frederick. 1996. *Art of the Baga: A Drama of Cultural Reinvention.* Baltimore: Museum for African Art and Prestel.

Lanaghan, Mrs. 1844. *Antigua and the Antiguans.* 2 vols. London: Saunders and Otley.

Latrobe, Benjamin. 1819/1969. *Journal of Latrobe.* Ed. J. H. B. Latrobe. New York: Negro Universities Press.

Leaf, Earl. 1948. *Isles of Rhythm.* New York: Barnes.

Leech, Keith. 1989. *Jack in the Green in Tasmania, 1844–1873.* London: Folklore Society.

Lekis, Lisa. 1960. *Dancing Gods.* New York: Scarecrow.

Leslie, Charles. 1739. *A New and Exact Account of Jamaica.* Edinburgh: Fleming.

Lewis, Matthew G. 1834/1999. *Journal of a West India Proprietor.* Oxford: Oxford University Press.

Lewis, Theresa. 1990. *Caribbean Folk Legends.* Trenton, N.J.: Africa World.

Lewisohn, Florence. 1964. *Divers Information on the Romantic History of St. Croix: From the Time of Columbus until Today.* [Frederiksted: St. Croix Landmarks Society.

Lid, Nils. 1928. *Joleband og Vegetasjonsguddom.* Oslo: Kommisjon Haus J. Dybwad.

Ligon, Richard. 1673/1970. *A True and Exact History of the Island of Barbadoes.* London: Cass, 1970.

Liverpool, Hollis. 2001. *Rituals of Power and Rebellion: The Carnival Traditions in Trinidad and Tobago.* Chicago: Frontline.

Lockhart, Alfred. 1979. Interview by Mary Jane Soule. T134, Soule Archive of St. Croix and St. Thomas Song and Dance, First Half of the Twentieth Century. Library of Congress, American Folklife Center and Von Scholten Collection, Enid M. Baa Library, St. Thomas, Virgin Islands.

Long, Edward. 1774. *The History of Jamaica.* 2 vols. London: Lowndes.

Lowe, Barbara. 1957. "Early Records of the Morris in England." *Journal of the English Folk Dance and Song Society* 8:61–82.

Luffman, John. 1789. *A Brief Account of the Island of Antigua: Together with the Customs and Manners of Its Inhabitants.* London: Cadell.

MacDonogh, Steve. 1983. *Green and Gold: The Wrenboys of Dingle.* Dingle, Ireland: Brandon.

Magnus, Olaus. 1555/1972. *Historia de Gentibus Septentionalisalibus.* Book 13, chapter 42. Copenhagen: Rosenkilde and Bagger.

Manuel, Peter. 1995. *Caribbean Currents: Caribbean Music from Rumba to Reggae.* Philadelphia: Temple University Press.

Mark, Peter. 1983. "Diola Masking Traditions and the History of the Casamance (Senegal)." *Paideuma: Mitteilungen zur Kulturkunde* 29:3–22.

———. 1992. *The Wild Bull and the Sacred Forest: Form, Meaning, and Change in Senegambian Initiation Masks.* Cambridge: Cambridge University Press.

Marsden, Peter. 1788. *An Account of the Island of Jamaica.* Newcastle: Hodgson.

Martin, Jane. 1982. *Kruman Down the Coast.* Boston: African Studies Center, Boston University.

Matheson, D. L. 1983. "The Folklore of St. Christopher's Island." Mimeographed manuscript. In possession of the author.

Mauldin, Barbara. 2004. "Ritual and Play: Carnaval in Nahua Indian Communities of Tlaxcala, Mexico." In *Carnaval!*, ed. Barbara Mauldin, 145–71. Seattle: University of Washington Press.

Maylam, Percy. 1909. *The Hooden Horse: An East Kent Christmas Tradition*. Canterbury: Cross and Jackman.

McCall, John C. 2000. *Dancing Histories: Heuristic Ethnography with the Ohafia Igbo*. Ann Arbor: University of Michigan Press.

McDaniel, Lorna. 1992. "The Concept of Nation in the Big Drum Dance of Carriacou, Grenada." In *Musical Repercussions of 1492: Encounters in Text and Performance*, ed. Carol E. Robertson, 395–411. Washington, D.C.: Smithsonian Institution.

———. 1998. *The Big Drum Ritual of Carriacou: Praisesongs in Rememory of Flight*. Gainesville: University Press of Florida.

McMurray, Joan F. 2000. "Mummies in St. Kitts and Nevis." Paper presented at The Islands in Between: Language, Literature, and History of the Eastern Caribbean, St. Croix, November.

———. 2001a. "The English Mummers and the West Indian Bull Play." *La Torre: Revista de la Universidad de Puerto Rico* 6(19): 37–49.

———. 2001b. "Evangelism and West Indian Folk Plays." *La Torre: Revista de la Universidad de Puerto Rico* 6 (19): 3–20.

McNaughton, Patrick R. 1982. "The Shirts That Mande Hunters Wear." *African Arts* 15(3): 54–58.

McNeal, Keith. 2010. "Pantheons as Mythistorical Archives: Pantheonization and Remodeled Iconographies in Two Southern Caribbean Possession Religions." In *Activating the Past: History and Memory in the Black Atlantic World*, ed. Andrew Apter and Lauren Derby, 185–244. Newcastle, England: Cambridge Scholars.

Messenger, John C. 1973. "African Retentions in Montserrat." *African Arts* 6(4): 54–57, 95.

Miller, Ivor L. 2005. "Cuban Abakua Chants: Examining New Linguistic and Historical Evidence for the African Diaspora. *African Studies Review* 14(1): 23–58.

———. 2009. *Voice of the Leopard: African Secret Societies and Cuba*. Jackson: University Press of Mississippi.

Millington, Peter. 1996. "Mrs. Ewing and the Textual Origin of the St. Kitts Mummies' Play." *Folklore* 107:77–89.

Millington, Peter, and Caspar James. 2011. "Mummies and Masquerades: English and Caribbean Connections." Paper presented at the Bath International Mummers' Unconvention Symposium, Bath, November.

Mills, Frank L., Simon B. Jones-Hendrickson, and Eugene Bertram. 1984. *Christmas Sports in St. Kitts-Nevis: Our Neglected Cultural Tradition*. N.p.

Monts, Lester. 1984. "Dance in the Vai Sande Society." *African Arts* 17(4): 53–59.

Moore, Francis. 1738. *Travels into the Inland Parts of Africa*. London: Cave.

Moore, Louis T. 1946. "Remember the John Kuner?" *North Carolina State Magazine*, June, 7.

Moore, Joseph "Paddy." 1979. Interview by Mary Jane Soule and Sylvester "Blinky" McIntosh. T061 and T062, Soule Archive of St. Croix and St. Thomas Song and Dance, First Half of the Twentieth Century. Library of Congress, American Folklife Center and Von Scholten Collection, Enid M. Baa Library, St. Thomas, Virgin Islands.

Moreton, J. B. 1790. *Manners and Customs in the West India Islands.* London: Richardson.

Moss, Barney. 1982. "A Mummers Play from Newfoundland." *In Folklore of Canada*, ed. Edith Fowke, 153-58. Toronto: McClelland and Stewart.

Musical Traditions of St. Lucia, West Indies. 1993. Liner Notes by Jocelyne Guilbault, Embert Charles, and Manfred Kreamer. Smithsonian Folkways Recordings SFW40416.

Newall, Venetia. 1993. "Up-Helly-Aa: A Shetland Fire Festival." In *Aspects of British Calendar Customs*, ed. Theresa Buckland and Juliette Wood, 57–74. Sheffield: Sheffield Academic.

Ndege, Conchita, and Robert Nicholls. 1990. *Through African Eyes: The Rhythm of Life and Art in Africa.* Winston-Salem, N.C.: Diggs Gallery, Winston-Salem State University.

Nicholls, Robert W. 1988. "Ensemble Music of the Igede." *Black Perspective in Music* 16(2): 192–211.

———. 1992. "Timing in West African Dance Performance: The Influence of Extramusical Factors on Rhythm." *Dance: Current Selected Research* 3:145–81.

———. 1993. "The Language of Drums: Africa's Traditional Broadcast Technologies." *The World and I: A Chronicle of Our Changing Era* 8(4): 244–55.

———. 1997. "Folk Media: Indigenous Learning Systems and Instructional Methodology." *Folklore Forum* 28(1): 49–82.

———. 1998. "Old Time Masquerading in the U.S. Virgin Islands." Report to the Virgin Islands Humanities Council. In possession of the author.

———. 1999. "The Mocko Jumbie of the U.S. Virgin Islands: History and Antecedents." *African Arts* 32(3): 49–61, 94–95.

———. 2001. "Old-Time Masquerade Costume Categories." *La Torre: Revista de la Universidad de Puerto Rico* 6(19): 21–36.

———. 2006a. "Omepa and Onyeweh Children's Masquerades." In *Playful Performers: Children's Masquerades of Africa*, ed. Simon Ottenberg and David Binkley, 129–50. New Brunswick, N.J.: Transaction.

———. 2006b. *Remarkable Big Trees in the U.S. Virgin Islands: An Eco-Heritage Guide.* St. Thomas: University of the Virgin Islands and Virgin Islands Department of Agriculture.

———. 2009. "Running John Bull: The Provenance of a Masquerade in the Lesser Antilles." *Folklore: The Journal of the Folklore Society* 120(2): 133–56.

———. 2010. "In Comes I: Performance, Memory and Landscape." *Folklore: The Journal of the Folklore Society* 121(1): 109–11.

———. Forthcoming. "Igbo Influences on Masquerading and Drum-Dances in the Caribbean." In *The Igbo in the Atlantic World: Slavery and Cultural Adaptation in the African Diaspora*, ed. Toyin Falola and Matt Childs.

Niles, Norma A. 1980. "Provincial English Dialects and Barbadian English." Ph.D. diss., University of Michigan.

Nissen, Johan Peter. 1838. *Reminiscences of a 46 Years' Residence in the Island of St. Thomas in the West Indies.* Nazareth, Pa.: Senseman.

Nissenbaum, Stephen. 1996. *The Battle for Christmas.* New York: Knopf.

Nketia, J. H. Kwabena. 1974. *The Music of Africa.* New York. Norton.

Nugent, Lady Maria. 1966. *Lady Nugent's Journal.* London: West India Committee.

Nunley, John W. 1985. "The Lantern Festival in Sierra Leone." *African Arts* 18(2): 45–49.

———. 1987. *Moving with the Face of the Devil: Art and Politics in Urban West Africa*. Urbana: University of Illinois Press.

———. 2010. "Jolly Masquerades of Sierra Leone and the Creole Histories of Atlantic Rim Performance Arts." In *Activating the Past: History and Memory in the Black Atlantic World*, ed. Andrew Apter and Lauren Derby, 139–56. Newcastle, England: Cambridge Scholars.

Nunley, John W., and Judith Bettelheim, eds. 1988. *Caribbean Festival Arts: Each and Every Bit of Difference*. Seattle: St. Louis Art Museum and University of Washington Press.

Oates, Caroline, and Juliette Wood. 1998. *A Coven of Scholars: Margaret Murray and Her Working Methods*. London: Folklore Society.

Ó Catháin, Séamas. 2007. "The Development of the Irish Christmas Mummers' Play." In *Masks and Mumming in the Nordic Area*, ed. Ed. Terry Gunnell, 743–54. Uppsala, Sweden: Royal Gustavus Adolphus Academy for Swedish Folk Culture.

Ogede, Ode S. 1994. "Counters to Male Domination: Images of Pain in Igede Women's Songs." *Research in African Literature* 3(25): 105–20.

Ogier, Darryl. 1998. "Night Revels and Werewolfery in Calvinist Guernsey." *Folklore* 109:53–62.

Oldendorp, C. G. A. 1770/1987. *C. G. A. Oldendorp's History of the Mission of the Evangelical Brethren of the Caribbean Islands of St. Thomas, St. Croix, and St. John*. Ed. Johann Jakob Bossart. Trans. Arnold R. Highfield and Vladimir Barac. Ann Arbor, Mich.: Karoma.

Oliver, Cynthia. 1995. "St. Croix Dancing: The Contemporary and Historical Path of Dance on the U.S. Virgin Island of St. Croix." Master's thesis, Gallatin Division of New York University.

———. 2009. *Queen of the Virgins: Pageantry and Black Womanhood in the Caribbean*. Jackson: University Press of Mississippi.

Oliver, Paul. 1970. *Savannah Syncopators: African Retentions in the Blues*. New York: Stein and Day.

Ortiz, Fernando. 1921. "Los Cabildos Carabali Afro-Cubanos." *Revista Bimestre Cubana* 16(1): 17–34.

Ottenberg, Simon. 1989. "We Are Becoming Art Minded: Afikpo Arts 1988." *African Arts* 22(4): 58–67, 88.

Ottenberg, Simon, and David A. Binkley. 2006. *Playful Performers: African Children's Masquerades*. New Brunswick, N.J.: Transaction.

Palmié, Stephan. 2010. "*Ekpe/Abakua* in Middle Passage: Time, Space, and Units of Analysis in African American Historical Anthropology." In *Activating the Past: History and Memory in the Black Atlantic World*, ed. Andrew Apter and Lauren Derby, 1–44. Newcastle, England: Cambridge Scholars.

Park, Mungo. 1799/1983. *Travels into the Interior of Africa*. London: Eland.

Payne, Timothy. 2005. "Village Life: Remembering Christmas of Long Ago." *Antigua Sun*, 17 December.

Pearson, Mike. 2007. *In Comes I: Performance Memory and Landscape*. Exeter: University of Exeter Press.

Peek, Philip M. 1980. "Isoko Arts and Their Audiences." *African Arts* 13(3): 58–60.

Pennant, Thomas. 1776. *Tour in Scotland in 1769*. London: White.

Petridis, Constantine. 2008. "Buffalo Helmets of the Tussian and Siemu Peoples of Burkina Faso." *African Arts* 41(3): 26–43.

———. 2012. "A 'Harley Mask' at the Cleveland Museum of Art." *African Arts* 45(1): 16–31.

Pettit, Tom. 1995. "Customary Drama: Social and Spatial Patterning in Traditional Encounters." *Folk Music Journal* 7(1): 27–42.

Picton, John. 1974. "Masks and the Igbirra." *African Arts* 7(2): 38–41.

Pinckard, George. 1806. *Notes on the West Indies*. Vol. 1. London: Longman.

Powers, A. M. 1988. "Mumming in Newfoundland." *The World and I: A Chronicle of Our Changing Era* 3(12): 652–59.

Ranung, Björn. 1973. *Music of Dawn and Day: Music and Dance Associations of the Igede of Nigeria*. Music album with notes. Helsinki, Finland: Love.

Rashford John. 1984. "Plants, Spirits, and the Meaning of 'John' in Jamaica." *Jamaica Journal* 17(2): 62–70.

Real, Katarina. 2004. "Evoe! The Carnaval of Recife and Olinda in Pernambuco, Brazil." In *Carnaval!*, ed. Barbara Mauldin, chapter 10. Seattle: University of Washington Press.

Rediker, Marcus. 1989. *Between the Devil and the Deep Blue Sea: Merchant Seamen, Pirates, and the Anglo American Maritime World, 1700–1750*. New York: Cambridge University Press.

Resnik, Judith, and Dennis E. Curtis. 2010. *Representing Justice: From Nascent City-States to Democratic Courtrooms and Guantánamo Bay*. New Haven: Yale University Press.

Rezende, Elizabeth, and Anne Walbom. 2009. *St. Croix: Historic Photographs*. St. Croix: Danish West Indian Society.

Richards, Anthony. 2006. "Our Dear, Disappearing Frizzled Fowl." *Liat Islander* 73:40.

Richardson, Evelyn. 1984. *Seven Streets by Seven Streets*. New York: Blyden.

Ridgwell, Gordon. 2003. "Straw Bears." *FLS News: The Newsletter of the Folklore Society* 39:8–9.

Rivera, Eulalie. 1987. *Growing Up on St. Croix: Recollections of a Crucian Girlhood*. St. Croix: Rivera.

———. 1992. Interview by Mary Jane Soule. Virgin Island Voices Audiotape Collection, St. Croix Landmarks Society, Frederiksted.

Roberts, John Storm. 1972. *Black Music of Two Worlds*. New York: Praeger.

Rouse, Irving. 1992. *The Tainos: Rise and Decline of the People Who Greeted Columbus*. New Haven: Yale University Press.

Rowley, William, Thomas Dekker, and John Ford. 1958. *The Witch of Edmonton*. In *The Dramatic Works of Thomas Dekker*, ed. Fredson Bowers, 3:481–568. Cambridge: Cambridge University Press.

Rudwin, Maximilian J. 1920. *The Origins of the German Carnival Comedy*. New York: Stechart.

Ruland, Josef. 1978. *Christmas in Germany*. Bonn: Hocwacht.

Russell, Ian. 1979. "A Survey of Traditional Drama in North East Derbyshire, 1970–78." *Folk Music Journal* 3(5): 399–478.

Sandys, William. 1852. *Christmastide: Its History, Festivities, and Carols*. London: Smith.

Schaw, Janet J. 1939. *Journal of a Lady of Quality: J. Schaw: Being the Narrative of a Journey from Scotland to the West Indies, North Carolina, and Portugal in the Years 1774 to 1776*. London: Oxford University Press.

Schrader, Richard A., Sr. 1989. *Notes of a Crucian Son*. St. Croix: Schrader.

———. 1993. *Fungi: More Crucian Stories*. St. Croix: Schrader.

———. 1996. *Under de Taman Tree*. St. Croix: Schrader.

Scoles, Reverend Ignatius. 1885. *Sketches of African and Indian Life in British Guiana*. Demerara: Argosy.

Scott, Michael. 1836/1999. *Tom Cringle's Log*. New York: Holt.

Scott, Sir Walter. 1810. *The Lady of the Lake*. Edinburgh: Ballantyne.

Shaw, Margaret Fay. 1955. *Folksongs and Folklore of South Uist*. London: Routledge and Kegan Paul.

Shekwo, Joseph Amali Yusuf. 1984. "Understanding Gbagyi [Gwari] Folktales: Premises for Targeting Salient Electronic Mass Media Programs." Ph.D. diss., Northwestern University.

Sidro, Annie. 1987. "Carnival in Nice." *The World and I: A Chronicle of Our Changing Era* 2(2): 454–63.

Siroto, Leon. 1969. "Masks and Social Organization among the Bakwele People of Western Equatorial Africa." Ph.D. diss., Columbia University.

Sloane, Hans. 1707. *A Voyage to the Islands Madera, Barbados, Nieves, S. Christophers, and Jamaica*. Vol. 1. London: B.M.

Smith, Fred T. 1987. "Symbols of Conflict and Integration in Frafra Funerals." *African Arts* 21(1): 45–51, 87.

Smith, J. B. 2010. "Pixies in Pembrokeshire." *FLS News: The Newsletter of the Folklore Society* 61:8.

Smith, James. 1840. *The Winter of 1840 in St. Croix*. New York: Osborn.

Smith, Keithlyn B., and Fernando C. Smith. 1988. *To Shoot Hard Labour: The Life and Times of Samuel Smith, an Antiguan Workingman, 1877–1982*. Scarborough, Ont.: Edan's.

Smith, Mary. 1981. *Baba of Karo: A Woman of the Muslim Hausa*. New Haven: Yale University Press.

Spencer, Flora. 1974. *Crop-Over: An Old Barbadian Plantation Festival*. Barbados: Commonwealth Caribbean Center.

Speaight, George. 1955. *Punch and Judy: A History*. London: Harrap.

Stedman, J. G. 1796/1971. *Narrative of a Five Years' Expedition against the Revolted Negroes of Surinam*. Amherst: University of Massachusetts Press.

Stegassy, Ruth. 1998. "John Cupid: We Have Been Called Carnival People." *Drama Review* 42(3): 96–107.

Stewart, John. 1823/1969. *A View of the Past and Present State of the Island of Jamaica*. New York: Negro Universities Press.

Story, G. M. 1969. "Mummers in Newfoundland History." In *Christmas Mumming in Newfoundland*, ed. Herbert Halpert and G. M. Story, 167–85. Toronto: University of Toronto Press.

Strother, Z. S. 1998. *Inventing Masks: Agency and History in the Art of the Central Pende*. Chicago: University of Chicago Press.

Strutt, J. 1801/1876. *Sports and Pastimes of the People of England*. London: White.

Stubbes, Philip. 1583. *The Anatomie of Abuses*. London: Iones.

Sullivan, Tom. 1980. *Salt Atlantic Chanties*. Folkways Records FW 37301.

Svabo, J. C. 1966. *Dictionarium Faeroense*. Copenhagen: Matras.

Tedre, Ülo. 2007. "Masks and Mumming Traditions in Estonia: A Survey." In *Masks and Mumming in the Nordic Area*, ed. Terry Gunnell, 367–448. Uppsala, Sweden: Royal Gustavus Adolphus Academy for Swedish Folk Culture.

Thomas, Louis-Vincent. 1958. *Les Diola: Essai d'Analyse Fonctionnelle sur une Population de Basse-Casamance*. Ifan-Dakar: Mémoires de l'Institut Français d'Afrique Noire.

———. 1965. "Bukut Chez les Diola-Niomoune." *Notes Africaines* 108:97–118.

Thompson, E. P. 1991. *Customs in Common*. New York: New Press.

Thompson, Robert Farris. 1974. *African Art in Motion*. Berkeley: University of California Press.

———. 1984. *Flash of the Spirit: African and Afro-American Art and Philosophy*. New York: Vintage.

Tiddy, R. J. E. 1923/1969. *The Mummers' Play*. Folcroft, Pa.: Folcroft Press.

Tombstone Feast: Funerary Music of Carriacou. 2001. Music CD with liner notes by Lorna McDaniel and Donald R. Hill. Rounder Records, Caribbean Voyage. 11661-1727-2.

Tree, Ronald. 1972. *A History of Barbados*. London: Davis.

Tuckerman, Joseph. 1837. *A Letter Respecting Santa Cruz as a Winter Residence for Invalids*. Boston: Massachusetts Historical Society.

Turner, Victor. 1969. *The Ritual Process*. Chicago: Aldine.

———. 1974. *Drama, Fields, and Metaphor: Symbolic Action in Human Society*. Ithaca: Cornell University Press.

Tydeman, William. 1978. *The Theatre in the Middle Ages: Western European Stage Conditions, c. 800–1576*. Cambridge: Cambridge University Press

Tyson, George F. 1995. "Jumpin' Up: Festivals and Masquerades in the Danish West Indies." Unpublished manuscript. In possession of the author.

Tyson, George F., and Arnold R. Highfield. 1994. *The Kamina Folk: Slavery and Slave Life in the Danish West Indies*. St. Croix: Virgin Islands Humanities Council.

Uchendu, Victor C. 1965. *The Igbo of Southeast Nigeria*. New York: Holt, Rinehart, and Winston.

U.S. Virgin Islands. Department of Education. 1972. *Looking Back on Carnival*.

Valls, Lito. 1981. *What a Pistarkle: A Dictionary of Virgin Islands English Creole*. St. John: n.p.

Vento, Urpo. 2007. "Masks and Mumming Traditions in Finland and Karelia: An Introductory Survey." In *Masks and Mumming in the Nordic Area*, ed. Terry Gunnell, 327–66. Uppsala, Sweden: Royal Gustavus Adolphus Academy for Swedish Folk Culture.

Virgin Islands Business Journal. 1991. "STX Courthouse Sculpture Is Cultural Link." August 12–25.

Visby-Petersen, Thora. 1917. *St. Thomas Tropeminder Fra De Vestindiske Oer*. Trans. Poul Erik Olsen. Copenhagen: Aarhus.

Vydrin, Valentin. 2009. "On the Problem of the Proto-Mande Homeland." *Journal of Language Relationship* 1:107–42.

Waddell, Hope Masterton. 1863/1970. *Twenty-Nine Years in the West Indies and Central Africa: A Review of Missionary Work and Adventure, 1829–1858*. London: Cass.

Waller, John Augustine. 1820. *A Voyage in the West Indies: Containing Various Observations Made during a Residence in Barbadoes, and Several of the Leeward Islands*. London: Phillips.

Warner, Elizabeth A. 1977. *The Russian Folk Theatre*. The Hague: Mouton.

Warren, Edward. 1885. *A Doctor's Experiences in Three Continents*. Baltimore: Cushings and Bailey.

Watson, Richard. 1817. *A Defense of Wesleyan Methodist Missions in the West Indies*. London: Cordeux.

Weed, Thurlow. 1866. *Letters from Europe and the West Indies*. Albany, N.Y.: Weed, Parsons.

Weil, Peter M. 1971. "The Masked Figure and Social Control: The Mandinka Case." *Africa* 41(40): 279–93.

———. 1988. "Fighting Fire with Fire: The Mandinka Sengko Mask." In *West African Masks and Cultural Systems*, ed. Sidney L. Kasfir, 151–96. Tervuren, Belgium: Musée Royal de l'Afrique Centrale.

Weiser-Aall, Lily. 1954. *Julenissan og julegeita i Norge*. Oslo: Norsk Folkemuseum.

Wentworth, Trelawny. 1834. *The West India Sketch Book*. London: Whittaker.

West, Hans. 1793. *Description of St. Croix with a Brief Overview of St. Thomas, St. John, Tortola, Spanishtown, and Crab Island*. Trans. Nina York. St. Thomas: Virgin Islands Humanities Council.

Westergaard, Waldemar. 1926. "Account of the Negro Rebellion on St. Croix, Danish West Indies, 1759." *Journal of Negro History* 11(1): 50–61.

Whistler, Henry. 1900. "Journal of a West India Expendition [*sic*]." In *The Narrative of General Venables, with an Appendix of Papers Relating to the Expedition to the West Indies and the Conquest of Jamaica, 1654–1655*, ed. Charles H. Firth, 146–47. London: Longmans, Green.

Widdowson, J. D. A., and Herbert Halpert. 1969. "The Disguise of Newfoundland Mummers." In *Christmas Mumming in Newfoundland*, ed. Herbert Halpert and G. M. Story, 145–64. Toronto: University of Toronto Press.

Wilkie, Thomas. 1815. "Ancient Customs and Ceremonies of the Lowland Scots." National Library of Scotland. MS 123.

Williams, Alfred M. 1896. "A Miracle-Play in the West Indies." *Journal of American Folklore* 9(33): 117–20.

Williams, Cynric A. 1826. *A Tour through the Island of Jamaica, from the Western to the Eastern End, in the Year 1823*. London: Hunt and Clarke.

Williams, Joseph J. 1932. *Voodoos and Obeahs: Phases of West India Witchcraft*. New York: Dial.

Willock, Wayne. 1996. "Tuk Bands." Lecture notes, August. In possession of author.

Young, William. 1807. "A Tour through the Islands of Barbados, St. Vincent, Antigua, Tobago, and Grenada in 1791 and 1792." In *History, Civil, and Commercial, of the British Colonies in the West Indies*, ed. Bryan Edwards, 3:241–84. London: Whittaker.

Zahan, Dominique. 1960. *Sociétés d'Initiation Bambara*. Paris: Mouton.

INDEX